Martha Brae's
TWO HISTORIES

Martha Brae's TWO HISTORIES

European Expansion and

Caribbean Culture-Building

in Jamaica

JEAN BESSON

Foreword by Sidney W. Mintz

The University of North Carolina Press

Chapel Hill & London

© 2002 The University of North Carolina Press
All rights reserved
Manufactured in the United States of America

Designed by Jacquline Johnson
Set in New Baskerville
By Keystone Typesetting, Inc.

The paper in this book meets the guidelines for
permanence and durability of the Committee on
Production Guidelines for Book Longevity of the
Council on Library Resources.

Library of Congress Cataloging-in-Publication Data
Besson, Jean, 1944–
    Martha Brae's two histories : European expansion and
Caribbean culture-building in Jamaica / Jean Besson;
foreword by Sidney W. Mintz.
        p. cm.
Includes bibliographical references and index.
ISBN 0-8078-2734-7 (cloth : alk. paper)
ISBN 0-8078-5409-3 (pbk. : alk. paper)
1. Martha Brae (Jamaica) — History. 2. Trelawny, Parish of
(Jamaica) — History. 3. Peasantry — Jamaica — Trelawny,
Parish of — History. 4. Blacks — Land tenure — Jamaica —
Trelawny, Parish of — History. I. Title: Martha Brae's 2
histories. II. Title.
F1895.M37 B48   2002
972.92 — dc21   2002006111

cloth   06 05 04 03 02   5 4 3 2 1
paper 06 05 04 03 02   5 4 3 2 1

In memory of

my father, "Lawyer,"

and for my family

and the people of

Martha Brae who

loved him too

CONTENTS

ILLUSTRATIONS, MAPS, AND TABLE

ILLUSTRATIONS

The emancipation plaque in the William Knibb
Memorial Baptist Church, Falmouth   *265*

Trelawny Rastafarians in a family-land house yard   *269*

MAPS

TABLE

FOREWORD
Sidney W. Mintz

Jean Besson's book does some things in the field of Caribbean anthropology that I believe no other such book has done. She manages this both by defining a problem area the scale of which sets it apart from earlier books and by bringing to her work both the concerns and the accomplishments of Caribbean anthropology. A look at anthropology itself may help me to describe her achievement.

Cultural (or social) anthropology, the last-born of the so-called social sciences, began by studying small, technically limited societies, mostly in world regions far removed from Europe's populous centers. Such societies, commonly labeled "primitive," differed greatly among themselves. But often those who studied them thought they shared a great deal, even if it was primarily in terms of what they lacked. The technological gap between them and the West, their want of writing (to which there are some startling exceptions), and their lack of large secondary institutions such as the state were all seen to mark them off from those large, modern societies from which the observers themselves had come.

The choice of such "primitive" societies for study was neither arbitrary nor haphazard. Alfred Kroeber tells us that anthropology studied those societies, rather than others, because they were the ones *in which no other discipline was interested*—neither political scientists, nor sociologists, nor economists. Missionaries, yes; and novelists, such as Joseph Conrad, might make passing references to "savage" or "simpler" peoples. But other than for the work of a few anthropologists, the images of these remote, non-Western societies were almost entirely imaginary.

Though studying what nobody else was interested in had its drawbacks, it also had its advantages. Anthropology, more than most fields of inquiry, was able to collect data to punch holes in wonderful theories about allegedly universal human propensities toward monotheism, the nuclear family, free enterprise, monogamy, and the waging of war. Using field data, it was Kroeber himself who convincingly savaged Freud's "theory" of the origins of the

xiii

incest taboo; Bronisław Malinowski had already done much the same for the Oedipus complex. Raymond Firth, among others, took useful critical aim at economic Robinson Crusoe–ism. At least partly because nobody else was that interested in how "primitive peoples" really did behave, anthropologists would identify genuine exceptions to supposedly universal behaviors and motives, thereby cutting off at the knees many of the riskiest imaginings of others about "human nature in the raw." Data from anthropological research with humans in dramatically different cultures made some grand theorists in other disciplines quite nervous. This was, for the most part, salutary.

All the same, few anthropologists ever claimed that they wanted to study *only* so-called primitive societies. An American anthropologist named Melville J. Herskovits, for example, initiated the anthropological study of peoples of African origin in the New World and began to define an Afro-America that stretched from Argentina to Nova Scotia. There was nothing primitive about the peoples who interested him and who lived in this vast region. They had little in common, other than their humanity, with the New Guineans, indigenous Australians, and Native Americans whom most anthropologists gloried in studying. And what they had in common behaviorally with their African ancestors was clearly cultural, not genetic — historical, not "natural." By and large, before Herskovits's work, nearly anyone who wrote about the New World descendants of Africans treated them as cultureless, or as of only limited anthropological interest, in contrast to the Native American peoples throughout the hemisphere.

Herskovits's interest was not grounded in some governing polarity between primitive and civilized, nor was he romantic about the same things as most of his contemporaries. Impressed by the massive, lengthy, and violent transfer of many millions of persons across the Atlantic in an earlier epoch of European expansion — the last known slaver to deliver its cargo to the Americas sailed in 1867 — Herskovits was led to ask some basic questions about the nature of anthropology's favorite concept: culture. What happens when enormous numbers of people, from hundreds of different communities, are dragged thousands of miles against their will and are then forced to reestablish themselves, under cruelly oppressive conditions, in a new setting? What becomes of their many different ways of life, their languages, customs, faiths, outlooks? From their terrible experiences, what can we learn about the fundamental principles by which cultures change or stay the same? By what means do people survive under such conditions? Are there any answers here that hold for our entire species?

In the 1920s when Herskovits first asked such questions, the majority of anthropologists; including many of his own classmates, associates, and friends, were supremely uninterested. The "primitive" peoples whom they chose to study spoke little-known languages, dressed in strange and colorful clothing, ate unfamiliar foods, worshiped curious gods in curiouser ways, got married and traced relationships by bewilderingly complex rules. For Western scholars, they were — to use a word that surely no anthropologist would have admitted using for them — *exotic*. In disappointing contrast, the people that Herskovits wanted to know about were, for the most part, not exotic at all. It was not that their cultures were terribly familiar, so much as that they seemed so pathetically *hybrid*. No matter from what perspective one observed them, what they did, and what they were supposed to think, they and their lifeways seemed faded: a patchwork, tattered, makeshift, and, worst of all, *mongrel*. Anthropologists generally wanted to study (though again, none would have used the word) *pure* cultures.

At about the same time that Herskovits began his lifelong effort to understand Afro-America, an astute young folklorist at Vassar College named Martha Beckwith began to travel to the Caribbean region to collect material. The decision to do so on Beckwith's part made good sense. Though cultural anthropologists may have seen nothing in the Caribbean to attract them, physical anthropologists, archaeologists, and folklorists did carry on research there. Perhaps because of their interest in history, scholars in those subfields, at least, made good use of their findings. Beckwith, whose training was anthropological, had made several field trips to the Caribbean for more specific, folkloric purposes. Then she published a kind of summary original essay on the culture of rural Jamaica, entitled *Black Roadways* (1929). Despite its occasionally condescending tone, and though it aspired to stand for the rural population of an entire country, it was based on Beckwith's work with particular persons in specific Jamaican villages and was a valiant first attempt to write an ethnography of a Caribbean people.

Black Roadways received very little notice. The Caribbean region remained intellectually remote from most anthropology of the time. Though rich in folklore, a sort of laboratory for physical anthropologists, somewhat interesting archaeologically, and the home of voodoo, the Caribbean region was peopled by groups who were almost the polar opposite of what anthropologists thought (or were told) they were supposed to study. Whereas New Guinea, Africa, and Amazonia offered kinship systems, costumes, coiffures, cuisines, languages, beliefs, and customs of dizzying variety and allure, to almost all anthropologists the Caribbean islands and their surrounding shores looked rather too much like a culturally burned-over, secondhand, unpristine world. Whether it was kinship or religion or language or anything else,

Caribbean people all seemed culturally midway between there and here—everything was alloyed, mixed, ground down, pasted on, the least common denominator. For most North American anthropologists, that sense of things was probably accentuated because racism and social separation in North America had made their black fellow citizens alien without making them exotic. With the major exception of religious behavior—and even in that regard, mostly just Haitian *vodoun*—the Caribbean region, in the view of nearly all cultural anthropologists, was irrelevant.

But in the years following World War II, leading anthropologists in Britain and the United States sent students to the Caribbean to carry out fieldwork, and the received view of the region began slowly to change. A series of new understandings was sinking in. People were finding out that the first European colonies were not African or Indian or Asian, but Caribbean; that the first planned economic production undertaken by Europeans outside Europe was in the Caribbean; that the first European-engineered flood of new foods and goods to Europe came from the Caribbean. The slavery system that the Europeans had built upon Africans and instituted in the Americas had really changed the shape of the world, and over several decades, that realization slowly took hold. It also turned out that Afro-Americans, as Herskovits had been insisting, *did* have a past, and that the peoples of the Caribbean *did* have cultures.

In recent decades, another old idea about the Caribbean has finally won acceptance. Because of its long and extraordinary colonial history, the Caribbean region had been regarded by most anthropologists as largely irrelevant to the really big theoretical questions that interested them. It had seemed improbable that studies of the cultures of those poor, anciently colonial, seemingly mongrelized and rootless peoples might actually have some value for understanding the dynamics of culture change, the cultures of other places, or the character of modern life. So improbable was it that, as recognition of the theoretical importance of the Caribbean grew, what it represented was rebaptized as an original idea among the students of Australia, Africa, and elsewhere. Today one can speak of "creolization" in Europe or Asia without so much as a nod toward the part of the world where creolization was born, and where the process that the word represents was first studied. (The price of borrowing words without learning what they mean is, in fact, high.)

What Caribbeanist scholars themselves would study also changed through time. After World War II, when cultural anthropologists first began systematic fieldwork in the Caribbean region, they looked for units of study that might correspond in some way to those that had guided earlier research among the "primitives." What happened was expectable: they chose for study communities that they saw as representing — "standing for" — societies. In one case, a group project on Puerto Rico, a whole series of communities was studied in the hope that their collective description (along with some additional institutional study) might result in a work that accurately described the society as a whole. Herskovits and his wife Frances produced community studies of their own in Trinidad, Haiti, and Suriname (Dutch Guiana). Other students looked at communities in Martinique, the Dominican Republic, Barbados, Cuba, and elsewhere.

Those community studies were a rich source of information on the peoples of the Caribbean region and on their widely variant cultural character. Nearly five hundred years of colonial rule by half a dozen powers, in various degrees of tight or loose control, resulted in enormous variety, half hidden by the touristic literature, the rum, the music, the beaches, and the palm trees. Serious, ethnographically sound community studies helped to delineate genuine samenesses and contrasts. Readers could get a deeper sense of how Caribbean peoples live, work, and think, in ways different from what we might learn from aesthetic invention, as in literature, and diarism, as in ethno-autobiography.

Yet those community studies, too, eventually lost much of their appeal. Descriptive, sometimes narrative in character, sometimes without substantial historical background, they rarely stood convincingly for anything bigger than themselves. Hence work in recent years has tended to shift toward urban studies, gender studies, race and race relations, factory studies, studies of gifted individuals, and the use of other Antillean settings in which to do fieldwork. Community studies continue to be made, but students of anthropology, hoping not to end up doing work that might prove redundant, have looked for other frames of research. There are vogues in the social sciences, as in much else; one senses a declining optimism about the wider value of the information that community studies can yield. It is in the light of such declining expectations that I wish to turn to the book before you.

Jean Besson gives us here the culmination of three decades of work, all of it essentially on different facies of the same problem, all of it ultimately on the same place. Yet it is definitely not a community study and should not be misread as one. It "originates" in one place, Martha Brae, within which there nest remarkable personal stories of individual men and women. Yet it reaches out not only to a region and to a whole nation, but also to the immense, centuries-old panorama of slavery, the plantation system, the colonial legacy, and the Atlantic world. But to define this book's analytic power, I wish first to add something more about the Caribbean region and about Jamaica.

The Caribbean was the first part of the New World to be discovered by the Europeans. We North Americans, if we reflect on our beginnings, naturally tend to think of Jamestown and Plymouth Rock. But by 1619, when the first enslaved Africans reached a port in what would one day become the United States, Caribbean Santo Domingo had already been shipping slave-made sugar to Spain for more than a century. Though the time between the colonization of the Caribbean region and the peopling of New England has been consigned to forgetfulness, by 1619 European colonialism in the Caribbean had been exterminating people and building different societies there for more than a century. From the European perspective the Caribbean islands were the first Americas, and only much later, North America.

In the fifteenth and sixteenth centuries and first decades of the seventeenth century, the "development" of the Caribbean islands by Spain's rivals was for the most part still to come. For nearly 125 years, Spanish rule was territorially unchallenged in the Caribbean. Beginning around 1625, under the Danes, Dutch, English, and French in particular, much of what the Spaniards had owned in the Antilles would soon be appropriated by their northern European neighbors. In that story the island of Jamaica stands out importantly. Spanish until seized by Oliver Cromwell's military in 1655, the Jamaican economy grew explosively after 1670 or so, becoming a premier producer of sugar, rum, and molasses, as well as a premier consumer of sugar machinery, instruments of torture, and men and women, both European and African. Cromwell had many enemies — Irish priests and patriots, labor organizers, petty thieves, women of ill repute. To them were added many thousands who were "barbadoesed." (In a later century other victims would be "shanghaied.")

But Jamaica would get more than Britain's overflow during the Commonwealth. For more than a century and a half after its fall to the British, Jamaica, in order to profit from feeding even more prodigally Europe's growing sweet tooth, gobbled up a million or more of Africa's children in a joyous frenzy. Enslavement, slave labor, and the state of slavery killed. When emancipation finally came, on 1 August 1834 — and was made official four years later — only some 330,000 slaves were left to be freed, of the million or so who had been landed there in the preceding 150 years.

After 1838, there began the ascent from slavery. But it would be misleading to suppose that, before freedom came, the slaves were passive victims of the plantation system. Not only had they resisted slavery in a score of ways, some peaceful and some violent, but they had also engaged successfully in the task of building their culture under the most inhuman conditions imaginable. With freedom, they would be able to realize in novel ways what they had already achieved. But, of course, freedom was not equality, and their fight for justice had to continue.

In what follows the author builds for us a rich picture of that struggle. A wide-ranging history, it centers on the intersection of two essential features of the Afro-American saga. One of those features is kinship; the other is land. Revealing step by step how the attachment of lineage to property embodied the real meaning of freedom makes for a monumental epic. Besson is able to demonstrate how anthropological analysis enriches the significance of history. For most human beings, being a person is an artifact of existing social links; we are born into a plexus of preexisting relationships. Over time, a network of kinship can take on the form of a collectivity that *owns something*. Who and what one is can be a precipitate of whom one is related to and what one owns by virtue of one's relationships. Besson's patient unveiling of the twinned dynamic of blood and land is first-rate anthropology and the keystone to this book.

What the author of *Martha Brae's Two Histories* has succeeded in doing here is to bring to light — and hence to interpretive consideration — the chronicle of a continuous struggle: the architecture of kinship and land turns out to be the latticework of freedom. The scale of the picture she draws can change — at times a family, at times a village, and at other times a far larger canvas. But what we learn from this depiction is that the boundaries that separate these concepts from each other change with time and circumstance. This book about Martha Brae is also a book about a world that Europe and Africa had made together — and not always unwillingly. Here we are afforded, by this daughter of two worlds, an inspiring and genuinely original vision of how the Jamaican people came into being and built their own society.

PREFACE AND ACKNOWLEDGMENTS

This book on Martha Brae's two histories is based on research in rural Jamaica over a period of thirty-three years, from 1968 to 2001.[1] Martha Brae was established around 1762 as a Euro-Caribbean colonial planter town in northwestern Jamaica, at the gateway to Europe's New World and at the heart of African slavery in the Americas. The town was transformed into an Afro-Caribbean peasant village at the vanguard of the ex-slaves' flight from the British West Indian estates after emancipation in 1838. The settlement of Martha Brae, which has persisted into the twenty-first century, therefore has both plantation and peasant histories. Yet only the Euro-Caribbean plantation history has been recognized. Moreover, most of this received Eurocentric history is scattered in general sources that, though useful, tend to be superficial and do not adequately situate the town in global, hemispheric, regional, and island contexts.

During the final stages of the preparation of this book, the importance of Martha Brae as a transatlantic slaving port has come to the attention of David Eltis et al. through their work on the *Trans-Atlantic Slave Trade Database: A Database on CD-Rom* (1999) at the W. E. B. Du Bois Institute at Harvard University. For Martha Brae, this database draws especially on David Richardson's (1996) study of the Bristol slave trade, which includes entries for this town. However, Atlantic historiography has not yet addressed the significance of colonial Martha Brae, despite its relevance to the European world economy, African American slavery, the Caribbean region, the British West Indies, and Jamaican plantation slave society. This book begins the task of integrating, developing, and contextualizing the town's Euro-Caribbean history and uncovers Martha Brae's hidden Afro-Caribbean cultural history through a methodology combining anthropological fieldwork, historical research, and the villagers' rich oral tradition.[2]

In these contexts the book, like the settlement of Martha Brae, also has two histories. My research began as a doctoral dissertation in the Department of Social Anthropology at the University of Edinburgh, Scotland, in

1968. The thesis was based on fieldwork in the village of Martha Brae, in the parish of Trelawny, from 1968 to 1969, with return visits in 1971 and 1972, and was submitted and accepted in 1974 (Besson 1974). That initial study focused on kinship and land tenure from the perspective of the theoretical controversy on family structure dominating the study of "West Indian" societies at that time. The analysis reflected the ahistorical methodology typifying the discipline of social anthropology in the 1960s and 1970s. From those viewpoints, the dissertation provided a synchronic study of a West Indian peasant community based on detailed analysis of data collected from 365 persons in seventy-eight households.[3]

The theoretical approach of the thesis was partly influenced by the Jamaican pioneers of the social anthropology of Jamaica, namely, Edith Clarke, Fernando Henriques, and Michael G. Smith. My thesis was also, however, partly a critique of their interpretation of Jamaican family structure. Both this critique and my indebtedness to these pioneers are evident in this book, which like those earlier studies is also influenced by Martha Beckwith's *Black Roadways* (1929), the seminal ethnography of the Jamaican peasantry.

Although my doctoral dissertation provided a useful starting point for the study of Martha Brae, this book goes well beyond that thesis and draws especially on my recurrent research from 1975 to 2001. This subsequent long-term study not only was based on a much wider range of material, including new information from a 100 percent census of 170 households (comprising over 800 persons), but also pursued new theoretical approaches. These perspectives partly draw on, critique, and develop the work of American anthropologist Sidney W. Mintz. In 1974, the year that I completed my doctoral dissertation, Mintz published *Caribbean Transformations*. This classic book, republished in 1989 and reinforced by his study with Richard Price on *The Birth of African-American Culture* (1992), revolutionized the anthropological approach to African America and brought the previously neglected Caribbean region to center stage. Mintz's anthropology is anchored in the social history of the Caribbean *oikoumenê*,[4] or societal area, as Europe's oldest colonial sphere, forged through the impact of plantations, slavery, and indenture at the core of African America (1996a). His ethnography on Caribbean plantation and peasant communities rang true with my professional and personal experience of the region, and his theoretical approach transformed my perspective on the Caribbean plantation-peasant interface. This led me to reassess and extend my methodology for the study of Martha Brae, a settlement at the heart of the Caribbean region, and resulted in my prolonged and more wide-ranging research on Martha Brae's two histories up to 2001. My research in Martha Brae also included a long-term study, from

1968 to 2001, of the peasant marketplace used by the villagers in the nearby urban center of Falmouth (Trelawny's present capital), a market established by their slave ancestors in the late eighteenth century.

In addition, my long-term research widened to the study of eight other Jamaican peasant communities surrounded by plantations (and by bauxite mines and luxury hotels) in the adjoining parishes of Trelawny, St. Elizabeth, and St. James, in the west-central area of the island, from 1979 to 2001. This comparative perspective has deepened my understanding of Martha Brae's two histories. The wider study, which likewise combined anthropology with historical research and oral history interviews, included in-depth fieldwork in three other Trelawny free villages established by ex-slaves in association with the colonial Baptist mission church—as occurred in postslavery Martha Brae. Information was collected from 120 households with some 600 individuals in neighboring Granville, 80 households with 415 people in Wilberforce/Refuge,[5] and 80 households with about 400 persons in Kettering. My archival and oral history research combined with fieldwork also identified The Alps as Trelawny's first Baptist-founded free village of New Birmingham, which with Sligoville (Jamaica's first Baptist free village) in the parish of St. Catherine provided the model for the Jamaican free-village system (Paget 1964; Besson 1984b; Reid 2000). I carried out this comparative study of Trelawny free villages in 1983 but continued research in Granville up to the year 2000. Further, recurrent fieldwork from 1968 to 2001 charted the founding and consolidation of Martha Brae's satellite squatter settlement of Zion, on neighboring Holland Estate. I draw on that wider study of Trelawny peasant communities in this book.

From 1979 to 2001 I also extended my fieldwork to the Leeward Maroon community of Accompong Town in St. Elizabeth, the oldest surviving corporate maroon society in the Americas descended from rebel slaves and consolidated after Jamaica's First Maroon War of 1725–39. From 1991 to 1999 my research included Accompong's neighboring community of Ockbrook/Aberdeen in St. Elizabeth, established by emancipated slaves in association with the Moravian mission church. In 1999–2001 I then undertook fieldwork in Maroon Town, St. James, a nonmaroon settlement that has evolved on the site of the historic maroon village of Cudjoe's Town/Trelawny Town whose inhabitants were deported to Nova Scotia after the Second Maroon War of 1795–96. The study of these three communities (Accompong, Aberdeen, and Maroon Town) at the maroon-nonmaroon peasant interface has likewise enhanced my understanding of Martha Brae's two histories. Due to constraints of space, however, this research in the parishes of St. James and St. Elizabeth is the subject of another book (Besson, forthcoming).

In addition to my research in these ten Jamaican communities, I undertook fieldwork in the Eastern Caribbean during 1992–94. This research reinforced my knowledge of the Caribbean regional context of Martha Brae's two histories. It included work with Caribs, East Indians, and Afro-Creoles in urban and rural areas of Trinidad and Tobago in 1992; interviews in Dominica, Antigua, and Barbuda in 1993; and visits to the British and American Virgin Islands (Tortola, Virgin Gorda, St. Thomas, and St. John), St. Kitts, Barbados, St. Lucia, St. Barts, and Martinique in 1993–94. (I also visited Guadeloupe in 2001.)

My interpretation of Martha Brae's two histories has also been influenced by my personal Caribbean background. The inclusion of this information departs from the traditional anthropological view, consolidated in the context of colonialism, of the anthropologist as an "objective" outsider-observer of "other cultures" (e.g., Malinowski 1922; Beattie 1964; Kuper 1976). Instead, I draw on more recent postcolonial developments regarding "positioned subjectivity" (Asad 1973; Rosaldo 1993; Whitaker 1998) and "anthropology at home" (Amit 2000). Although the concept of anthropology at home usually refers to Europeans and Euro-Americans conducting fieldwork in Europe or North America, I use it here to include so-called Third World anthropologists like myself undertaking research in their own society.[6]

In a powerful and moving book, *Culture and Truth: The Remaking of Social Analysis*, Renato Rosaldo argues for the transformation of ethnographic writing from a so-called objective analysis of a "culture" as a coherent whole, with a timeless present, to a recognition that the ethnographer is "a positioned subject" who "occupies a position or structural location and observes with a particular angle of vision," and who therefore "grasps certain human phenomena better than others" (1993:19). The ethnographer's age, gender, sexuality, "race," class, culture, "life experiences," and "outsider" or "insider" status all influence her or his interpretation of the "life processes" that form the basis of a diverse reality. As such, even "so-called natives are also positioned subjects who have a distinctive mix of insight and blindness," and an ethnography is always provisional and incomplete (19, 8). This book on Martha Brae is no exception. I therefore attempt to delineate my positioned subjectivity in relation to my fieldwork and to my interpretation of the settlement's two histories.

By way of introducing myself in relation to my research, I first clarify that I am neither a Frenchman as some eminent scholars first concluded, nor a black Marxist writer as others initially assumed. I am a Jamaican woman, born (as Jean McFarlane) in the island's capital city of Kingston in 1944, and through marriage now have a creolized Trinidadian surname (Besson

1989a:18). I grew up in Trelawny, the rural parish where Martha Brae is situated, and received my secondary education (1953–62) at St. Hilda's Diocesan High School, Brown's Town, an Anglican school in the adjoining parish of St. Ann. At that time, unknown to me, Sidney Mintz (1955, 1957, 1958) was undertaking his groundbreaking studies of St. Ann's Baptist free village of Sturge Town and the related Brown's Town marketplace. In the Jamaican color-class system of social stratification I am classified as "fair colored" and "middle class," but in Britain I am regarded as "white" (with a "perm") and in the southern United States as "African American."

My Jamaican roots reflect the plantation-peasant interplay and the process of creolization or "indigenization" that are central to Martha Brae's two histories. My paternal background originates partly in the McFarlane planter family, of Scots descent, in the parishes of St. Elizabeth and St. James, dating back to the mid-eighteenth century.[7] My grandfather, George Lindsay McFarlane (1870–1957), a fifth-generation Meso-creole descendant of the McFarlanes in Jamaica (Besson 2001b), was, however, a self-made planter. He purchased estates in St. James, from Spring Garden (a few miles outside Montego Bay) to Great River (near Montpelier Estate),[8] and in the parish of St. Catherine. In the early twentieth century "Mas George" introduced the first private land settlement schemes for the peasantry of St. Catherine and St. James.

My father, Kenneth Murdoch McFarlane (1910–86), was George McFarlane's third son and fourth "legitimate" child. He entered the Jamaican legal profession, studying law in the colony and obtaining his external degree from the University of London in 1933. At the time of his death, he was the longest-serving attorney-at-law on Jamaica's North Coast, having worked for fifty-three years in the parishes of Hanover, Trelawny, and St. James;[9] much of his legal work was based in Falmouth, the second capital of Trelawny, which eclipsed the planter town of Martha Brae. As the youngest son of a planter family in a British West Indian plantation society based on primogeniture (chapter 2), he did not inherit his father's estates. Nevertheless, from a professional base he reestablished himself among the planter class—in Trelawny, where I spent my childhood on the "properties" of Southfield, Merrywood, Top Hill, Holland, Maxfield, and Irving Tower, all former slave plantations in the vicinity of Martha Brae.

Having purchased and resold such plantations at various times, however, Ken McFarlane was soon creating the first private land settlement schemes for the Trelawny peasantry and setting up his own dole system for the destitute of the parish, who nicknamed him "Lawyer" and "Champion of the Poor." He was invited to become *custos* of Trelawny—in a context that would have led him, as the island's senior custos at that time, to become acting governor-general of Jamaica.[10] But he declined and continued to farm and to work as an attorney until the age of seventy-five (by which time he had returned to his hometown of Montego Bay). Known as "The Sage" in the legal profession, he greatly enriched my understanding of the interplay, in Martha Brae, between customary land tenure and Jamaica's colonially derived agrarian legal code (chapter 4). His role as a philanthropist and patron to the peasantry not only contributed to my appreciation of its emphasis on land acquisition but also facilitated my acceptance as a researcher in the Trelawny peasant communities, particularly in Martha Brae and Granville. This book is dedicated especially to him.

My membership through Lawyer in the local planter class and my "structural location" as the daughter of a patron were therefore significant in positioning my relationship with the peasantry, especially in the discussion of land issues. Yet I was fairly naive about agrarian relations when I began my fieldwork, being preoccupied with the academic debate on family structure, despite the villagers' frequent references to their problems of "land room." My plantation upbringing also inhibited my involvement in village life in the early stages of my research. For example, as a member of the Falmouth Anglican planter church, I did not attempt to participate in the Afro-creole Revival cult until after many years of fieldwork.

The plantation strand of my background might also have positioned my subjectivity entirely against the view of Caribbean peasantries as a mode of "resistant response" to the plantation system (Mintz 1989:131–250) and completely in favor of the interpretation of the flight from the estates in terms of an attachment by freed slaves to the plantations, a preference of ex-slaves for remaining as estate-based peasants in peaceful coexistence with benevolent planters, and an exodus caused only by some draconian postslavery planter policies and legislation (Paget 1964; D. Hall 1978; Marshall 1979). My perspective on the "flight" and on the plantation-peasant interface (the contexts in which Martha Brae was transformed, chapters 1 and 3–6), which evolved in the later years of my research, was "repositioned" (Rosaldo 1993:7) not only by a growing appreciation of my own partial peasant background, but also by my anthropological training and experience. These factors led me to interpret Caribbean peasant cultures as "oppositional" to the plantation system and other forms of land monopoly and as "diagnostic" of such complex and historically shifting power relations.[11]

My maternal family is rooted partly in the peasantry of the parish of St. Elizabeth. My mother's father, Albert Angelo Myers (1878–1966), son of David Solomon Myers and Margaret Elliot, was from an Afro-Jewish peasantshopkeeping family in the village of Top Hill, where their house yard, provision ground, and family land can still be seen.[12] David Solomon's paternal grandfather, Michael S. Myers (ca. 1786–1870), is said to have been a second-generation German Jew who emigrated from Portsmouth, England, to Jamaica about 1801. According to his obituary in the *Colonial Standard*, he lived in Jamaica for sixty-nine of his eighty-five years, mainly as a magistrate at Portsea in St. Elizabeth, though he was granted a patent around 1824 for three hundred acres of land in the District of Look Behind in northeastern St. Elizabeth.[13] Some of Michael Myers's descendants became small farmers in St. Elizabeth, married into the Jamaican peasantry, and became Christianized. David's mother, for example, was a *sambo* of three-quarters African and a quarter European descent, and his wife Margaret (from Ballards' Valley) was "colored." Albert Angelo Myers's maternal grandfather was English and his maternal grandmother was a sambo who claimed some Arawak blood. Albert Myers was therefore descended from Afro-Jamaican slaves, and he knew persons who had been enslaved. He attended the government primary school in Top Hill, where he won a scholarship to Munro College (then known as Potsdam) around 1887.[14]

In 1897, just over one hundred years ago, Albert Myers became one of the first colored Jamaicans to win the Jamaica Scholarship. This colonial award enabled him to study medicine at King's College, London. There he met my maternal grandmother, Elizabeth Murton Philpott (1877–1966), who had departed from her genteel Victorian background to become a nursing sister at King's. Elizabeth's family in Cranbrook, Kent, was of English gentry descended from Sir John Philpott, lord mayor of London (1378–79), who owned a manor in Gillingham, Dorset.[15] Albert Myers, after working as a doctor for many years in England (where he was denied an officer's commission in World War I on the grounds of his color), returned to the British West Indies and served in Dominica (where he married my maternal grandmother and where my mother was born) and Jamaica. My paternal grandmother, Edith Adair McFarlane (née Baxter, 1880–1935) from St. Catherine, had links with the Jamaican peasantry as well. Her branch of the Baxter family in eastern Jamaica was of Scots-maroon descent, the Scottish Baxters having settled in Fort George, St. Mary, adjoining St. Catherine, near the Windward Maroons.[16]

My work for this book is indebted to many others, too, only some of whom can be mentioned here. My mother, Meg (Myers) McFarlane, encouraged and helped me in so very many ways throughout the years of my research, which she enriched with her own knowledge of the Jamaican peasantry. In addition, her provision of regular motor transport for the market women of

Martha Brae who traveled to and from Falmouth (chapter 6), before the era of the minibus, transcending the social distance of Jamaican color-class relations,[17] contributed to my acceptance in the village and further influenced my "positioned (and repositioned)" subjectivity (Rosaldo 1993:7). My husband, Dr. John Besson, whom I met in 1963, when he was a medical student in the Edinburgh University West Indian Students' Association (founded by his father in 1923), not only broadened my Caribbean regional perspective through the knowledge of his paternal and maternal homelands of Trinidad and Guyana, but also repeatedly rearranged his professional life to support my teaching and research.

My university teachers, colleagues, and the many students whom I have taught and from whom I have learned likewise helped to shape my interpretation of Martha Brae's two histories; my students in particular probed the complexities of adaptation, resistance, and opposition by Caribbean slaves and their descendants to changing power relations. My supervisor at the University of Edinburgh, Professor James "Jimmy" Littlejohn — a specialist on West Africa, rural Scotland, social stratification, and peasant societies — guided my doctoral study of Martha Brae at a time when the anthropology of the Caribbean region was virtually nonexistent in the United Kingdom. He then encouraged me to embark on an academic career and facilitated my first teaching post, at Edinburgh University. There, in addition to tutoring in the Social Anthropology Department from 1974 to 1976, I established an extramural course on "West Indian Societies" (Lowenthal 1972), possibly the first course on the anthropology of the Caribbean in Britain.

I subsequently developed, from 1976 to 1990, an ethnography course on the societies and cultures of the Caribbean region at the University of Aberdeen, Scotland, in the wider context of teaching anthropology in the Sociology Department, where I found common interests with anthropologists of Africa and Asia, and with sociologists such as Robert Moore who worked among West Indians in Britain and on class, "race," and ethnicity. My position at Aberdeen as the only female lecturer in a distinguished department of fifteen heightened my awareness of gender in society, a theme that became increasingly important in my research. Since 1991 the Anthropology Department at Goldsmiths College, in the University of London, has provided a fruitful context for expanding my teaching and research on the Caribbean region and diaspora.

Scholars elsewhere in the United Kingdom, Europe, the Caribbean, and the Americas have provided valuable opportunities for discussing my research in seminars, workshops, conferences, and informal contexts. These include former colleagues, such as Professors Sidney Mintz, Michel-Rolph Trouillot, and Franklin Knight in the Departments of Anthropology and History at the Johns Hopkins University, in the United States, where I held a visiting appointment as associate professor in anthropology and participated in the Program in Atlantic History and Culture in 1989–90; the Society for Caribbean Studies in the United Kingdom, in which I am a founding member (1976–77) and past chair (1987–89); the Caribbean Societies Seminar at the Institutes of Commonwealth Studies (ICS) and Latin American Studies (ILAS), University of London; the Caribbean Studies Association, Trinidad; the European Society of Caribbean Research, Berlin, Utrecht, and Vienna; the International Congress of Americanists, Stockholm; and colleagues at all three campuses of the University of the West Indies: Mona in Jamaica, St. Augustine in Trinidad and Tobago, and Cave Hill in Barbados. Especially rewarding was my participation in the international conference on "The Meaning of Freedom" at the University of Pittsburgh, held in 1988 to commemorate the centenary of the abolition of slavery in the Americas and 150 years of freedom in the Commonwealth Caribbean (McGlynn and Drescher 1992), themes directly relevant to Martha Brae's "new" history as an Afro-creole community.[18]

I am particularly indebted to Professor Sidney Mintz and Professor Pat Caplan, former director of the ICS, for reading and commenting on an earlier draft of the manuscript, and I am honored by Professor Mintz's foreword to the book. I also thank Elaine Maisner, editor, for her guidance in bringing the manuscript to completion and the two readers, Professors Jerome S. Handler and Kevin A. Yelvington, whose intellectual rigor and knowledge of the Caribbean enriched my research. However, the responsibility for the final outcome is, as usual, mine alone.

I am grateful to a range of institutions for helping to fund the research: the Ministry of Education, Jamaica; the Social Science Research Council, United Kingdom; the British Academy; the British Council; the Carnegie Trust for the Universities of Scotland; the University of Aberdeen Travel Fund; the St. Augustine Campus at the University of the West Indies, Trinidad and Tobago; Goldsmiths College, University of London; and the Nuffield Foundation, which provided both a fellowship and a small grant for completing an early draft of the book. In addition, I thank the library staff at the Universities of Aberdeen, Edinburgh, and London (Goldsmiths, the ICS, the Institute of Historical Research [IHR], the School of Oriental and African Studies, and Senate House), as well as at the National Library of Jamaica and the Institute of Jamaica in Kingston, and the Carnegie Library in Falmouth, Trelawny. I especially appreciate the help of the University of London libraries (at ICS/ILAS, IHR, and Goldsmiths) for installing the Trans-Atlantic Slave Trade Database (Eltis et al. 1999) ahead of schedule to facilitate my research.

My greatest debt of all is to the Jamaican peasantry and especially to the free villagers of Martha Brae. Many individuals assisted my research, but constraints of space permit me to mention only a few of the "older heads" in Martha Brae — whose identity I protect by pseudonyms. My landlady, Victoria Robertson (aged eighty-six in 2001), who was then the "oldest head" of the village's central family line and a second- and third-generation descendant of the emancipated slaves who established the free village, provided me with hospitality throughout my fieldwork and guided my participation in the community — thereby also influencing my positioned subjectivity. William Tapper, a great oral historian, skilled cultivator, and grandson of emancipated slaves, perhaps more than anyone else taught me the significance of the rich oral traditions of the Jamaican peasantry as well as the local meaning of "a good planting day" (chapters 5–6). Rupert Bailey, who in his nineties in the 1990s was the oldest living member of Martha Brae's Old Families, particularly illuminated my understanding of free-village life including the "burial society" of which he was president for decades (chapters 6–7). "Miss Loretta," "Miss Ruth," "Miss Madeline," "Miss Angela," "Miss Nora," and "Miss Pam," along with "Miss Victoria,"[19] especially taught me about women's lives in the community, while Pastor and Mother Jackson revealed to me the ideology, rituals, and dynamics of "reputation" central to the Revival religion, which articulates with Baptist Christianity. Through the Jacksons, I was sometimes drawn into the factionalism of Revival, but they greatly increased my knowledge of this Afro-creole ideology in which they have been involved for over fifty years (chapter 7). Some of these key figures have since died and are believed to have joined the ancestors in the Revival spirit pantheon, but their influence will continue to play a central role in Martha Brae's new history for many years to come.

As in this preface, I use fictitious names throughout the book for living and recently deceased individuals in Martha Brae and other Trelawny peasant communities. In my doctoral dissertation I also used a pseudonym for Martha Brae itself (Besson 1974). However, at the villagers' request, I subsequently revealed the identity of the community,[20] a view not only paralleling the perceived significance, in all the communities studied, of empowering the hidden history of the Jamaican peasantry but also reflecting their perception of my repositioned subjectivity. Consistent with these perspectives, I have retained the names of the Old Families: that is, the central family lines or cognatic descent groups, descended through both genders from former female and male slaves, that have perpetuated the peasant communities and their family lands in the wider contexts of Jamaican colonial and postcolonial society and the capitalist world system (chapters 3–5 and 8). I have also, for this reason, used the names and nicknames of the ancestor-heroes and -heroines of these family lines.

In addition to contributing to the discipline of social anthropology and the cultural history of the Caribbean region, this book advances Jamaica's national history—including that of the free villagers of Martha Brae and other Trelawny peasant communities. It is a portrait of their creative Afro-creole culture-building in the face of European expansion, transatlantic slavery, New World plantations, and continued Euro-American land monopoly, themes that form the central focus of Martha Brae's two histories as planter town and peasant village.

Martha Brae's
TWO HISTORIES

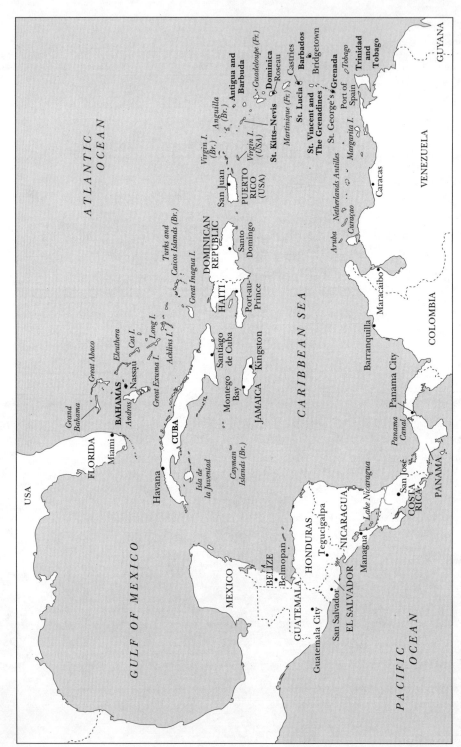

Map 1. The Caribbean Region. Adapted from *Jamaica Road Map*, new ed. (Oxford: Macmillan, 1999); Macmillan Education Ltd.

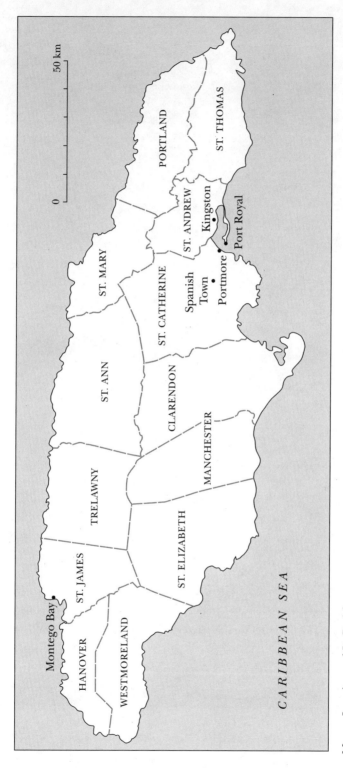

Map 2. Jamaica and Its Parishes

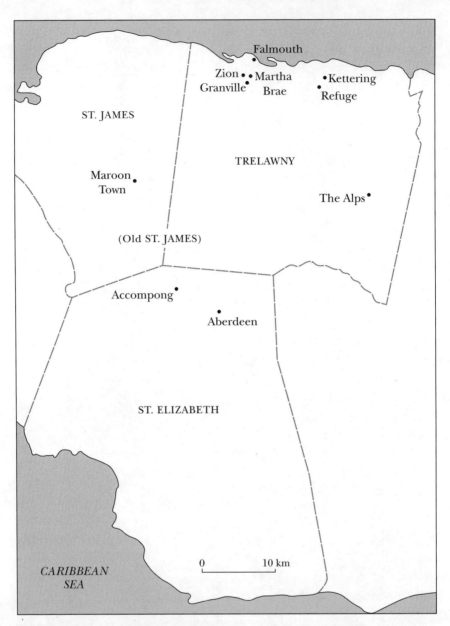

Map 3. The Ten Communities Studied in the Parishes of Trelawny, St. James, and St. Elizabeth

CHAPTER ONE

Caribbean Controversies
and Anthropological Theory

In the last three decades of the twentieth century, an explicit agenda emerged among anthropologists and historians to rectify the neglect of subaltern social and cultural history. For example, writing on the southern United States in the 1970s, Eugene Genovese observed that "the history of the lower classes has yet to be written" (1971:102), whereas Herbert Gutman (1976a, 1976b) addressed the social history of the American working class, including Afro-American slaves and their descendants. In the 1980s Eric Wolf wrote of *Europe and the People without History*, arguing that "we . . . need to uncover the history of 'the people without history' — the active histories of 'primitives,' peasantries, laborers, immigrants, and besieged minorities" (1982:x). In 1992 academics, journalists, and Native Americans all felt it necessary to point to the hidden histories of the post-Columbian Americas in the context of the New World quincentenary. This theme was again highlighted in 1994 by the Forty-eighth International Congress of Americanists on "Threatened Peoples and Environments in the Americas." In the late 1990s Roger Keesing and Andrew Strathern still maintained that anthropologists have frequently regarded peasant communities "as more or less closed and self-contained, and often as devoid of known history" (1998:401).

Anthropology, History, and the Caribbean Region

The slighting of "the people without history" was perhaps nowhere more pronounced than in the Caribbean region, variously described as the "Third World's third world" (Naipaul 1973), the First World's first annex, and the "core area" of African America (Mintz 1989:22, 1996a:304). Here the Native Americans were virtually wiped out and post-Conquest societies were manufactured through European colonization,

5

American plantations, African slavery, and Asian, African, and European indenture. From the 1970s to the 1990s Sidney Mintz highlighted the neglect of African American history and emergent Caribbean cultures. In the first entry on the Caribbean in the *Annual Review of Anthropology*, Michel-Rolph Trouillot (1992a:35) wrote of the region as "an open frontier in anthropological theory" and identified the continuing marginality of Caribbean anthropology where "few dare to bring explicitly to the discipline the political or metatheoretical lessons learned on the frontier."[1] In the *Encyclopedia of Social and Cultural Anthropology*, Kevin Yelvington (1998:86) stated that "the social and cultural anthropology of the Caribbean has been made peripheral to the core of the discipline." At the start of the twenty-first century there were still few courses on the anthropology of the Caribbean region in British universities.

Nevertheless anthropologists, historians, and specialists in creole languages and literature have begun to uncover the processes of accommodation, opposition, and resistance by Caribbean peoples to colonization, slavery, indenture, and neocolonial land monopoly. Much of this process has been effected through open and violent struggle, such as slave rebellion and the maroon wars of runaway slaves. But much has been hidden, subtle, and creative, including the reconstruction of new cultures and identities. Anthropology therefore has a crucial role to play in uncovering post-Conquest Caribbean cultural history. This cultural history, in turn, is central to anthropology, for it illuminates "the nature of culture, understood as a continuous process of retention and renewal" (Trouillot 1992a:30) and "memorializes, by the careful documentation of small events, the most remarkable drama of culture-building in the modern world" (Mintz 1980:15).[2]

Caribbean Peasantries and Martha Brae

Some themes in Caribbean cultural history have now received considerable attention, such as the varying responses of the enslaved. Nevertheless, Mintz recognized the persisting neglect of Caribbean peasantries, who "represent *a mode of response* to the plantation system and its connotations, and *a mode of resistance* to imposed styles of life" (1989:132–33). Mintz defined "peasantry" in general as "a class (or classes) of rural landowners producing a large part of the products they consume, but also selling to (and buying from) wider markets, and dependent in various ways upon wider political and economic spheres of control" (132). He later qualified the criterion of land ownership by noting that peasants are "small-scale cultivators who own or *have access to* land" (141, emphasis mine). He further argued that "Caribbean peasantries are, in this view, *reconstituted* peasantries, having begun other than as peasants—in slavery, as deserters or runaways, as plantation laborers, or whatever—and becoming peasants in some kind of resistant response to an externally imposed regimen" (132). For Mintz this process of peasantization occurred even in the slavery era, beginning almost immediately after the Conquest, a view that contrasts with Woodville Marshall's (1985:2) assertion that the British West Indian peasantry "starts at emancipation in 1838."

From this perspective Mintz (1989:146–56) identified, in addition to postslavery peasantries, four types of peasant adaptation in the colonial slavery period: post-Conquest "squatters," "early yeomen," the "proto-peasantry," and "runaway peasantries" or maroons. The "squatters" were escaped slaves, free persons of color, and white deserters, drawing on Arawak, European, and African cultural heritages, who from the sixteenth century squatted illegally in remote interiors of the Greater Antilles colonized by Spain. This adaptation was sooner or later wiped out by the escalating plantation system. However, Martha Brae's satellite squatter settlement of Zion, established on "captured land" on Holland Estate during the period of my fieldwork (1968–2001), represents a new variant of Caribbean squatter peasantry. The "early yeomen" were Euro-Caribbean peasants who emerged in the Lesser Antilles in the seventeenth century, when postindentured laborers left the plantations and acquired small land grants. But these peasants, too, were soon wiped out by the burgeoning slave plantation system. The "proto-peasantry" consisted of African and creole or local-born slaves who developed a peasantlike adaptation within the plantation system itself from the eighteenth century, especially in British Jamaica and French Saint Domingue. The "runaway peasantries," or maroons, were rebel slaves who established virtually autonomous communities in almost inaccessible terrain during the entire slavery period throughout African America, especially in Dutch Guiana (Suriname) and Jamaica. Protopeasants and maroons laid the foundations for postslavery peasants, including those of Martha Brae.

Mintz's work on peasantization and aspects of the peasant lifestyle (the house-yard complex, production, consumption, and exchange) has illuminated economic and political anthropology. His studies have generated further research, and in the second edition of *Caribbean Transformations* he observed that "two scholars in particular have significantly advanced our understanding of Caribbean peasant societies in recent years" (1989:xxvii). Here Mintz noted Trouillot's (1988) study of the Dominican banana peasantry in the world economy and my own articles on land and kinship in the free villages of Trelawny Parish, Jamaica. Mintz (1989:xxvii) pointed to the need for a book-length study of one of these Trelawny communities, Martha Brae, where ex-slaves had transformed a colonial planter town at the heart of the Caribbean region into a postemancipation peasant village at the vanguard of the flight from the British West Indian plantations. He also restated that "the fact is that too few observers have analyzed the peasant life-style with the seriousness it deserves," and "relatively few books and papers have dealt with the origins and history of peasant subcultures and the similarities and differences among them. Even rarer are historical studies which deal in a detailed fashion with one or another aspect of rural life in the region as a whole" (144, 230). This book on Martha Brae's two histories seeks to contribute to these neglected areas of study and to show their wider relevance to African American studies, Caribbean cultural history, and social anthropological theory.

First, the book contextualizes, integrates, and develops Martha Brae's Euro-Caribbean "plantation" history and uncovers its Afro-Caribbean cultural history by analyzing "the peasant life-style with the seriousness it deserves" (Mintz 1989:144). In so doing, it provides a wholistic account of this settlement at the very center of African America and at the gateway to Europe's New World. Second, the book contributes to documenting "the origins and history of [Caribbean] peasant subcultures and the similarities and differences among them" (230) by situating Martha Brae's Afro-creole cultural history within the wider context of a comparative study of five other peasant communities in Trelawny Parish at the heart of the Caribbean peasant interface with plantations, bauxite mines, and the tourist industry. Third, Martha Brae's Afro-creole cultural history and its comparative context leads to a detailed analysis of a central "aspect of rural life in the region as a whole" (230), namely, customary land tenures reflecting kinship and community, interweaving with creole cosmologies and oral traditions, and rooted in the slavery and postslavery past. Central to the continuity of Martha Brae as a free village is the "family-land" institution, a customary kin-based tenure that exists not only in other Trelawny free villages but also throughout Jamaica and in many other Caribbean territories. My analysis reveals that family land is not a cultural survival from either Africa or Europe, as conventional theories contend. Instead, it is a creole institution created by the peasantries themselves through Caribbean culture-building in the face of Euro-American land monopoly. This conclusion advances Mintz's perspective on Caribbean peasantries and reinforces Mintz and Richard Price's (1992) thesis of African American institution-building, recently restated by Price (2001).

My analysis of such customary land tenures and of Martha Brae's two histories modifies Mintz and Price's creolization thesis in two important and related ways. First, Mintz and Price posit that the birth of African American culture was effected by slaves creating institutions "*within* the parameters of the masters' monopoly of power, but *separate from* the masters' institutions" (1992:39). In contrast, Martha Brae's two histories reflect the *appropriation and overturning* of European institutions by African American slaves and their descendants, paralleling the peasant transformation of the planter town — and the current transformation of part of Holland Estate into Martha Brae's satellite squatter settlement of Zion. This process of reversal is most clearly manifested in the family-land institution, which is rooted in the institution-building of male and female slaves who appropriated slave village yards and plantation provision grounds in a customary system of tenure, use, and land transmission to all of an individual slave's descendants regardless of age, gender, or legitimacy. This customary system of unrestricted nonunilineal or cognatic descent overturned and reversed exclusive European primogeniture, whereby only "legitimate" children inherited, males had precedence, and the eldest son had primacy. This nonexclusive cognatic descent system, which continued after emancipation to the present, has maximized scarce land rights and formerly forbidden kinship lines among the descendants of chattel slaves — who were not only legally landless and kinless, but were also regarded as property themselves. In addition, it has changed aspects of state law and contributed to Caribbean nation-building.

Second, Mintz and Price (1992:68–70) assert that such overlapping, nonexclusive cognatic descent groups (traced through both genders and including all of an individual's descendants) could not function for landholding in the postslavery Caribbean. Yet my analysis reveals that such landholding systems are widespread in contemporary Caribbean societies, where they articulate with even more inclusive common tenures and with circulatory migration and transnational identities — and thereby with the Caribbean diaspora in North America and Europe. Paradoxically this critique, with its evidence of a cultural re-creation that also transformed the restricted unilineal landholding kin groups derived from West and Central Africa,[3] develops Mintz and Price's creolization or Caribbeanization thesis, for my analysis uncovers a culture-building process even more creative than the one they identified.

My interpretation also unravels the so-called mysteries of Caribbean landholding kin groups referred to by Mintz and Price (1992:75). It likewise clarifies other Caribbeanist controversies including the flight-from-the-estates and family-land debates, arguments concerning the definition and developmental potential of Caribbean peasantries, issues in the interpretation of Jamaican religion and the Afro-Caribbean family system, and the disagreement on the articulation of race, class, culture, and gender in the Caribbean region.

Race, Class, Culture, and Gender in the Caribbean

Over the past fifty years social scientists have sought to identify, through various theoretical perspectives, the interrelation of race, class, and culture in Caribbean societies. Particularly resilient has been the functionalist-pluralist debate.[4] This controversy has focused especially on the non-Hispanic Caribbean, particularly on the anglophone variant and Jamaica — the major English-speaking territory. There have also been attempts to synthesize the two opposing views. Martha Brae's two histories illuminate and engender this debate.

The Functionalist-Pluralist Debate

Fernando Henriques (1968) advanced an early functionalist perspective of Jamaican society and culture, paralleled by Lloyd Braithwaite's (1975) and Hyman Rodman's (1971) studies on Trinidad and Raymond Smith's (1956) analysis of British Guianese free villages. This functionalist approach, developed in Smith's later studies of kinship and class in Guyana and Jamaica (1988, 1996), draws on Talcott Parsons's (1952) view of social stratification in the United States, which emphasized consensus and common values integrating various classes in the social system. In the Caribbean context, functionalists assumed that a white bias integrated different color classes through common adherence to European cultural values. Thus Henriques portrayed the Jamaican social system as a hierarchy of color classes, defined by the complex variable of *color* and economic criteria, held together by Eurocentric values originating in slave society. However, he did not adequately address the capitalist class relations that are central to Martha Brae's two histories.

In an attempt to deal with power, conflict, and cultural diversity, Michael Smith (1965a, 1965b, 1984) advanced his "plural society" theory of the Commonwealth Caribbean as an explicit challenge to the functionalist approach. He developed J. S. Furnivall's (1945, 1948) view of South-East Asian colonial societies, in which different "racial" and cultural groups were portrayed as held together only through the power and domination of a European colonial elite. In a case study of Jamaica, Smith (1965a:162–75) contrasted the European culture of the white minority elite with the folk culture of the black majority stemming from Africa and slavery. His discussion included an analysis of the differences in "property concepts and distribution" that highlighted the significance of family land: "Among the economically dominant section, property takes the typical form of productive enterprise, such as commercial businesses, firms, factories, estates, or the like. . . . Among the lowest section, the dominant property form is 'family land,' that is, land held without proper legal title, and without precise personal distribution of rights, by the members of a family and their dependants" (169). But despite his "institutional analysis" (80), he recognized neither the dynamic process of institution-building in family land nor the complex interplay between this customary tenure and the legal code, while his interpretation of West Indian family structure (1962b) oversimplified the family system of the Jamaican peasantry.

Lambros Comitas's (1962, 1973) studies of five coastal communities in Jamaica, including Duncans (adjoining the free village of Kettering) near Martha Brae, adopted Michael Smith's plural society approach. However, Comitas's contention that there was no peasant adaptation in Jamaica slighted the significance of the reconstituted peasantries of Trelawny Parish. Erna Brodber's (1983) study of oral history in the parish of St. James, adjoining Trelawny, was also presented from a pluralist perspective — a static model that overlooked dynamic creolization and constrained her analysis of the oral traditions so central to Afro-Jamaican peasant communities like Martha Brae (Besson 1989a:18, 1992b).

Functionalist-Pluralist Syntheses

Various attempts have been made to resolve or synthesize the functionalist-pluralist debate. George Beckford's plantation society thesis (1999) includes an implicit synthesis. He argues that Third World plantation societies, such as those of the Caribbean region, are plural societies typified by a white bias and "class-caste" stratification. However, although Beckford also explores the persistent poverty generated by capitalist class relations, he contends that the plantation system resulted in weak families and communities, a perspective that does not accurately portray Martha Brae and other Trelawny villages, with their strong communities and kin groups persisting in the face of the world's most pronounced plantation system. Nor does Beckford sufficiently acknowledge the historical and ethnographic specificity of the Caribbean region.[5]

A more extensive synthesis was advanced by David Lowenthal (1972:76–

212) in his analysis of West Indian or non-Hispanic Caribbean societies as characterized by white-biased color classes and social and cultural pluralism. Using a fivefold classification, he analyzed forty-five societies as variants on these themes (76–87). His main variant, the "standard Creole structure," comprised the majority of such societies, including Jamaica; his discussion of pluralism included family land (103–4). Although Lowenthal's analysis reinforced both the functionalist and pluralist perspectives, he moved beyond them in highlighting the variations among the non-Hispanic territories. Elsewhere (Lowenthal 1961, 1987), he provided perceptive interpretations of Caribbean attitudes to land that illuminate both histories of Martha Brae, though, like Michael Smith, he did not consider the dynamic interplay between legal and customary land-tenure systems. Drawing on Lowenthal's analysis of West Indian societies, Harry Hoetink (1985) further widened and elucidated the regional context with a comparison of "race" and "color" in non-Hispanic and Hispanic Caribbean variants. For Hoetink, whereas non-Hispanic territories are typified by social and cultural pluralism and color-class hierarchies, Hispanic Caribbean societies have homogeneous cultures and a continuum of color, a difference resulting from contrasting histories of colonialism, slavery, and plantations.

Reputation and Respectability

Another synthesis of the functionalist-pluralist controversy is Peter Wilson's (1969, 1973, 1995) still-influential thesis of "respectability," "reputation," and "crab antics," which considers gender as a major theme. Wilson focuses on anglophone Afro-Caribbean societies, but his analysis of reputation draws on the concept of machismo or manhood in Hispanic Caribbean territories. Wilson seeks to resolve the opposing views of shared or separate value systems; he also aims to shift attention from the Afro-Caribbean family and household, with its emphasis on women and the "matrifocal family," to the total social system (including the elusive dynamics of community) and the behavior of the so-called marginal lower-class Afro-Caribbean male. His thesis centers on the ethnography of the tiny island of Providencia, which he views as similar to rural communities elsewhere in the English-speaking West Indies. Though politically tied to Catholic Spanish-speaking Colombia, Providencia has a Protestant anglophone Caribbean culture, having been settled in the eighteenth century by Euro-Jamaican planters and their Afro-Jamaican slaves. It can therefore be regarded as particularly like Jamaican rural communities, and Wilson argues for the Jamaican origin of Providencian family land (1995:56).

Wilson suggests that the essence of Providencian society is a dialectic between "respectability" (the shared value system of the functionalists) and "reputation" (the separate value system of the pluralists). Respectability is rooted in colonial social stratification based on class, color, wealth, and Europe-centered culture, lifestyle, and education and is perpetuated especially by the white churches, the European institution of legal marriage, and Eurocentric educational systems. In contrast, reputation is an "indigenous" or creole counterculture based on the ethos of equality and personal, as opposed to social, worth. In Providencia, island identity and equality and the associated value system of reputation are ingrained in the symbolism of land, reflected especially in the ideology of equal inheritance by siblings of house-spots and gardens and in undivided family land. Another important basis of island equality is kinship, and, in its more literal sense, reputation is based on verbal skills and anti-establishment activities.

Reputation and respectability are, Wilson maintains, differentially subscribed to in terms of race, class, gender, and age. He identifies two color classes in Providencia: a small, richer, whiter "high class" and a larger, poorer, blacker "other class." Respectability is especially the concern of the "high class," which sees its respectable lifestyle as a rationale for its elite status and wealth. Although the "other class" shares this value system of respectability, it is more fully oriented to reputation with its egalitarian ethos. For Wilson, men and women vary in their orientation to reputation and respectability. Women, even those of the "other class," are the bearers of Eurocentric respectability. Wilson attributes this orientation of Afro-Caribbean women to their closer association with the master class during slavery as concubines and domestic slaves.[6] Women are also more involved in the white churches, with their secular concern for the propriety of domestic life and European marriage. Men, on the other hand, particularly those of the "other class," subscribe especially to egalitarian values. In Providencia, land—the symbol of island identity and equality—is essentially controlled by men, and brotherhood provides a model for kinship solidarity outside the female domestic domain.

It is here—his pursuit of the existential focus of the so-called marginal Afro-Caribbean male—that Wilson's main theoretical contribution lies. The locus of this existentialism is the small, informal groups of men of similar status and generation called "crews," who have often sailed, fished, or worked together and who meet regularly beyond the household. Crews gather especially in rum shops, where the dynamics of reputation, in the more literal sense of informal ranking based on personal worth, can be observed. The basis of a man's reputation is his virility, manifested in sexual conquests and the fathering of many children — "poor men's riches" (Wilson 1995:74) — and established by boasting in this public domain. But virility is only one of a wider class of expressive skills that contribute to a man's reputation, which is also derived from entrepreneurial activities and recognized by the bestowing of titles and nicknames. Wilson further hypothesizes that reputation is rooted in Afro-Christian cults that, in contrast to the female-oriented secular white churches concerned with domestic morality, are male-centered and more involved with power and the sacred. Moreover, the variable of age influences the differential orientation to respectability and reputation in that as men grow older, they have less interest in the dynamics of reputation and more regard for respectability. This is evidenced by fewer visits to the rum shop, more interest in the church, and a greater commitment to legal marriage.

Wilson contends that in Providencia the dialectic between reputation and respectability is manifested in "crab antics," behavior designed to level claims to superior status, citing a Providencian proverb that is also found in Martha Brae.[7] A major context for such crab antics is the inheritance of land, for, as Wilson notes, land is not only a source of equality, but also of differentiation and prestige. Thus, despite the ideology of equal inheritance, coheirs maneuver to secure a greater share of land and thus of island identity. This is manifested in two island attitudes to land, namely, "covetousness and contentiousness" (Wilson 1995:58), and in land disputes, which occur especially among men. Other leveling mechanisms include ridicule and gossip, as both reputation and respectability may be destroyed by words.

Reputation and Respectability Reconsidered

Wilson's study is in many ways a significant contribution to Caribbean anthropology, with wider implications for development and change. It identifies a creole counterculture to colonialism, rooted especially in land, and draws attention to male Afro-Caribbean life, while the concept of "crab antics" is useful in relation to land disputes, such as those that sometimes occur in Martha Brae. But his theory has weaknesses when considered from the perspective of Afro-Caribbean peasant women (Besson 1993). First, the male value system of reputation, which Wilson advances as a model for development, is partly based on unequal and exploitative gender relations. Second, he mistakenly assumes that opposition to colonial culture is the preserve of Afro-Caribbean men and that black Caribbean women are perpetuators of Eurocentric values. Third, Wilson's conclusion that reputation is primarily male-oriented overlooks the fact that women, too, compete for status, both among themselves and with men. Fourth, his analysis of contemporary gender relations is based on the argument that slave women upheld the values of the master class, an untenable perspective.[8]

Despite these flaws in Wilson's theory, his view of Afro-Caribbean women is reflected in other studies of gender in the region. Thus Roland Littlewood (1993:295 [n. 42]) defends Wilson's thesis, and his own use of it, in response to my critique based on preliminary data from Martha Brae (Besson 1993): "Jean Besson . . . has pointed out that the respectability-reputation dichotomy undervalues the very real idea of resistance by Black women against slavery . . . my own reading (and I think that of Peter Wilson) is that his bipolarity is to be read as polythetic: women are respectable, not as a fixed characteristic but relative to men." My appraisal questions Wilson's interpretation of the respectability-reputation paradigm precisely as defined by Littlewood. Moreover, in the book in which my article appears, three other contributors of both genders disagree with Wilson's thesis (see Brana-Shute 1993, McKay 1993, and Yelvington 1993). Other critical assessments of his perspective have been advanced by Barbara Bush (1990:1–3), Karen Olwig (1990), Michel-Rolph Trouillot (1992a:26), Daniel Miller (1994:259–64), Kevin Yelvington (1995, 1996, 1998:88), and Virginia Young (1993:115, 154), some of whom draw on my critique. My evaluation of Wilson has also been supported elsewhere (Kossek 1995:198; Constance Sutton, personal communication 1996); Sutton's (1974) own review of Wilson's work expressed an early unease.

More recently, focusing on Jamaica from 1834 to 1865 (from the abolition of slavery, through apprenticeship and emancipation, to the Morant Bay Rebellion), Mimi Sheller (1998) draws on my work to advance the critique of Wilson and illuminate the role of black women with particular reference to political protest and public leadership (these women included ex-slaves on Trelawny plantations and in the parish capital of Falmouth, where they were sometimes sent for punishment). She identifies three important areas of such female participation. First, black female agricultural workers opposed "coercive plantation labour policies, especially during the apprenticeship period" on the grounds of their roles as wives and mothers, thereby manipulating Eurocentric domesticity and respectability to serve their own ends: the consolidation of free villages and access to land (90, 98–99). Second, black women challenged "white male control of religion," especially through Revival leadership as "Mothers" and "Queens"; at this time about two-thirds of Baptist class leaders were female (90, 100–103). Third, black women utilized urban popular culture and outdoor space, dominating streets and marketplaces to channel flows of information and mobilize political action. Such female street culture included political protests in Falmouth in 1840 and 1859 and the initiation of the Morant Bay Rebellion in 1865, after which several women were hanged (105–11).

Gender in Culture-Building

The critique of Wilson's thesis is reinforced by Martha Brae's new history, which underscores the culture-building of both female and male slaves and the opposition to the plantation system by ex-slaves and their descendants of both genders who appropriated the planter town. Although women (and men) in Martha Brae play a significant role in the Christian Church, this is the Nonconformist Baptist Church, which is the free villagers' formal symbol of opposition to the Established Anglican Church that reinforced the plantation slavery system. The house yard (the spatial dimension of the domestic domain) is another symbol of autonomy from the surrounding plantations. The yard is also the nucleus of the peasant economy, as in the protopeasant past. Although provision grounds are mainly a male domain, some women cultivate them.

In Wilson's model of respectability, the house yard and the Christian Church are linked through the domestic domain and a focus on European legal marriage. The link between the Christian Church and the domestic domain can be identified in Martha Brae, where women sometimes remark that the Baptist Church condemns "sinful living" and baptizes illegitimate children on special days. This does not, however, reflect a commitment to early European legal marriage among the women of Martha Brae, who, with their men, have forged a creole family system grounded in the protopeasant adaptation.[9]

In Martha Brae females, as well as males, participate in all the major dimensions of Wilson's model of reputation, namely, landholding, creole cults, entrepreneurship, oral culture, procreation, titles, and nicknaming. Both genders are involved in acquiring land of their own. Through the cognatic descent system both women and men transmit land rights, serve as family-land trustees, create new family estates from purchased land, and sometimes engage in crab antics or land disputes. Family land also provides a significant context for oral culture and its transmission by both genders, and both ancestor-heroes and ancestress-heroines feature in such oral traditions. Whereas men are prominent in the Rastafarian movement, women are central to the Revival cult and the related dynamics of reputation based on verbal skills. Similarly, both genders are significant in the friendly society, which integrates Revival and Baptist Christianity. Females, like males, keep shops and are the vanguard of the peasant marketing system; both genders participate in rotating savings and credit associations, occupational multiplicity, and migration.

Women as well as men have titles and nicknames reflecting their reputations in and around Martha Brae. The male titles of "Captain" and "Prof" are based on seafaring skills and "professing Science" respectively;[10] male nicknames include "Sam Isaacs" for the village's mortician (after one of the island's leading funeral parlors) and Rastafarian nicknaming. The title "Miss" combined with the female Christian name, regardless of conjugal status (like the feminist "Ms."), refers to women of reputation, such as landholders, shopkeepers, and market higglers; the title "Mother" is used for female Revival leaders. In addition to Revival Mothers in Martha Brae, oral tradition in the neighboring free village of Granville suggests that the ex-slave "Mother Lawrence" may have been a leader in the Myal cult at the heart and height of Myalism.[11] Trelawny free-village oral tradition likewise includes male and female nicknames, such as the emancipated slave "Queenie," who may have been a Kumina "Queen,"[12] and her ex-slave brothers "Poor Man" and "Hard Time" in Refuge. "Nanny," the Windward Maroon leader who also features in Leeward Maroon oral history, is a further illustration of female nicknaming (Besson 1997, 1998a, 2000). Many women and men have "pet-names," in contrast to their Christian names, to convey their individuality and protect them from Revival spirits. Cognatic descent group titles are created and transmitted by both genders.

Motherhood is also a basis of reputation, with the positive evaluation of female fertility paralleling the valorization of male virility. As elsewhere in plantation America, the children of Trelawny slave women were not legally their own, despite the inheritance by offspring of an enslaved mother's status. Yet Caribbean slave women, as well as men, created and continued cognatic descent lines that appropriated and transmitted customary rights to land. In Martha Brae today, children continue to be "poor men's riches" (Wilson 1995:74) for women as well as men: they contribute significantly to a woman's status, symbolize her womanhood, and, potentially, represent the beginning and continuance of her landholding family line. From this perspective the shaming ritual at an unmarried girl's first pregnancy, identified by Edith Clarke (1966:99) for Jamaica and highlighted by Peter Wilson (1995:128–29) for Providencia, may be reinterpreted as a "ritual of reversal" (Besson 1989a:164–65, 1993:29) establishing female reputation, rather than reflecting a concern with loss of respectability as Wilson contends. The use of the title "Mother" for female Revival leaders also underlines the symbolic significance of motherhood. For both genders, then, titles, nicknames, and procreation are aspects of an internal status system based on personal, rather than social, worth — a mode of ranking established within the peasant community in the face of the island's Eurocentric system of social stratification.

The analysis of gender in Martha Brae therefore modifies Wilson's androcentric thesis of reputation and respectability; it reveals that women as well as men have been prominent in Caribbean culture-building and development since slavery days. In addition, Martha Brae's new history, with its examination of Revival and Rastafari, provides some of "the necessary research" urged by Wilson (1995:233) on the relations between creole cults and the community. Martha Brae's Afro-creole cultural history also develops Wilson's thesis regarding the need for a new Caribbean history to replace the region's Eurocentric history and highlights the role of land in this new engendered history.

Kinship and Class

Raymond Smith's (1988) study of kinship and class in Jamaica and Guyana returned to the functionalist-pluralist debate. In this work, published thirty-two years after his classic (1956) book on the Negro family in British Guiana (which applied Meyer Fortes's concept of the developmental cycle in West African domestic groups to Afro-Caribbean households and advanced a functionalist analysis of the "matrifocal family"), Smith sought to develop aspects of his earlier study and to explore the wider West Indian kinship system. Drawing on case studies from the "Old Middle Class," "New Middle Class," and "Lower Class" in Jamaica and Guyana, based on in-depth interviews eliciting informants' kinship concepts through the genealogical method, he questioned "certain orthodox assumptions about class differences in West Indian kinship" (1988:ix). His analysis was a critique of plural society theory but shifted from his earlier (1956) explanation of the matrifocal family in terms of economically marginal Afro-Guyanese males to a recognition of creolization in Guyana and Jamaica. He argued that these former colonies were not plural societies where black, white, and brown "social segments" had distinct cultures and institutions. Instead, "the family structure of different classes and racial groups can be understood as variations on a common structural theme" (1988:7), namely, a creole kinship system rooted in colonial history, social hierarchy, and legal and nonlegal marital unions, and generating "matrifocality" and extensive kinship ties.

As a critique of plural society theory, Smith's study was convincing and significant, shifting attention to Caribbean class relations, but as an analysis of Caribbean kinship it was less so. Whereas his earlier classic offered perspectives derived from African societies, this work was overly influenced by Euro-American urban kinship models (Besson 1990). It portrays West Indian kinship as structurally similar to English kinship and as based on noncorporate ego-focused bilateral kinship networks, an interpretation subsequently reinforced in the continuing context of his antipluralist functionalist perspective (R. T. Smith 1996:27–28). This aspect of Caribbean kinship has, however, long been recognized. What is needed now is an analysis of its articulation with the ancestor-focused unrestricted cognatic descent system — as in this book.

Such cognatic descent systems are widespread throughout the Caribbean region, especially in association with customary landholding, and are prominent in the church-founded peasant villages of Trelawny, a parish that is not only the immediate focus of Martha Brae's new history but was also one of the areas examined in Raymond Smith's Jamaican study. Smith stated that "the most important development affecting domestic life after the abolition of slavery was the establishment and growth of church-based village communities," though he rejected the peasant concept with little validation (1988:161, 126). His data also pointed to the importance of cognatic descent lines, grounded in family land, for his Afro-Caribbean informants, despite methodology biased toward ego-focused kinship and the exclusion of "the poorest of West Indians" from his study (114).

Consideration of the cognatic descent system would have been pertinent to Smith's analysis, for not only are the kinship concepts of this system explicit in Caribbean oral history, but also family land itself originates in themes central to his thesis, namely, colonial history, Caribbean class relations and culture-building, and the modern world system. Rather than being a survival from either Africa or Europe as Raymond Smith (1971, 1990) and others have suggested, or indicative of plural societies as Michael Smith (1965a) contended, family land is a creole institution created by Caribbean peasantries in the face of Euro-American land monopoly in the capitalist world economy. Such an analysis would also have aided Raymond Smith's (1988:176) search for a new term for Afro-Caribbean "yard"-based kin relations, for these are often generated by the unrestricted descent system at the heart of family land. This conclusion would, however, have fitted uneasily into his thesis. Although he touched on "class warfare" and the plantation-peasant conflict (167, 161–62), his focus was hierarchy and cultural uniformity in the Caribbean class system rather than the capitalist class relations that are central to Martha Brae's two histories.

Malcolm Cross (1979) and Diane Austin (1984), focusing on urbanization, provided more useful analyses of Caribbean and Jamaican capitalist class relations and their articulation with race and culture. But neither Cross nor Austin examined the process of culture-building that lies at the heart of Martha Brae's Afro-Caribbean history.

Class and Culture-Building

In contrast to the functionalists and pluralists, Mintz and Price (1992; Price 2001) consider the process of culture-building as it relates to capitalist class relations generated by European expansion and the world economy. Within this framework they provide a more dynamic perspective on the re-creation of Afro-American cultures than Melville Herskovits's African-retention thesis (e.g., 1937, 1990; M. J. Herskovits and F. S. Herskovits 1947), reasserted by Roger Bastide (1972) and Mervyn Alleyne (1996). Mintz and Price's argument includes five central points. First, the Africans of the New World came from diverse ethnic groups, preventing the conveyance of a generalized African cultural heritage to any single plantation colony (1992:2, 8). Second, accordingly, their African heritage is not reflected in retentions of surface form, as Herskovits (1990) contends, but in underlying meanings or "cognitive orientations" (ways of perceiving the world and its social relations) comparable to deep " 'grammmatical' principles" (Mintz and Price 1992:9–11, 14). Third, therefore, "the organizational task of enslaved Africans in the New World was that of creating institutions — institutions that would prove responsive to the needs of everyday life under the limiting conditions that slavery imposed upon them" (19). (Mintz and Price defined "institution" as "any regular or orderly social interaction that acquires a normative character, and can hence be employed to meet recurrent needs. Thus broadly defined, a particular form of marriage, a particular religious cult, a particular pattern for establishing friendships, a particular economic relationship that is normative and recurrent — all would be examples of institutions" [23].) Fourth, the slaves engaged in rapid institution-building, such as the creole language and religion in Suriname,[13] as well as establishing the fictive-kinship shipmate bond that was pronounced among Jamaican slaves (43–50).[14] And fifth, "the institutions

created by the slaves . . . took on their characteristic shape *within* the parameters of the masters' monopoly of power, but *separate from* the masters' institutions" (39), a contention that is modified in this book.

In her analysis of the Afro-American slave family on the Danish West
Indian island of St. John, Karen Olwig (1981a) adopted Mintz and Price's
view of entirely separate institutions. She argued that the slave family system
(based on extraresidential conjugal relations and bilateral kinship networks
of exchange) was created within the masters' sphere of power but was distinct from their European nuclear family (349), and that the "slave family
embodied both 'a mode of response' and 'a mode of resistance' to the
plantation system" (356).

Monica Schuler (1979a) both supported and qualified Mintz and Price's
argument in her portrayal of Jamaican slave religion. She agreed that the
Jamaican slaves constructed their own way of life " '*within* the parameters
of the masters' monopoly of power, but *separate from* the masters' institutions' " (121). Nevertheless, she argued, a creole culture developed more
slowly in Jamaica than in Suriname. The various African ethnic groups
among the Jamaican slaves gradually evolved into a pan-African society and
then into a Caribbean social system. The creation of the Afro-Jamaican
religion, Myalism, played a central role in this process by drawing on African
cultural principles and evolving in response to slavery. According to Schuler, the slaves perceived the master as an evil sorcerer, and Myal developed as a community-based, antisorcery religion. Myalism also "drew semi-
autonomous plantation slave villages or [after emancipation] free villages
together through shared ritual" and symbols (128). Elsewhere, she identified the "parishes of St. James and Trelawny" as the "center of Myalism in
the 1820s, 1830s, and early 1840s" (1979b:71, 1980:40).

Mary Karasch (1979) endorsed Schuler's thesis that African American
slave religion was a mode of cultural resistance. She also reinforced Schuler's emphasis on the significance of African principles in Afro-American
slave religion. But, she argued, slave religion was not always entirely "separate from" the slave owners' religion, for the slaves sometimes *manipulated*
the masters' religious symbols — as in urban Brazil, where the slaves used the
masters' Catholic lay brotherhoods to represent and regulate relations
among African ethnic groups. The brotherhoods also served as burial and
mutual aid societies, and their symbols were perceived as powerful charms
that protected the slave communities against the masters' sorcery. Karasch
concluded that, to resist slavery, the slaves hid their own creole religion (the
basis of contemporary Umbanda) behind the masters' symbols.

For Karasch, therefore, a significant research goal in African America "should be an evolutionary study of the development of value systems and institutions forged during the centuries of slavery to the present" (1979:141). Such a study of culture-building was crucial to uncovering Martha Brae's Afro-creole cultural history. The two histories of Martha Brae illuminate the process of culture-building that occurred in the Caribbean region in the context of capitalist class relations generated by the world economy. These plantation and peasant histories, at the heart of African America, highlight how ex-slaves and their descendants *appropriated and overturned the masters' institutions* in a creative process of creolization and reversal that paralleled the transformation of the planter town. This approach has similarities with Richard Burton's (1997) analysis of Afro-creole cultures, which draws on my research.

Naming, Power, and Contention

In his analysis of power, opposition, and play in the Afro-Caribbean cultures of Haiti, Trinidad, and Jamaica, Burton (1997:93–94), citing Mintz and myself, highlights a theme central to Martha Brae's two histories, namely, the contribution of the Jamaican peasantry to "the development of a dynamic creole culture" (93). Drawing on my earlier work, Burton notes that "the core of this reconstituted peasant culture was the possession of land" (93), a perspective developed further in this comprehensive analysis of Martha Brae's two histories. This text explores the centrality of land to the Jamaican peasantry as well as the articulation of their landholding systems with the village, national, and global economies, and with state law, kinship, gender, and religion.

In his "consideration of cultural resistance in the Caribbean," and (quoting Bolland 1992:72) in his analysis of creolization as " 'a process of *contention*' between different racial and social groups" rather than "a homogenizing process," Burton's (1997:6) distinction between "resistance" and "opposition" is pertinent to Martha Brae's two histories. For Burton, drawing on Michael de Certeau (1980) and paralleling Michel Foucault (1978:95–96), "resistance" refers to "those forms of contestation of a given system that are conducted from *outside* that system, using weapons and concepts derived from a source or sources other than the system in question," whereas "opposition" involves "those forms of contestation of a given system that are conducted from *within* that system, using weapons and concepts derived from the system itself" (Burton 1997:6). This contrast is similar to Mintz's analysis of "adaptation" and "resistance," which, he believes, is often based on "prior *adaptation*" (1989:76), and is illuminated by Mintz and Price's (1992:39) thesis of slave institution-building "*within* the parameters of the masters' monopoly of power." However, Burton's focus on "opposition" finds closer parallels with my modification of Mintz and Price, namely, my analysis of Afro-Caribbean culture-building as a process of *engaging with, appropriating, transforming, and reversing* European institutions, rather than being entirely "*separate from*" the masters' style of life (Mintz and Price 1992:39). This modification also has parallels with Lila Abu-Lughod's (1990) analysis of variants of "resistance" as diagnostic of complex and historically shifting power relations.

In his argument on Afro-creole oppositional cultures, Burton (1997:163–69) engages Wilson's (1973) crab antics thesis, drawing on my reconsideration of reputation and respectability (Besson 1993), a critique developed in this book. Burton recognizes my point that Afro-Caribbean peasant women have played a central role in opposing colonial cultures. In this context, he annunciates an Afro-creole female culture of respectability characterized by "double oppositionality": that is, of being "opposed to a male culture that is itself opposed to the dominant culture" (1997:168). Though his "double oppositionality" derives from Littlewood (1993:295), Burton does not totally accept Littlewood's view of a black female respectability based on a closeness "to White men in a 'double opposition' . . . , through sexual relations between masters and household slaves, and through their opportunity to enter domestic work, teaching and nursing" (295; quoted in Burton 1997:168 [n. 24]). Nevertheless, while Burton does not "think that Littlewood grasps that the culture of respectability is in fact in opposition to the colonial culture it so resembles," he concludes that "the general thrust of his [Littlewood's] argument seems to me to be valid" (168 [n. 24]). On the other hand, Sheller (1998:116 [n. 32]) asserts that, although "Richard Burton argues for a more complex understanding of the reputation/respectability dialectic," he "does not abandon the emphasis on a *masculine* culture of play and opposition."

In a related essay, "Names and Naming in Afro-Caribbean Cultures," Burton (1999) focuses on the significance of nicknames (and given names), a theme central to Wilson's (1973, 1995) concept of reputation and to the understanding of Caribbean creolization. Many of Burton's points are consistent with my analysis of Martha Brae's two histories. Such points include the masters' denial of "generational continuity and adulthood" among the slaves (Burton 1999:41), the taking by slaves of new names to protect them from evil spirits and the slaves' manipulation of Christian baptism, the creativity of the slaves and their descendants in naming, the significance of recreating fictive and consanguineal kinship among the slaves, the role of

23   Caribbean Controversies

naming in creolization and in the re-creation of Afro-creole identities, the significance of Rastafarian nicknames, the significance of names and titles in an oppositional culture in which the slaves and their descendants appropriated and transformed dimensions of European culture, and "the multiplication of names and identities" in "oppositional tactics" (52). Burton also raises the important point (for American slaves) that secret surnames, which were unlikely to have been the masters', were used as titles but indicates the need for clarification on this point (42).[15] For the British Caribbean, Burton notes the appropriation of the owners' surnames by slaves and former slaves as the arrogation of the masters'/ex-masters' status and power (52–53) and speculates, in relation to Jamaican ex-slaves taking on their former master's surname after the 1831–32 slave rebellion, that "in appropriating the *surname* of the Other, they symbolically appropriated the selves that, by giving them a first name but withholding the dignity of a surname, Massa had stolen from their forebears" (53–54).

In its repeated emphasis on the *male* Afro-Caribbean culture of oppositionality (e.g., 1999:43), however, Burton's analysis of naming returns to Wilson's (1973, 1995) androcentric view of reputation and culture-building and reasserts "the respectability orientation of female Afro-Caribbean culture" (1999:49), assumptions that are questioned by Martha Brae's Afro-creole cultural history. One illustration, from Martha Brae and other Trelawny villages, of the limitations of Burton's perspective is the appropriation by *female* as well as male slaves, and by their descendants of both genders, of slave masters' surnames to serve as titles of the Afro-creole cognatic descent groups forged during and after slavery with their powerful symbolism of generational continuity, freedom, personhood, empowerment, and re-creation of identity. This appropriation, which still transmits the title of the unrestricted descent group (and wherever possible a family-land estate) through women as well as men (regardless of the surnames of individual members of the kin group), not only reversed patrilineal surnaming and primogeniture among the planters but also overturned the imposition of the masters' surnames on the slaves as property. This Afro-creole transformation of androcentric European surnaming in the re-creation of gendered identities is also reflected in the titles of female trustees in some of Martha Brae's landholding Old Families, who are known by the titles of their main descent group rather than by their legally married surnames.

In his analysis of oppositionality and naming, Burton overemphasizes the dependence of Afro-creole culture-building on Euro-creole culture, a view that may account for his uncritical acceptance of Douglas Hall's (1978) perspective on the flight from the estates. Referring to slaves' appropriation of the surname of their master M. G. "Monk" Lewis in Jamaica and citing "the important article by Hall 1978," Burton states (1999:53):

> For slaves to take over the name of this demi-god — and Lewis must be among the twenty or thirty commonest surnames in Jamaica — was, on the one hand, symbolically to take over his power and to signal that they were as free and as worthy as he, and, on the other, to acknowledge, and to force *him* to acknowledge, the existence of a continuing bond between them, an important prudential consideration, especially when, as is now clear, few slaves *initially* intended to leave "their" plantations when they obtained their "full free."

In this and other respects Burton underplays the agency of the slaves, ex-slaves, and their descendants of both genders in building their Afro-creole cultures and communities, not only in free villages such as Martha Brae, but also in maroon societies like Accompong and Congo Town/Highwind-ward/Me No Sen You No Com some miles inland from Martha Brae.

Likewise, Burton (1999:54) refers to the "magical nominalism" whereby the slaves and their descendants sought, in appropriating European names, to "actively embody the moral and other qualities of the person so designated," illustrating with reference to abolitionist William Wilberforce: "Thus Phillippo (1969:202) records the following revealing statement by a slave: 'Wilberforce — dat good name for true; him good bukra; him want to make we free; and if him can't get we free no oder way him *will by force*. . . . To take over, therefore, the name Wilberforce, as many slaves did, was not only a mark of gratitude and a recognition of symbolic paternity . . . but an appropriation of the very will and force embodied in the syllables that made up his name" (Burton 1999:54). However, an overemphasis on such Euro-centric onomastics not only overlooks the transformation of some of the English abolitionists' names by ex-slaves in their dual naming of free villages (chapter 3) — such as replacing Baptist missionary William Knibb's imposed name of "Wilberforce" with the symbolic "Refuge," or (for a time) Knibb's "Granville," after Granville Sharp, by "Grumble Pen" (referring to land disputes) in Trelawny — but also disregards the slaves' own contribution to abolition through rebellion, revolution, marronage, the "Quashee"/"Qua-sheba" trickster complex, and culture-building.

My assessment of Burton's androcentric and Eurocentric analysis of Afro-creole names and naming is reinforced by Jerome S. Handler and JoAnn Jacoby's (1996) exploration of slave names and naming systems in Barbados (the most important British West Indian colony in the seventeenth century). Their study emphasizes the agency of both female and male slaves in naming themselves and the role of such naming in creolization, cultural disguise, and opposition, including the rebuilding of self-esteem and the re-creation of identity. Drawing on a wide range of evidence, the authors high-light not only the creolization of African names, but also the taking of African names by creole slaves; the existence of multiple names among the slaves, including names and nicknames given in the plantation slave com-munities; and the role of both namesaking and the appropriation of Euro-pean surnames (not usually those of slave masters' and especially in the decades immediately preceding and following emancipation) in relation to the assertion of status and the reckoning of descent. Though Handler and Jacoby are inconclusive on the nature of such descent among the slaves, and are preoccupied with establishing links to West African matrilineal descent systems, their evidence suggests that Caribbean cognatic descent groups with creole titles were consolidating in the later stages of slavery and were significant in relation to postslavery landholding (711–24).[16]

This conclusion is strengthened by Michael Craton's (1994) data from the Bahamas, exemplified by "the troublesome slaves of Lord Rolle in Exuma" (28) and their descendants. "In the 1820s the Rolle slaves claimed that they had been promised the land on which they lived by Lord Rolle's father . . . and resolutely refused to agree to be transferred to Trinidad" (28). After emancipation, these ex-slaves retained their customary rights to this land, reinforced by the claim that it had been bequeathed to them by Lord Rolle. "Wittily encapsulating the ambivalences of all such 'paternalistic' rela-tionships, the Rolle ex-slaves all took their former owner's name" (29). This surname became a title for the landholding cognatic descent group: "Thenceforward, in an absolute converse of the system of primogeniture upon which aristocratic European tenures depended, any person with the surname Rolle — today more than 4,000 persons — *or anyone who could prove descent from a Rolle on the male or female side* — a veritable host — could theoreti-cally claim house-plot and subsistence allotment upon the 5,000 acres of Exumian common land" (Craton 1987:96–97, emphasis mine).[17] Though Craton (99) interprets such customary tenure as an African retention, this land appropriation and transmission reflects Caribbean culture-building through the overturning of British colonial plantation primogeniture.

Kinship, Land, and Religion

On the large Jamaican plantations, including those of old St. James and new Trelawny, a more complex creole kinship system evolved among the slaves than just the bilateral networks of exchange identified by

Olwig (1981a, 1981b, 1985) for the small estates on Danish St. John. The kinship system of the Jamaican slaves was also more coherent and wide-ranging than Orlando Patterson's (1973:159–70) analysis portrayed. This Afro-creole kinship system included three dimensions: a *dynamic complex marriage system*, based on multiple conjugal forms and sequential unions or serial polygamy;[18] *ego-focused bilateral kinship networks*, recognizing relatives for each individual on both parental sides; and *ancestor-oriented nonunilineal or cognatic descent lines*, traced from a common ancestor of either gender through both males and females. These cognatic family lines crystallized through the customary tenure and transmission of land rights and related burial patterns, which in turn were reinforced by the magico-religious Obeah-Myal complex.

Patterson's analysis of the Jamaican slave family focused on the destruction of African patterns of kinship and marriage, the presence of "promiscuity," and the absence of European marriage and the nuclear family (1973:159–62, 167). However, his study did provide evidence of the ship-mate bond as a basis of fictive kinship, including the incest taboo (150). Indeed, much of the evidence for Mintz and Price's (1992:43) discussion of shipmates derives from the Jamaican case. From this fictive kinship ship-mate bond a creole marriage system was created on the Jamaican slave plantations, as shown by a reinterpretation of Patterson's material on the "cycle of mating" (Besson 1995b).[19] This new marriage system, forged in opposition to slavery, drew on both African cultural values and a transformation of European marriage to create a Caribbean system of conjugality and procreation.

In the African societies from which the slaves imported to Jamaica came, marriage did not always entail coresidence; marriage was also a dynamic process of increasing stability and incorporation and was not necessarily based on monogamous relations. There was likewise respect for age. These African cultural values were the seedbed of the creole marriage system, though the latter was not a passive African cultural survival, but a dynamic Caribbean cultural re-creation. This creole marriage system was built on three conjugal forms, linked within the wider parameters of serial unions and reflecting an internal status system based on age. Short-lived duolocal or extraresidential unions typified the younger slaves, involving minimal conjugal rights and obligations but distinguished from promiscuity and casual mating. Older slaves lived in consensual cohabitation, reflecting increasing conjugal commitment. These two conjugal forms were linked not only sequentially in the same relationship, but also in a pattern of sequential unions, while some prosperous male slaves practiced polygyny. In the nineteenth century, with the increasing influence of Baptist missionizing and the planters' need to reproduce the slave population after the abolition of the slave trade, the slaves were allowed to marry legally. But rather than adopting the European custom of early legal marriage, they transformed this marital status in the contexts of their creole conjugal complex and cosmology. Legal marriage — the third conjugal form of the creole marriage system — marked proven conjugal commitment among the oldest slaves and the culmination of an internal status system based on increasing conjugal stability and age. Their Obeah-Myal and Native Baptist worldviews did not require early "Christian" marriage as a prerequisite for conjugality and procreation. Indeed, this status was regarded as inappropriate for younger slaves, who were ridiculed by the slave community if they attempted to enter European legal marriage.

Therefore, out of the kernal of the shipmate bond was created a dynamic, "exogamous" marriage system (in which individuals did not marry close relations) whereby numerous diverse conjugal and "in-law" relationships were forged, maximizing conjugality and affinity among the slaves. This represented an elaboration of a "complex" marriage system in Lévi-Straussian terms (1969), namely, a nonprescriptive, unrestricted system of exchange. This creole marriage system generated extensive ego-focused bilateral kinship networks of exchange and mutual aid elaborating biological ties on both parental sides, as evidenced in the kinship terms "Tata," "Mama," "Sister," "Boda," "Uncle," "Aunty," "Cousin," and "Grannie," the latter used for both grandparent and grandchild.

To complement this ego-focused bilateral kinship system there emerged on the Jamaican slave plantations an ancestor-focused nonunilineal or cognatic descent system (traced from each gendered slave through both women and men), articulating with customary land rights to plantation provision grounds and slave village yards with family burial grounds (Besson 1992a, 1995b; and chapter 3). For example, John Stewart (1823) observed the significance of such customary rights to yards, provision grounds, and family cemeteries: "Adjoining to the house is usually a small spot of ground, laid out into a sort of garden, and shaded by various fruit-trees. Here the family deposit their dead, to whose memory they invariably, if they can afford it, erect a rude tomb. Each slave has, beside this spot, a piece of ground (about half an acre) allotted to him as a provision ground. . . . If he has a family, an additional proportion of ground is allowed him, and all his children from five years upward assist him in his labours in some way or other" (267, quoted in Mintz 1989:187). Similarly, as early as 1793 Bryan

Edwards noted a system of customary inheritance, including the transmission of land rights, among the Jamaican slaves:

> I do not believe that an instance can be produced of a master's interference with his Negroes in their peculium thus acquired. They are permitted also to dispose at their deaths of what little property they possess; and even to bequeath their grounds or gardens to such of their fellow-slaves as they think proper. These principles are so well established, that whenever it is found convenient for the owner to exchange the negro-grounds for other lands, the Negroes must be satisfied, in money or otherwise, before the exchange takes place. It is universally the practice. (1793, 2:133, quoted in Mintz 1989:207)

Despite Stewart's androcentric focus on male slaves, his statement that "each slave" had customary land rights suggests full female, as well as male, participation in this customary system of land tenure, use, and transmission.

Discussing "our ignorance of the extent, if any, to which land-use privileges were granted to female slaves on the Jamaican plantations," Mintz (1989:216–17) states that he "has no evidence that land use was ever afforded other than to male slaves—though their families . . . commonly helped them on provision grounds." However, Mintz and Price (1992:78) later note, in their analysis of gendered marketing roles in Haiti and Jamaica, that "both men and women had worked provision grounds and done field labor during slavery."[20] Roderick A. McDonald's (1993) study of the economy and material culture of Jamaican slaves, including those on Georgia and Braco Estates in Trelawny a few miles from Martha Brae, confirms that provision grounds were allocated by law for the use of both female and male slaves and that patterns of customary inheritance existed among them (23–26). This gender equality provided the foundation for the system of cognatic descent and land transmission that transformed privileges to customary rights,[21] especially given the significance of women as field slaves and the matrilateral emphasis in slave yards and communities. In addition, Barry Higman's (1998) study of Montpelier Plantation in St. James provides evidence of multiple-house yards or "compounds" or "family villages," and of customary patterns of descent and land transmission,[22] as well as burial and tombing in slave villages (115–45, 248–49).

The emergent unrestricted cognatic/nonunilineal system, traced from slaves of both genders through female and male descendants, paralleled in part the African concept of landholding kin groups but departed in the New World context from African restricted unilineal descent traced through one gender only. This cognatic system maximized forbidden kinship lines and scarce land rights among the chattel slaves, who were not only legally kinless and landless but also property themselves. It would burgeon in the family-land institution among emancipated slaves and their descendants, including those in Trelawny's free villages such as Martha Brae, in the contexts of the flight from the plantations and the related conflict between planters and ex-slaves.

The Afro-Jamaican magico-religious complex of Obeah and Myal, with its elaborate mortuary ritual reflecting the perception of an active spirit world including ancestral kin, reinforced the customary land-transmission system with its cognatic descent-based burial pattern. In describing burial in Jamaica's slave village yards, Stewart noted the pouring of "libations at funerals and sacrificing fowls on the graves of the newly dead — a tribute that mourners afterwards occasionally repeat" (Alleyne 1996:81, citing Stewart 1823). Philip Curtin (1970:31) observed that "the Negro preoccupation with the spirits of the ancestors . . . led to a special attachment for the family burial place." This interrelation of magico-religious beliefs and ritual with customary land transmission would have been especially marked in the parishes of Trelawny and St. James, which had pronounced protopeasant adaptations and were the stronghold of the Obeah-Myal complex (Schuler 1980:40; Higman 1988:265–66). The journal of Thomas Thistlewood, a small-scale slave plantation owner, provides further evidence, from elsewhere in western Jamaica, of this relationship between Obeah-Myal and customary kin-based land transmission among the slaves and indicates the cognatic nature of this system (D. Hall 1989:184–86, 214, 217).

Integral to the Obeah-Myal complex, which was both a belief system and a religious organization similar to West African secret societies, was the belief in a dual spirit or soul. One spirit, the *duppy*, was believed to leave the body at death and, after remaining for a few days at the place of death or burial, to journey to join the ancestors. The elaborate funeral ritual was practiced to mark and effect this transition. Another spirit was thought to be the *shadow* of the living person (buried with the corpse at death) that could be caught, harmed, and restored by Obeah/Myal-men and -women.

Patterson (1973:185–95) contrasted Obeah and Myal on the Jamaican slave plantations as being derived from West African concepts of "bad" and "good" medicine. In this dichotomy, "Obeah was essentially a type of sorcery which largely involved harming others at the request of clients, by the use of charms, poisons, and shadow catching. It was an individual practice, performed by a professional who was paid by his clients. . . . Myalism, on the other hand, was obviously a form of anti-witchcraft and anti-sorcery" (188). It was "organized more as a kind of cult with a unique dance ritual" (188) that honored the African-derived minor deities of a spirit pantheon (rather than the distant Supreme Deity) and the departed ancestors and ancestresses whom, it was believed, could possess the living. However, Alleyne (1996:84) observes that

> in Africa good and evil are not always clearly antithetical. This was even more true of Jamaica, where magic designed to harm members of the White ruling class and slaves loyal to them occupied that nebulous area between good and evil. Certainly the British viewed such magic as obeah. . . . But for Africans, resorting to the power of spirits in order to resist slavery was a positive expression of religion. Those writers who reported that myal was hostile to obeah and undid obeah's evil work show clearly how Myalmen harnessed spiritual forces to resist slavery.

Schuler (1979a, 1979b, 1980) argued that the Myal cult united the slaves in their resistance to slavery and European values and was thought to protect their communities from internal and external harm, and that the shared body of Myal ritual and belief provided a mode of integration among slave plantation villages, whereas Curtin (1970:29) concluded that "essentially obeah was neither good nor bad: it could be used either way." Kenneth Bilby (1993) has questioned the widespread dichotomization of Obeah and Myalism. He suggests that Obeah originally most often referred to morally neutral magical/spiritual power that could be accessed through spirit possession or Myal and used for protection and healing. Moreover, this morally neutral magical spiritual power (in some places still referred to as Obeah) was and remains central to Afro-Jamaican religion as well as varying throughout the Caribbean in time and space.[23] Even Patterson observed that "Obeah in its myal form served certain important medicinal functions during slavery," thereby indicating the overlapping of Myalism and Obeah. Obeah was also important as a source of perceived protection in the context of slave rebellion (1973:191–92). Bilby's (1993) analysis of Obeah is drawn on and developed by Handler (2000) and Handler and Bilby (2001).

The creation of the customary system of land transmission, rooted in cognatic descent and reinforced by burial and by the slaves' cosmology and ritual, was a major aspect of institution-building among the Jamaican slaves. This system was created "*within* the parameters of the masters' monopoly of power" and was to some extent "*separate from* the masters' institutions" (Mintz and Price 1992:39). It was also a mode of "cultural resistance" or opposition "built upon prior *adaptation*, involving the slaves in processes of culture change and retention of a complicated kind" (Mintz 1989:76). However, the protopeasant adaptation and its cognatic mode of descent and land transmission *appropriated* aspects of the plantation system — which was the masters' primary institution. Moreover, the slaves' culture-building in relation to land and kinship involved a *reversal* of the principles of the plantation institution, namely, monoculture, legal freehold, chattel slavery, the nuclear family, and primogeniture. The dynamics of this creole institution-building were therefore *not* entirely "*separate from* the masters' institutions" but entailed a *direct engagement with, and overturning of* their Euro-creole lifestyle.

The Obeah-Myal complex, which articulated with cognatic family lines and customary land transmission including ancestral burial grounds in the slave communities (and after emancipation interrelated through Revival with family-land cemeteries in free villages), was initially more separate from the masters' institutions — namely, the planters' Anglican Christianity — than the slaves' Afro-creole kinship and land-tenure systems. In eighteenth-century Jamaica, the Anglican Church was the only church allowed by law to function on the island and, as the official religion of the slave masters, supported the status quo of slavery. At that time the planters neither attempted, nor wished, to convert the slaves. Even after an act in 1816 to propagate the gospel among the enslaved, the impact of the Established Church on the slaves was largely superficial and ineffective. In slave communities, however, Myal complemented Obeah and articulated with slave rebellion and marronage (as well as with burial and customary kin-based land transmission). In these contexts, the slaves sought to use their Obeah-Myal complex to reverse the masters' plantation institution by protecting themselves from the owners' "sorcery" of enslavement (Schuler 1979a).

With the arrival of Nonconformist missionaries (many of them from Britain) in the late eighteenth and early nineteenth centuries, the slaves would hide their Obeah-Myal institution behind Baptist Christianity. In so doing, they would not only continue to oppose the planters and slavery but would also covertly transform the colonial religion of their missionary allies (through the control of Baptist Christianity by Obeah and Myal in the Native Baptist variant in the slave communities) while attending the Baptist Church. This strategy of engaging with and overturning colonial Baptist Christianity through both alliance and subversion continues in Jamaican free villages, manifested in simultaneous adherence to Revivalism (which evolved from Obeah, Myal, and Native Baptist Christianity) and the orthodox Baptist Church.

Kinship, Law, and Land

In *Recharting the Caribbean: Land, Law, and Citizenship in the British Virgin Islands*, Bill Maurer (1997b:167–207) reinforces the significance of the Caribbean family-land institution, which forms the core of Martha Brae's Afro-creole cultural history. Drawing on my early essays, he further highlights the role of family land in creating Caribbean identities. However, he sees his analysis as shifting ground in the so-called family-land debate, which includes the questions of whether family land is an "institution" and whether the cognatic landholding kin groups are restricted or unrestricted; that is, whether or not some descendants of the original ancestor are excluded — for example, whether migrants lose or retain land rights. Substituting "phenomenon" for "institution," Maurer argues that British Virgin Island (and Barbadian) descent groups are restricted, emphasizes the centrality of law in creating Caribbean identities, and highlights the link between British common law and Caribbean "custom." He also asserts that my analysis of unrestricted descent depends "on a weak notion of 'family,' "[24] whereas Charles Carnegie (1987) stresses ambiguous "genealogy," contends that neither view explains "how Caribbean peoples talk and think about Caribbean family land," and concludes that the "family/genealogy distinction maps almost too neatly onto the so-called plural society debate" (203–4).

Yet both Carnegie and I advanced "intersystem" analyses of "law" and "custom" in contrast to Michael Smith's plural society approach. I have also argued that, even at a conceptual level, law and custom in Jamaica are not as separate as Edith Clarke and Smith contended, for Jamaica's legal system not only differs from but also draws on English common law in certain ways. In addition, I have shown that since the days of slavery family land has overturned colonial primogeniture and is shaping the writing of Caribbean law through such culture-building.[25]

Citing Sidney Greenfield's (1960) data as well as his own, Maurer attempts to show that Barbadian and British Virgin Island (BVI) landholding kin groups are "potentially restricted . . . since limiting inheritance to the 'heirs of his body' " excludes in-marrying spouses (1997b:198). In addition, citing no reference, he argues that I conclude that "outside children (either illegitimate, or not of the father's household)" would not necessarily be included (201). Yet the issues raised by Maurer reveal further evidence that Caribbean landholding descent groups are unrestricted in three main ways. First, the exclusion of in-marrying spouses in inheritance in Barbados and the British Virgin Islands is based on the principle of *affinity*, rather than of descent, and is entirely consistent with an unrestricted *descent* system.[26] Second, as I have always argued, *all children* and all descendants of a landholder, including those regarded as "illegitimate" in the Eurocentric social system, are coheirs to family land; only a *spouse's* "outside children" are excluded on the basis of *affinity* rather than of either descent or "illegitimacy." Third, Maurer's delineation elsewhere of BVI land tenure richly portrays a landholding system recharted through creolizing unrestricted cognatic descent, including both genders of descendants and regardless of whether these are absent or resident (1996:353–54).

Maurer's analysis of the centrality of law in constructing Caribbean identities and his argument that " 'custom' and 'law' are . . . mutually constitutive" and "are continually reinvented by Caribbean people" (1997b:192, 201) likewise reinforce my interpretation of Martha Brae's new history, which shows the significance of Caribbean culture-building in creating, shaping, and transforming the law itself. But Maurer might have taken more account of the interplay between such law and custom by exploring the process of institution-building rooted in the protopeasant past and its contribution to the "explanation" of how Caribbean people regard contemporary family land. Moreover, had he followed through the development of this culture-building thesis beyond 1988, he would have found it difficult to overlook my continuing portrayal of the strength of Caribbean kinship (ego-oriented and ancestor-focused genealogy, complex marriage exchange and affinity, and the entire family system), themes that are further developed in this book.

Martha Brae's Two Histories and Anthropology

In addition to accelerating theoretical debates on the interpretation of Caribbean societies and cultures, including the illumination of culture-building, *Martha Brae's Two Histories* contributes to several areas of anthropological theory. As well as promoting the exploration of the dynamic nature of culture through a study of creolization at the core of Europe's oldest colonial sphere, it significantly advances the comparative study of kinship, which lies at the heart of the discipline. The analysis of unrestricted cognatic descent, which is a central theme of the book (and which links land to kinship, gender, law, religion, migration, history, oral tradition, and identity), elevates the cross-cultural study of descent: unrestricted descent groups were long regarded by anthropologists as unworkable and are even now considered rare, with examples usually confined to the Pacific region and a few East African societies. Moreover, Martha Brae's three-dimensional family system, which integrates cognatic descent with bilateral kinship (whereby individuals trace male and female relatives on both parental sides) and with sequential conjugal unions by both women and men, reveals a new variant of Hawaiian-Eskimo kinship terminology in the cross-cultural study of how various societies classify "kin."[27] This terminology, expressed in the Jamaican creole language created by the slaves, highlights the significance of half siblingship and serial polygamy, combined with respect for both gender equality and age. The analysis of the conjugal system, in which serial polygamy (whereby individuals of both genders may have a series of spouses) is combined with multiple conjugal forms, uncovers a marriage system more complex and elaborate than even Claude Lévi-Strauss (1969) envisioned in his pathbreaking comparative study of marriage exchange.

Other contributions of the book to anthropological theory concern the cross-cultural study of ecology, economy, land, and mortuary ritual; the anthropology of gender, power, law, identity, and ethnicity; the documentation of peasantries and their histories; and the advancement of the world-historical-political-economy approach to interpretive ethnography. The analysis of Martha Brae's two histories also contributes to correcting the overemphasis in dependency and world-systems theories on "metropolitan-satellite" and "core-periphery" relations (Frank 1969; Wallerstein 1974, 1980), which focus on the impact of the First World capitalist countries on postcolonial Third World societies, by revealing the internal class dynamic and the importance of "agency" or cultural creativity (Giddens 1976:75; Wulff 1995:8–14) in a settlement at the very core of the so-called periphery.

The following chapters elaborate these themes. Chapter 2, "Martha Brae's Euro-Caribbean History," contextualizes, integrates, and develops the historical anthropology of Martha Brae as a colonial planter town at the heart of the Caribbean region, generated by European expansion and New World slave plantations. Chapter 3, "The Origins of Martha Brae's Afro-Caribbean History," resolves the debate on the reasons why ex-slaves fled the British West Indian estates and reveals the roots of Martha Brae's post-slavery cultural history in Caribbean slave opposition and resistance as well as in postslavery peasantization, including the free-village system in Jamaica and Trelawny.

Chapter 4, "The Free Village of Martha Brae," looks directly at the transformation of the town by ex-slaves in the plantation heartlands of Trelawny (at the vanguard of the flight from the British West Indian estates). It examines the continuing significance of gaining and retaining land rights, through customary as well as legal tenures, among the contemporary Martha Brae peasantry, which persists on a scarce land base at the crux of the Caribbean peasant-plantation/tourism interface. We also see how this intense land scarcity has spawned Martha Brae's satellite squatter settlement of Zion, on a part of Holland Estate adjoining the free village, and explore the complex articulation of customary landholding with Jamaica's colonially derived agrarian legal code. Chapter 5, "Martha Brae's Free-Village Oral Tradition," provides four case studies of Old Families (unrestricted cognatic descent groups) descended from the ex-slaves who appropriated the planter town and who created and transmitted family land in the free village. This chapter also demonstrates the importance of the oral tradition of these Old Families when combined with my anthropological fieldwork and historical research.

Chapters 6 to 8 explore Martha Brae's contemporary peasant economy and community in the wider contexts of postcolonial Jamaica and the modern capitalist world system, including further themes of continuity and change in relation to slave and postemancipation culture-building. Chapter 6, "Elaborations of the Peasant Economy," examines Martha Brae's socioeconomic system of production, consumption, and exchange: house yards, provision grounds, marketing, occupational multiplicity (including river-rafting tourism), migration, and mutual aid. Chapter 7, "The Baptist Church, Revival Ideology, and Rastafarian Movement," considers the coexistence of these three religious forms in Martha Brae, rooted in the process of creolization and interrelated with landholding, and shows that cosmology and ritual are crucial to maintaining the peasant community. Chapter 8, "Households, Marriage, Kinship, and Descent," uncovers the dynamic and elaborate transnational family system of the Martha Brae villagers and reveals how it reflects Caribbean culture-building and links the peasant community with migrants elsewhere in the island and overseas. The conclusion in Chapter 9 highlights the implications of Martha Brae's two histories for anthropology, which has generally marginalized the region.

CHAPTER TWO

Martha Brae's
Euro-Caribbean History

Western European overseas colonization began with the establishment of the plantation complex in the offshore Atlantic islands of the Canaries and Madeira in the fifteenth century, modeled on plantations pioneered during the twelfth century in the eastern Mediterranean islands. The expansion of Europe's nation-states intensified with the introduction and escalation of the plantation system in the Americas, especially in the Antilles or islands of the Caribbean Sea after 1492. This transatlantic colonial expansion was generated by the emergence of a capitalist world system, based on Europe's distinctive view of commodity production in the so-called satellites or periphery of the European "metropolis" or "core."[1]

European Expansion and Caribbean Plantations

The plantation system was transplanted to the Caribbean region with the introduction of sugarcane to the New World (from Spain's Canary Islands) by the Spanish in 1493. It has remained a major theme throughout some five hundred years of post-Columbian history — now reinforced by new forms of land monopoly such as bauxite mining and tourism. Differences in Hispanic and non-Hispanic (British, French, Dutch, and Scandinavian) colonial control shaped Caribbean plantations, and seven variants can be identified (Mintz 1978; Hoetink 1985). The first was the sixteenth-century Hispanic sugar plantation system in the Greater Antilles, including Jamaica (colonized by the Spanish in 1509, following Christopher Columbus's encounter with the island in 1494), worked by enslaved indigenous Arawak/Taino peoples and imported African slaves. The second variant (ca. 1640–70) saw the introduction and intensification of sugar plantations by England and France in the Lesser Antilles, especially in Barbados

37

(colonized by the English in 1627), worked by enslaved native Caribs and imported Africans and indentured laborers from Europe.

The third and very significant variant was the burgeoning, in the Greater and Lesser Antilles, of the non-Hispanic plantation system — for example, in Barbados and later in Jamaica (which was seized by the English in 1655) and neighboring French Saint Domingue (after 1697 with the capture of the western third of Hispaniola from Spain). These plantations reached their zenith in the later eighteenth century, when Saint Domingue and Jamaica were the two most profitable dependencies based on the slave plantation system that the world has ever known. In Saint Domingue, this system was aborted by a slave revolution (1791–1804), but it continued in France's Lesser Antillean colonies until emancipation in 1848. Jamaica's enlarged plantation system declined with the onset of emancipation in 1834–38 — except in the parish of Trelawny, where colonial Martha Brae was situated; in Trelawny, plantations continued to expand beyond the abolition of slavery (Jacobs 1970:16).[2] Such non-Hispanic agricultural schemes, based on African slave labor, developed on a smaller scale in the British Leeward and Windward Islands. In Trinidad, following Britain's conquest of the island from Spain in 1797, sugar plantations dominated the economy by 1810 (Brereton 1981); Trinidad, with British Guiana, became the expanding southern frontier of the British West Indian slave plantation system. During this period, the Dutch likewise developed Caribbean sugar plantation colonies with African slave labor, especially in Suriname, until emancipation in 1863, while the Danish developed the slave plantation system in St. Croix and St. John until emancipation in 1848 (Olwig 1985).

The fourth variant (ca. 1770–1882) was the revival and escalation of the Hispanic plantation system in those Greater Antillean colonies (Cuba and Puerto Rico) retained by Spain, simultaneous with the weakening of the slave plantation system in the non-Hispanic territories. The intensified Hispanic plantations used African slave labor, forced labor (of mixed racial origins in Puerto Rico), and contract labor (imported Chinese in Cuba) due to the declining slave trade. In these Hispanic colonies, emancipation did not occur until 1876 in Puerto Rico and 1886 in Cuba — where slavery continued longer than in any other New World colony except Portuguese Brazil, where emancipation came in 1888.

The fifth variant included the plantations of the postemancipation era, which began in 1834–38 in the British West Indian territories but differed among the colonies of the Caribbean region throughout the nineteenth century: after 1848 in the Danish and French colonies (except for postrevolutionary Saint Domingue, which became independent Haiti in

1804), after 1863 in the Dutch West Indies, and after 1876 and 1886 in the remaining colonies of Spain. These plantations utilized free wage labor (ex-slaves and their descendants) and the labor of indentured Africans and Asians.

The sixth variant saw the consolidation of a waged rural proletariat on technologically sophisticated corporate sugar plantations pioneered by the United States in Cuba and Puerto Rico after the Spanish-American War in 1898 and developed by European powers in the non-Hispanic territories after 1899. This type of plantation (sometimes state-owned, as in post-revolutionary Cuba) has continued in parts of the Caribbean region, including Puerto Rico, Trinidad, Jamaica, and St. Kitts, and still engrosses the fertile land of Trelawny surrounding Martha Brae. The seventh and final variant is a modification of this theme: increasing mechanization of plantations from the later twentieth century has reduced the number of jobs for plantation laborers and exacerbated poverty among rural proletarians who are often embedded in peasant communities such as contemporary Martha Brae. Such marginalization has contributed to rural-urban and overseas migration into the twenty-first century.

The Transatlantic Slave Trade and New World Slavery

The Caribbean plantation system was independent of slavery, though, as elsewhere in plantation America, imported slave labor from Africa dominated the early Caribbean plantations. Before 1800 most transatlantic migrants to the New World were enslaved Africans, and "in the 1820s, . . . 90 percent of those coming across the Atlantic were African," the peak of the transatlantic slave trade being 1680–1830 when it formed the basis of the plantation complex (Eltis 2000:12, 17, 27). In addition, plantation slavery and the responses of the enslaved played a major role in shaping Caribbean societies and cultures at the heart of African America.

Recent scholarship has emphasized cultural as well as economic factors in the rise of African slavery in the Americas, the agency of Africans as well as Europeans in the transatlantic slave trade, and the racial nature of New World slavery (Blackburn 1997; Eltis 2000). Robin Blackburn (1997:350) argues that "the slave plantation was the most distinctive product of European capitalism, colonialism and maritime power in the late seventeenth and early eighteenth centuries, with racial sentiment acting as a crucial binding agent." He observes that "the acquisition of some twelve million captives on the coast of Africa between 1500 and 1870 helped to make possible the construction of one of the largest systems of slavery in human history" and that "by 1713 plantation slavery had been established on a racial basis in Brazil, the Caribbean and North America," with "black" skin color and phenotype (including variations of "racial" classification) being associated with slave status (3, 14–15, 25), a persisting legacy in the Caribbean, Latin America, and the southern United States today.

David Eltis (2000) highlights the paradox of slavery and freedom in the early modern world, raising the question of how Western societies with a highly developed sense of liberty could create the harshest systems of enslavement in the later seventeenth and eighteenth centuries (1650–1800). Eltis contends that, in addition to the economic element of European enslavement of Africans, the colonists' values and social relations, especially regarding property, labor, ethnicity, and gender, were crucial to creating this paradox, particularly among the English and the Dutch, who intensified the initial Iberian imposition of the European worldview on non-Europeans. According to him, colonial expansion occurred in conjunction with a growing emphasis on individualism, which, combined with capitalism, shifted property rights (including owning one's own person as the basis of freedom and having rights in other people as laborers) from communities and kin groups to individuals. Combined with the perception of Europeans as "insiders" and non-Europeans as "outsiders," this resulted in free labor for whites and the exclusive enslavement of Africans, for "European conceptions of the other ensured that only non-Europeans could be slaves" (280). The colonial insider/outsider dichotomy was also reflected in contrasting transatlantic shipping conditions for Europeans and Africans, the latter as chattels who endured far more severe overcrowding and intense suffering. Eltis concludes that this Middle Passage "was probably the purest form of domination in the history of slavery as an institution" (117). Blackburn (1997:3) notes that more than one and a half million slaves died on the transatlantic crossing — in addition to the many who perished before leaving Africa or within a year of arriving in the Americas; some mortality also resulted from slave resistance, including suicide and revolt.

The emergence of racial chattel slavery in the context of European expansion intensified after 1650, with the dominance of the English in the Atlantic and the Dutch in Asia. Factors contributing to these developments included the early appearance of the nuclear family and nonfeudal land tenure, in England and the Netherlands, which led to the growth of capitalist agricultural productivity and international trade in the first half of the seventeenth century and facilitated transoceanic migration. The paradox of slavery and freedom was most pronounced among the English, who dominated the transatlantic slave trade with the expansion of their plantation system from 1650 to 1700 — initially in Barbados.

Western androcentric attitudes to gender roles supported these trends, institutionalizing another form of social inequality shaping New World slavery. As Eltis (2000:16) observes: "The scope for individual action that evolved in northwestern Europe in the early modern period was greater for males than for females. Women . . . were hugely underrepresented in all skilled occupations and professions in seventeenth-century England and the Netherlands. . . . *Primogeniture practices throughout the West — to take just one example — denied them anything approaching a legal status that matched that of males*" (16, emphasis mine). Therefore, European women went to the New World mainly as members and reproducers of nuclear families. A much greater number of black females crossed the Atlantic as enslaved migrant labor, due to their economic importance in their own societies and then in the slave trade for both African sellers and European buyers. But African women were confined to field or domestic labor and were excluded from the skilled occupations learned by some enslaved men. The culture-building that would occur among enslaved Africans and their descendants in the vicinity of Martha Brae and elsewhere in Jamaica and the Caribbean, through the creation of customary systems of land tenure and transmission based on cognatic descent (including both genders and their female as well as male descendants), would thus oppose and transform European attitudes toward class, ethnicity, kinship, economy, property, and gender.

Eltis (2000) underscores not only the significance of African women in the slave trade and plantation slavery (and therefore their enormous impact on the demography and cultures of the New World), but also the prominence of children in this forced migration: "a higher proportion of children left Africa for the Americas than left Europe," and "before 1800 it is likely that at least four-fifths of the females and over 90 percent of the children sailing to the Americas were not European" (97). For these reasons, "the traditional view of the slave traffic as comprising mainly males and mainly adults needs revision" (96). Blackburn (1997:330) reinforces this reassessment, emphasizing the prominence of women and children in the Atlantic slave trade in contrast to the preponderance of adult males in European (and Asian) indentured labor.

Shipping technology and costs were crucial to the productivity of the transatlantic slave trade. Drawing on the Trans-Atlantic Slave Trade Database (TSTD) (Eltis et al. 1999), which provides information on approximately 70 percent of the slave trade to the New World (27,233 voyages from

1595 to 1867, especially those between 1660 and the last recorded crossing of 1867), Eltis (2000:118) shows how the English dominated the transoceanic shipment of people, including slave trading, to the Americas from the later seventeenth to the early nineteenth centuries. English slave traders comprised especially the Royal African Company, based in London, and after 1700 this company and Bristol traders. Liverpool also became an important slaving port in the eighteenth century. The English "traded on all parts of the African coast that sold slaves and traded all over the Caribbean," especially in Jamaica (128).

African agency was significant in the transatlantic slave trade, where Europeans and Africans traded as equals, as well as in deflecting the plantation system to the New World. Europeans had been unable to expand the Old World plantation system from the offshore Atlantic islands to Africa, due to the ability of African societies to resist European colonization before the nineteenth century, and had therefore transplanted it across the Atlantic in the wake of the European conquest in 1492. Similarly, "African resistance resulted in Europeans taking slaves away in ships as a second-best alternative to working slaves on African plantations or mines. From this perspective the slave trade was a symptom of African strength, not weakness" (Eltis 2000:149 [quotation], 162). African attitudes toward ethnicity also contributed to transatlantic slave trading, for, in contrast to European traders, the perception of "outsiders" by African enslavers was not based on continental/subcontinental definitions as the modern concepts of "Africa" and "Africans" did not then exist (150).

Estimates of the transatlantic slave trade vary. A conservative consensus is that 11.4 million slaves left Africa and 10 million disembarked in the Americas (Eltis et al. 1999:5); a higher estimate gives 15.4 million departures, with 14.9 million setting out for the New World (Inikori 1993:686, quoted in Eltis et al. 1999:6, 37 [n. 20]). For a variety of reasons, West African societies differed in their involvement in the transatlantic slave trade. Six regions of West Africa supplied most of these slaves, but two of these, Senegambia and Sierra Leone–Windward Coast, "are estimated to have supplied only 10 percent of the slaves" (Eltis 2000:192). Drawing on the TSTD project, Eltis and David Richardson (1997a:6) show that four-fifths of the slaves taken from Africa on the Middle Passage from 1662 to 1867 came "from just four regions — the Gold Coast, the Bights of Benin and Biafra, and West-central Africa." Most of these slaves were shipped from a small number of ports, especially "Cape Coast Castle and Anomabu on the Gold Coast; Whydah in the Bight of Benin; Bonny and Calabar in the Bight of Biafra; and Cabinda, Benguela, and Luanda in West-Central Africa." During this period, over 90 percent of these slaves disembarked in the Caribbean region and Brazil, with the Caribbean receiving nearly 50 percent and the British West Indies over 20 percent (6). Of these, in the eighteenth and early nineteenth centuries, Jamaica imported over 800,000 enslaved Africans and reexported about 200,000 slaves (P. D. Morgan 1997:133). The Jamaican port of Kingston was prominent in such trading, with 190,000 known arrivals; it was the sixth most important point of disembarkation in the Americas (132–33). The TSTD shows that other leading Jamaican ports for disembarking slaves included Montego Bay, Martha Brae, and Falmouth in the parishes of St. James and Trelawny. Port Royal was also a noted slaving port (Burnard 1996).

Drawing on the TSTD project, Eltis and Richardson (1997a:7) state that for Jamaica and the British Leeward Islands "the Bight of Biafra was easily the largest source of supply of slaves." In addition, Eltis (2000:109) observes that a considerable number of females were exported from Old Calabar, New Calabar, and Bonny. Regarding the hinterland of the Bight of Biafra, home of the Igbo and Ibibio (108), Eltis and Richardson (1997a:10–11) refer to an essay by Douglas Chambers (1997):

> Concentrating on the Bight of Biafra, Chambers argues that most of the slaves shipped from the region were Igbo-speaking and, because they were largely taken by the British, they tended to be landed in British American colonies. Within the British Americas, he suggests, particularly large numbers of Igbo-speaking slaves were to be found in Jamaica, the Leeward Islands and Virgina. . . . In the course of his analysis, he challenges claims that slaves from the Gold Coast, notably Akan groups, had a dominant influence on Jamaican slave communities, arguing that important local institutions and practices such as *jonkonu* and *obeah*, which are sometimes attributed to Akan connections, were probably of Igbo origin.

Chambers (1997:83) further maintains that "after 1760, when the tide of Igbo exiles was at its height, it is likely that Igbo were shipped in relatively large numbers to the islands of the Lesser Antilles and to areas around Montego Bay and Savannah la Mar in western Jamaica." Moreover, Igbo slaves, in areas such as western Jamaica, "tended to resort to resistance" (i.e., opposition), rather than rebellion, "within small-scale communities to force the *buckra* to abide by unwritten but well-known plantation customs" (86–87). Chambers asserts that the concept of buckra itself, to denote the evil white slave master, was an Igbo creation. Nevertheless, citing the TSTD, Eltis and Richardson (1997b) emphasize the significance of Gold Coast imports to Jamaica, which was "the major single destination" for such slaves,

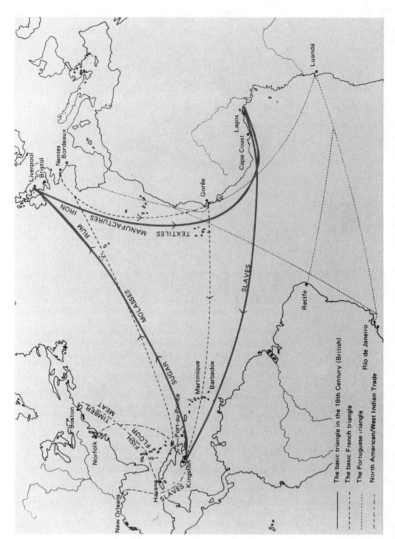

Map 4. The Triangular Trade. From "The Triangle of Trade," in Peter Ashdown and Francis Humphreys, *Caribbean Revision History for CXC* (London: Macmillan, 1988), 19; Macmillan Education Ltd.

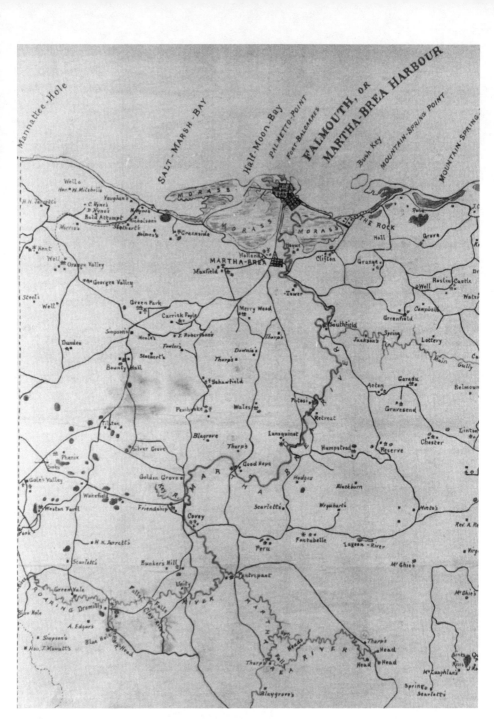

Map 5. Martha Brae and Its Surroundings. From James Robertson's map of the parish of Trelawny, 1804, National Library of Jamaica, Kingston.

especially in the eighteenth century. They point out that "Akan cultural prominence in Jamaica (including Ahanta, Fanti, Akim and Asante peoples among others) is well rooted in the slave trade according to this data set" (20).

Philip Morgan (1997:126), however, believes that "broad summaries of aggregate patterns disguise marked shifts over time," and that the regions supplying the British trade including Barbados and Jamaica, and therefore the African cultures influencing these colonies, varied (a telling point for the debate on African retentions and Caribbean culture-building):

> David Eltis has provided a detailed chronological analysis of the British trade before 1714. A close, decade-by-decade examination of this trade reveals that the leading African provenance zones that supplied Africans to Barbados and Jamaica were constantly changing. In the 1660s the Bight of Biafra was the leading supplier; in the 1670s the Gold Coast, Bight of Benin and Bight of Biafra were roughly equal providers; in the 1680s the Bight of Benin was the leader; in the 1690s again the Bight of Benin dominated the trade, but with strong infusions from West-Central Africa into Jamaica and from the Gold Coast into Barbados; in the 1700s and early 1710s, the Bight of Benin and increasingly the Gold Coast were pre-eminent. David Richardson has explored the aggregate eighteenth-century British trade. He reveals, for example, that from the 1710s through 1730s British shipments of slaves from Senegambia reached an all-time high; during the 1760s and 1770s about a third of British Africans came from the Windward Coast; and from the 1780s through 1807, the Bight of Biafra and West-Central Africa accounted for about 70 per cent of British slave exports. *A dynamic, diasporic approach indicates how slaves came from a changing series of African coastal regions. The aggregate picture masks a fluid, evanescent reality.* (Emphasis mine)

New World plantation slavery was intense in the Caribbean and Brazil. In fact, the Caribbean region received nearly half of the enslaved Africans who arrived in the Americas, with over one-fifth of the slaves transported across the Atlantic disembarking in the British West Indies (Eltis and Richardson 1997a:6). In the 1660s, when annual African arrivals began to exceed those of Europeans in the English Americas, Barbados was the leading sugar producer in the West Indies and was probably the world's most productive economy in the second half of the seventeenth century; Barbados remained unrivaled as a British West Indian sugar colony into the first part of the eighteenth century. During this period the Leeward Islands group was the second most lucrative sugar producer in the English Americas, with Jamaica developing as a plantation colony fairly slowly due to weak internal and external security including buccaneers and pronounced resistance by rebel slaves through revolt and marronage. However, in Jamaica, "England's largest Caribbean island," would emerge "the sugar and slave system in its starkest and most exploitative form" (Dunn 2000:151). In March and June 1739 treaties were made with the Leeward and Windward Maroons, and by the 1750s Jamaica had swept ahead as the leading British West Indian sugar-producing colony, while Jamaica's Port Royal had overtaken Bridgetown, Barbados, as the largest English town and port in the Americas (Blackburn 1997:404–5; Eltis 2000:195–219).

The Jamaican sugar and slave economy reached its height between 1783 and 1815; after the collapse of the slave plantation system in neighboring French Saint Domingue in the 1790s, Jamaica became the world's leading sugar producer. With these developments, "the slave trade to Jamaica was greatest, in both value and volume, between 1783 and 1808, the year Britain abolished the slave trade to its colonies, when 354,000 slaves — the island's largest-ever slave population — lived on Jamaica" (McDonald 1993:2). By 1800 Trelawny Parish, in which colonial Martha Brae was situated, had more sugar plantations than any other parish in the island and 27,827 slaves (Karras 1992:126).

Jamaican Plantation Slave Society

Following the English capture of Jamaica in 1655, the colony was administered from the metropolis, as elsewhere in the English Americas, "by a governor, council, and representative assembly, with parish churches, vestrymen, and justices of the peace at the local level, and a militia for protection" (Dunn 2000:xxi). Higman (1976, 1984, 1988, 1998) has delineated the contours and dynamics of the plantation slave society that developed within this framework and its articulation with global capitalism and the Atlantic world. Colonization and the establishment of the planta-tion system through land grants initially focused on the southern and east-ern areas of the island, with plantations expanding into the north and west after a colonial treaty was executed with the Leeward Maroon rebel slaves in the Cockpit Country in March 1739. Sugar plantations, consolidated throughout Jamaica from the mid-eighteenth century, were first established on the coastal lowlands and river deltas and then in the intermontane val-leys. These plantations competed with coffee estates (and, to a lesser extent, with pimento walks) for land and slaves, especially from the 1790s, and there were also livestock pens that predated the sugar industry (Shepherd

1998:177; Shepherd and Monteith 1998). In addition to enslavement on these plantations, estates, and pens, some African and creole slaves worked in urban centers, such as port and market towns.

By emancipation in 1834–38, "Jamaica had 670 sugar plantations with an average population of 223 slaves, accounting for one-half of the island's 312,000 slaves" (Higman 1998:2). In the second half of the eighteenth century the colony possessed even more sugar plantations, which increased "from 535 in 1750 to 900 in 1790, together with a doubling or trebling of the size of the average estate" and a threefold increase in productivity (Blackburn 1997:407). At this time the largest sugar plantations were between 1,000 and 2,000 acres. In 1754, 467 planters commanded estates of that size (with 214 plantations holding more land in reserve), "accounting for 77.8 per cent of the land available for cultivation" (406). In the same year, 303 planters held medium-sized estates of between 500 and 999 acres, and 566 planters had smaller estates from 100 to 499 acres, with "only 263 landholders with less than 100 acres" (407). There was a high degree of absenteeism, especially among English planters, and "in 1770 about a third of Jamaica's estates, accounting for 40 per cent of sugar output, were administered by agents or attorneys on behalf of absent owners" (406). Many of these attorneys were Scots (Karras 1992:65–71).

Higman's (1998) detailed study of Montpelier Plantation in St. James Parish illustrates the land-use system of a Jamaican slave estate. By the 1820s the pattern of production at Montpelier was "based on four essential land use types: cane pieces, surrounded by pasture, provision grounds, and an outer ring of woodland" (96). Atypically, however, woodland, with ruinate and the slaves' provision grounds, dominated Montpelier Plantation's space in the Great River Valley: 44 percent of the property (3,000 acres) consisted of woods, contrasting with an average of 14 percent for other Jamaican sugar estates. In 1825 provision grounds comprised 467 acres of Montpelier's approximately 10,000 acres (80, 94–95).

In Jamaica, as in many other Caribbean colonies, the slaves' provision grounds were usually on the marginal hilly backlands of plantations, as were trees for timber. But in some western parishes, including St. James and Trelawny, provision grounds were sometimes on separate "mountains" in the interior (even more than ten miles away), especially for coastal plantations. This pattern of land use, which continued throughout the period of apprenticeship from the abolition of slavery in 1834 until full emancipation in 1838, was clearly documented for Trelawny by Joseph Sturge and Thomas Harvey in 1837: "The parish of Trelawny is one of the largest and wealthiest in the island. It is almost exclusively planted with canes. The estates occupying plains and undulating lands near the coast, and the negros' provision grounds being situated in the mountain woodlands of the interior, at distances varying from three to even twenty miles from their homes" (1838:221–22, quoted in Higman 1988:266).

In the central area of a Jamaican slave estate was the plantation community, dominated by the owner's Great House — usually constructed of cut stone on high ground overlooking the slaves' house yards from which signs of rebellion could be observed. In the 1950s the Great House ruins of Trelawny's Southfield Estate near Martha Brae could still be seen on a hill above the remains of the slave village on a ridge below, near the overseer's bungalow. As at Southfield, there were also residences for white staff and, on the majority of estates, the sugar works. These comprised a mill, a boiling and cooling house, a distillery, a trash house, tradesmen's shops, and generally a cattle yard. Some plantations also provided a hospital for their slaves, and most plantation doctors were Scots. In the case of Montpelier (which comprised three estates), there were by 1825 at least 332 buildings, "of which 88 percent were contained within the close works-village-great house complexes. . . . Some 268 or 81 percent were the houses of slaves located within the villages: 137 at Old Montpelier, 89 at New Montpelier, and 42 at Shettlewood. . . . At Old and New Montpelier the slave villages each occupied 16 acres, and at Shettlewood 7 acres" (Higman 1998:103).

The personnel on the plantations reflected the basic dichotomy of powerful white masters and powerless black and (over time) colored slaves. Each group was, however, stratified within. For example, at Montpelier, in addition to the plantation owners — including the Ellis dynasty, from 1752 to 1912, which lived in Britain for 130 years from 1782 to 1912 (Higman 1998:61–77) — "there was a constant turnover of white overseers, bookkeepers and artisans" (40). Many such staff on Jamaican plantations were also Scots (Karras 1992:49).

Extending Richard Sheridan's (1974, 1977, 1985) work on the Scots in the West Indies, Alan Karras (1992) shows that Scottish ethnicity, professional education, and limited opportunities for employment and social mobility (resulting partly from primogeniture) generated a significant flow of transient migrants from Scotland to Jamaica and the Chesapeake from 1740 to 1800. From 1750 to the end of the eighteenth century 65 percent of the estimated 9,000–10,000 Scots who emigrated to these destinations, hoping to make their fortunes and return to Scotland, went to Jamaica (44–45). These industrious and thrifty sojourners were artisans, bookkeepers, overseers, doctors, lawyers, estate attorneys, and merchant planters. Despite their aim of returning home, Scottish migrants became enmeshed in debt and credit networks and found it difficult to remove capital from the island. Many sojourners therefore became settlers, investing in land and slaves; some estate attorneys, overseers, and doctors purchased their own plantations. In 1754 at least 10 percent of the landowners in Jamaica were Scots; by 1774 about one-third of the island's white population was from Scotland or of Scottish descent, and approximately two-thirds of Jamaica's doctors were Scots (54–60).

The Scots tended to settle in the growth areas of Jamaica, particularly in the parishes of St. James (including Trelawny), Westmoreland, and Hanover but also in St. Mary and St. Ann. In such areas they clustered in pockets and neighborhoods, linked and reinforced by islandwide networks and patron-client relationships based on kinship, friendship, and ethnicity. By 1804 Trelawny had the highest percentage of Scots, who comprised 35.5 percent of the parish's total population — residing especially in the vicinity of Martha Brae (122–31, 140). By 1817 Scottish settlements had spread throughout the island, and Scots represented between 12 and 29 percent of the white slaveholders in various parishes and possessed more-than-average numbers of slaves, with Trelawny having "the highest numbers of slaves per Scot" (177).

The Jamaican slaves also became internally differentiated and stratified. In addition to the ethnic differences between imported Africans and local-born Creoles, sociolegal racial distinctions emerged among the Creoles resulting from miscegenation between white men and black or colored female slaves. As Fernando Henriques (1968:44) explained: "Inside the coloured group distinctions had grown up very early. Sir Hans Sloane, writing in the early years of the eighteenth century, divides the population into: white; blacks; mulattoes — the offspring of white and black; quadroons — the offspring of mulattoes and whites; mustees — the offspring of whites and quadroons." About a century later, "M. G. Lewis, in his *Journal of a West India Proprietor*, published in the 1820's, has this entry for January 15th: 'The offspring of a white man and a black woman is a mulatto; the mulatto and black produce a sambo; from a mulatto and white comes the quadroon; from the quadroon and white comes the mustee; the child of a mustee by a white man is called a musteffino, while the children of a musteffino are free by law, and rank as white persons to all intents and purposes' " (46). Richard Hart (1994:128–29) has recorded the classifications of Negroes, sambos, mulattoes, quadroons, and mustees from 1817 to 1832 for the slave population on Good Hope Plantation in Trelawny, about five miles from Martha Brae.

The main occupational distinctions among the enslaved were supervisory, skilled, domestic, and field slaves. Supervisory and skilled slaves were generally male and colored rather than black. Domestic slaves were also often colored, but female, and it was from this category that planters typically selected concubines. Field slaves included both genders, with a predominance of women. There were at least three field gangs on each estate, with four on the larger plantations such as Montpelier in St. James and Green Park in Trelawny, a few miles inland from Martha Brae (Patterson 1973:56–65, 156–58; Higman 1998:41–43). The first or first and second gangs comprised the main body of field slaves. The third gang consisted of weak, elderly, sick, and pregnant slaves. The fourth gang, the "hogmeat gang," capitalized on the labor of young boys and girls, between four and ten years old, who weeded cane and collected grass to feed the hogs or pigs. Oral traditions in Trelawny's free villages tell of ancestral slave children of both genders in such hogmeat gangs.

In Jamaican plantation slave society, as in Western Europe and elsewhere in the British West Indies, the transmission of property within the master class was based on primogeniture (Craton 1987; Karras 1992:50; Higman 1998; Eltis 2000:16; R. A. Barrett 2000:172). Accordingly, "property in plantations and slaves descended through free families according to rules which gave precedence to the male line. Slave status, on the other hand, descended through the female line" (Higman 1998:2). As a result, "males dominated the plantation world in terms of ownership, management and the consumption of the income produced" (75).

The transplantation of such English law to Jamaica, and to other English colonies in the Americas, not only served as an instrument of domination and control but also defined the identity of the colonists as "English" and, after 1707, as "British"—including the Scots, despite their distinct ethnicity. The metropolitan/colonial legal system, which emphasized the absolute right of British men to property and liberty, including representative law—reinforced by racist dogmas defining Negroes as a separate species lacking the moral essence of humanity—was used to rationalize enslavement of Africans and trading of chattel slaves. This legal fiction "resolved" the paradox of slavery in societies based on freedom, defining distinct categories of persons as either entitled to liberty or suited to enslavement, especially among the English/British and Euro-creole slaveholders in Jamaica and Barbados (Greene 2000). The issue became explicit in 1772–73, when planters on these islands (Jamaican Edward Long and Barbadian Samuel Estwick) challenged the decision of a British court to free a slave named Somerset who had been transported to England. Their proslavery pamphlets argued that African slaves were comparable to English medieval villeins, that the British legislature was itself involved in the slave trade, and that the whole British nation profited from West Indian slave plantations.

In the long term, however, such arguments backfired as the massive slave regimes constructed on these dogmas resulted in an extreme "philosophy of fear" among the planters based on intense negrophobia or "simple, direct fear of their slaves and their capacity for resistance" (Steel 1993:4). This was especially true in Jamaica, which "had the highest ratio, ten to one, of blacks to whites in British America" (Mullin 1994:20). This "world view of the Jamaican plantocracy" was rooted in the maroon resistance of the Spanish slaves at the time of the English conquest of the island and was reinforced by "one of the highest rates of servile rebellion in the New World" (Steel 1993:5), maroon wars, and the "Quashee" stereotype of dissembling dangerous slaves. Negrophobia led to an ambivalent stance toward the free colored, Jamaica being "unique in publicly transforming coloureds into whites," with "any free coloured person more than three generations removed from pure African ancestry" being "granted full citizenship and legal equality with whites," despite a basic distrust of even the smallest degree of Negro ancestry (13–14).

The Jamaican planters' perception of their slaves not only hardened an exceptionally severe slave regime but also creolized their own British identity, with a shift by the later eighteenth century from an emphasis on liberty to a concern for safety. This transformation was manifested in the Jamaica Assembly's confession to its parent state in 1774 (in the context of the stamp duty crisis preceding the American Revolution) that the colony's small white minority could never resist British rule and needed metropolitan military protection against the constant threat of slave and maroon rebellion (Steel 1993:13–14; Greene 2000:27–28). This was particularly the case in western Jamaica, where slave rebellion was rampant and planters kept extensive records of slave ethnicities "in order to control the blacks while making white society more secure" (Mullin 1994:26, 33).

Drawing partly on my own work, Higman's (1998:290–305) overview of social relations at Montpelier Plantation during slavery and then freedom (1739–1912) focuses on the primacy of land for both masters and slaves (who had differing views of property) and on the significance of "community" in the plantation context. He contrasts this perspective with earlier views of historians on Jamaican plantation slave society such as Edward Brathwaite (1971), Orlando Patterson (1973), Michael Craton (1978), and Douglas Armstrong (1990), who made little or no analytic use of the concept of community. Higman's own analysis also highlights the links between the Montpelier Plantation community and wider contexts, including the

Great River Valley and the Atlantic world. Similar linkages were central to the plantation communities surrounding the colonial town and trading port of Martha Brae, established in old St. James by 1762 and consolidated in the new parish of Trelawny.

Higman's (1984) analysis of urban slavery in the British West Indies and his Montpelier study (1998) underline the importance of creolization in Jamaican communities during slavery, as well as the significance of plantations and their slave villages in this process even compared to towns. British Caribbean urban slave populations peaked in the early nineteenth century, when (ca. 1830) 8 percent of slaves lived in urban settlements. At that time, almost 6 percent of the slave population resided in the eight largest towns (with over 2,000 slaves), including Kingston (the largest urban center) and Spanish Town in southeastern Jamaica and Montego Bay in the northwest, in St. James Parish. Most urban slaves were in domestic service, and most of these were female. In 1834, on the eve of the abolition of slavery, 66 percent of the slaves in Kingston were domestics in contrast to about 10 percent on the estates. Other urban female slaves in the British West Indies were hucksters or sellers, whereas enslaved urban males tended to be in skilled trades. According to Higman, the internal contradictions of slavery were more apparent in the towns, manumission was more common in urban settlements, and the interaction of enslaved and free persons was more clearly manifested in urban centers than on the plantations. However, "the towns were not necessarily in the vanguard of creolization" (1984:54), as Craton (1976) suggested for Jamaica and Peter Hogg (1979) for African America. Higman's research reveals that the early-nineteenth-century British Caribbean urban slave population was more heterogeneous than on the plantations, especially in the older sugar colonies like Jamaica, and indicates that the estates were the vanguard of creolization in Jamaican slave society.

The parishes of old St. James and new Trelawny, at the heart of Jamaica's rural plantation slave economy, would therefore have been at the forefront of the process of creolization—as Higman's (1998) study of Montpelier shows. Reinforcing this view is Craton's (1971) observation that in 1817 approximately 62 percent of Trelawny's slave population were Creoles: "17,692 of the parish's 28,497 slaves had been born in Jamaica, 10,791 had been born in Africa, 13 in America and one at sea" (15 [n. 22]). These statistics indicate that the Trelawny slave population was by this stage highly creolized, for nearly two-thirds of the slaves were Jamaican-born.

Yet in St. James and Trelawny there was significant interaction between slave plantations and towns, as well as among estates. Trelawny slaves engaged in such interaction when they went to the marketplace, attended the

Baptist mission church, and became involved in the Obeah-Myal religious complex. Planters also had a network of relationships among the estates and in the parochial capitals of Montego Bay, Martha Brae, and Falmouth. This network reinforced the planter class in old St. James and new Trelawny, which were the immediate contexts for Martha Brae's Euro-Caribbean history. These parishes reflected the contours of Jamaican plantation slave society in microcosm, and plantation slavery was especially highly developed there.

The Establishment of Old St. James, New Trelawny, and Colonial Martha Brae

After the English conquest of Jamaica in 1655, the area now known as Trelawny Parish in the northwest was colonized as part of old St. James in Cornwall County.[3] Named in honor of the Duke of York (later King James II), St. James was first settled as a precinct in 1665, following Charles II's proclamation of that year. It was established as a parish in 1671, when the island's second group of parishes was founded. With an area of some 566 square miles, old St. James was bounded on the north by the sea, on the west by the parishes of Hanover and Westmoreland, on the east by the parish of St. Ann, and on the south by the parish of St. Elizabeth (Shore and Stewart 1952:16; Ogilvie 1954:1–3; Wright and White 1969:185; Black 1979, 1984:5). Initial settlement of old St. James, like that of Jamaica generally, was effected through land patents from the Crown. A number of the early settlers patented land near the Martha Brae River, including Colonel Charles Whitfield, who in 1674 acquired Southfield property about a mile from the site that would become Martha Brae.

Despite this early colonization, settlement of the parish was initially slow. In 1673 its population consisted of only 124 whites and 22 Negroes (Goodwin 1946:184), and as late as 1711 St. James still had "no towns, few inhabitants and little commerce" (Wright and White 1969:185). Exposure to attack from the Leeward Maroons in the Cockpit Country Mountains to the south, in addition to buccaneers and pirates from the north, exacerbated the hindrances to early settlement in the island as a whole.

By the second half of the eighteenth century, however, settlement in old St. James was extended and the nature of this growth changed. Although some early patentees had received extensive land grants, the predominant mode of early colonization of the parish, as of Jamaica generally, was smallholdings. Following a transformation that typified the island from the late seventeenth and early eighteenth centuries, the smallholding began to give way to the large-scale plantation. For example, Montpelier was established in the Great River Valley in 1739 after execution of the Leeward Maroon treaty, and, with the escalation of the plantation system in St. James, the number of sugar mills in the parish "increased from 20 to 115 between 1745 and 1774" (Higman 1998:14).

With this shift to large-scale plantations, St. James's capital, Montego Bay, in the western part of the parish, prospered and became a free port. It was important both for exporting plantation products and importing slaves. The TSTD (Eltis et al. 1999) records a total of 125 shiploads of enslaved Africans disembarking at Montego Bay during the slave trade. Montego Bay had been founded in the early eighteenth century by Captain Jonathan Barnett (1677–1744), a wealthy planter who led the parish's defense against pirates and maroons. However, because Montego Bay was nearly sixty miles from St. James's eastern border, planters in the east pressed for a new parish to be created from the eastern portion, with its own capital. Despite strong opposition from western St. James, a petition to this effect was submitted to the Jamaica Assembly as early as 1733, but on the bill's third reading it was thrown out.

Nevertheless, continued pressure to create a new parish led to the establishment by 1762 of Martha Brae, the first British colonial town in eastern old St. James, on the site of reputed precolonial Arawak and post-Conquest Spanish settlements.[4] The town was situated on the Martha Brae River, about one mile inland and two and a half miles upstream from the coast, at a point where the sugar plantations of Holland and Irving Tower adjoined. Holland was owned by Henry Cuniffe, an English planter and surveyor who had also acquired Merrywood Plantation bordering Holland and Irving Tower. The archives show that Irving Tower had been established three years before Martha Brae by Scottish planter James Irving (of Bonshaw Tower in southwestern Scotland), in 1759.[5] However, the TSTD reveals that at least one shipload of slaves disembarked at Martha Brae Harbor as early as 1754 (Eltis et al. 1999), indicating that the site of Martha Brae was significant for plantation trade even before the founding of the town in 1762. The town of Martha Brae, which was to serve as a supply point for the surrounding plantations, was laid out by Cuniffe on about thirty acres of land on a marginal ridge on the eastern edge of his Holland Estate.

Ray Fremmer (1968) described the founding of the town and its significance to the planters of eastern St. James:

He [Cuniffe] laid out this town on the easternmost portion of his own sugar plantation, Holland, bordering the Martha Brae river. That point on the river was then merely the unloading point for the barges carrying supplies up-river from the ships anchored out in the harbour at Rock [at the mouth of the river], destined to Cuniffe and other planters in the interior. That was the furthest point upriver to which a barge could navigate without hitting rocks.

Other planters urged Cuniffe to sell them a small piece of land where they might build a shelter for their supplies from the barges when the roads were too wet for the drays to manage. Accordingly, he laid out a town with two streets running east to west, Queen Street and King Street, and three streets running north to south, Church, Duke and Princess Street, with eighty-five lots for sale. And eventually every lot did sell, probably making Henry Cuniffe the first successful subdivider on the north coast.

Cuniffe named his town Lyttleton after William Lyttleton, who became governor of Jamaica in that year, 1762. But "gradually, the name of the new town, Lyttleton, faded away, losing out to the much older name of the adjoining point in the river, Martha Brae."

The derivation of the town's name, Martha Brae, is controversial. Dan Ogilvie (1954:6) asserted that "the name is traditionally associated with 'Mart,' a centre for the sale of goods and 'Brae,' the Scottish name for 'Hillside Bank.' In process of time it became Martha Brae as more colloquial to the ordinary people." Fremmer (1968) disagreed, concluding instead that "Martha Brae" derives from the Spanish name "Multiberon" Cove — Bay of Many Sharks — for the bay at the mouth of the river, marked on a map of 1670 in Edward Long's *History of Jamaica* (1774). This was successively corrupted (as the name of the river) to "Rio Matiberion" on Whitfield's 1674 Southfield land patent, "Para Mater Tiberen Rio" on a map of 1683, and "Para Mater Tiberones River" and "Mater Tibero Cove" on Harris's 1721 map of Jamaica. Fremmer's argument seems convincing for the evolution of the Spanish name for the bay and the river, prior to the founding of the British colonial town. However, the significance of Scottish settlement in the area by 1754 (Karras 1992:122–31, 140) and the town's role as a plantation supply point (including the trading of slaves), as well as the subsequent development of marketing by the slaves themselves, support Ogilvie's hypothesis, especially as the town's name was changed from Lyttleton to Martha Brae and as Martha Brae appears in the TSTD from 1754. The Multiberon River may then have been renamed after the town, particularly given the full meaning of "Brae," namely, "the [hill] slope bounding a riverside plain" (*Chambers 20th Century Dictionary* 1983:149). Long's map of 1774 clearly shows the name "Martha Brea [*sic*]" at the mouth of the river, and Craskell and Simpson's map of 1763 (reproduced in Karras 1992:128) shows the town of Martha Brae. The name of the British settlement may therefore have evolved along with its role as a riverside-hill market town for both masters and slaves. Even today food produce is traded at the crossroads in Martha Brae known as "River Hill."

In November 1770 a successful petition for the subdivision of old St. James was presented to the House of Assembly by the inhabitants of the eastern part of the parish. By formal writ the parish was to be divided by a line running due south to the northern boundary of St. Elizabeth from a point at Long Bay, approximately twelve miles east of Montego Bay. The lands to the east and west of this line respectively were henceforth to be known as the separate parishes of Trelawny and St. James. The new parish was named after Sir William Trelawny, Jamaica's governor. In January 1771 the formal writ announcing these changes was published, and Trelawny — with 333 square miles, more than half the area of old St. James — became the fifth largest parish on the island. With the publication of the formal writ, Martha Brae became the first capital of Trelawny. Henry Cuniffe, the town's founder, later became Trelawny's custos (Fremmer 1967, 1968), serving as chairman of the local government known as "the Justices and Vestry." The vestry was comprised of freeholders who were the leading planters of the parish.

The creation of Trelawny was marked by celebrations among the new parishioners, especially among the inhabitants of Martha Brae, as Dan Ogilvie (secretary to the Trelawny Parochial Board, which replaced the vestry) Eurocentrically portrayed: "This was an event which created internal exhilaration and a variety of joyous and predictable display. It was a manifestation of extraordinary public rejoicing. A real holiday was proclaimed. Places of business were closed and even the slaves who had but a vague appreciation of the importance of the enactment were allowed to enter, unconsciously, or otherwise into the patriotic celebrations. The then chief town, Martha Brae, was a scene of revelry" (1954:3).

H. P. Jacobs (1970:14) stated that on its creation in 1771, Trelawny contained "about half of the population, but much less than half the sugar production" of old St. James. In 1774 Edward Long (2:221) wrote that "Marthabrae" stood "about two miles above the mouth [of the 'Marthabrae' River], on a rising ground not far from the bridge," and consisted "of about thirty houses or more; as the late partition of St. James has of consequence tended to the establishment of a new town here, which may grow in size in proportion as the lands, at present unsettled in the parish, are brought into culture." Yet Craton's (1978:36) retrospective figures for Trelawny in 1768 (six years after the founding of Martha Brae, but three years before the creation of the new parish) show that, although there were fewer sugar estates in this eastern portion than in the west of old St. James, the east already had the higher sugar productivity.[6] By 1800 Trelawny had more sugar plantations than any other parish, and in 1832 it was still the island's leading sugar producer (Karras 1992:125–26).

Western Trelawny (including the fertile Queen of Spain's Valley, watered by the Martha Brae River, straddling the boundary of Trelawny and St. James), the immediate hinterland of the town of Martha Brae, developed rapidly and by 1804 was producing more sugar than did all of Trelawny thirty years before. In 1804 the parish exported 13,295 hogsheads and 1,229 tierces of sugar, produced by its 94 sugar estates,[7] the largest amount of sugar that had ever been exported from the island. Even after the abolition of the slave trade in 1808 and the subsequent decline of the British West Indian planter class, Trelawny's planters continued to prosper for many years, as fortunes could still be made from sugar and the soil in this parish was not yet exhausted.[8] In 1829, five years before the abolition of slavery in the British colonies in 1834, Trelawny, with a slave population of 25,654, possessed more slaves than any other parish in Jamaica (Ogilvie 1954:150). Trelawny's slave population had been even higher in 1820 and 1811, with totals of 27,000 and 27,550 respectively (19, 154) and higher still in 1800 with 27,827 slaves (Karras 1992:126). Trelawny's continuing sugar productivity without the use of slaves is reflected in the "Agricultural Reports" of the *Falmouth Post* in the years following emancipation.[9]

The Plantation Hinterland of Colonial
Martha Brae: The Tharp Estates

The most important plantations in the hinterland of colonial Martha Brae were the consolidated Tharp estates. In 1767 — five years after the founding of Martha Brae and shortly before the subdivision of old St. James — John Tharp (1744–1804, educated at Eton College and Trinity College, Cambridge), the Euro-creole son of a fairly prosperous planter in the parish of Hanover, bought Good Hope, a three-thousand-acre plantation bordering the upper reaches of the Martha Brae River. This purchase, combined with his ownership of nearby Wales and Lansquinet Estates and a part interest in Potosi, an adjoining plantation, made Tharp at age twenty-three the largest landowner in old St. James. Good Hope would become the biggest slave plantation in the new parish of Trelawny and Tharp, Trelawny's most prominent freeholder and one of the wealthiest planters in Jamaica.

Tharp continued to consolidate his landholdings, purchasing all the real estate that became available in the area during the next thirty-five years, as well as Dean's Valley Estate in the parish of Westmoreland and Chippenham Park in St. Ann. His property in new Trelawny included such large estates as Windsor, Covey, and Pantre Pant, and by 1791 Tharp owned almost all of the land bordering the Martha Brae River. He became the largest slave owner in the island, with a total of over three thousand slaves, and one of "the wealthiest planters in Anglo-America" (Mullin 1994:26). The average production of Tharp's estates between 1795 and 1800 was just over 1,500 hogsheads a year. Moreover, he received the highest prices ever paid for Jamaican sugar, at a time when the slave plantation system was most productive. In 1805, the year after John Tharp's death, the Tharp estates produced 2,500 hogsheads of sugar (Wright and White 1969:215; Tenison 1971:14, 18–20). From 1781 Tharp himself engaged in the trade of African slaves, "whom he sold at a considerable profit to other planters in Jamaica," and "in 1802 he was one of the original investors in the West India Dock Scheme in London" (Hart 1994:51). Also in 1802 he bought Merrywood Estate (his last land purchase), located a mile southwest of Martha Brae; Merrywood adjoined Holland and Irving Tower and bordered his Top Hill Plantation (Tenison 1971:18; Craton 1971:19).

Tharp's lavish lifestyle at Good Hope Great House—a "fine Palladian Great House," built by the previous owner, Colonel Williams, in 1755 (Tenison 1971:6–7), which commanded a splendid view of the Cockpit Country Mountains—exemplified the opulence of Trelawny's slave-owning plantocracy. Fine silver plate, engraved with the head of an African man, and china decorated with a similar head of a male African slave enclosed by sheeves of sugarcane, were imported from England, as were wine and champagne. Tharp "would send gifts of live turtles to his family and business associates in England" (16–17). The estate buildings included, in addition to the Great House (on a hill overlooking the other buildings) and Tharp's office (behind the Great House), the overseer's house; the sugar works, with a waterwheel turned by the Martha Brae River; a church; a slave hospital; a school for the slaves' children; and houses for the slaves. In John Tharp's lifetime Good Hope was a central meeting place for Trelawny planters, both for social occasions and for discussions related to the sugar industry.

As was customary for the leading plantocrats of the day, Tharp took an active part in the affairs of his parish and colony. He was a member of the

John Tharp's Good Hope Great House near Martha Brae. Photo by Jean Besson.

House of Assembly, custos of Trelawny, and a "mediator" in the Second Maroon War of 1795; among his responsibilities as custos, he served as "Guardian of the Maroons in his parish" (Robinson 1969:84). For a period when he resided in England as an absentee proprietor, Tharp was also deputy lieutenant of Cambridgeshire and campaigned for a seat in the House of Commons. At the time of his death in 1804, he "owned almost all the riverside land in Trelawny from the mountains to the sea, Chippenham Park in St. Ann and Dean's Valley in Westmoreland. He also owned several houses in Falmouth [Trelawny's second capital], and in England a 6,000 acre estate in Cambridgeshire which he also called Chippenham Park and a beautiful London house in Portland Place. He owned over 3,000 slaves and left instructions in his will that there should never be less than 2,800 on his estates. His Jamaican property was valued at £500,000 and was left to his young grandson" (Tenison 1971:18–19). John Tharp was buried in the family burial ground on Good Hope Estate. Good Hope, which remained in the Tharp family until the mid-nineteenth century, was a prosperous sugar plantation for a hundred years after John Tharp's death, until 1904 (10). It has persisted, through changing ownership, as a thriving estate based on agriculture, pen keeping, and tourism to the present day. In 2001 it was owned by a member of the island's Euro-creole merchant elite, and the three-thousand-acre estate in England belonged to a descendant of John

Tharp. In the entrance hall of Chippenham Park in England there is a portrait of Tharp and a map of Good Hope Estate.

The English Plantocracy in the Vicinity of Martha Brae

Further examples, focusing first on the estates of the English planters, some of whom were absentee, elaborate this portrait of the slave plantation hinterland of colonial Martha Brae, the parochial and island economy and society of which it was a part, and its relationship with the British metropolis and Atlantic world. The second largest sugar plantation in the parish, after Tharp's Good Hope, was Orange Valley in western Trelawny; along with Good Hope and Green Park, it was one of only three sugar estates in the parish to provide a hospital for its slaves. Orange Valley was purchased from the Allen family in 1757 (five years prior to the founding of Martha Brae and fourteen years before the creation of Trelawny) by Herbert Newton Jarrett II (1724–90), of Westmoreland, a member of one of Jamaica's oldest planter families. Jarrett married Ann Allen, the previous owner's sister, as his second wife. Their son, Herbert Newton Jarrett III (1765–1829), inherited Orange Valley and lived as an absentee proprietor among the English gentry (where he was known to Queen Charlotte), with a mansion in Norfolk and a house in London (Wright and White 1969:30–32; Fremmer 1984b). Herbert Jarrett II gave Kent sugar estate adjoining Orange Valley to John Jarrett, his elder son from his first marriage, who was also an absentee proprietor. At his death in 1809, his Trelawny sugar estates — Kent and Golden Grove on the banks of the Martha Brae River — produced an income of £20,000 sterling per year. By the early nineteenth century, too, Orange Valley had the largest number of slaves of any single Trelawny estate: 615 in 1817 and 641 in 1828 (Craton 1978:42–45). In 2001 Orange Valley was a livestock pen owned by a Euro-creole family.

Green Park in western Trelawny, with around 559 slaves, was the third largest sugar plantation in the new parish. With this large slave population, Green Park had the full complement of four field gangs and a slave village of at least thirty houses. Between 1740 and 1761 it had passed by sale through the hands of several owners, the last of whom bequeathed it to William Atherton, who inherited it in the late eighteenth century. Atherton spent much time as an absentee proprietor in England but frequently returned to his Trelawny plantation, where he completed its third and largest Great House.

Another Englishman who divided his time between his Jamaican plantation and his home in Britain was planter-historian Bryan Edwards (1743–1800), who in 1769 bought the 1,500-acre estate he called Bryan Castle in eastern Trelawny and built its magnificent Great House. Originally from Wiltshire, Edwards returned to England in 1793 and settled as a West Indian merchant and banker, dying there in 1800. During his time in Jamaica he represented Trelawny as a member of the Assembly from 1788 but also made frequent return trips to England.

Sir Simon Clarke (1727–77), ninth in line of baronet in the Clarke family of Hyde in Cheshire, was also a member of Trelawny's English plantocracy. He owned Hampshire, Mahogany Hall, and Long Pond Estates in eastern Trelawny and additional plantations in Westmoreland. Another member of the Clarke planter dynasty was Edward Clarke, who acquired the nearby sugar estates of Hyde and Swanswick in eastern Trelawny (Sibley and Ogilvie 1980). Long Pond, originally patented to William Reid in 1709 and established as a sugar estate in 1753, has been Trelawny's longest surviving sugar factory — having operated for nearly 250 years — and in 2001 comprised the core of Lond Pond Estates.

One of the parish's most prominent English planter families were the Barretts (cousins of John Tharp), whose plantations straddled Trelawny and St. James, dominating the rich coastal lands of the "Northside"; they also acquired estates in Hanover and St. Ann (R. A. Barrett 2000). Theirs would be one of the longest surviving planter dynasties in Jamaica, enduring for seven generations, from the early days of British colonization until the postemancipation era. The founder of the dynasty was Hearcie Barrett, an officer in Cromwell's Army of Occupation in 1655, an early patentee of land in old St. James, and a member "of the old Cornish family of Barrett of Tregaren and Penquite" (Shore and Stewart 1952:64). Hearcie Barrett received grants of land from Charles II in several parishes in Jamaica but settled on his property in Clarendon. He had two sons: Hearcie Barrett II, who lived on the family's land in Spanish Town, and Samuel Barrett, who was killed in the French invasion of the island in 1694. Samuel's son, Samuel Barrett II, settled his grandfather's lands in old St. James in 1715 and married Elizabeth Wisdom, the daughter of early patentees with land to the east of the Martha Brae River. On his death in 1760, Samuel II left his property to one of his sons, Edward Barrett (1734–98), who completed the Barrett Great House at Cinnamon Hill, St. James, and established the Barrett family fortune on the Northside.

The Barrett dynasty, though of English origin, consisted mainly of resident planters. Edward Barrett "the Builder" visited England but lived mostly in Jamaica, where he married Judith Goodin, the daughter of William and Sarah Goodin of Trelawny's Spring Estate. One of Edward and Judith's grandsons, the Honorable Richard Barrett (1789–1839), was a planter, supreme court judge, custos of St. James, and Speaker of the Jamaica Assembly. He lived at Barrett Hall in St. James but built the much grander Greenwood Great House in Trelawny for entertaining guests.

In 1781 Elizabeth Barrett, Richard Barrett's paternal aunt, married Charles Moulton, the son of an English gentleman commanding a man-of-war stationed for defense in the West Indies. Their sons, Edward and Samuel Barrett-Moulton, acquired the additional surname of Barrett by royal license when they inherited the property of their maternal grandfather, Edward Barrett "the Builder," at his death in 1798. This inheritance included the Barrett townhouse in Trelawny, completed in 1799, as well as the family's plantations there. Edward Barrett-Moulton Barrett (1786–1857), the father of poet Elizabeth Barrett Browning, was the only absentee proprietor of the Barrett dynasty. He inherited the family seat of Cinnamon Hill and, at Wimpole Street in London, lived off the profits of his Jamaican property generated by the labor of his two thousand slaves.

The mid-1800s saw the decline of the Barrett family fortune, but the extensive family burial ground has remained in the Barrett family. In 2001 English members of the Barrett dynasty, with British and Euro-creole descendants of other Northside planter families — the Palmers of Rose Hall, the Lawrences of Running Gut, the Scarlets of Trelawny, and the Tharps of Good Hope — were active in the Friends of the Georgian Society of Jamaica (which centers on Trelawny) in London, over 345 years after the Barrett dynasty was established in Jamaica.

The Scottish and Creole Planters around Colonial Martha Brae

Trelawny's slave-owning planter class comprised not only English families such as the Barretts, Jarretts, Athertons, and Clarkes, in addition to the Anglo-creole Tharps, but also Scots and colored Creoles. The area that became Trelawny Parish was the heart of Scottish sojourning and settlement in Jamaican slave society, with dense networking around colonial Martha Brae (Karras 1992:66–80, 122–31, 139–49). Even though Scottish sojourning diversified to other parts of the Caribbean and the world after 1800 (8), it continued in Jamaica into the nineteenth century; Scottish ethnicity was still strong in Trelawny after the abolition of slavery, as evidenced in a series of letters from a Scotsman to fellow Scots appearing in the *Falmouth Post* in 1836.[10] Especially significant in the eighteenth century were the Scots who established and consolidated Hampden and Georgia sugar plantations, which formed the core of Hampden Estates and Long Pond Estates — the two vast corporate plantations in Trelawny in 2001. Scottish expatriate networks clustered around these two plantations up to the late twentieth century.

In 1757, five years before the founding of Martha Brae, Robert and James Stirling, two younger sons of James Stirling of Keir, Perthshire, central Scotland, financed by their older brother Sir Archibald Stirling, jointly purchased land in the fertile Queen of Spain's Valley a few miles inland from the site of Martha Brae, beneath the Cockpit Country Mountain range, and established Hampden sugar plantation. Robert had traveled to Jamaica in 1742, first trading as a merchant and then buying Frontier Estate in St. Mary around 1748; James had followed in 1753. James soon sold his share of Hampden Plantation to Robert and returned to Scotland in 1761. Robert died in 1764, enmeshed in debt, and James went back to Jamaica by 1765. By 1774, the Stirling brothers' cousin, Patrick Stirling, was managing the Jamaican estates, James having returned to Scotland. In 1780, three years before Sir Archibald Stirling's death in 1783, Hampden was "valued at around £35,000 with 300 slaves, after its debts were paid" (Karras 1992:78–79). Sir Archibald was childless, and on his death his estate passed to his brother William's three sons, two of whom, Archibald Jr. and John, inherited Frontier and Hampden respectively. These two nephews of Archibald Sr. arrived in Jamaica in 1789 and were trained as planters by Scotsman Francis Grant, who was now manager of Hampden.[11]

In 1787, a few years after Sir Archibald Stirling's death, his heirs in Jamaica invited their cousin Phillip Ainslie out from Scotland to visit Hampden Estate. Ainslie, who remained in Jamaica and became a bookkeeper at Retirement Plantation in St. James, recorded his visit to Hampden in some detail. He included observations on the distinction between African and creole slaves, the self-assumed superiority of the Afro-Creoles, the presence of mulatto slave children on the estate, and the re-creation of descent lines among the enslaved:[12]

> I frequently visited the negro village. . . . The great portion of the negroes on Hampden estate were born upon it, and, in several instances, could prove their descent from grandfathers and grandmothers. As such, they were designated creoles, of which they were exceedingly proud, and looked down with immeasurable contempt on those they called "New Niggers," and those freshly imported from Africa. There were a few

mulattoes, children of European fathers, such as overseers, book-keepers, and tradesmen. The females of these were employed in the household work of the great house, and as seamstresses, whilst such as were of mature age were employed as nurses during visitations of sickness, and always proved themselves invaluable in this capacity, being full of tenderness, kind, patient, and unwearied. (Quoted in Fremmer 1984a)

Some of these mulatto children were reputedly fathered by Ainslie's deceased cousin Patrick Stirling, who had been an attorney at Hampden Estate. In fact, Stirling's will of 1776 stated: "As every person resident in this country any time has children begot on the bodies of Africans or their descendants, and as you know I have some supposed or laid to my charge under the predicament, I request that you will procure that freedom of those not free in the first place and leave them entitled to all rights and privileges of Englishmen and one thousand pounds sterling to the male if his freedom can be procured, and another thousand pounds sterling to the daughter" (quoted in ibid).

In 1823 the Stirling family, along with their Scottish friend William Stehart, the owner of Trelawny's nearby Dundee Estate, invited the Scottish Missionary Society (SMS) to conduct missionary work in that area. The Stirlings "gave a part of Hampden Estate as a site for a church," and the Stirlings and Stehart "offered to pay half the expense of erecting it" (Sibley 1978:70). In 1824 the SMS sent Reverend George Blythe to Hampden, where he established Jamaica's first Presbyterian church in 1827. In 2000 the plantation persisted as the core of Hampden Estates,[13] having been sold in 1852 by Sir William Stirling-Maxwell (grandnephew of Archibald) to an ancestor of the present owners—who, like the Barretts and other planter dynasties, maintained an ancestral burial ground on the estate (71; "Hampden Estates" 1995).

Georgia sugar plantation in eastern Trelawny had been purchased for Charles Gordon of Aberdeenshire, Scotland, by his fellow northeastern Scottish sojourner and attorney John Grant "in 1778 for £26,000" at which time it "produced 140 hogsheads of sugar per year"; Gordon had traveled to Jamaica "to settle his deceased merchant uncle's affairs in the early 1770s" (Karras 1992:66).[14] Gordon did not remain long in Jamaica, touring North America in 1773 and returning permanently to Scotland in 1781, at which time he reappointed John Grant (a lawyer who would become Jamaica's chief justice in 1784 and a Scottish landowner by 1791), with his brother Francis Grant as his attorneys and employed Francis as his manager. Francis Grant (who likewise became manager of Hampden) also acted as an agent for the sale of hundreds of slaves disembarked by several slaving vessels at Martha Brae and Montego Bay between 1789 and 1792, and at Falmouth in 1793 (D. Richardson 1996).

Other planters from Scotland, or of Scottish descent, in Trelawny included James Stewart I and II and John Cunningham. James Stewart I went from Scotland to Jamaica in the mid-eighteenth century and acquired 167 acres of land in Trelawny, then still part of old St. James, a few miles east of Martha Brae. There he built a cut-stone Great House called Stewart Castle. James Stewart II (1766–1828), a Scots-Creole born in Jamaica and a planter-historian like Bryan Edwards, inherited Stewart Castle and, apart from some years in England lobbying Parliament against the abolition of the slave trade, spent his life in Trelawny.

John Cunningham was born in Scotland in 1738. On arriving in Jamaica, he became an attorney for Maxfield Estate, which adjoined Holland Plantation and bordered Martha Brae. Cunningham not only later became owner of Maxfield, but also of neighboring Greenside Estate and three other Trelawny sugar plantations — Hopewell, Biddeford, and Roslin Castle. His sons, one of whom was James Cunningham, a custos of Trelawny, inherited his Trelawny plantations. In 2001 in Martha Brae's neighboring free village of Granville, bordering Maxfield, an Old Family descended from ex-slaves still used the Cunningham surname as its title (other Old Family names in Granville being those of the Barrett and Jarrett planter families).

Although the English, Scots, and Euro-Creoles dominated Trelawny's planter class, miscegenation and manumission sometimes resulted in the paradox of a slave-owning planter of slave descent. Such was the case of Hugh Barnett, a quadroon with one-quarter Negro ancestry, the son of Captain Jonathan Barnett (the founder of Montego Bay) and his mulatto mistress Jane Stone. Hugh Barnett inherited what is now the eastern two-thirds of Montego Bay and, at his death in 1779, controlled five plantations including Sportsman's Hall, Biddeford, and Hopewell in Trelawny. After his death most of the Barnett real estate was inherited by his son Hugh II, who, along with his father's sister's children, now controlled six plantations: Catherine Hall and Catherine Mount in Montego Bay and four in Trelawny. This wealth enabled the Barnett family to be considered "structurally white," despite their Negro ancestry. The case of Hugh Barnett was later paralleled in postemancipation Trelawny by quadroon Henry Sewell (son of William Sewell, proprietor of Arcadia Estate, and a mulatto slave woman), who inherited the Sewell "sugar empire" in 1872 (Fremmer 1980) and whose descendants lived at Arcadia until the late twentieth century.

The Consolidation of the Trelawny Planter Class
and the Slaving Port of Martha Brae

Trelawny's planter families were closely interrelated through a network of kinship and marriage, which strengthened the monopoly of power by the planter class and consolidated its land base. For example, John Tharp of Good Hope was a cousin of the Barretts and married into the Partridge family of Potosi Plantation adjoining Good Hope. The Barrett family intermarried with the Wisdoms, early patentees of land east of the Martha Brae River, and with the Goodins of Spring Estate. The Wisdoms, in turn, intermarried with three other Trelawny families — the Mintos, the Gallimores, and the Virgos — who owned neighboring plantations in Trelawny's eastern foothills. (In Martha Brae in 2001, the central Old Family descended from ex-slaves still used the title Minto, and the Gallimores were a central family line in the Trelawny free village of Kettering.) Similarly, Ann Virgo Gallimore, the widow of Matthew Gallimore (who died in 1792), married John Tharp's son, John Tharp II, and settled with him in England.

Trelawny's planter families were linked not only by consanguinity and affinity (relations of blood and marriage alliance), but also through sales of land and slaves, cooperation in the face of slave rebellion and maroon wars, ties of friendship, and even legal disputes. The dense networks among the Scottish sojourners and settlers in the parish and beyond, based on ethnicity, kinship, friendship, acquaintance, debt and credit, and patron-client relations — such as the interpersonal web of Francis Grant, manager of Georgia and Hampden Plantations (Karras 1992) — further intensified the consolidation of Trelawny's planter class.

This plantocracy of the new parish of Trelawny — English, Scots, and Creoles; white and colored; and consolidated through kinship, conflict, cooperation, and exchange — was now the stronghold of Jamaica's planter class, a position it would maintain for many years to come, as the Trelawny plantations continued to prosper well beyond emancipation (Jacobs 1970:15; Craton 1978:24; Karras 1992:125). It was against this backdrop of Trelawny's plantation slave society that colonial Martha Brae flourished as a slaving port and planter town.

For Trelawny's first thirty years, Martha Brae, the capital, was the center of parochial government and the hub of its plantocracy, reflecting the prosperity of a parish that had become the leading sugar-producing area of Jamaica at the meridian of the island's Golden Age. At this time the parish vestry, court, and militia were located in Martha Brae, where every Trelawny planter of note had a townhouse, and where ships bound for metropolitan ports, such as Bristol and Liverpool, loaded Trelawny's slave-grown sugar. By around 1774 there were about thirty grand townhouses — two-story and Georgian in style — in Martha Brae. The year 1800 saw the construction of a courthouse, where, in addition to holding court, the Scottish plantocracy celebrated "Burns Supper" (Long 1774, 2:221; Fremmer 1967, 1968; Jacobs 1970:14.) [15]

Accounts of Martha Brae's received history focus on the splendor of the eighteenth-century town, [16] as typified by Fremmer's (1967) description:

> For the first twenty years of the life of the new parish of Trelawny, Martha Brae was the centre of the government and all social life. The Vestry met there; every plantation squire of importance in the area had a town house in Martha Brae. . . .
>
> The ship captains who carried their sugar to England and brought out their supplies preferred not to travel too far from their ships, especially not over bad roads to outlying sugar estates. William Atherton, owner of Green Park sugar estate, had a house on Queen Street, Henry Cuniffe, who owned Merrywood, Holland, Lisworney, and Garredu sugar estates, had a house in Martha Brae, John Fowler, who owned Grange plantation, had a house in Martha Brae.
>
> Fowler was the Martha Brae agent for the ship *Lion*, Captain James Steel, bound for Liverpool from Martha Brae in November, 1780. Other ships that called at Martha Brae were the *Brothers*, Captain Alexander Campbell, and the *Harriet*, Captain Montgomerie.
>
> Sometimes, for instance on 28 April 1780, there were as many as four ships in the Martha Brae Harbor, the *Sally*, the *Chubb*, the *Good Hope* and the *Munt*.
>
> The following account comes from the *Royal Gazette* for 1781: "The *Molly*, Captain Jordan, which sailed from Montego Bay last Saturday night for Martha Brae, where she arrived last Tuesday, carried in a prize of war, a schooner pickaroon, mounting ten swivels, having on board thirteen Spaniards which she took near Martha Brae harbour, and received the bounty of one hundred pounds sterling in conformity to an order of the Vestry of the parish of Trelawny."
>
> This same publication customarily listed such news items as: "July 14, 1781: Saturday last, arrived at Martha Brae, the brig *Pearl*, Captain Phillips, from New York in 24 days. June 30: arrived Martha Brae from Barbados, the brig *Swift*, Captain Bryson."

In addition to these ships, which Fremmer tells us were exporting sugar from Martha Brae to the metropolis and bringing supplies to the colonial town, the TSTD (Eltis et al. 1999), drawing especially on information provided by David Richardson (1996), identifies eight transatlantic slaving vessels arriving at Martha Brae as the first and principal port of disembarkation in the Americas for approximately forty years—from 1754 (a few years before the consolidation of the town in 1762) to 1793.

According to the TSTD data, the earliest of these eight vessels disembarking African slaves at Martha Brae was the sloop *Swallow* (captain, Thomas Gamon; seven crew members), constructed and registered in Liverpool in 1753. The *Swallow* sailed from that metropolitan port on 7 April 1753 intending to purchase 170 slaves for the six owners of the venture (John Welch, Nicholas Southworth, John Cheshire, Edward and Roger Parr, and John Gorell). The following year it embarked on the transatlantic Middle Passage carrying 130 enslaved persons bought at the West African port of Gambia in Senegambia, such trading having started on 31 March 1754. *Swallow* unloaded 113 surviving slaves at Martha Brae later that year, returning to Liverpool on 10 September after a "successful voyage" in which the captor "delivered slaves for original owners." Likewise, the brig *Maria* (captain, William Amos; eighteen crew members), built in Britain and registered in London, left that port on 25 April 1773, bought slaves in Gambia, and later set out on the Middle Passage with 189 slaves, disembarking with 165 slaves at Martha Brae in the same year. The brig completed a successful voyage for the captor, delivering slaves for the original owners. In between these transactions in 1754 and 1773 (two years after the new parish of Trelawny was created), and even after the subdivision of St. James, it is likely that slaves were supplied to Martha Brae from Montego Bay (as in the case of John Tharp discussed later in this chapter), the main slaving port in St. James Parish.

Following the *Maria* in 1773, six more slaving vessels arrived at Martha Brae while the town was the capital of Trelawny (TSTD, Eltis et al. 1999): the *Daniel* in 1789 and 1792, the *Crescent* and the *Wasp* in 1790, the *Royal Charlotte* in 1791, and the *Jupiter* in 1793. The brig *Daniel* (captain, Richard Martin; thirteen crew members who increased to sixteen by the end of the voyage; owner of venture, James Rogers), constructed in Bristol, England, in 1783 and registered there in 1788, departed from that port on 31 July 1788 and purchased slaves from Calabar on the Bight of Biafra, intending to disembark at St. Vincent. However, of the 121 enslaved Africans who began the Middle Passage, the 117 survivors (4 died en route) were unloaded at Martha Brae on 1 March 1789 and the ship returned to Bristol in June, the voyage from origin to disembarkation having taken 215 days. On 2 November 1791 the *Daniel* (captains, Henry Laroche and John Langdon; owners of venture, James Rogers with Sir James Laroche and Richard Fydell) sailed again to Calabar, this time from Grenada. The brig now carried two guns and initially had a crew of 18, which increased to 21 in West Africa with a subsequent reduction to 14 (5 died before the Atlantic crossing and 2 apparently disembarked in the New World). The captor purchased slaves starting on 17 January 1792, left Calabar on 18 March, and unloaded slaves in Martha Brae on 27 May. When the ship left West Africa there were 211 slaves on board (129 males and 82 females), but at disembarkation only 171 remained (98 men, 55 women, 12 boys, and 6 girls who were delivered for the owners), there having been 40 deaths on the Middle Passage which lasted sixty-nine days. The ship returned to Bristol on 2 September 1792, the "successful voyage" having taken 210 days from origin to disembarkation.

In 1790 the *Crescent* and the *Wasp* both unloaded enslaved Africans at Martha Brae. The ship *Crescent* (captain, William Roper; owners of venture, James Rogers, Sir James Laroche, Richard Fydell [who would all own the *Daniel* venture of 1791–92 and the *Jupiter* venture of 1792–93], and Thomas Walker), had 26 crew members, later decreased to 23 and then to 12 (11 apparently remaining in the New World), carried two guns, and was constructed in Liverpool in 1787. It sailed from Bristol on 4 October 1789, purchasing slaves primarily in Sierra Leone (from Rio Nuñez to Cape Mesurado) but also en route from the Bananas Islands and Los Islands. The *Crescent* sailed from Africa in 1790 with 270 slaves (3 less than intended) at the outset of the Middle Passage and disembarked 263 of them at Martha Brae on 15 July, there having been 7 deaths en route. It is unknown whether there was a slave revolt on board, but the record states that "European vessel's boats cut off from the African coast." The *Crescent* returned to Bristol on 12 October 1790, having "delivered slaves for original owners"; the voyage from origin to disembarkation lasted 286 days. The ship *Wasp* (captain, William Hutcheson; owner of venture, Thomas Jones) had 25 men in its crew, later reduced to 19 and then to 12 (7 apparently remaining in the Americas), carried four guns, and was built in the United States in 1776. It departed from Bristol on 6 March 1790 and purchased slaves at New Calabar on the Bight of Biafra. The *Wasp* left Africa with 282 slaves on board and unloaded 228 at Martha Brae on 29 August. The ship returned to Bristol on 20 November, with the "voyage completed as intended" (i.e., slaves delivered for the original owners); the journey from origin to disembarkation took 173 days.

The brig *Royal Charlotte* (captains, William Peale and James Souter; 34 crew members reduced to 30, then to 27 in the New World; four guns; owner of venture, James Jones) sailed from Bristol on 21 October 1790. It purchased slaves in Bonny, Bight of Biafra, and set out across the Atlantic with 386 enslaved Africans. Only 312 slaves survived the Middle Passage, disembarking at Martha Brae on 11 May 1791. The *Royal Charlotte* returned to Bristol on 19 July, the voyage from origin to disembarkation having taken 205 days and being "completed as intended" for the original owner of the slaves. The ship *Jupiter* (captain, John Goodrich; owners of venture, Rogers, Laroche, and Fydell [see above]) had 38 crew members at the outset; that number, which increased to 39 from Africa, reduced to 29 by arrival in Jamaica, then to 20 before returning to England. Carrying six guns, the *Jupiter* left Bristol on 24 October 1792, and started purchasing slaves at Bonny on 3 January 1793. It embarked on the transatlantic crossing with 400 enslaved Africans (211 males and 189 females, including 88 children — 175 men, 137 women, 36 boys, and 52 girls); 355 slaves disembarked at Martha Brae on 16 June 1793. Forty-five slaves died on the Middle Passage, including 18 women. Nevertheless, the voyage was regarded as successful for the captor with most slaves being delivered. The *Jupiter* returned to Bristol on 27 September, the length of voyage from origin to disembarkation having been 237 days. David Richardson reports that other slave vessels disembarked slaves at Martha Brae, such as the *Dragon* via Barbados, St. Vincent, and Montego Bay; the *Favourite* via St. Vincent; the *Rodney* via Grenada; and the *Sarah* via Barbados — all in 1791 (1996:164, 184, 195, 197).

The involvement of John Tharp of Good Hope (Trelawny's largest landowner and one of the wealthiest planters in Jamaica) in the life and slave trade of Martha Brae further underlines the town's role as the parochial capital. Tharp shipped his sugar to England from a wharf at Martha Brae (Tenison 1971:11). Research by Richard Hart (1994) on Good Hope Plantation (1744–1994) reveals that this wharf was established by Tharp himself, who in 1771 (the year in which Trelawny was created and Martha Brae became its capital) "bought, for £380 currency, 150 feet of land known as the Martha Brae Wharf"; in the same year he also acquired, for £5,000, 2,831 acres " 'near Martha Brae' " (47). In addition to exporting sugar, Tharp shipped rum, coffee, fustic, and other plantation products from Martha Brae (50).

From 1781, when he engaged in the African trade, Tharp resold slaves at a substantial profit to other planters in Jamaica. Hart (1994) has established that Tharp conducted some of his trading at Martha Brae — as, for example, in January–February and December 1784 — and that some slaves were transported to this area via Montego Bay:

> An item in the *Supplement to the Cornwall Chronicle*, published in Montego Bay on Saturday 24 January 1784, stated that on the previous Wednesday a ship had arrived in that port, with 450 Gold Coast slaves consigned to John Tharp and his partner. The advertisement for their sale read:
>
> "Martha Brae, Jan. 27 . . . For SALE . . . Wednesday the 4th of February on board the ship THARP Captain Fisher (From Anamaboe) 440 Choice, Young Fantee, Ashantee, and Akim NEGROES By Tharpe [*sic*] & Campbell."
>
> A similar advertisement appeared in the *Supplement to the Cornwall Chronicle* of 4 December 1784. The ship on this occasion was the Gascoyne and the sale aboard the ship on 13 December was of "425 fine Young Coromantee, Fantee, and Ashantee Slaves." In this venture there were three partners — Tharp, Campbell and Charles. (57–58)

Hart (1994) found evidence of further trading by Tharp in 1785 and again in 1802 for his "friends at Martha Brae":

> There is evidence that he [Tharp] was again trading in 1802. Caleb Fletcher, a Liverpool slave trader, wrote to him in February of that year to say that a letter that Tharp had written to the firm of R. Walker & Co., "respecting their sending . . . a Cargo of Slaves for Sale," had been referred to him. The surviving partners of that firm, wrote Fletcher, "wish to confine themselves . . . to the Jamaican Commission Trade" but "I will . . . send you a Cargo of Slaves from Bonny direct to your friends at Martha Brae provided you will get a House in England to accept the Bills." (58)

The TSTD (Eltis et al. 1999) provides complementary evidence that the slaving ship *Tharp* (captains, Cobb Taylor and Duncan Fisher; owner of venture, John Coughlan; departed London on 9 January 1785) purchased 450 Africans from the Gold Coast, Cape Coast Castle, Anomabu, Adja, and Agga, disembarking (after deaths on the Middle Passage, which lasted ninety-eight days) 388 slaves at Montego Bay on 10 February 1786. Richardson (1996:164) further shows that John Tharp sold around 80 slaves imported to Martha Brae in June 1791, brought by the *Dragon* via Barbados, St. Vincent, and Montego Bay, some from Anomabu and some purchased on the Gold Coast from the *Jupiter*.

The Eclipse of Martha Brae as
Parish Capital and Planter Town

Despite the initial prosperity of Martha Brae, dissatisfaction with its suitability as Trelawny's capital was made known almost from the start. It was felt that a parish with a seacoast (especially a parish whose plantations participated in the triangular trade between Europe, Africa, and the Americas) needed a seaport for its chief town, yet Martha Brae was over a mile inland and two and a half miles upriver. Furthermore, a bar of silt at the entrance to the river created difficulty for all but the shallowest vessels reaching Martha Brae directly, and barges plied between the town and its harbor at the river mouth. In addition, the town's site on a ridge constrained its expansion. A committee, under the chairmanship of Samuel Barrett of the Barrett planter family, was therefore appointed to consider an alternative site for Trelawny's capital. Rock, at the mouth of the river, was first suggested, as it already had five stone piers for unloading and loading cargo to and from the town of Martha Brae. Moreover, the gentle slope of Florence Hall Pen, behind the harbor, could be developed for residences. But Rock had shallow water.

The site finally selected for Trelawny's second capital was Palmetto Point Pen, one of the properties of Edward Barrett "the Builder" of Cinnamon Hill. This site, about a mile west of Rock, offered flat, level land, a good harbor, and — with the trade winds by day and land breeze at night — excellent health conditions. In fact, Barrett had already begun a subdivision there named Barrett Town. The justices and vestry of Trelawny purchased 170 acres at "Point" from Edward Barrett, who himself donated the land for the Trelawny Anglican Parish Church near the center of the proposed town. The site was surveyed and planned with amenities for a township, to be called "New Town." Thirty streets were laid out and the land was sold off in lots, mainly as residential sites for townhouses, to the parish plantocracy.

The exact date of the establishment of Falmouth, as the new town was soon to be named, is disputed — as is the origin of the name itself.[17] Fremmer (1967, 1968) gives 1771 and 1774 as significant dates in the town's development. Patrick Tenison (1979) also cites 1774, whereas Ogilvie (1954: 118), Philip Wright and Paul White (1969:206), and Clinton Black (1979) all give 1790. Robert Assheton Barrett (2000:35), a descendant of Hercie Barrett, states that "by 1771, ten ships set sail from Falmouth each year" and that "in the 1780s, development of the town of Falmouth began on Barrett land." It seems that the project may have been begun in 1771 (the date of the founding of Trelawny), when Edward Barrett started to plan his township (cf. Blain 1989:107), and that the ships were trading with the town of Martha Brae until around 1792. The year 1774 appears to be the date when Barrett provided the first deeds for the sale of lots, in which he called the town Barrett Town. At this time there was only one house there. Around 1781, when there were about eight or ten houses in Falmouth, two roads were cut to serve the township: one through the swamps to Martha Brae and the interior, the other a coast road from the mouth of the Martha Brae River, with bridges built and improved by the vestry in 1782 and 1790 (Ogilvie 1954:33).[18] By 1790 the town was sufficiently developed for the vestry to consider transferring the parochial capital there. By 1793 or 1794 Falmouth contained at least 150 houses (120; Blain 1989:107).

The new port's deeper harbor for transatlantic slaving vessels, as well as for ships exporting slave-grown sugar, was a major factor in the development of Falmouth and the eclipse of colonial Martha Brae. For example, Robert Barrett (2000) notes that Colonel George Barrett, who leased Oxford Estate in Trelawny from Edward Barrett for eight years (1789–97), and his partner Leonard Parkinson sold twenty-six shiploads of slaves from 1789 to 1792 (34–35, from *Proceedings of the House of Assembly*, app. IV and V, 1789–92). From the *Eliza*, for instance, 512 slaves sold at an average of forty-seven pounds, five shillings, and sixpence sterling (£47 5/6) on 24 February 1791 (Barrett 2000:35). Complementing this record, the TSTD (Eltis et al. 1999) shows that nine slaving vessels (ranging from 92 to 386 tons), including the *Eliza*, arrived at Falmouth, Jamaica — the principal port of disembarkation in the Americas — from 1792 to 1808. For eight of these nine vessels, Falmouth was also the first port of disembarkation in the New World (one vessel arrived via Barbados).

For these nine shiploads of enslaved Africans imported to Falmouth, the TSTD shows that the *Eliza*, a brig from Liverpool, purchased 484 slaves from Anomabu, Adja, Agga, and Cape Coast Castle (Gold Coast), embarked on the Middle Passage (which lasted forty-seven days) with 137 slaves, and disembarked 119 (61 men, 40 women, 11 boys, and 7 girls) at Falmouth on 30 April 1792. The brig returned directly to Africa. The *Recovery*, a ship from Bristol carrying 316 slaves purchased in Calabar on the Bight of Biafra, arrived in Falmouth on 3 November 1792 with 216 surviving slaves (80 men, 69 women, 27 boys, and 40 girls), sailing back to Bristol on 28 January 1793. The *Courier*, a brig from Liverpool that bought 366 slaves in Sierra Leone and set out on the Atlantic crossing with 277 slaves, 24 of whom (including 7 women) died on the Middle Passage, arrived with 257 slaves at Falmouth on 8 June 1793. These numbers suggest that there were 4 births

Market Street, Falmouth, ca. 1840, by Adolphe Duperly. National Library of Jamaica, Kingston.

on the transatlantic crossing. This vessel had been "captured before disembarking slaves," was subsequently "recaptured or released," and returned to Liverpool on 5 November. The *Sarah*, a ship from Liverpool that purchased 632 slaves from Bonny on the Bight of Biafra, disembarked 511 slaves at Falmouth on 26 February 1799 before also heading back to Liverpool. The *Rio Nova*, a ship from London that had embarked with 544 slaves from the Gold Coast, disembarked 471 slaves at Falmouth on 7 July 1799 and returned to London that year. (Robert Barrett [2000:35] states: "The [Barrett] deed book records that, on 18 November 1791, John Deffell sold Edward [Barrett] a ¹⁄₁₆ part of that 'good ship or Vessel called Rio Nova, Square Sterned River Built,' now lying in the River Thames.") The *Ariel*, a schooner constructed in Liverpool and departing from Kingston, Jamaica, set out on the Middle Passage with 162 slaves from the Gold Coast and disembarked 140 slaves at Falmouth on 23 January 1800. The *Rufus*, from Philadelphia, embarked with 159 slaves from Senegal (Senegambia) and arrived at Falmouth with 137 slaves in 1804. On the *Perseus*, a ship from Liverpool, 290 slaves embarked from the Congo in West-Central Africa. *Perseus* sailed into Falmouth with 265 slaves on 26 January 1808, the year of the abolition of the slave trade throughout the British Empire, and then returned to Liverpool. The *Hinde*, a ship from Liverpool with 265 slaves from the Windward Coast of West Africa, sailed via Barbados into Falmouth carrying 240 slaves on 11 February 1808 — again, the same year that the slave trade was abolished.

With the growth of Falmouth, John Tharp acquired extensive property there — three townhouses, a foundry, and his own wharf and wharf buildings — and began to ship his sugar from Falmouth instead of Martha Brae; at Falmouth he received at least one shipload of Ibo slaves.[19] Tharp Street in present-day Falmouth (which is still regarded as the best laid-out town in Jamaica) commemorates Tharp's role in the town's development. His foundry remains a prominent landmark in Falmouth.

In 1791 the vestry met in Martha Brae to consider plans for building the Anglican Parish Church of St. Peter the Apostle in Falmouth, on the site donated by Edward Barrett. This building, the first church in Trelawny, was started in 1794, completed in 1796, and marked its bicentenary in 1996. Meanwhile, in 1793 a Dr. Coke, who had formed the Methodist mission in Jamaica in 1789, visited Martha Brae with the idea of organizing a mission, though a Methodist mission did not appear until 1816 — and in Falmouth — after the establishment of a Baptist mission there by John Rowe (the first English Baptist missionary in Jamaica) in 1813.

In 1794 the plantocracy petitioned for the removal of the court from Martha Brae to Falmouth and for the enactment of Falmouth as a port of entry and clearance. In 1797 the vestry transferred its meetings from Martha Brae to Falmouth (Fremmer 1968), and in 1798 Scottish planters founded the exclusive Athol Union Masonic Lodge of the Scottish Constitution in Falmouth, possibly the first lodge established in Jamaica (Sibley and Ogilvie 1975a). In 1799 the Falmouth Water Company was formed to supply water to the town and to shipping in the harbor. The company acquired lands on the eastern edge of Martha Brae, bordering the river, where it constructed a diversion canal; built a dam, aqueduct, and sluice gate; and erected a twenty-foot Persian Wheel, which emptied water into a wooden trough that flowed through a six-inch main into a large reservoir in Falmouth's town square. By 1814 Falmouth had the first domestic water supply in the Americas. In 1800 a shed for a Sunday market — which was mainly in the hands of Trelawny's plantation slaves — was erected in Falmouth near the reservoir, completing the eclipse of Martha Brae as a market town as well as the parish capital. Before this, "people squatted anywhere along the streets [of Falmouth] to sell their food-stuffs, especially was it so at where we now call the Market Square" (Ogilvie 1954:43) — actually called Water Square (*Falmouth Post*, 14 December 1836).

In 1805, when Falmouth became a port of entry and clearance with a

Trelawny ex-slaves in Falmouth's Water Square ("Market Square"), ca. 1840, by Adolphe Duperly. National Library of Jamaica, Kingston.

customhouse, the town became firmly established as Trelawny's new capital. The vestry sold the Martha Brae Courthouse, and the court now met in Falmouth. In 1809, Falmouth became a free port and the vestry began in earnest to plan the building of a new courthouse there. The structure was completed in 1815 on a site purchased from Edward Barrett-Moulton Barrett, the absentee proprietor who lived in London's Wimpole Street.

For about its first fifty years Falmouth enjoyed increasing prosperity as it became firmly entrenched as the new capital of Jamaica's leading sugar-producing parish, even into the postemancipation era. Georgian buildings were erected from stone and brick that had served as ballast for the English sailing ships. Many homes had two stories so that residents could live on the second floor and open shops for the sale of imported goods below,[20] and Jewish merchants flocked to Falmouth. The Falmouth Courthouse and Town Hall were now the center of social life for the parish plantocracy, which entertained British governors and royalty and held large formal balls with Scottish dancing. At such times, the planters stayed in their townhouses, the most famous of which was the Barrett townhouse at Number One Market Street; completed in 1799, it endured until the 1990s. The year 1835 saw the founding of the town's historic newspaper, the *Falmouth Post and Jamaica Advertiser*. Owned and edited by John Castello from 1835 to

The Persian Wheel at Martha Brae, erected in 1799, which provided the first domestic water supply (to Falmouth) in the Americas in 1814. Photo by Jean Besson.

1876 (Jacobs 1970:15), it covered parochial, island, European, and Atlantic news (such as the case of the Spanish slaving schooner *Amistad* reported on 8 January 1840) for several decades after the abolition of slavery.

With Falmouth's burgeoning prosperity in the early nineteenth century, Martha Brae was eclipsed as a slaving port and colonial town. At this point, the settlement's Europe-centered history concludes with observations on

An Afro-creole cottage and a Euro-Caribbean ruin, reflecting Martha Brae's two histories. Photo by Jean Besson.

its decline into a ghost town. Fremmer's (1968) account exemplifies this perspective:

> The founding of Falmouth in 1771 by Edward Barrett cancelled any future Martha Brae may have had at that time. Although thirty houses had already been built there, few more were constructed, due to the preference for Falmouth. In fact, many people who had built in Martha Brae sold out and bought in Falmouth, as the records show. Out of respect for Custos Cuniffe's wish that his new town, Martha Brae, be the new Parish's capital a court-house was built there in 1800, but it was a futile gesture. Only five years later the court-house at Martha Brae was sold and Court was held in Falmouth. The Vestry had already transferred its meetings to Falmouth in 1797, and the older town fell into a state of progressive decline.

Fremmer (1968) summed up contemporary Martha Brae in a single paragraph:

> Today, a hundred and ninety-seven years after the historian Long [1774] wrote that there were then about thirty houses in Martha Brae, there are 95, but only one is two-storey, as all were in 1771 and the majority of them

are only one or two roomed frame dwellings set on piers. The town has changed, and the people have changed. The English occupants of the original thirty houses have long since died and been forgotten; not an Englishman is left in town. Even the names of the streets were forgotten in the social upheaval of two hundred years, and only a few months ago all the streets were given new names.

Other sources were even briefer. They provided no hint of Martha Brae's postemancipation history and dismissed the present-day settlement as "a mere scatter of houses" (Wright and White 1969:46; Black 1979; cf. Sherlock 1984:119).

In 2001, while Falmouth's architecture was the focus of the Georgian Society of Jamaica and its Friends in London in the context of Jamaican heritage tourism, Martha Brae showed little architectural evidence of its colonial history. Other than the urban grid of streets, there was only one Georgian ruin, another Georgian-style house built by an emancipated slave, two old tombstones (one with a late-eighteenth-century inscription) in house yards, and the Persian Wheel, though some fifty years ago other Georgian ruins could be discerned. Yet Martha Brae has become a vibrant Afro-creole peasant village. More than eight hundred persons live in about 170 households,[21] established and consolidated by ex-slaves and their descendants on the site of the former slave-trading planter town. The rest of this book uncovers that hidden history, with its central theme of culture-building, through a methodology combining anthropological fieldwork, historical research, and the villagers' rich oral tradition. Chapter 3 begins the task by locating the origins of this "new" Afro-creole history in Caribbean slave opposition and resistance and postslavery peasantization—including the flight from the British West Indian estates, the context in which the colonial town of Martha Brae was appropriated and transformed.

CHAPTER THREE

The Origins of Martha Brae's
Afro-Caribbean History

Martha Brae was transformed from a Euro-Caribbean planter town into an Afro-Caribbean peasant village in the contexts of the exodus of emancipated slaves from the British West Indian plantations and the free-village movement in Jamaica and Trelawny. A full understanding of the appropriation of colonial Martha Brae by former slaves and their descendants must therefore start with a consideration of the classic flight-from-the-estates debate: did the British West Indian ex-slaves wish to leave the plantations, or would they have preferred to remain there but were prevented from doing so by planter policy and legislation?

The Flight-from-the-Estates Debate

A useful starting point for this debate is the "reconsideration" by Douglas Hall (1978:8), who summarized the extant views:

The prevailing impressions conveyed in the general body of literature on the history of the [British West Indian] post-emancipation period are: that the majority of ex-slaves wished to remove themselves from the estates on which they had suffered so much in the days of bondage; that the ex-slaves were, apparently with some reluctance, forced to leave the estates because of the harsh attitudes and demands of their masters, the ex-slave owners; and, in either case, that their movements clearly depended on the availability of somewhere else to go.

These impressions, as Hall showed, derived respectively from the opposing views of Rawle Farley (1964) on British Guiana and Hugh Paget (1964) on Jamaica.

Hall's reconsideration, based on an examination of evidence given before the Select Committee of the House of Commons on the West India Colonies

81

in 1842, developed his earlier view, following Paget, of the Jamaican case (D. Hall 1959). Hall argued that the ex-slaves who left the British West Indian plantations were not rejecting the horrors of the slavery system but the inequities of early freedom, reflected in planter policies restricting the use of estate houses, gardens, and provision grounds in order to retain the ex-slaves as a dependent labor force. This involved either imposing high rents on houses and provision grounds or rendering continued occupation conditional on daily work for the plantations (D. Hall 1978:17). Hall further concluded that while there was hatred of the plantation, there was love of home on the estate (23–24). The crucial factor in the flight from the plantations was therefore planter policy regarding land and labor among the former slaves.

The debate surfaced again in two complementary publications by Sidney Mintz and Woodville Marshall in 1979. In "Slavery and the Rise of Peasantries," Mintz (1979) elaborated his earlier thesis that Caribbean peasantries represented a mode of resistant response to the plantation system (1989 [1974]:132–33), exploring the rise of the postslavery peasantries against the backdrop of postemancipation planter power and the link with the protopeasant past. Marshall's commentary conceded that reconstituted peasantries in the Caribbean region represented a resistant response to the plantation system. However, citing Hall (1978) and focusing on the anglophone Caribbean, Marshall argued that Mintz underplayed the significance of labor recruitment policy, the ex-slaves' response to planter policy, and the role of the provision grounds in the flight from the estates. If these were stressed, Marshall contended, rather than the ex-slaves' desire for independence from the plantations, "the patterns of development [of the postslavery peasantries] would emerge more clearly" and the resistant response would be seen in more complex terms (1979:245).

Marshall posited that the ex-slaves expected to have continued access to the plantation yards and provision grounds and perhaps intended to increase provision ground cultivation to the detriment of labor on the estate. This conflicted with planters' interest in retaining a cheap full-time labor force, which led to the introduction of a labor recruitment policy based on "long contracts, low wages and conditional occupancy of houses and provision grounds" to keep the ex-slaves tied to the estates (1979:246). The conditional occupancy of provision grounds, dependent on supplying cheap regular plantation labor and sanctioned by eviction, was the key element in this policy. Nevertheless, though the policy succeeded in the short term, it backfired as a long-term strategy; the ex-slaves responded by challenging wage rates, by going on strike, by sometimes violently resisting, and, eventually, by leaving the estates. Marshall also argued that "where planters sold surplus estate land or rented land to ex-slaves there was no significant desertion" of labor from the plantations (248). Like Hall (1978), Marshall focused on the conflict of interests between planter policy and the expectations of the former slaves, and the peaceful coexistence of plantation and peasantry where this conflict did not occur. In a study of an estate-based peasantry in Dominica, Russel Chace Jr. (1984) also argued Hall and Marshall's case.[1]

Marshall, Hall, and Chace contributed valuable perspectives in stressing the role of planter policy regarding land and labor in triggering and shaping the exodus from the plantations and in highlighting the role of the provision grounds. Yet to focus too closely on these factors, and on the postemancipation era, underplays the significance of the long, complex history of opposition and resistance in the ex-slaves' flight from the estates. Such a view underestimates the agency of the enslaved in favor of the planters' hegemony. Moreover, Marshall's evidence shows that the ex-slaves' attachment to estate provision grounds was rooted in the belief that these lands were in fact their own — or in the actual purchase or rental of these lands (1979:246, 248).

Nor would a sharper focus on postemancipation planter policy and the role of provision grounds have sharpened Mintz's overview of postslavery peasant development. Instead, the contours of postslavery peasantization would have emerged more clearly if Mintz had drawn more fully on his earlier analysis regarding the contrasting plantation-peasant interplay in the Hispanic and non-Hispanic Caribbean variants (1959, 1971a:29, 1989: 146–56). Although the declining plantation system in the nineteenth-century–non-Hispanic territories enabled the transformation of protopeasants into postemancipation peasants, the simultaneous escalation of the Hispanic Caribbean plantations destroyed the squatter peasantries.[2] Soon after emancipation occurred in Puerto Rico (1876) and Cuba (1886), the establishment of modern plantation *centrals* by the burgeoning imperial power of the United States, following the Spanish-American War when the United States seized these colonies from Spain in 1898, resulted in the consolidation of the postemancipation Hispanic-American plantation system. This consolidation severely constrained the emergence of postslavery peasants in the Hispanic variant.[3] The non-Hispanic territories, therefore, provided the main arena for the growth of Caribbean postemancipation peasantries and for the consolidation of land rights, kinship, and community as bases of economic, social, and cultural autonomy among the former slaves and their descendants.

Drawing on these background themes of slave opposition and resistance, and the differential plantation-peasant interplay in the Hispanic and non-Hispanic colonies, I reassert and develop Farley's view on British Guianese free communities and its wider relevance to the British West Indies (and to other non-Hispanic areas of the Caribbean region) to illuminate the transformation of Martha Brae. Farley (1964:52) argued:

> The establishment of the village settlements of British Guiana forms one of the most remarkable phases of the whole of Caribbean economic development. It has been customary to regard the rise of these freeholds in British Guiana as peculiarly related to the history of that part of the Caribbean. This is, however, wholly to misunderstand the total history of British Caribbean historical change. The economic history of British Guiana is not a separate aspect of Caribbean history: it is part and parcel of the same history. British Guiana is no more than the under-developed southern economic frontier of the British Caribbean. . . .
>
> So far, the rise of the village settlements is usually recorded as a post-emancipation phenomenon. Considered as such, the exciting story of the settlements becomes a mere record entirely drained of its real historical colour. The roots of the village settlements are to be found in the days of slavery. The forces which were fundamental to the establishment of these settlements were, *for the most part*, the same economic and social forces which led to the end of slavery as such on August 1st, 1838.
>
> The most decisive and continuous of these forces was the desire, on the part of the slaves, for personal liberty and for *land of their own*. (Emphases mine)

I show that British West Indian (and other non-Hispanic Caribbean) post-slavery peasant formations are indeed a creative response to the plantation system, rooted in slave opposition and resistance including the protopeasant adaptation and marronage. I further argue that planter policy and state legislation constrained as well as triggered the flight from the estates, and that estate-based peasantries therefore reflected both opportunity and constraint. In addition, I extend Farley's perspective on the ex-slaves' desire for autonomy and "land of their own" by showing that such land acquisition included customary as well as legal tenures. These customary tenures consolidated systems of land use and transmission, based on kinship and community, that originated in protopeasant institution-building and included unrestricted cognatic or nonunilineal landholding kin groups (traced through both genders and including absent and resident descendants), which maximized land rights and family lines and enabled migrants to return. Evidence for this thesis comes from both sides of the flight-from-the-estates debate and from throughout and beyond the British West Indies (Besson 1992a, 1995d), for the complex processes generating and inhibiting the exodus recurred sequentially in the British, French, Danish, and Dutch West Indies and were predated in revolutionary French Saint Domingue/Haiti. Hall's argument, however, neither fully recognized the agency of the enslaved nor moved beyond the British West Indian case.

Land, Kinship, and Community: Caribbean Slave Opposition and Resistance

From the inception of the plantation system in the British West Indies, as elsewhere in the Caribbean region, enslaved Africans and Creoles sought to establish autonomy and community,[4] often based on customary as well as legal rights to land that correlated with the Afro-creole kinship systems created by plantation and rebel slaves. This quest for autonomy and the reconstruction of identity was manifested in various forms of slave opposition and resistance: protopeasant adaptations, rebellion, revolution, and marronage. Long, continuous histories of slave rebellion typified the Caribbean region, Brazil, and, to a lesser extent, the southern United States. Slave rebellion particularly characterized the non-Hispanic Caribbean, where the early development of large-scale plantation slavery was most pronounced. This was especially true in the British West Indian colonies, which were the vanguard of European colonial agrarian capitalism, and "the greatest slave revolts in the Western hemisphere, except for the world-shaking revolution in Saint-Domingue, took place in Guiana and Jamaica" (Genovese 1981:33).

Marronage — escaping slavery and founding autonomous communities — also typified New World slavery and was widespread throughout African America. As Richard Price (1996:1) notes, "For more than four centuries, the communities formed by such runaways dotted the fringes of plantation America, from Brazil to the southeastern United States, from Peru to the American southwest." Maroon societies lived under constant threat of war from plantation-military regimes and were thus established in almost inaccessible areas such as mountains, forests, and ravines, where the topography facilitated guerrilla warfare and the establishment of customary rights to land. In other cases, maroons hid in towns or escaped by sea.

Some maroon communities were wiped out in war; others won freedom and legal rights to land through treaties with colonial governments forced to sue for peace. Such treaties were forged in Brazil, Colombia, Cuba, Ecuador, Hispaniola, Jamaica, Mexico, and Suriname. The Jamaican Leeward and Windward Maroon treaties of March and June 1739 with the British provided a model for the treaties of the 1760s between the Dutch and Surinamese Maroons, and the most distinct and longest lasting maroon communities were in these non-Hispanic Caribbean territories of Jamaica and Suriname. Here (and elsewhere), although customary land rights were transformed to legal freehold by the treaties, customary land-tenure principles have continued to evolve. For example, in Accompong Town in St. Elizabeth, the oldest corporate maroon society in the Americas and the only surviving community of the Jamaican Leeward Maroon polity (where from 1979 to 2001 I undertook fieldwork some miles inland from Martha Brae), legal freehold treaty land has been transformed into sacred space by oral traditions, burial sites, and rituals. This sacred landscape is reinforced by overlapping, unrestricted cognatic descent lines with usufructuary rights to house yards, provision grounds, and emergent family cemeteries within the wider framework of the commons with their African and Afro-creole community burial grounds (Besson 1997). This land tenure has parallels with that of the Jamaican Windward Maroons, as well as similarities and differences with the customary matrilineal landholding systems of the maroons of French Guiana and Suriname.

The widespread protopeasant adaptation was a more subtle mode of slave response, based on customary rights to land. Here a peasant lifestyle was established by slaves within the constraints of the plantation system (Mintz 1979, 1989; and chapter 1). Protopeasantries especially typified the non-Hispanic colonies (particularly the British West Indies and French Saint Domingue), from the eighteenth century. As the plantation system intensified, planters faced the problem of feeding their slaves, especially with increasing warfare among colonial powers in the region and the rising cost of importing food. Therefore, wherever topography allowed, planters allocated land unsuited to sugar monoculture as provision grounds for the slaves to grow subsistence crops, in addition to the yards for kitchen gardens in the plantation villages. The slaves, however, developed the provision ground system well beyond what the planters intended, producing surpluses for sale in public marketplaces.

Such protopeasant adaptation was most striking in Jamaica (which was the first Caribbean colony to introduce the system), with its hilly plantation backlands and separate estate mountains and flourishing Sunday markets.

In 1774, the meridian of Jamaican slavery, protopeasant slaves controlled 20 percent of the island's currency (mostly in small coinage) from their marketing activities and were the island's main suppliers of food and crafts. This protopeasant adaptation was highly developed in the parish of Tre-lawny, where the slave plantation villages reflected the general pattern of house yards throughout the island (Armstrong 1990; Higman 1998), and the provision ground system — for example, on estate mountains — was espe-cially pronounced (Higman 1988:265–66). From the later eighteenth cen-tury, such cultivation fed into the thriving protopeasant market in Falmouth (Wright 1973:56; Simmonds 1987:34) and, before that, almost certainly into a slave marketplace in the planter town of Martha Brae.

Protopeasantries also emerged in other British West Indian colonies with mountainous or marginal land such as the Windward Islands (Dominica, St. Lucia, St. Vincent, Grenada, and Tobago), British Guiana, the Bahamas, and Barbuda. There were also petty protopeasants (slaves who cultivated tiny kitchen gardens and did some huckstering) in Barbados and some of the Leewards. A highly developed protopeasant adaptation was established in French Saint Domingue, neighboring Jamaica, and elsewhere in the French West Indies, especially mountainous Martinique. There were also protopeasant adaptations in Dutch Guiana and St. Eustatius, and in Danish St. John (Besson 1995d).

The existence of these protopeasantries throughout the non-Hispanic Caribbean was a tremendous paradox within the slavery system, challenging the notion of slaves as property and making visible the humanity and cre-ativity of the enslaved. Moreover, the skills and capital acquired through these activities provided a basis for the subsequent development of post-emancipation peasantries, such as those of Martha Brae. Evidence of the significance of the protopeasant adaptation as a mode of opposition to slavery comes from both sides of the flight-from-the-estates debate. Mintz interpreted the protopeasantry as a form of slave *"resistance"* based on *"prior adaptation"* (1989:76, 131–56; cf. Farley 1964). Similarly, Douglas Hall (1978:24) referred to the "self-asserted independence" of the slave "in the privacy of his house and garden and the circle of his family," and to "reports of the slaves' attachment to their dwelling-places and to the burial plots of their relatives and their sense of belonging to the 'negro-house' community of the estate" (cf. Paget 1964:40; Turner 1982:55). Thus cus-tomary rights to yard and ground, and the interrelationship of kinship and land, became important bases for the reconstruction of identity and com-munity among slaves.

British West Indian Jamaica, where the protopeasant adaptation was most pronounced, provides clear evidence of such customary rights to land as a basis of slave autonomy and community, and as a reflection of an ancestor-oriented cognatic descent system (traced from slaves of either gender, through both male and females), articulating with customary land rights to plantation provision grounds and slave village yards with family burial grounds (chapter 1). Evidence from other Caribbean territories (e.g., the British Windward and Leeward Islands, the French West Indies, Dutch Guiana, and Danish St. John) supports the conclusion that female as well as male protopeasant slaves appropriated plantation land and that customary cognatic systems of descent and land transmission were being created by them and were perpetuated by their descendants in the flight from the estates (Besson 1992a, 1995d).

In the British West Indies, unusually isolated protopeasant adaptations, bordering on marronage, emerged in the Bahamas and Barbuda at the margins of plantation slave society. These cases provide a notable illustration of the interrelationship of kinship, community, and customary rights to land and their role in Caribbean slave opposition and resistance. Here, well-developed customary tenures, based on actual or fictive kinship and squattage/commonage, provided the foundations of virtually autonomous protopeasant communities. These customary tenures were also the basis of the slaves' opposition to formal work and to their owners' attempts to move them to more profitable plantation colonies in the region.

From these wider perspectives, estate-based peasantries and the flight from the estates can be seen as transformations of two related modes of slave opposition and resistance, namely, protopeasantry and marronage, both based on customary land rights. Protopeasants evolved into estate-based peasantries when ex-slaves were able to retain rights to yards and grounds, or when a colony's size or topography, planter policies, or state legislation regarding land and labor constrained movement off the estates. Free communities were established beyond plantation boundaries when planter policies, state legislation, availability of land, and peasant capital combined with the traditions of slave opposition and resistance to trigger a flight from the estates paralleling earlier marronage. In many colonies, including Jamaica, both variants of postslavery peasantry coexisted (as well as persisting maroon communities) as did protopeasant and maroon adaptations in the slavery past.

Kevin Smith has emphasized the importance of this link between the postslavery exodus and pre-emancipation slave opposition and resistance, especially marronage. Referring to the essay where I first advanced this view (Besson 1992a), he states:

> Besson's apt recognition of the close connection between pre-emancipation marronage and the post-emancipation "flight from the estates" acknowledged the increased choices that legal emancipation offered to the former slaves as it underscored the continuity in the pre- and post-emancipation struggle between planters and workers to determine the terms of estate labour and the nature of Caribbean society. Besson's interpretation . . . linking the pre- and post-emancipation struggle between workers and owners and placing it at the centre of the post-emancipation story, provides a strong foundation for scholars seeking to examine the outcome of that struggle as it unfolded in continued competition for control of the labour process in the British Caribbean throughout the nineteenth century (K. D. Smith 1995:113).

In addition, Smith observes:

> By the early 1990s, then, historians had made important strides in improving our understanding of the conflict between competing segments within Caribbean society. Besson's recognition that the freedmen's response to the post-emancipation attempts of planters to create a docile and reliable work-force in the form of a landless peasantry was linked to marronage, a form of pre-emancipation slave resistance, underscored both the depth of the post-emancipation conflict between planters and former slaves and the multi-faceted roots of that conflict in the period of slavery. (121–22)

Also drawing on my work, Sheller (1998:115 [n. 16]) has reinforced "the importance of access to land" for the freed slaves in Jamaica, highlighting the significance, in this context, of the Baptist free villages in Trelawny (98), whereas, in relation to my argument, Kevin Smith further underlines the relevance of customary land rights in the continuity between the slavery period and family land in Caribbean postslavery peasant communities (1995:113, 129 [n. 28]).[5]

With this resolution of the flight-from-the-estates debate in the British West Indies, we can look more clearly at the contours of postslavery peasantization throughout the non-Hispanic Caribbean including the small-scale tenures by which the ex-slaves and their descendants acquired or retained land of their own — particularly through customary landholding systems based on community and kinship, especially those rooted in unrestricted cognatic descent systems that maximized scarce land rights. These regional contours, in turn, reinforce my interpretation of the exodus of former slaves from the British West Indian plantations in terms of slave opposition and resistance as well as postslavery opportunities and constraints. This regional perspective also situates the transformation of Martha Brae in a Caribbean context.

Caribbean Postslavery Peasantization

Haiti and Jamaica

French Saint Domingue and British Jamaica were the two most profitable Caribbean slave plantation colonies in the later eighteenth century, and both had pronounced traditions of rebellion and marronage. Protopeasant adaptations were also the most highly developed in these two territories. These adaptations evolved into postslavery peasantries with customary land tenures in Haiti after the revolution of 1791–1804 and in Jamaica after emancipation in 1838, and were complemented in Jamaica by persisting maroon societies. The case of revolutionary Saint Domingue/postrevolutionary Haiti highlights the significance of slave opposition and resistance in Caribbean postslavery peasantization and raises the questions of the provenance and nature of Caribbean landholding kin groups.

In Saint Domingue, slaves cultivated provision grounds on the mountainous backlands of plantations and provided food for the entire colony through public marketplaces. Saint Domingue also had notable traditions of slave rebellion and marronage. These themes fueled the great slave revolution in 1791 and established independent Haiti in 1804. Protopeasant cultivation and food marketing "continued to flourish during the Revolution itself, and to expand thereafter" in postrevolutionary peasant communities (Mintz 1979:227). After the revolution ex-slaves acquired property through squatting and government land partition and sale. Mintz observed that "had the plantations been restored in Haiti, they could have produced wealth. But those who would have done the work *could not be driven back onto the plantations*" (80, emphasis mine).[6]

Mintz highlighted the economic and symbolic importance of land and the customary system of land use, tenure, and transmission that evolved among the postrevolutionary Haitian peasantry. He noted the question of possible African cultural provenance of the *lakou* or landholding kin group but concluded that more work was needed to resolve this issue (1989:242). Elsewhere he referred to "the adoption of the French tradition of equal inheritance" by Haitian peasants (274). Mintz and Price (1992:75) suggested that the lakou is patrilineal but indicated the need for further research on the nature of Caribbean landholding kin groups, especially in Haiti and Jamaica. Nevertheless, Mintz (1995:80) subsequently reasserted the "patrilineal, patrilocal" structure of the lakou. Serge Larose (1975), however, showed that the lakou is based on unrestricted cognatic descent — a *Caribbean* theme (Besson 1979, 1987b; and chapter 8).

After postrevolutionary Haiti, Jamaica manifested the most conspicuous postslavery peasantization in the Caribbean region. As in Haiti, the exodus of former slaves from Jamaican plantations after emancipation in 1838 originated in strong traditions of slave opposition and resistance, including protopeasant adaptation, rebellion, and marronage, but it was triggered by state/planter legislation that obstructed the ex-slaves' customary rights to land on the estates. Jamaica had experienced the most "continuous and intense servile revolts" (Patterson 1973:273) in the Caribbean, and the great slave rebellion of 1831–32 in the western parishes of the island catalyzed the abolition of slavery throughout the British colonies. Marronage had also been pronounced, the Leeward Maroon treaty (signed near Martha Brae in March 1739) had "marked the first act of collective emancipation for formerly enslaved blacks in the Caribbean" (B. C. Richardson 1992:164), and the Jamaican Maroon polities persisted after emancipation. In addition, through the highly developed protopeasant adaptation, emancipated slaves possessed cultivation and marketing skills to establish free communities and generate capital to acquire land.

The potential availability of land for a Jamaican postslavery peasantry was, however, severely constrained by planter policies and practices, and by legislation of the planter-based Jamaica Assembly to keep the ex-slaves tied to the plantations. The initial strategy was to provide a period of apprenticeship, as elsewhere in the British West Indies (except for Antigua, where freed slaves had little option but to remain on or near the estates). The apprenticeship system, which was intended to last until 1840, had the overt aim of "preparing" the former slaves for freedom (Holt 1992:56). But with their strong tradition of slave opposition and resistance, the Jamaican slaves had long been carving out their own autonomy and were ripe for a departure from the plantations. Apprenticeship was essentially designed to contain this expected exodus and to ensure sufficient labor for the estates.[7]

After the early end of apprenticeship in 1838,[8] the planters anticipated a labor problem resulting from both the withdrawal of women, young children, and old people from estate labor and the withdrawal of labor due to the continued cultivation of, and sale of produce from, the provision grounds on the backlands and mountains of the estates.[9] In the parish of Trelawny, this apprehension had been manifested during the period of apprenticeship by the development of plans to import white settlers to counteract settlement in the mountains by ex-slaves (Holt 1992:75). This policy, paralleled elsewhere in the island, did not mature, though recently arrived German immigrants and subsequent indentured Asian and African labor were variations on this theme.

In the aftermath of full freedom, attempts to counteract the expected withdrawal of labor included the Ejectment and Trespass Acts passed by the Jamaica Assembly. These acts, which imposed high rents on estate houses and provision grounds sanctioned by ejection and imprisonment, were designed to create dependency on the low wages paid by the estates. The legislation was reinforced by a virtual veto on selling land to former slaves. Ejection was sometimes followed up by the sale of estate mountain lands (but not to ex-slaves) as a further strategy to create a landless proletariat.[10] This obstructive planter policy was striking in the parish of Trelawny, which had been the heart of the Jamaican slave plantation system and where the estate economy remained strong after emancipation. The strategy of creating a landless proletariat tied to the plantations was made explicit in Trelawny, where this policy "was stated baldly enough by a meeting of the freeholders, proprietors, and managers of the properties in the parish of Trelawny held in February, 1839: 'It is the opinion of this Committee that the people never will be brought to a state of continuous labour while they are allowed to possess the large tracts of land now cultivated by them for provisions, which renders them perfectly independent of their employers' " (Paget 1964:42).

Planter policy to some extent backfired, however, triggering as well as constraining a flight from the estates, because, to establish some bargaining power regarding wages, ex-slaves began buying land for house-spots wherever possible. This outcome was apparent in Trelawny, as Edmund Lyon reported from the parish in July 1839, one year after emancipation:

Many proprietors have advertised for sale their mountain lands heretofore cultivated as provision grounds by their labourers, from an assumption that their produce, by rendering the people independent of estates' labour for sustenance, has a tendency to prevent that regularity of labour they deem necessary for sugar culture; this in conjunction with the irritation produced on some properties by the indiscriminate service of notices to quit, has reduced a very large proportion of the best class of agricultural labourers in this parish to become purchasers of land, thus producing an effect the very reverse of that contemplated by their masters, in rendering them more independent of daily hire than before. (Quoted in Paget 1964:42)

This outcome had not been anticipated by the planters, who failed to take adequate account of either the tradition of slave opposition and resistance or the continuing alliance between the Nonconformist missionaries and the former slaves. Although the policies and practices of most planters continued to obstruct peasant development, the Nonconformist missionaries acted as covert intermediaries on the land market between planters and ex-slaves, establishing church-founded village communities. In addition, "from the impetus provided by church sponsorship, other free villages grew without the deliberate patronage of the missionary churches" (Mintz 1989: 161). As well as these nucleated villages, dispersed settlements were established by ex-slaves who managed to acquire land through purchase, rental, or squatting, for some planters did sell land to former slaves, sometimes hoping to win an advantage in the labor market; other planters even made grants of land to their ex-slaves. While land scarcity was exacerbated by the absence of Crown lands for sale, there was also some squatting on Crown lands. In addition, some mountainous backlands forfeited to the Crown by colonists through failure to pay quitrents could be purchased or rented, though such forfeiture was discontinued after 1838.

Meanwhile, after emancipation some estate-based peasantries remained through choice; others stayed because planter policies and practices and state legislation, including the machinations of the Crown Colony government after the Morant Bay Rebellion of 1865 (Satchell 1990, 1992, 1999), inhibited as well as triggered the flight from the estates. Don Robotham (1977) highlighted these continuing constraints on estate-based peasants in Jamaica up until the labor protests of 1938, a century after emancipation:

Since after emancipation only a small minority of the people settled in free villages and these continued to work on the plantations, what was the fate of the mass of the people? ...

After emancipation the mass of the people in Jamaica were converted from the state of slavery neither to become an independent peasantry nor to become a proletariat; instead they became dependent *tenants* renting house and grounds from the planters at a rate of two days' labour per week payable in cash or labour and subject to eviction by the planters at one week's notice.

... In general what was never altered until after 1938 was the tenure of the people — many remained tenants at will, subject to eviction with a week's notice and firmly *bound to work on the estates on which they lived* on pain of eviction. (50–51)

Even in the case of those ex-slaves who managed to purchase land, "it was only a house spot; or when they did purchase 'grounds' these were miniscule" (49). It was in this context that family land, rooted in the protopeasant adaptation, was re-created in postslavery peasant communities.

Elsewhere in the British West Indies

Like Jamaica, British Guiana (now Guyana), the largest British Caribbean territory, manifested the themes of postslavery village settlements and customary tenures originating in slave opposition and resistance, including the slaves' desire "for personal liberty and for land of their own" (Farley 1964:52), and reflected the constraining impact of state/planter legislation on the flight from the estates. A long history of slave rebellion, protopeasantry, and marronage combined with the accumulation of peasant capital and relative availability of land to trigger and sustain a major movement from the estates into free-village communities. Free villages were often created on the narrow empoldered coastal plain through land purchase; others were based more on the maroon tradition through squatting on Crown land. By the 1860s, however, legislation to control the sale of land — "clearly intended to decapitate the peasant movement" — stemmed the tide of these villages (Mintz 1979:235). In these contexts, Guyanese free villagers established "children's property" that enabled all descendants of the land purchaser to have inalienable land rights, often in a joint estate (Besson 1995d).

Trinidad reflected an attenuated parallel of the Guyanese case. After emancipation, there was a substantial exodus of former slaves from the Trinidadian estates and a drive to establish villages. This was due to a desire on the part of the ex-slaves "to make freedom meaningful, to achieve a measure of economic and social independence of the planter . . . accentuated by the tenancy system, the withdrawal of allowances in 1842, the reduction in wages after 1846, and countless other irritants" (Brereton 1981:80). The relative availability of land was constrained by the general reluctance of planters to sell to ex-slaves, high prices, and state policy obstructing the sale of Crown lands to former slaves. Within this context a customary system of equal inheritance to land among descendants evolved in peasant communities (Rodman 1971:16).

Along with Jamaica, Guyana, and Trinidad, the Windward Islands provided the most opportunity for postemancipation peasant settlement and reflected further variations on the themes of opportunity and constraint. There had been protopeasantries in Tobago, St. Lucia, Grenada, and St. Vincent in addition to some maroon communities—for example, in St. Vincent and St. Lucia. Small plots of land allocated to male and female slaves had been worked by family groups, with customary transmission (Marshall 1991b). During apprenticeship, the continued occupancy of house and ground became contentious, with the apprentices claiming possession of houses, yards, and provision grounds. But as planter policies became more oppressive, former slaves, when possible, left the estates, founded postemancipation settlements, and established legal and customary tenures including family land, though some ex-slaves remained tied to the estates as tenants. In St. Lucia, former slaves were unsuccessful in their attempt to reestablish the old ruined town of Dauphin (Henshall 1976:38).

Dominica, the largest and most mountainous of the British Windwards, showed both similarities to, and differences from, the other Windward Islands. A protopeasantry had coexisted with maroon communities (Trouillot 1988:28, 68–75). Emancipated slaves did not face obstructive legislation, but the fact that coastal estates occupied most of the arable land initially curtailed flight from the plantations (81). In addition, planters ensured that the ex-slaves remained tied to the estates through task work, métayage (sharecropping), and rental (Chace 1984). This suggests, in contrast to Chace's thesis that Dominica's former slaves were not concerned with independence from the plantations (9), that the ex-slaves had little opportunity to leave. In the later postemancipation period, however, a peasantry became established through small purchases of land (Trouillot 1988:95–96). By the twentieth century, when peasants had virtually replaced plantations, a significant number of smallholdings constituted family land, providing autonomy and permitting circulatory migration.

Barbados, most of the Leewards, and British Honduras (now Belize) more fully repressed peasantization; in the Bahamas and Barbuda, constraints operated even within benign neglect. In the smaller or more gently sloping islands of Barbados, Antigua, St. Kitts, Montserrat, and Nevis, all of which contained dense populations, plantation agriculture was extremely dominant. Nevertheless, during slavery petty protopeasant adaptations were created (Besson 1995d), and interment in slave villages and plantation burial grounds has been richly documented for Barbados (Handler and Lange 1978:173–78). There was also rebellion and marronage, as on Barbados and Nevis. After emancipation, notable migration traditions developed in these colonies, but some ex-slave communities were established on marginal land in Barbados, Antigua,[11] and St. Kitts (Greenfield 1960; D. Hall 1971); where land was purchased, family land developed and enabled migrants to return (Besson 1995d).

On the other hand, in the immediate aftermath of emancipation, peasantization in Montserrat and Nevis was almost entirely stifled by land monopoly, and estate-based peasantries consolidated. A relatively independent peasantry did become established in Montserrat in the 1850–70 period, and customary "family land" and "generation land" evolved (Philpott 1973). In Nevis, protopeasant customary tenure consolidated among estate-based peasants and later continued in colonial land settlements (Momsen 1987).[12] In the late nineteenth century, some family land developed in a few small villages (Olwig 1993, 1997).

The cases of Montserrat and Nevis were paralleled, in some respects, by British Honduras. There, despite the potential availability of land, labor legislation and land monopoly by the mahogany planters prevented the development of a postemancipation peasantry (Bolland 1981:600–611). But among the Black Caribs, descendants of Caribs and maroons deported by the British from St. Vincent in 1797 due to a colonial struggle for land, a cognatic system (similar to Vincentian family land) developed in the context of postslavery land scarcity (Solien 1959; Gullick 1985:18).

In contrast to the extreme control of ex-slaves in Montserrat, Nevis, and Belize, there was benign neglect, or more room for maneuver, in the Bahamas and Barbuda where the autonomy of protopeasants had approximated that of maroons. After emancipation in the Bahamas, when legislation to restrict ex-slaves' access to land proved impractical to enforce, protopeasantries evolved into free communities. However, emancipated slaves were not entirely free from coercion, as "credit and truck" systems were introduced to keep them "in a position of 'practical slavery'" (Johnson 1991a:84). In this context Bahamian customary tenures, merging aspects of "generational property" and commonage, provided some autonomy (Craton 1987).

From 1680 to 1870 Barbuda had not been a plantation island but a private fief of the Codrington family, which owned Antiguan sugar plantations and lived in England. But Barbuda was not entirely isolated from the plantation system, and Barbudan slaves "died when removed by force to Codrington estates in Antigua" (Berleant-Schiller 1987:123). Nevertheless, Barbuda's emancipated slaves did not have to find land but only to retain it. House yards were transmitted either to all descendants or on the basis of household participation; bushland was used as commonage, except for fruit trees (and the immediately surrounding land), which could be passed on to an individual's descendants. However, throughout the postemancipation period and after Crown Colony government was established in 1899, there were successive external attempts to impose commercial agriculture on the island. Barbudans successfully resisted these attempts through their customary tenures (Berleant-Schiller 1977, 1978, 1987).

Parallels in the Danish, French, and Dutch Caribbean

The Danish West Indies, where slavery was abolished in 1848, clearly showed the primacy of slave opposition and resistance for shaping postslavery peasantization. The flight of ex-slaves from the St. Johnian estates originated in protopeasant adaptation, slave uprisings, and marronage; it was both triggered and constrained by state/planter legislation (Olwig 1985:82–93). Drawing especially on the protopeasant tradition, free villages developed in the 1870s and 1880s on marginal mountain land acquired by ex-slaves through purchase or deeds of gift, then were transformed into family land held by all descendants. However, in flatter St. Croix slaves could not create a protopeasantry due to land engrossment by sugar estates. After emancipation the strong plantation system was reinforced by a labor code that kept workers on the estates until a labor uprising in 1878. In the 1880s the Danish colonial government failed in its attempt to establish a land settlement and create a cottar class: Crucian laborers, with no strong protopeasant tradition, had no desire to become a landholding peasantry. Instead, they formed "a rural proletariat that organized industrial action" (95).

After 1848, the French West Indies likewise mirrored the continuing significance of pre-emancipation peasantization for postslavery peasant communities, especially in mountainous Martinique, which had a tradition of marronage and pronounced protopeasant adaptation during slavery including customary land (and tree) transmission based on unrestricted cognation (Tomich 1991; Horowitz 1992; Debien 1996). While postemancipation peasant villages (rooted in both maroon and protopeasant origins), with customary cognatic land transmission, were being established in the mountains of Martinique, the Boni or Aluku Maroons became strengthened in French Guiana (after an agreement with the colonial government in 1860) and continued to consolidate customary matrilineal landholding in the remote interior (Bilby 1989; Hoogbergen 1989).

Peasantization rooted in slave opposition and resistance also continued in some Caribbean colonies of the Netherlands after emancipation in 1863. In St. Eustatius, which had a small-scale plantation system and protopeasant adaptation, agriculture "came [almost] totally into the hands of the freed slaves who, as time went by, reserved small pieces of plantation ground to grow subsistence crops" through tenantry; as "in the Dutch Antilles no regulations were passed to facilitate the selling of land to former slaves" (van den Bor 1979:127, 133–34). In addition, a flight from the Statian estates occurred through migration, especially to St. Croix (van den Bor 1981:55–56). Customary land transmission evolved among the Statian peasantry (who were now constrained by land speculation and high land prices) in relation to undivided "succession-ground." This customary system, based on unrestricted cognatic descent, was compatible with overseas migration by allowing migrant kin to retain land rights.[13]

In Dutch Guiana (now Suriname), which was the main slave plantation colony of the Netherlands, differences and similarities to both St. Eustatius and the French West Indies occurred. In the vast forested interior the largest post-treaty maroon societies in African America, including the Saramaka, had consolidated communities, ancestral rituals, and landholding systems based on matriliny. Simultaneously, in the Para coastal plantation region, protopeasant slaves had formed overlapping nonexclusive cognatic kin groups, comprising all descendants of each original enslaved African, for ancestral ritual (Mintz and Price 1992:68–70). The question of how these groups evolved for landholding in postemancipation peasant communities is interwoven with Martha Brae's new history (chapter 8).

The Baptists and the Jamaican Free-Village System

As well as occurring within the setting of Caribbean post-slavery peasantization, the transformation of Martha Brae took place in the context of the Jamaican free-village system, which involved an alliance between ex-slaves and English Baptist missionaries. This alliance originated in the slavery era with the complex relationship between the slaves and the Baptists, who were especially active in the parishes of St. James and Trelawny — also the heart of the Obeah-Myal complex in Jamaica.

The Baptist Missionaries

The planters' Established Anglican Church in Jamaica had little impact on the slaves. In the later eighteenth and early nineteenth centuries, however, English Nonconformist missionaries (Moravians, Methodists, and Baptists) sent to the colony had more influence on the non-white population. The Established Church and most planters largely op-

Obeah-Myal funeral ritual in a slave plantation community, Eurocentrically portrayed. National Library of Jamaica, Kingston.

posed the preaching of these missionaries. The Baptists had the most success in converting slaves, as the Baptist faith had been introduced by Negro preachers. The most prominent of these black preachers were George Lisle (or Liele), an ex-slave from Virginia and Georgia, who went to Jamaica in 1784, and Moses Baker, another American ex-slave, who was baptized by Lisle in 1787. In 1788 Baker began preaching in St. James adjoining the new parish of Trelawny and also taught Trelawny slaves (Turner 1982:11; Little 1995).[14]

In 1813 the Baptist Missionary Society (BMS) in England dispatched its first missionary to Jamaica, the Reverend John Rowe, to reinforce the work of Lisle and Baker (Lisle had called on the BMS in response to the subversion of the Baptist faith by the slaves' Obeah-Myal beliefs and rituals). After he was met by Baker in St. James, Rowe took up residence in Falmouth, Trelawny. Following Rowe's death from yellow fever in 1816, a number of other Baptist missionaries went to Jamaica and established churches. Falmouth, however, remained without a Baptist minister until the Reverend Thomas Burchell formed the Falmouth Baptist Church in 1827. Burchell's assistant, James Mann, was the first pastor of this church, whose membership increased to about six hundred, until his death from malaria in 1830. By then he had organized two other Baptist churches in Trelawny: at Rio Bueno and Stewart Town.

Mann was replaced in Falmouth in 1830 by the Reverend William Knibb, from Kettering, Northamptonshire. The appointment of Knibb, an outspoken opponent of the Established Church and slavery, was enthusiastically received by the members of the congregation, the majority of whom were slaves from the surrounding Trelawny plantations. At this time there were eighty-eight sugar plantations in the parish and approximately 26,000 slaves (Sibley 1965:80; Wright 1973:57). During Knibb's first year the membership of the Falmouth Baptist Church increased to 700, with an additional 2,000 "inquirers"; in the scattered congregations of the parish as a whole, he served over 5,000 people. At the time of his arrival in Falmouth there was no Baptist chapel or mission house in Trelawny, but he soon became involved in acquiring land and building on behalf of the churches at Falmouth, Rio Bueno, and Stewart Town. Soon, however, Knibb's work among the Trelawny slaves was interrupted by the "Christmas Rebellion" of 1831–32, the great slave revolt that became known as the "Baptist War."

Obeah-Myal and Baptist Christianity: Manipulating Colonial Symbols

To contextualize the Christmas Rebellion of 1831–32, which was the largest slave uprising in the British West Indies and the most spectacular slave revolt in Anglo-America (Craton 1982:291–93; Mullin 1994:254), it is important to understand the relationship between the slaves and the Baptist Church and between the Obeah-Myal complex and Baptist Christianity. The social significance of the Baptist Church among Jamaica's slaves was twofold. First, "the slave saw the Baptist missionaries as his allies against the planters in their fight for freedom" (Patterson 1973:214). Second, the Baptist class-leader system, whereby influential slaves became class leaders, opened up positions of leadership among the slaves and facilitated the continuity of Obeah and Myal.[15]

The slaves therefore embraced the Baptist faith at a formal level and attended the Baptist Church, including Trelawny slaves in the vicinity of Martha Brae who comprised Knibb's Falmouth congregation. Nevertheless, the slaves remained committed to Obeah and Myal and interpreted Baptist Christianity through Afro-creole traditions (Schuler 1979a, 1979b). As a result, two variants of Baptist faith emerged: the "Orthodox" form, taught by the missionaries and practiced by the slave congregations in the churches, and the "Native" or "Black" Baptist form, controlled by Obeah and Myal, taught by Negro class leaders on the plantations. This latter variant played a central role in the 1831–32 slave rebellion.

It was a combination of these various factors that led to this rebellion being named the Baptist War. The revolt was widely thought to have been led by slave headmen (who were usually class leaders) from estates in the hinterland of Montego Bay, St. James, and by a domestic slave, "Daddy" Sam Sharpe (or Tharp),[16] who was a Native Baptist class leader in Burchell's congregation in Montego Bay. Moreover, the planters were convinced that the rebellion had been instigated by the Nonconformist — especially Baptist — missionaries, although the missionaries denied any involvement.

Controversy surrounds the specific cause of the revolt, but (in addition to being the culmination of a strong tradition of slave resistance in the western part of the island) it appears to have been closely linked to the slaves' belief that emancipation had been granted by the British government and was being withheld by the planters in Jamaica. Although details of the various accounts differ, the main facts of the rebellion seem clear. Two days after Christmas, a large number of slaves (estimates vary from 20,000 to 60,000) broke free, burning over 150 estates. The revolt started "with the firing of Kensington estate, high above Montego Bay, on the night of Tuesday, December 27, 1831" (Craton 1982:293), and spread swiftly throughout the western parishes including Trelawny and the vicinity of Martha Brae (303). Martial law was declared, and the Falmouth Baptist Chapel was taken over as a barracks for the military-plantation regime. The uprising, which lasted for two weeks, was largely under control by mid-January 1832 and martial law was lifted on 5 February. Only fourteen whites died in the conflict, but several hundred slaves were either killed in action (estimates vary from 200 to 400) or executed (100 to 500), and a hundred more were flogged. The Native Baptist rebel slave leader, Sam Sharpe, was tried on 19 April and hanged on 23 May 1832 in front of the courthouse in Montego Bay.[17]

In addition to reprisals against the slaves, the planters took revenge on the Nonconformist missionaries, especially William Knibb, who (with Sharpe) was regarded as a ringleader of the revolt. Knibb was arrested, imprisoned, and threatened with death. On his release he found that the Falmouth Baptist Chapel, along with thirteen other Nonconformist chapels, had been destroyed by the Colonial Church Union (a planter-based organization) following the lifting of martial law.

After the rebellion, the Jamaica Assembly appointed a committee to inquire into the causes of the revolt. A deputation, including the Hon. Richard Barrett (Speaker of the Assembly and owner of estates in Trelawny and St. James), went to London in 1832 to represent the planters' case (R. A. Barrett 2000:87). The missionaries also sent deputations to Britain in 1832, and the Baptist Church selected Knibb to report on conditions in the

William Knibb's Falmouth Baptist Chapel. National Library of Jamaica, Kingston.

churches (Sibley 1965:9; Wright 1973:111). In England Knibb contributed to the antislavery campaign, assisted by Burchell. Indeed, under the leadership of Baptist missionary William Knibb and planter Richard Barrett the final stages of the abolition movement in England were partly played out by representatives from Trelawny; when slavery was abolished throughout the British Empire on 1 August 1834, Knibb's base at Falmouth, one and a half miles from Martha Brae, became known as "the cradle of the abolition of slavery" (Black 1979).[18]

Knibb and Burchell returned to Jamaica at the end of 1834 and, with the help of a grant from Parliament and churches in England, rebuilt the Falmouth Baptist Chapel. The new chapel, seating 1,600 persons, was dedicated in 1837. Knibb continued to work for full emancipation of the slaves, attacking the apprenticeship system. Two years earlier than planned, on 1 August 1838, the slaves were fully freed. In the period directly following emancipation, the membership of the Baptist Church in Jamaica rapidly increased.

The Nonconformist missionaries fought not only for the abolition of slavery and full emancipation of the slaves, but also for a new society. With the end of slavery, they became involved in negotiations for fair wages on behalf of the ex-slaves and in establishing land settlements. The Baptists, especially William Knibb, were at the forefront of these reforms. For exam-

The interior of Knibb's Falmouth Baptist Chapel. National Library of Jamaica, Kingston.

ple, through his negotiations with the absentee planter Edward Barrett (owner of Oxford and Cambridge Estates in Trelawny), Knibb secured the first wage settlement on the island (R. A. Barrett 2000:103). And with Baptist minister James Phillippo (who founded Jamaica's first free village of Sligoville in the parish of St. Catherine between 1835 and 1838),[19] Knibb initiated the island's church-founded free-village system. The Reverend John Clark, who established Sturge Town in 1839 in the parish of St. Ann, adjoining Trelawny,[20] was also prominent in the free-village movement.

This free-village system, the outcome of slave opposition and resistance and the Nonconformist antislavery struggle, and triggered by postemancipation state/planter legislation obstructing rights to plantation house yards and provision grounds, mushroomed in Trelawny and was the vanguard of the flight from the British West Indian estates. However, the Baptist missionaries were not revolutionaries but reformers, and the free villagers were their captive congregations. The ex-slaves had a separate agenda for full freedom (including the consolidation of their Afro-creole kinship and land-tenure systems, and related Obeah-Myal beliefs and rituals). Their agenda would unfold within, appropriate, and transform the colonial Baptist mission model of free villages, just as Obeah and Myal had appropriated orthodox Baptist Christianity and fueled the Baptist War.

The Free-Village System

William Knibb had been at the forefront of the Baptist antislavery struggle, and after emancipation his leadership in the free-village movement (with James Phillippo) was a continuation of his reformer's role. The germ of Knibb's idea for church-founded villages was expressed as early as July 1838, on the eve of emancipation, at a meeting of apprentices in Falmouth, Trelawny's capital, one and a half miles from Martha Brae: "The Rev. William Knibb . . . saw clearly enough before the slaves were completely emancipated that settlement on their own land was the only course open to the people evicted from the estates. On 19th July, 1838, he told a meeting of 2,500 Jamaican apprentices at Falmouth, that, 'if they (the planters) are blind to their own interests, and drive you from their properties, there is plenty of crown land in Jamaica [a misconception explained below], and you can resort to that in case of extremity' " (Paget 1964:43). Knibb went on to tell the apprentices that " 'I have had an offer of a loan of £10,000 from a friend in England; and if it be necessary, that sum shall be appropriated towards the purchase of lands on which you may locate yourselves if your present employers force you to quit the properties on which you now live' " (quoted in ibid:46).

The loan Knibb spoke of did not, at this point, materialize, and on investigation it turned out that the Crown had no lands to grant. But in September 1838, a few weeks after emancipation, Knibb wrote to Dr. Hoby, a member of the Baptist Committee in England, outlining his plans for a free village and emphasizing the opportunity this would provide for Baptist missionizing:

> The complete emancipation of the inhabitants of this colony has opened a glorious door for the extension of the gospel in the interior of the island. . . . Most of the labourers' grounds are on the borders, or in the heart, of these mountains, so that they are perfectly acquainted with the most advantageous spots. . . . Many have already either purchased or settled on lands, and I believe that I could now, if I had the means, purchase from 500 to 1,000 acres, in one of the most lovely spots on earth, where scarcely human foot has trod, for about £2 or £3 sterling per acre. This I would purchase at once. I could soon re-sell to families, in lots of from two to four acres each, which would enable the worthy members of my church, with others who are fearfully oppressed, to settle, and form a village of their own. (Quoted in Wright 1973:167)

On 13 November 1838, shortly after writing to Hoby, Knibb informed Joseph Sturge, a Birmingham Quaker and now the leading abolitionist in

England, about the planters' victimization of the Baptist ex-slaves, the scarcity of land for peasant development in Trelawny, and his determination to obtain property in the parish on which to establish a free village. Knibb's plan was soon realized, as reported to Hoby and subsequently to Sturge:

> Two weeks later he [Knibb] was able to tell Hoby that he had been offered five hundred acres in his cousin Dexter's district, with a good house on it, for £1,000 sterling. "I shall buy it today and I earnestly beg you to procure me the loan of £500 or £600 for twelve months. Do take this to Mr. Sturge, and I am sure he will assist." The following day he wrote Sturge that the land was bought; the village was to be called Birmingham. More land was expected to come on the market shortly, but the terms would be cash, and he asked for further loans. (Wright 1973:167–68)

Knibb's "cousin Dexter" was Baptist missionary Reverend Benjamin Dexter, stationed in Stewart Town in southeastern Trelawny.

On its establishment Knibb's village was named New Birmingham in honor of Joseph Sturge's English hometown, and "by January 1839, over seventy families had already purchased land in the village and were erecting homes" around a Baptist church and school (Wilmot 1982:46–47).[21] Cross fire the next month between the *Falmouth Post* and William Dyer of the *Cornwall Courier*, in an article published in the *Post* on 13 February (p. 6), illuminates the continued evolution of this free village:

> Now, we, who know somewhat more of Mr. Knibb, than William Dyer will ever have the honor of knowing, positively declare, that he has not been recalled; . . . we beg to assure him [Dyer] that the large tract of land lately purchased by Mr. Knibb, in this parish, is to be surveyed, and laid out in the course of a few days in small lots. *A town is to be built called New Birmingham; and the streets are to be named after our excellent Governor, Wilberforce, Sturge, Clarkson, Burchell, Knibb, Hill, Lyon, Lewin, Facey, Carnaby, Finlayson, Castello* [the editor of the *Falmouth Post*], *and other friends of Freedom.* (Emphasis mine)[22]

This village, which was the first free village in Trelawny, along with Sligoville, St. Catherine, Jamaica's first free village founded by Phillippo, served as a model for the island's free-village system.

An "Agricultural Report" published on 5 June 1839 in the *Falmouth Post* throws further light on this process of peasantization, stating that "Messrs. Knibb, Clarke, Dexter, and Dendy, have succeeded in buying large tracts of land, and assisted as these Reverend Gentlemen will be, by the West India Land Investment Company, in the course of a short time, Townships will be built, and the proprietors made as they ought to be, entirely independent of their present employers. . . . 'The Free Village System' must be encouraged, and when successfully established, will be the terror of those who seem at present desirous to accumulate wealth by uncompensated labour." By 1840 Knibb estimated that there were nearly eight thousand cottages in two hundred such free villages throughout Jamaica, though in 1842 he observed that there were only 3,000 Baptist freeholders out of a potential 150,000. By 1845,[23] Knibb speculated that 19,000 ex-slaves had purchased land and were erecting cottages. Trelawny was at the center of these developments, he believed, with twenty-three free villages containing 1,590 houses.

Other villages founded by Knibb himself in Trelawny included Piedmont, eleven miles inland from Martha Brae in the foothills of the Cockpit Country (where ex-slaves had cleared land, purchased by Knibb, for a Baptist chapel in 1836 [*Falmouth Post*, 25 May 1836]); Hoby Town, named in honor of Dr. Hoby of the Baptist Committee in England; and Unity, a name symbolizing the solidarity of the ex-slaves. Still other Trelawny villages he organized were Refuge, originally named "Wilberforce" after abolitionist William Wilberforce, seven and a half miles east of Martha Brae; Kettering, which bears the name of Knibb's Northamptonshire hometown, ten and a half miles east of Martha Brae; and Granville, so called in honor of abolitionist Granville Sharpe, just one mile southwest of Martha Brae. As Knibb anticipated, such free villages provided the basis for some political power, which was tied to freehold land rights, as well as a limited economic independence from the plantations and a bargaining position for higher wages when working on them.[24] Church-founded villages also served as religious congregations, and prayer houses (known as class houses as they were linked to the Baptist "Class System") were erected in each community.[25] In some villages, there was also a Baptist church.

Jamaican postslavery peasantization occurred mainly in the years immediately after full freedom. At the time of emancipation in 1838, there were only 2,014 freeholders on the island. In 1840, just two years later, this figure had risen to almost 8,000 (7,848), demonstrating an increase of nearly 6,000 (5,834) (Paget 1964:49–50). By 1860 there were 50,000 landholders with under fifty acres. From 1860 the peasantry produced cash crops (especially coffee and bananas) for export, in addition to cultivating for subsistence and internal peasant markets. These developments partly coincided with the "period of consolidation" of the British West Indian peasantry from 1860 to 1900 (Marshall 1985:6). However, the Morant Bay Rebellion of 1865 in southeastern Jamaica underlined the continuing scarcity of land among the ex-slaves (Heuman 1994). Moreover, under Crown Colony government (introduced in 1866 after Morant Bay), the state's "land lease policy was not conducive to peasant development" (Satchell 1999:60), and the island's plantation economy was reestablished by the 1880s through the banana industry, while sugar estates persisted uninterrupted in the western parishes and in south-central Clarendon. The plantation system thus continued to inhibit peasantization.

Since the 1880s the Jamaican peasantry has been severely constrained (despite the labor protests of 1938, universal adult suffrage in 1944, political independence in 1962, and land settlement schemes on marginal land) by the development of corporate plantations and (after World War II) new forms of land monopoly in the bauxite mining and tourist industries (Beckford 1975, 1999; Stolberg and Wilmot 1992). This parallels the "period of saturation" and possible contraction of the anglophone Caribbean peasantry since 1900 (Marshall 1985). In these contexts free villages, with their core of family lands, have continued to provide a foothold for the Jamaican peasantry, while the unrestricted cognatic descent system at the core of family land has enabled migrants to return.

In the immediate aftermath of emancipation, peasant-planter competition was especially acute in the west-central area of Jamaica. In Trelawny, which had been the heart of the Jamaican slave plantation economy, emancipated slaves became the vanguard of the island's free-village system through their alliance with Baptist missionary William Knibb in a land/labor struggle with the planters that was the bitterest on the island (Underhill 1862: 377–78).[26] It was in this parochial setting that Trelawny's first capital, Martha Brae, would be appropriated and transformed into a postslavery peasant community (chapters 4–5) both similar to and different from other Trelawny free villages — such as those where I conducted fieldwork: The Alps, Refuge, Kettering, and Granville.

The Alps (New Birmingham): Trelawny's First Baptist-Founded Free Village

When researching the comparative framework of Martha Brae's new history, I sought to identify Trelawny's first free village of "New Birmingham," referred to in Knibb's letter of November 1838 (Hinton 1847:299–300; Wright 1973:167–68). But my fieldwork inquiries failed to locate a village of that name. Therefore, pursuing a hypothesis of a dual naming system suggested by the Trelawny Baptist villages of Wilberforce/ Refuge and Granville/Grumble Pen (Besson 1984b), as well as by the triple names of Angwin Crawl/Birmingham/Sturge Town in St. Ann (Mintz

1989:157–79), I looked for a village of another name that had originally been called New Birmingham.

Knibb's letter provided the initial clue as to the approximate location of this village: "in the mountains, in my cousin Dexter's district" (Hinton 1847:300). This was the Stewart Town area, in southeastern Trelawny, where Baptist missionary Reverend Benjamin Dexter was stationed (Wright 1973: 145). Edward Underhill (1862:359–61) identified The Alps—ten miles south of Stewart Town beyond Mahogany Penn, deep into the northern Cockpit Country—as a free village founded by the Reverend Dexter and occasionally visited by the Reverend E. Fray of Falmouth (Knibb's son-in-law). In a speech to the Baptist Missionary Society at Exeter Hall, England, in 1842, Knibb had indicated that New Birmingham was officially established by his cousin Dexter (*Speech of the Rev. William Knibb*, 1842:41). Inez Knibb Sibley (1978), a descendant of Knibb and Fray, observed of The Alps that "the London Baptist Missionary Society began missionary work here in 1835," with a Reverend Dexter in charge, and that at that time "the only place available for worship was an old coffee house which was repaired and used for this purpose" (9).

These indications that The Alps might be New Birmingham, with an evolution from Knibb's chosen name (honoring the hometown of abolitionist Joseph Sturge) to a colloquial one derived from the spectacular topography, were pursued through my archival research on land deeds recording conveyances of subdivided land by both Dexter and Knibb. One of these, a conveyance by the Reverend B. B. Dexter to one Robert Campbell, provided the conclusive clue: "All that . . . parcel of land *situate and being at the Alps in the Parish of Trelawny* . . . which is distinguished on the plan of the said property executed by Richard Wilson Esqr surveyor as comprehending lots number ninety four and ninety five *in the town of New Birmingham . . .*" (*Deeds* 1842, emphases mine). It appears, then, that from Dexter's time the settlement had two names and that, based on the wording of the deed, The Alps may already have been the name of the property (a coffee plantation) purchased by Knibb in the name of Dexter for the establishment of his "little Birmingham." The evidence is clear that this original name, "The Alps," superceded that of "New Birmingham," though reference to the latter can now only be found in the early land deeds and in history books. One such book records, in its "[L]ist of Chapels, Mission Houses, and School-Rooms Erected since the Year 1835, with the Cost of Each, and Debts Due upon Them," that the cost of the chapel at New Birmingham built by Dexter was £500, with accommodation for 550 persons, and that the mission house cost £600 (*Speech of the Rev. William Knibb*, 1842:41). Another entry lists the deacons and leaders for New Birmingham. One of these leaders bears the surname Brissett (20), the title of a prominent Old Family or unrestricted cognatic descent group in The Alps today. This Brissett family overlaps with the village's central family line, which uses the surname Campbell as its title.

In this and other ways, fieldwork in The Alps reinforced my historical research. The isolated location of the village, in this otherwise uninhabited northeastern area of the Cockpit Country, and the beauty of its alpine slopes and flowers exactly coincides with Knibb's description of the site of his first land purchase "in one of the most lovely spots on earth, where scarcely human foot has trod" (quoted in Wright 1973:167).[27] The focus of the village is the Baptist church on a mountainside; the ruins of the mission house appear nearby, with house yards on the slopes and in the valley below. Interviews with villagers tapped a rich oral tradition concerning the establishment of The Alps as Trelawny's first Baptist-founded free village. One of my informants was shopkeeper Sylvester Bonner, born around 1917, whose shop and house yard were situated closest to the church. On his maternal side he was descended from a former slave on The Alps coffee plantation, Archibald "Archie" Campbell, from whom many villagers traced unrestricted descent through either males or females. Archie's old cottage and tombstone can be identified, and his gravestone underwrites the oral tradition that he was born in 1813 during slavery (and was therefore 25 years old at emancipation) and died in 1924 at the age of 111.

Another descendant of Archie Campbell was Egbert Edwards, who lived farther from the center of the settlement in the area of The Alps known as "Chrichton's Mountain," and who extended Sylvester Bonner's oral history one further ascending generation into slavery. Born in The Alps in 1892, Egbert was ninety-one when I interviewed him in 1983. During World War I he had fought in England, Belgium, Italy, and France. He subsequently returned to The Alps, where he cultivated bananas, sugarcane, and yams. His wife, late mother, and himself would take such produce by donkey to markets elsewhere in Trelawny.[28]

Egbert's late mother, Eliza Campbell, was one of Archie Campbell's thirteen children. Egbert himself was born in Archie's cottage and grew to know his ex-slave grandfather, "who used to wear long shirt,"[29] and who spoke of his boyhood experience in a plantation hogmeat gang: "Sometimes they sent him to look for hog feeding when he was in slavery, as a slave child." Egbert had learned that Archie's ex-slave father (Egbert's great-grandfather), who was also named Archibald Campbell,[30] had purchased several acres of land from the Reverend Dexter in New Birmingham after emancipation. This suggests internal differentiation among the ex-slave settlers, based in part on access to land, perhaps perpetuating earlier economic stratification among the slaves. The great-grandfather, Archibald Campbell I, transmitted his freehold land rights to his son Archie Campbell II (who also knew the Reverend Dexter) and, through him, to his numerous descendants traced through both males and females, thereby creating an unrestricted cognatic landholding kin group, the Campbell Old Family (including members with other surnames), which was now partially dispersed through migration. These descendants included Egbert Edwards and his five children (four daughters and a son), who were the great-great-grandchildren of the ex-slave who purchased land of his own.

Egbert further recounted that Archie Campbell II and his parents (Archibald Campbell I and his spouse) had been slaves at Mahogany Hall, a nearby cattle pen in Trelawny with 133 apprentices in 1837 (Craton 1978:42). He said that they had also been enslaved on an estate in the adjoining parish of St. Ann, as "sometime they change places"; that is, the slaves were sometimes sold or moved about. The settling, after emancipation, of the ex-slaves Archie Campbell II and his parents in the free village of New Birmingham therefore contrasted with their enforced mobility as slaves. The postslavery migration of some of their descendants, such as one of Egbert's daughters and his son who moved to the United States (but who retained freehold land rights in The Alps), likewise contrasted with the controlled mobility of the former slaves.[31]

Archibald Campbell I's family line was interrelated with other Old Families in The Alps, including the Brissetts and the Fergusons, all descended through male or female links from emancipated slaves and partially dispersed through migration but retaining their roots in the free village as an important basis of transnational identity.[32] Although land could be bought and sold in the village (as at the time of the founding of New Birmingham), oral histories, genealogies, and burial patterns identify the family lines and family lands that evolved after emancipation. These overlapping family lines became embedded in the land through their burial grounds, marked by cairns and tombs. The kin-based cemeteries, which were similar to those of some other Trelawny villages (and to those in the postslavery village of Ockbrook/Aberdeen in St. Elizabeth, neighboring Accompong [Besson 1995b, 1997]), were the most extensive I have seen; one of these cemeteries contained at least thirty-four graves.

The significance of these family-land graveyards as symbols of identity, and therefore representing cultural opposition to the plantation system, was underlined by the oral tradition of a "cholera ground" in the village. Here, overgrown by alpine flowers, reputedly lay the remains of 150 slaves who died in a cholera epidemic on The Alps Plantation. Unlike the entombed slave master and the graves of the emancipated slaves and their descendants, the burial places of the slaves were unmarked.[33] Thus they remained "invisible men" (Craton 1978) and women (Dadzie 1990), lacking formal identity in death as they did in life on the slave plantation. In contrast, the ex-slaves and their descendants were able to forge visible identities within their free-village community through the creation or consolidation of enduring family lines, family lands, and family burial grounds.

The endurance of the free village itself, founded by ex-slaves in alliance with Baptist missionaries deep in the mountains of Trelawny near the Leeward Maroon polity, underscores the tradition of slave opposition and resistance and antislavery struggle in the flight from the estates. The family-land institution in The Alps (as in other Jamaican and non-Hispanic Caribbean postslavery peasant communities) drew on the institution-building of proto-peasant slave ancestors of both genders who established customary cognatic land-transmission systems. In the case of Trelawny's Baptist-founded free villages, such as The Alps and those discussed below, family land transformed the legal freeholds purchased from the English Baptists. This transformation, by the ex-slaves and their descendants, of the missionaries' imposed land settlements continued the process of Caribbean institution-building through the appropriation and reversal of colonial institutions begun in slavery.

Refuge (Wilberforce): Another Early Exodus

The village of Refuge is about six miles southeast of Falmouth, where the Reverend William Knibb was stationed, and seven and a half miles from Martha Brae. Originally named Wilberforce after the abolitionist, Refuge was founded by Knibb around a Baptist church on about ninety acres of hilly land bordering Oxford Plantation. The inscription on the cornerstone of the large cut-stone Wilberforce/Refuge Baptist Church reads "Church Founded 1838," suggesting the formation of the village in the year of emancipation shortly after the founding of New Birmingham. However, the process of establishing the church-founded community reached back to the abolition of slavery. In a letter dated 24 November 1834, Knibb referred to "the Refuge as a desirable second station for Falmouth," noting that "the purchase of land is completed, and the title enrolled" and that "I am exceedingly desirous of immediately putting up a strong wood chapel" (Hinton 1847:214). In another letter, dated 1 January 1835, Knibb wrote, "On every estate in the neighbourhood of the Refuge, there are members of my church" (215), and the *Falmouth Post* of 24 August 1836 reported that the "Wilberforce Chapel" had been enlarged that year. In a letter of 8 May 1838, Knibb announced that another enlargement of Wilberforce (costing no more than £300) was "nearly completed," with the church to be reopened the following Sunday (quoted in Hinton 1847:216).[34]

After emancipation the new village of Wilberforce provided a refuge for freed slaves, not only from Oxford (which in 1837 had 207 apprentices, about one-third of whom were Baptists) but also from other nearby estates such as Etingdon, Hyde Hall, and Stewart Castle which in 1837 had 216, 222, and 219 apprentices respectively (Craton 1978:43).[35] The names Wilberforce and Refuge were both used from 1838 to 1842 (Hinton 1847:270–382), but on 26 June 1839 the *Falmouth Post* referred to the "Baptist Chapel at Refuge." By 1842 the village had taken on the colloquial name of Refuge (Wright 1973:216–17), and in 1842 in his speech to the BMS in Exeter Hall Knibb reported his founding of the "Refuge" chapel (likely to have been the later cut-stone church) at a cost of £1,400, able to accommodate 1,500 persons, and a schoolroom costing £200 (app. 1, *Speech of the Rev. William Knibb*, 1842:41).[36]

According to oral history, there was also a prayer house in Refuge in the area known as Stewarton. This belief was reinforced by the fact that the family land of one of the village's central family lines (the Lyon Old Family) was situated in this area;[37] the oral tradition of another Old Family (the Bells) refers to land in Stewarton.[38] In addition, older villagers claimed to know the exact site where the class house was located, and there were ruins here. The steep climb from Stewarton to the Baptist church, at the center of Refuge, provides a convincing rationale for the location of the prayer house in this remote part of the isolated, dispersed, and extremely hilly settlement.

At the time of my fieldwork, Refuge had a population of around 415 persons in about eighty households; still strongly Baptist, they were proud of their history as a free village founded by William Knibb. Pictures of Knibb and the two Reverend Ellis Frays (Sr. and Jr., Knibb's son-in-law and grandson), who all ministered at Refuge, hung inside the church; the oldest Baptist villager proudly recalled that she was baptized in 1911 by the younger Ellis Fray. The ruins of the old Baptist mission house could be discerned on a plot of land referred to by the villagers as "Mission."

In 2001 Oxford Estate still ran up to the southern boundary of Refuge and stretched southward into the plateau of rich cane lands that, in 1983, comprised the 20,000-acre holdings of the National Sugar Company (Long Pond). These consolidated plantations, of which Oxford was a tributary, were previously the corporate holdings of Trelawny Estates, owned by Seagrams (the world's largest alcohol multinational) from around the 1950s until nationalization in 1978. By 1995 the Jamaican government had been forced by the World Bank and the International Monetary Fund to divest National Sugar, which became Long Pond Estates. The major shareholder was a pan-Jamaican group in the private sector, which owned the factory and leased most of the cane lands from the Jamaican state for forty-nine years starting on 1 January 1994.[39] At the time of my field research many of the older people in Refuge had been plantation laborers at Oxford, and some villagers still worked there, as their slave ancestors did before them on the plantations that now formed the tributaries of Long Pond Estates.

Oral tradition in Refuge focused especially on the Old Families, the landholding kin groups traced through unrestricted cognatic descent (including both genders and absent as well as resident descendants) from the ex-slave ancestors who settled the free village. The two Baptist deacons were members of the two most prominent family lines (the Bell and Lyon Old Families), whose descendants included much of the village population. In 1983 the Bell family traced its ancestry four ascending generations from its oldest living members (who were in their seventies) to an African slave woman, one of three "sisters" (or fictive shipmate sisters) said to have been brought from Africa; she worked on Oxford Plantation and, after emancipation, was one of the original settlers of Wilberforce/Refuge. This woman's granddaughter was "Queen" Elizabeth Bell-Merchant, the grandmother of several contemporary villagers, who may have been a Myal/Revival "queen" (cf. Sheller 1998:102). One of "Queenie's" elderly granddaughters narrated the following account of enslavement and emancipation, including the acquisition of freehold land through Knibb:

My grandmother told me that her people were from Africa, and she even had the mark on her knee. And when I asked my grandmother about it, she told me it was her mother who marked her there and they call it "a negro mark."[40] Queenie's father's mother was from Africa. She always said it was like three sisters came out: one went to Westmoreland [Parish] as a slave, and one stay in Oxford, and another in the east—not in Trelawny. Long ago some people [came] from that way and say that we are family here, as their grandmother told them so.

Queen Elizabeth's father cooked Freedom Dinner [at emancipation]. It was cooked at Oxford, as they were up there [as slaves], and after that everybody came to Refuge, and the lands cut up and given to the ex-slaves. Queen Elizabeth's father' mother came here [to Oxford] as a slave and he came with her [from Africa as a child], and then he grew here . . . in slave days. They were at Oxford and after Freedom they came to live in Refuge. . . . My grandmother's father' mother came to Refuge and got the land. The land where I live and the land at Stewarton, Queen Elizabeth had those pieces. . . . Those two pieces were got by that woman who was a slave, from Knibb, and when the grandmother died it was left for Queenie's father, and when he died it was left for Queenie.

Queenie's father is said to have lived to the age of 101. He had two other children, both sons, but "they bought land" of their own. Another of Queenie's elderly granddaughters knew these granduncles as a child and recalled that they were nicknamed "Hard Time" and "Poor Man." They too had been slaves, and "they told me how they [the slave drivers] used to beat them and work them. They were on Oxford Estate." Queenie sold one of the two plots (the piece at Stewarton), but her descendants retained the other as family land, as is another 1 ¼-acre plot purchased by Queenie and her husband. Their tombs and those of two of their children and two grand-daughters could be seen on this land, and Queenie's inscribed tomb could also be identified. As Queenie's elderly grandchildren had grandchildren of their own, the unrestricted cognatic family line descended from the African slave ancestress numbered at least seven generations; many family members had lived in Refuge.

Queenie and her ancestors passed down to their descendants not only freehold land rights, but also accounts of slavery. The following story told by a grandson of Queenie illustrates the anonymity of plantation slaves as faceless members of a labor force geared solely to producing profits for their masters, an anonymity (underlined by the recurring theme of a cholera ground with unmarked graves, as in The Alps)[41] that would be partially dispelled by the creation of family lines and family lands in the free village:

Of course my grandmother Queenie, she knew a little [of slavery], as the Bells were born in the days of slavery. The old people told me that in the days of slavery, the slaves lived in little huts, and in the mornings they are called up into a big yard, and they call it a big pen, like how you gather up animals,[42] and you are taken out to work, by a task master. The people were working on the sugar plantation in the cutting and cleaning of the cane. And they had the food in a big trough for the people; when the food is ready they knock a piece of iron and everybody come. Also told me that once a disease broke out among the people called cholera. Plenty people died of this contagious disease, and there are some spots in the sugar plantation, they call it "cholera ground," where the people were buried;

and some of the people they tried to push them in the ground before the breath left the body. And many people were beaten with whips when they did not work, and of course they had a very hard time.

At the time of my fieldwork the Lyon Old Family traced its ancestry four ascending generations — from the oldest living members (who were in their eighties) to an African-born slave couple and their son "Old John Lyon, an old slave fellow," a creole slave on Hyde Hall Estate. Old John Lyon, one of the original settlers of Refuge, had obtained land from William Knibb in the Stewarton area of the village. This land has remained as family land among the ex-slave's descendants and, with several households of his descendants clustered there, forms the core of Stewarton. John Lyon had three children and five grandchildren, and the Lyon family comprised eight generations of cognatic descendants: four generations of deceased ancestors, whose graves and tombs were embedded in the land (there were fifteen such graves and tombs including John Lyon's), and four living generations. Despite the dispersion of many of the living members of the kin group through migration to other parts of Jamaica, the United States, and England, the family's identity remained focused on the family land in Stewarton.

The Lyon Old Family overlaps with the Bell family and with other unrestricted cognatic landholding kin groups, traced through both genders from ex-slaves and using descent group titles despite varying individual surnames, such as the Spencers, who trace their ancestry to "a slave girl" at Etingdon Estate entombed along with four of her descendants on their family land in the "Spencer Hill" district of Refuge; similar family-land burial grounds embroider the village landscape. The Lyons are also related through affinity to one of Granville's central Old Families. In addition, kinship ties exist between Refuge villagers and those of Kettering. Family lines, family lands, and family burial grounds are recurring themes in Kettering and Granville as well.

Kettering: A Home for Ex-Slaves and Knibb

The village of Kettering, overlooking Duncans Bay and named after Knibb's Northamptonshire hometown (*Falmouth Post*, 5 June 1839), is about three miles northeast of Refuge. Kettering was founded by William Knibb in 1841 on a former pimento estate bordering the town of Duncans. The land was sold in lots to ex-slaves from surrounding plantations such as Braco: "Seldom any person bought more than two lots; each lot was 52 feet by 108 feet"; the village was established with eighty houses for

278 persons (Robotham 1977:49; *Speech of the Rev. William Knibb*, 1842:45). It was in this "new village settlement" that the freed slaves of the Baptist church built Knibb a home, in gratitude for his efforts in the abolitionist cause and for the persecution he had endured on their behalf: "a substantial two-storey stone house, costing £1,000, and described in the now hostile *Falmouth Post* as 'one of the most comfortable mansions in the parish of Trelawny' "; and it was here that Knibb died of yellow fever in December 1845 (Underhill 1862:369; Wright 1973:199, 243). Knibb's widow, Mary Knibb, who survived him by twenty years, continued to live at Kettering, and some of their descendants became creolized.[43]

Writing in 1845, Knibb gave some idea of the development of Kettering:

> The village is now assuming a very interesting appearance, and in a few years will be a flourishing little town. It is laid out in four hundred building lots, which, with very few exceptions, are sold. Regular streets intersect each other, and neat cottages are rising on every hand. My own dwelling-house stands in the centre, with a neat chapel and school-room adjoining, and already nearly two hundred of the members of my church have here fixed their abode. The grand road through the island, from Kingston to Montego Bay, runs close to the land, and a village named Duncans, where there are a post-office and a market, is situated on the other side of the road. The village is about two miles from the sea, a part of it commanding an extensive view of the ocean, while the distant mountains of Cuba can sometimes be distinctly seen. Thus I dwell among my own people, though in a foreign land, blessing, I hope, that God who has hitherto provided me a table in the midst of mine enemies. (Hinton 1847:466–67)

Seventeen years later Underhill (1862:378), following his tour of the West Indies in 1860 on behalf of the BMS, reported that Duncans, with Kettering forming its northern side, "is now one of the most flourishing towns in the interior. It has an excellent weekly market, which is attended by peasants from the mountains in large numbers."

Kettering today is, at first sight, indistinguishable from the town of Duncans and in this respect contrasts with the more dispersed settlements of The Alps and Refuge. However, the inhabitants of Kettering have a strong sense of identity as a free village established by William Knibb. As one Kettering villager observed: "If it was not for Knibb, the blacks would not have any go in this area. . . . And Knibb start cut his land and save up the hill [for his own home], and sell it to the people. The whole of this land for Knibb and he sell it bit by bit." On closer examination Kettering, with its family lands, also manifests the appearance of a free village. This is especially so in those areas farthest from the Duncans town center, as a significant variation occurs among the component districts of Kettering with respect to burial in the house yard. The area of Kettering known as "Red Earth Bottom," near the town center, and the more central part of "Kettering Top" now fall within the Duncans town limits for the purpose of burial in the Duncans cemetery. This prohibition on yard interment, imposed by the Trelawny Parochial Board through burial legislation around the mid-twentieth century,[44] during the lifetime of older Kettering villagers, illuminates the transformation of burial patterns in the free village of Martha Brae, where interment in the village cemetery has now replaced yard burial (chapters 4 and 5). The more distant part of Kettering Top, as well as "Kettering Bottom," are outside this limit, and here burial in house yards persists.[45] As in other Trelawny villages, Kettering's Old Families and their family lands are interspersed with migrant newcomers, purchased land (from which new family lands are being created), and tenancy. Tenants include two branches of the Lyon Old Family from Refuge. There are also kinship ties with the free villages of Granville and Martha Brae.

My fieldwork in Kettering focused on about eighty households with around four hundred persons (roughly half of Kettering's total population), in Kettering Top and Kettering Bottom, and in the central block of the village that contains the site of Knibb's house on "Kettering Hill" and the Baptist church below bordering the main road from Kingston to Montego Bay. Immediately opposite the gate of Kettering Hill is an acre of family land deriving from the time of Knibb and belonging to the Scott Old Family, one of Kettering's central family lines. (Two other plots of Scott family land in Mid- and Bottom Kettering had been sold.) At the time of my fieldwork a cluster of households lived on the family land, which served as a basis of identity for the descent group that was partially dispersed through migration to the United States and Canada as well as to other parts of Trelawny and Jamaica. In addition, some members of the descent group lived on their own small plots purchased elsewhere in Kettering. One of these plots, one square chain in size,[46] was bought around 1938 before universal adult suffrage (1944) and enabled voting rights, as well as providing freehold rights for descendants.[47] Still other members of the kin group lived on rented land in Kettering and Duncans.

The family land includes a family cemetery, where at least fourteen members of the Scott Old Family were interred prior to the Duncans town limits burial prohibition. The family land was purchased by Emanuel Scott, the paternal grandfather of the oldest living generation (and the great-great-

great-grandfather of the youngest of the five descending generations), who "was in the time of slavery." He "got [bought] the land from old arrivance [an old-time person, perhaps another ex-slave], but the old arrivance got the land from Knibb." There was no title for the land, but a "registered paper" was provided, as was the custom at that time. Emanuel Scott was buried in the family cemetery. Others interred there include his two daughters and two sons, who lived in Kettering in the 1890s. The last members of the kin group to be buried in this graveyard were interred in 1944–45, and family members now have to be buried in the Duncans cemetery.

Oral histories were recounted by heads of four households that comprised four living generations of the descent group. They explained that the family land is "not only for those living on the land alone, anyone [of the Old Family] could come," "if they even go to America and come back." In addition, the family land "will remain for grand and great-grandchildren, and go on into generations, and it could [should] not be sold." The Scott Old Family is therefore a dispersed and expanding unrestricted cognatic landholding corporation (traced through both genders and including absent as well as resident kin), whose family land symbolizes the identity and continuity of the family line descended from the ex-slave Emanuel Scott and provides a nonexclusive residential base for some of his descendants.[48]

Similar Old Families or unrestricted cognatic descent groups rooted in family land, and with titles, ancestral graves, and tombs, were found throughout the districts of Kettering that I studied, and their oral histories shed further light on their slave and ex-slave ancestors. For example, Josie Bennett, who was born in 1921 and had been a market higgler, lived in Kettering Bottom on a quarter acre of family land that was so rocky it was almost impossible to cultivate. Her paternal grandfather "used to carry wood when they were making the Baptist Church"; the family land originated with this grandfather's paternal grandmother, who, with several other members of the family line, was buried on the land. Josie's paternal half brother lived nearby on a half-acre of family land originating more recently from their paternal grandfather. In addition to the histories of these two plots, Josie recounted the experience of her father's maternal grandmother's mother (her own great-great-grandmother) as a pregnant slave who was flogged, for refusing to work, on Harmony Hall Estate bordering Kettering. Josie was told this by her paternal grandmother: "She seh [said] when her grandmother was expecting, she did a lot of work and she did not want to work. [So] them dig a hole and put her in there and lick [whipped] her with the cattanine [cat-o'-nine-tails]. And it [the whip] catch her in the back and the baby born with a bad eye."

Another example is Sandra Jenkins, whose family land had been passed down from her maternal grandmother's mother, an ex-slave who was buried on the land and is said to have bought the land. This great-grandmother told Sandra of her experience as a slave child in a hogmeat gang:

I know my great-grandmother, she was Sarah Wilson, [my] mother's mother' mother. When slavery abolished she was twelve years old. She told me, after living for one hundred and five years. She told us, according to it, they used to send her in the pasture to look meat, on the estate, meat to feed pigs. She used to get bush to feed the pigs. They used to have estate at Lancaster, also Harmony Hall, and also Braco [estates persisting to the present]. So, in those days now, those people [the slaves] used to work on the estates that side, so it was one of those.

The experience of Sarah Wilson as a slave girl paralleled that of Archie Campbell II, of The Alps, who had been a slave boy in a hogmeat gang.

Granville (Grumble Pen): Martha Brae's Neighboring Free Village

Granville, two and a half miles inland from Falmouth and one mile southwest of Martha Brae, was founded by William Knibb in the year of his death, 1845, in the main plantation area of Trelawny. The village was established on about ninety acres of hilly land, on a former livestock pen, bought by Knibb (Besson 1984b).[49] This free village, named after abolitionist Granville Sharpe, was founded to absorb dispossessed slaves from the surrounding estates of Merrywood, Maxfield, Green Park, and Holland, which in 1837 on the eve of emancipation had 140, 119, 409, and 120 apprentices respectively (Hinton 1847:466; Craton 1978:42–44).

Underhill (1862:369–70) observed that earlier free villages established in Trelawny by Knibb (such as Refuge and Kettering) were diminishing the congregation of his large Baptist church in Falmouth and identified the founding of Granville by Knibb (a few days before his death) as a strategy to counteract this by ensuring "that a portion of the people might be near enough" to provide "a good congregation at the parent chapel." Initially, therefore, there was only a prayer house in Granville, though this was replaced in the 1940s by a Baptist church that was enlarged in the 1980s. After Knibb's death, Granville was consolidated by his widow; one Old Family showed me a treasured land conveyance to an ex-slave ancestor signed by Mary Knibb.

At the time of my research, Granville comprised about six hundred persons in approximately 120 households. The core of the population, as in The Alps, Refuge, and Kettering, belonged to overlapping Old Families or unrestricted cognatic family lines (traced through males and females, and including both residents and migrants), with kin-group titles, descended from ex-slave settlers and usually transmitting family lands. As in other Trelawny peasant communities, Granville villagers are strongly aware of their free-village history, and their oral accounts complement historical sources and provide more insight into Granville's development than do written records.

This oral tradition has four interrelated themes: the establishment of the free village by William Knibb; the subdivision of land by Knibb's "land butcher" or surveyor "Sergeant Wallace," a mulatto police sergeant of mixed African and European ancestry and a Baptist, probably a class leader,[50] whose descendants have the largest and most fertile landholdings at the edge of the village; the histories of the Old Families (some of whom interweave with those of neighboring Martha Brae) and their family lands; and the evolution of the settlement's name from the colloquial "Grumble Pen" to Knibb's chosen name of "Granville." These themes are outlined in turn, beginning with the founding of the village and the subdivision of its land.

When I began my fieldwork in Granville, a Mr. Carey, born around 1908, was a former plantation cooper who had retired to his family land adjoining the Wallace Old Family's landholding. His paternal grandparents were both from Granville, "and they go back to Knibb." Here is his account of the founding and subdivision of Granville:

> This Granville is connected to Knibb, also Kettering. The parson them get so much acres — I hear Granville was 100 acres — they get it for the church members after the abolishing of slavery, and the members could be settled in the different areas. They cut up the land in lots. Some of the lots are 2½ squares [square chains], and some don't get full 2 squares, and after when they started to measure, from this section down there come up to this end, some of the people don't get more than 1½ squares, according to the amount of land for them. I hear that all over there, and this area [Wallace's land] were connected to the church people — them call them Leaders — and those get a little bigger section when it come to the last than the rest, but further down only little, little lots amounting to 2 squares each lot.

Another Granville oral historian was Eugene Norris, born in 1916, who elaborated the theme of Sergeant Wallace and his subdivision of the Granville lands including a subsidiary Wallace landholding named "Dispute":

The cutting up of the land, it was a man them call Sergeant Wallace was the man in those days to cut up the land. A piece of land up there what him have, when somebody to get the land it was a contention, so the cutter-man Wallace take that piece, and him give it name "Dispute." . . . The contention was between two persons said they did not want it, because it was too narrow to the road, the street is up there and the road side it, so it caused contention, so the cutter-man said he would take it since they did not want it. Wallace got more than one piece of land; that piece of land go through five Wallace generation until now. . . . Those were the great people in those times, so they were Baptist people, so Knibb gave him the office to sell. . . . Wallace was a "red-man," a *mulatto*, and his forefathers were slaves; was a Baptist, that's why he get the opportunity to cut the land, and Wallace was a police sergeant, and because he was in a position, Knibb gave him access to cut up the land.

In 2000 Sergeant Wallace's descendants had the largest landholdings in Granville, and (except for Dispute) their land was the most fertile and gently sloping. Combined with the case of Archibald Campbell I in The Alps, this indicates that there was internal differentiation within Jamaican church-founded free villages even at the time of their establishment. This was based partly on access to land and partly on status in the Baptist Church, themes that the oral tradition of Sergeant Wallace suggests may have been closely related.[51]

The case of the Wallace Old Family illustrates the theme of Granville's unrestricted cognatic landholding kin groups. In 1983 the Wallace Family was entirely dispersed through migration (e.g., to Falmouth, where I interviewed an elderly grandaughter of Sergeant Wallace, and to England), and a tenant, Stanley Smith, was caretaker for the land. However, the rights of absentee descendants to the land were highly visible in the substantial concrete house being built there, with migrant remittances, to replace the old wooden cottage from the postemancipation period. By 1995 there were two large concrete houses, built through remittances and circulatory migration. One of Sergeant Wallace's great-grandsons, Sam Walker (a Baptist, born in 1936), had returned in 1992 to live there after thirty-five years in London and was still residing there in 2000 (as was Stanley). Sam's oral history, tracing the transnational family line seven generations and providing information on some of the living members of the dispersed descent group, is summarized below.

Sam Walker's great-great-grandfather was a Scotsman surnamed Wallace, who is likely to have been a member of the Trelawny planter class. This

Scotsman's son, Sam's great-grandfather, was a sergeant major and sub-divided the Granville lands. This is consistent with the accounts, by older villagers, of the mulatto Sergeant Wallace who cut up the Granville land for William and Mary Knibb. Sergeant Wallace's mother may have been enslaved, and the sergeant may have been an emancipated or manumitted slave. He is said to have acquired twelve acres of land at the edge of Granville. This is now the Wallace family land, and the sergeant and his wife were buried behind the cottage. The sergeant's daughter, Sam's grandaunt, was also interred there. But the sergeant's son, Sam's grandfather, was buried (at his own request) in the parish of St. Catherine, where he died in 1955, for, as Sam explained on his behalf, "where the tree fall, there shall it lie." However, the grandfather's son and daughter-in-law, Sam's parents, lived in the cottage on the land (where Sam himself grew up) and were buried in the yard. Sam's father, who knew the sergeant, died in 1974; the mother died in 1995. The grandfather's four daughters, Sam's paternal aunts, migrated (one to Falmouth, the others overseas including to the United States), but all visited the family land in Granville. Sam's six siblings of both genders all resided in London but could return to live on the land; in fact, "they came here the other day." His three adult children and three grandchildren, all in England, may likewise return and there is now ample accommodation in the two large houses, which serve as family-land "hotels."

Eugene Norris's Old Families, on both maternal and paternal sides, likewise stretch back to the time of Knibb and further illuminate the creation of ever-increasing unrestricted cognatic descent lines and the expression of their identity through family land. His case also illustrates the miniscule scale of most family lands in Granville. On his maternal side he traces his Old Family four ascending generations to his great-great-grandmother, a slave on Merrywood Plantation (a former Tharp estate), adjoining Granville, who participated in the celebration of emancipation and "the singing of the freedom songs." Eugene knew her daughter, his great-grandmother "Mother Lawrence" (who may have been a Revival Mother), who was "a slave child" at emancipation: "She told me that when Knibb came home from England and get these things straightened out to free the people, I remember the song she told me about—like you would say Independence—and the song says that everybody tie them head with a red handkerchief for delivery from slavery, and they sang it all around the place beating drum, like Jonkonnu: 'And they starve us, they beat us, but One above will punish them.' "[52]

Mother Lawrence's mother was one of Granville's ex-slave settlers who bought half an acre from Knibb. At her death "the land was passed to Mother Lawrence," her only child; "and then Mother Lawrence dead and lef' it for her pickney, for her four children, one of whom was my grandmother." It still remained as family land among the ex-slave's descendants, who now comprised six generations. Some, like Eugene Norris and one of his brothers, lived in Granville on their own small plots of purchased land. Many more were scattered beyond the village through migration. The twenty children of another of Eugene's brothers, who lived in Falmouth, illustrate the migration theme: they were "scattered all over Portland [Parish], Clarendon [Parish], America [the United States], Falmouth, and Kingston." The family land, on which no one presently lived, should not be alienated and is for all of the ex-slave's dispersed descendants: "Not to be sold. It is for when anyone [of the Old Family], who does not have any land, to go and cotch on the land . . . so the whole of us are owner of the land. So that land is there, like we pay the taxes, to rescue the one who does not have anywhere and want to come, without war."[53]

The case of Eugene's brother, who lived as a tenant in Falmouth and had no bought land of his own, illustrates this role of family land as providing security for those in need. Eugene was building a house on the family land for this brother to live in. But residing there would not give him exclusive land rights: "Only living there to make himself comfortable, until when him dead. He can't stop any children or grandchildren of his brothers and sisters from going on the land and picking [fruit], so he not owner of the land. Just that he does not have land anywhere [else]." The tradition of intestacy that typifies much family land will continue with respect to this landholding: "for you could not make will for half an acre of land, so it just stay there and we all go in and pick off the land." There are five ancestral graves there and "anyone in the Family can be buried on the land." Because Eugene's maternal Old Family overlaps with the Anderson Old Family in Martha Brae (chapter 5), those Martha Brae villagers also have rights to this family land in Granville.

Eugene's paternal Old Family is likewise traced back to an emancipated slave, his great-grandfather, who bought half an acre from Knibb. This too is regarded as family land for the ex-slave's descendants, some of whom lived elsewhere in the village (e.g., Eugene and his paternal uncle both lived on purchased land) but many of whom had migrated. At the time of my research no one lived on the family land, though Eugene's paternal grandparents once lived there and there are family tombs. The land is regarded as the family burial ground, and any of the great-grandfather's descendants "could use the land and pick anything." At the time, Eugene's paternal uncle cultivated the land. Both Eugene and his uncle intended to leave their own small purchased house yards for their descendants, demonstrating the ongoing process of creating family land in Trelawny's free villages.

The case of Stanley Smith, the tenant on the Wallace family land, further illustrates the theme of overlapping Old Families in Granville that also overlap with unrestricted cognatic descent groups in Martha Brae. Stanley, who had established some independence from his family lands, traces descent in two overlapping landholding cognatic descent groups in Granville. One of these further overlaps with the Minto Old Family, the central cognatic landholding kin group in Martha Brae (chapter 5). Moreover, his paternal grandfather, who died in 1992 and could have been buried on family land in Granville, was interred at his own request in the Martha Brae cemetery. In 1995 both Stanley and his landlord Sam remarked to me that there was an emerging (though as yet sporadic) trend for Granville villagers to be buried in Martha Brae. In addition, they had heard that there may soon be a Trelawny Parish Council prohibition on yard burial in Granville, as was introduced to parts of Kettering and to Martha Brae earlier in the twentieth century.[54] In 2000, however, the traditional burial pattern still persisted in Granville, where the landscape (like that of The Alps, Refuge, and parts of Kettering) is embroidered with graves of varying style and age (sunken earth graves, boulders, cairns, old stone tombs, and modern concrete vaults) charting continuity and change in the free village, as well as both the passing and the augmentation of its generations.

Some elderly members of Granville's Old Families remarked on the consolidation of the village's name from the colloquial "Grumble Pen" to Knibb's "Granville." I cite four such accounts:

> Granville was a property [estate], and they cut it up and sell it to the black people; here and Refuge, they were bought at one time. The place was not called Granville, but Grumble Pen, and from the people come occupy it, them call it Granville.

> My father's mother told me that they used to call this district Grumble Pen, as worries is always in the district. My grand-aunt live over 90 years, tell me same thing.

> I know Granville when it was called Grumble Pen. Name told it from generation. My parents had eighteen of us, and we were told so, but some in the village don't know this. It was one property . . . and one man named Parson Knibb — and through the time was slavery — Mr. Knibb go to En-

gland to ask the King, and cut up this place and everybody place. The poor people grumbled and Mr. Knibb cut off a piece from York Pen and call it Grumble Pen, but we just call it now Granville.[55]

According to what we come and hear our people, older ones say, this district here was in the time of Mr. Knibb, and they were quarelling to get a piece of land to build a home — the people did not have anywhere — so him as minister, the people go to him . . . they get to have a spot each. The younger ones call it Granville now.

The oral tradition on the evolution of the name of the free village, from Grumble Pen to Granville, highlights the struggle for land that occurred at the postemancipation peasant-plantation interface including the land disputes among the land-hungry peasantry, issues that persist to the present.

This central theme of gaining and retaining access to land by ex-slaves and their descendants, which recurs in Granville and the other Trelawny Baptist free villages that I studied, lies at the heart of Martha Brae's Afro-creole cultural history. However, in contrast to The Alps, Refuge, Kettering, and Granville, where the colonial Baptist Church created captive congregations through imposed land settlements on marginal land, Baptist ex-slaves themselves appropriated the colonial town of Martha Brae, which had been at the center of the slave plantation heartlands of Jamaica. Yet, though glimpses of the establishment of the four Trelawny Baptist-founded villages where I conducted fieldwork are apparent in colonial publications, there is little indication of the transformation of Martha Brae in either the received history of the island and the settlement or in Baptist records. Chapters 4–5 uncover and interpret this transformation, drawing on a combination of my historical research and anthropological fieldwork, including the Martha Brae free villagers' oral tradition.

CHAPTER FOUR

The Free Village
of Martha Brae

The transformation of Martha Brae from a Euro-Caribbean planter town to an Afro-creole peasant village, effected by emancipated slaves, drew on the strong traditions of slave opposition and resistance in west-central Jamaica, combined with an ambivalent alliance with the Baptist mission church. This transformation took place at the vanguard of the flight from the estates throughout Trelawny, Jamaica, the British West Indies, and the Caribbean region; was consolidated within the wider context of Caribbean postslavery peasantization, especially the free-village system in Jamaica and Trelawny; and was triggered by draconian planter policy and legislation, particularly in Trelawny, regarding land and labor following emancipation. This momentous metamorphosis of Martha Brae contrasted with the "unsuccessful attempt by the ex-slaves to re-establish the old ruined town of Dauphin" in the British Windward Island of St. Lucia (Henshall 1976:38); it was facilitated by Falmouth's eclipse of colonial Martha Brae as Trelawny's capital in the early nineteenth century.

The Transformation of Martha Brae

Historical sources give little indication of either the changing nature of Martha Brae or its significance as a free village at the heart of the Caribbean peasant-plantation interface. Paradoxically, some initial clues to this transformation can be found in Eurocentric accounts of Trelawny's history, which regard the settlement as a colonial Georgian town and dismiss the contemporary village as "a mere scatter of houses" (Wright and White 1969:46; Black 1979).[1] In a discussion of taxation, revenues, expenditures, and financial economies and savings by the Trelawny Parish Vestry between 1838 and 1840, Dan Ogilvie (1954:24–25) reported that "Messrs. Reeves, Vermont and Anderson, assisted by the Parish Solicitor, were ap-

127

pointed a committee to make enquiries respecting sundry lots of land at Martha Brae belonging to the Parish and that they furnish a diagram of the same if necessary. Quite a few of the holdings at Martha Brae, the property of the Vestry, were taken by squatters due to sheer neglect on the part of the Officers responsible."[2] Ray Fremmer (1968) similarly noted: "As early as 1839, many of the lots at Martha Brae which were the property of the Vestry had been taken over by squatters, so far had the town declined out of neglect. A committee headed by the Parish Solicitor was formed to furnish the Vestry with a diagram as a first step in retrieving the captured lots." These accounts, related from the perspective of the vestry, indicate that the beginnings of the appropriation of the planter town by ex-slaves occurred through squatting in the immediate aftermath of full freedom between 1838 and 1840.

This period of squatting by emancipated slaves in Martha Brae coincided with the earliest stage of the postslavery flight from the Jamaican plantations and the Baptist free-village system in Trelawny, sponsored by Baptist missionary William Knibb in Falmouth just one and a half miles from Martha Brae. In 1838 the parish's first Baptist free village of New Birmingham/The Alps had been established in southeastern Trelawny, followed by Wilberforce/Refuge six miles southeast of Falmouth. By 1841 Kettering existed nine miles east of Falmouth, and by 1845 Granville/Grumble Pen had been founded two and a half miles inland from Falmouth and one mile southwest of Martha Brae.

The transformation of Martha Brae through squatting was clearly different from the purchase and subdivision of marginal properties for Baptist free villages by Knibb. However, the strategy of squatting had been used successfully by runaway slaves in the nearby Cockpit Country and provided the framework for the 1739 Leeward Maroon treaty, which gave the rebel slaves legal land rights and consolidated the maroon communities of Trelawny Town in St. James and Accompong Town in St. Elizabeth. Oral tradition in Accompong's neighboring postemancipation Moravian community of Ockbrook/Aberdeen regarding initial settlement by ex-slaves through squatting around 1845 and subsequent colonial planter government land retrieval, registration, sale, and taxation, in combination with my archival and field research, suggests a further parallel with the transformation of Martha Brae: that is, the retrieval of land by a planter vestry concerned with taxation would have laid the basis for the resale of land. The recent (1990s–2001) process of surveying and subdividing Zion, Martha Brae's satellite squatter settlement on nearby Holland Plantation, by the Trelawny Parish Council (which succeeded the Parochial Board, successor to the vestry) with a view to land sales and taxation (discussed later in this chapter) provides a vivid illustration of the type of transformation that occurred less systematically in postslavery Martha Brae.

I have found no documentary evidence that the village of Martha Brae was established by the Baptist Church. Yet there are indications of Baptist involvement in the slave plantation communities surrounding the settlement and in Martha Brae itself around the time that slavery was abolished. Names of Martha Brae residents, as well as those from the surrounding sugar estates of Irving Tower and Holland, appear in the membership book of the Falmouth Baptist Church kept by William Knibb himself about the time of apprenticeship (and as early as 1831) and emancipation. In a letter from "Falmouth, Nov.10th, 1835" (quoted in Hinton 1847:218–20), Knibb referred to Martha Brae as a small village, and he mentioned nearby plantations emphasizing the large number of apprentices in Trelawny:

> The parish of Trelawney [*sic*] contains the greatest number of apprentices of any in the island, the children under six years of age alone numbering 8000 on the 1st of August, 1834, and the entire population of apprentices being about 27,000. Its destitution is such that I am not aware of one public school in the whole parish, except one or two small ones recently established.
>
> The town of Falmouth contains nearly 5000 inhabitants, and near it are situated the *small villages of Martha Brae, Salt Marsh, and the Rock*. Within three or four miles are a number of sugar estates and pasturage pens. It is in the town of Falmouth that I have purchased a piece of ground, in a central part, and have commenced the erection of a school-room. . . .
>
> *The apprentices connected with my church and congregation in the town, most of whom come from the country round, amount to full three thousand*, and at the laying of the corner-stone twelve hundred children of apprentices were present. (218–19, emphases mine)

The foundation stone of the school in Falmouth had been laid on 26 September 1835 by two magistrates, J. R. Vermont and John Kelly (Hinton 1847:217–18), whose Kelly surname serves as a title for one of Martha Brae's Old Families (chapter 5).[3] The school, named the Suffield School "in honour of Lord Suffield, a large proprietor who had promoted beneficial measures," was opened in March 1836 (Hinton 1847:220). The two magistrates, "Messrs. Kelly and Vermont," also offered to collect contributions for the school, which provided a "British System of Education" (*Falmouth Post*, 1, 8 June 1836).

All of this suggests that ex-slave apprentices from the neighboring estates of Holland and Irving Tower were already appropriating the site of colonial Martha Brae by 1835, and that they were closely involved with Knibb's Baptist church and school in Falmouth. This link was highlighted during my fieldwork, when the William Knibb School was established at the site of the slave village on Holland Plantation, across the road from Martha Brae. Although New Birmingham was Trelawny's first *Baptist church-founded* village established in 1838, the appropriation of colonial Martha Brae and its transformation into a free village by *ex-slaves* may have predated the founding of New Birmingham. The free village of Martha Brae, consolidated at the vanguard of the flight from the estates, may thus deserve a place in Jamaican history equivalent to Sligoville, St. Catherine, organized during the period of apprenticeship. Moreover, the transformation of Martha Brae by the apprentices themselves, without the direct assistance of the Baptist Church, more fully demonstrates the agency of the ex-slaves than do the Baptist-founded villages of New Birmingham and Sligoville.

The association of emancipated slaves in Martha Brae with the Baptist Church is again indicated by local records of 1839 and 1843. A "Report of Working Classes Connected with the Church under the Pastoral Care of the Rev. William Knibb, Baptist Missionary," appearing in the *Falmouth Post* of 27 March 1839, includes a list of men, women, and children "At Work" and "Not at Work" on Holland and Irving Tower sugar estates bordering Martha Brae. Just one and a half miles inland from Falmouth, Martha Brae was in the plantation heartlands between Falmouth and Granville, which was founded by Knibb in 1845 (with only a prayer house) to provide a satellite congregation for the Falmouth Baptist Church. In a letter to his absent wife Mary from "Falmouth, August 4, 1843," Knibb, referring to the annual emancipation celebrations on 1 August "at Falmouth and its dependent churches," wrote of a parade from Martha Brae village to the Baptist chapel in Falmouth:

> Today I have returned from our August festivities, and they have never been so interesting since 1838. . . . You would have enjoyed the Falmouth scene. The chapel was crowded to excess. . . . *Several hundred horsemen with palms in their hands, assembled at Martha's [sic] Brae,* and a little before twelve o'clock I went in the shandy adorned with ribbons. . . . In we came round by the wharf . . . and to the chapel. . . . The children paraded the streets, and the hurrahs of the good folks were deafening. (Quoted in Hinton 1847:458–59, emphasis mine)

The presence of an old Baptist Prayer House in Martha Brae, which the oldest villagers (including members of the Kelly Old Family) remembered as always having been there and which oral history locates as far back as the late nineteenth century and probably earlier, suggests that postslavery Martha Brae provided a similar satellite congregation to that of Granville, through the "Class System," for the parent Baptist chapel in Falmouth, especially as oral tradition states that land in Martha Brae was acquired by the Baptist Church in the 1840s (chapter 5). Such a satellite relationship would also have had similarities with the Stewarton Prayer House in relation to the Refuge Baptist Church.[4] Today, most Martha Brae villagers are Baptist and regularly attend the William Knibb Memorial Baptist Church, in Falmouth (as well as the Revival tabernacle in Martha Brae), a church that replaced the chapel, built by Knibb, that was destroyed by a hurricane in 1944 (Wright 1973:244–45). Moreover, throughout my fieldwork (1968–2001), the Martha Brae Baptists have been categorized as "Class 5" of the Falmouth Baptist Circuit, just as the Refuge church is now part of the Kettering Baptist Circuit.

After the abolition of slavery Martha Brae, situated on a ridge of marginal land where the two sugar plantations of Holland and Irving Tower adjoin, would (from a colonial perspective) have provided a particularly appropriate location for a reservoir of ex-slave plantation labor. On the eve of emancipation, in 1837, Holland and Irving Tower had 120 and 81 apprentices respectively (Craton 1978:43), whereas Hague Estate, just beyond the Persian Wheel and river bridge at Martha Brae, had 174 apprentices (44). The concern about a continuing plantation labor supply was an explicit part of Knibb's free-village strategy, for he was a reformer, not a revolutionary. In 1842 Knibb informed the Select Committee at Exeter Hall, England, that "whenever I had to do with buying a place for a free village, I have tried to select a spot surrounded by a number of estates," illustrating this policy with reference to Kettering — "a Pimento Walk at Duncans in Trelawny which was surrounded with sugar estates" — established the previous year, 1841 (British House of Commons, "Select Committee on West India Colonies, 1842," quoted in Robotham 1977:49). Refuge, even closer to Martha Brae, was another example of this strategy used in 1838, as Granville (Martha Brae's neighboring village) would be in 1845. The postemancipation village of Martha Brae offered an even more "ideal" site for a plantation labor supply, as it was located at the very core of the plantation heartlands of northwestern Trelawny and within a few miles of the Tharp Estates, which persisted until 1867 (Tenison 1971:22). Martha Brae's oral tradition reflects an acute awareness of this continuing role as a reservoir of labor for surrounding estates, and the ethnography of the free village further underlines this theme.

In addition to Knibb's 1835 reference to Martha Brae as a small village and the indications of ex-slaves squatting there between 1838 and 1840, there is brief historical evidence that the village of Martha Brae was firmly established, with a population of 372 persons, by 1861 (D. Hall 1959:211). This date coincides with the watershed between the "Period of Establishment" (1838–60) and the "Period of Consolidation" (1861–1900) of the British West Indian peasantry (Marshall 1985), which was constrained in Jamaica by the reestablishment of the plantation system throughout the island from the 1880s (Satchell 1990, 1999). The oral histories of Martha Brae's Old Families that directly descend from the ex-slave settlers of the free village, reinforced by my anthropological fieldwork and Trelawny land tax records, provide detailed insight into this process of transformation, establishment, and consolidation (chapter 5). The ethnography of Martha Brae (the remainder of this chapter and chapters 6–8) reveals further evidence of such consolidation. This ethnographic study also demonstrates the increasing land scarcity that the villagers have faced during the "Period of Saturation" of the anglophone Caribbean peasantry since 1900 and that Jamaican peasants have experienced since the 1880s (Marshall 1985; Stolberg and Wilmot 1992), a situation further reflected in the overflow of the village into its satellite squatter settlement of Zion between 1968 and 2001.

Martha Brae's Contemporary Context

The free village of Martha Brae now has a population of at least eight hundred persons in around 170 households,[5] most of whom reside on a small ridge of about thirty acres (the site of the colonial town) surrounded by estates. After emancipation, Trelawny continued to be one of the island's chief sugar-producing parishes throughout the nineteenth and twentieth centuries and into the new millennium. Plantations still monopolize the parish's fertile intermontane valleys and coastal plains, but many of the former ninety-four individually owned sugar estates are now tributaries of two vast consolidated corporate sugar plantation *centrals* or "land-and-factory-combines." Other estates remain as "properties" or large farms either raising livestock (especially cattle), monocroping in sugarcane or fruit (such as papayas) for the world economy, or growing winter vegetables for export.

In addition to these themes of parochial continuity and change from the slavery and postemancipation past, Trelawny's contemporary agrarian structure should be seen within the wider context of Jamaica's national economy — in which the rural sector continues to play a major role. After emancipation the plantation economy was reestablished throughout the colony by 1900; in the twentieth century the island's agrarian structure remained essentially the same despite government freehold land settlement schemes on marginal land in the 1930s and 1940s, decolonization and political independence in 1962, and Project Land Lease in the 1970s (Stolberg and Wilmot 1992; Besson 1995e). In the 1990s agriculture comprised 46 percent of land use in Jamaica: 503,240 hectares of the island's 1.1 million hectares or 10,940 square kilometers.[6] Within this framework, large-scale monoculture (on flat, fertile land) for the world economy continued to take precedence over small-scale diversified farming (on hilly, marginal land) for local use, as Marjorie Allen-Vassell and Wintlett Browne (1992:53–54) explain:

> There are about 200,000 farms in Jamaica. These range from the very small, that is less than .4 hectare, to farms that are thousands of hectares in size. Most of our farms are under 2 hectares. . . . The small farms, however, occupy only 16 per cent of the agricultural land. These farmers produce most of the crops that are sold locally. They practice both multi-cropping or mixed cropping and mixed farming. . . . The large farms make up only 1 per cent of the total number of farms but they are on 60 per cent of the agricultural lands. These farms tend to practice mono-culture . . . mainly for export.

Table 1 provides a detailed breakdown of Jamaica's agrarian structure by parish and size. To summarize, of the island's 214,297 farmers, 201,200 had less than 10 acres (with 176,418 having less than 5 acres and 105,075 less than 2 acres); only 13,097 farmers had 10 acres or more, and only 532 had over 100 acres. This structure was mirrored in Trelawny: of the parish's 15,463 farmers, 14,891 had less than 10 acres (with 13,557 having less than 5 acres and 8,772 less than 2 acres); only 572 had 10 acres or more, and only 25 had over 100 acres.

This representation of the agrarian structure, which has continued into the twenty-first century, does not entirely reveal the land concentration in Trelawny, which contains two of Jamaica's eight remaining land-and-factory combines (and two of the island's ten vast consolidated sugar estates, all now either owned by or leased to the private sector), namely, Long Pond Estates and Hampden Estates.[7] Long Pond (which was owned, as Trelawny Estates, by the Seagrams multinational from the 1950s until nationalization in 1978 and which has mostly been divested by the state to the private sector since 1994), comprises 20,000 acres on the fertile lands of the northeastern plateau flanking the hilly village of Refuge. At the end of the twentieth

TABLE 1. Number of Farmers by Parish and Size of Farm (in Acres), Jamaica, 1988

Parish	0–.5	.5–1	1–2	2–3	3–5	5–10	10–25	25–50	50–100	>100	Total
St. Andrew	1,987	1,071	1,637	1,206	1,195	782	255	37	22	8	8,200
St. Thomas	1,874	1,454	2,640	1,967	1,977	1,016	397	63	20	30	11,438
Portland	1,105	1,296	2,912	2,195	2,357	1,329	635	128	63	47	12,067
St. Mary	2,863	2,867	5,402	4,087	4,311	3,071	1,043	176	81	82	23,983
St. Ann	1,442	2,091	3,976	2,850	2,936	2,043	918	182	50	49	16,537
Trelawny	1,477	2,885	4,410	2,514	2,271	1,334	437	75	35	25	15,463
St. James	1,958	1,977	2,809	1,617	1,358	1,183	531	94	37	36	11,600
Hanover	1,110	1,254	2,139	1,619	1,781	998	470	78	24	45	9,518
Westmoreland	2,300	2,756	3,719	2,584	2,505	2,055	1,080	196	65	55	17,315
St. Elizabeth	1,653	2,668	4,709	3,299	3,118	2,236	1,029	234	53	27	19,026
Manchester	1,149	2,717	5,828	4,259	3,874	2,642	1,189	221	52	21	21,952
Clarendon	4,404	3,651	6,408	4,559	4,700	3,541	1,151	162	55	51	28,682
St. Catherine	2,982	1,936	3,559	2,881	3,323	2,552	1,021	155	51	56	18,516
Total	26,304	28,623	50,148	35,637	35,706	24,782	10,156	1,801	608	532	214,297

Source: Ministry of Agriculture, Data Bank and Evaluation Division, "Farmers' Register, 1988." Kingston, Jamaica, 3 September 1991, p. 1.

century Hampden Estates, a few miles directly inland from Martha Brae and Granville, was owned by a Scots-creole and expatriate family corporation, whose ancestor Dr. George MacFarquhar Lawson (who was entombed in the plantation's family burial ground) in the last of five ascending generations purchased Hampden from Sir William Stirling-Maxwell (grandnephew of Archibald Stirling, the Scots planter who established Hampden sugar plantation in the eighteenth century) in 1852. Lawson's grandson, who inherited the plantation, consolidated Hampden with seven smaller adjoining plantations — among them, Gayle's Valley, Golden Grove, and Western Favel — and expanded the distillery. Hampden Estates, which became a limited liability company in 1949, dominates the fertile Queen of Spain's Valley limestone basin (beneath the northern foothills of the Cockpit Country) straddling northwestern Trelawny and northeastern St. James. The parochial boundary runs through the sugar factory, but approximately two-thirds of Hampden's seven thousand acres are in Trelawny.

Like Long Pond, Hampden Estates produces sugar and rum for the world economy. Also similar to Long Pond, Hampden exports its sugar through the Jamaican sugar industry mainly to Tate and Lyle in London.[8] But unlike Lond Pond, which sells much of its rum to North America, Hampden exports 90 percent of its rum to Europe (Germany, Holland, and the United Kingdom), and, in contrast to Long Pond's world-famous bottled rums, much of Hampden's rum is used for blending in the rum and food industries. Trelawny villagers who produce sugarcane as a cash crop sell their canes to the Long Pond and Hampden factories; in fact, 50 percent of the sugarcane ground by Hampden Estates is supplied in this way.

Despite the persistence of plantation agriculture, the Jamaican economy diversified after World War II through the manufacturing, bauxite mining, and tourist industries. Most manufacturing takes place in urban areas, especially in the capital city of Kingston, but some small factories operate in rural areas such as Trelawny — for example, the garment factory at Hague and the Carib Metal Factory near Zion, both in the vicinity of Martha Brae. In both bauxite mining and tourism, the island plays an important international role. Jamaica is "the world's second most abundant producer of bauxite, after Australia, and the leading exporter of alumina," the white-powdered aluminum oxide derived from bauxite ore (*Caribbean Eye Exhibition* 1997). Bauxite ore, and its processed alumina, is opencast mined by four companies: Kaiser, Jamalcan, Clarendon Alumina Productions, Ltd. (CAP), and Alpart. All were originally foreign-owned, but the Jamaican state now has part ownership in these companies, which rent or lease large tracts of land for forty-year periods. Bauxite is found in the red earth covering limestone in the island's central parishes including Trelawny, but the main bauxite operations are in Trelawny's neighboring parishes to the east and south: St. Ann, St. Elizabeth, Manchester, and Clarendon. Alumina and bauxite are exported to the United States, Canada, Norway, Sweden, the United Kingdom, and the former Soviet Union for the manufacture of aluminum.

Jamaica is one of the main tourist destinations in the so-called Third World. This industry, which dates back to the nineteenth century but escalated after World War II, is based especially in the North Coast parishes of St. James, Trelawny, St. Ann, and St. Mary; the northeastern coast of Portland; and the western coasts of Hanover and Westmoreland around Negril. In Trelawny, the Trelawny Beach Hotel outside Falmouth and the Silver Sands Hotel near Duncans/Kettering exemplify this theme, and by 1995 there was also a large hotel complex, the Grand Lido Braco Hotel, between Duncans and Rio Bueno on a part of Braco Estate. Some plantations near Martha Brae have also become the basis of tourism. Southfield Estate is now the site of Rafters' Village (owned by the Jamaica Tourist Board but divested to the private sector in 1995), which controls rafting on the Martha Brae River and is one of the island's three main river-rafting projects.[9] Good Hope Estate runs an exclusive Great House hotel, set in the now 2,000-acre plantation/pen, financed by Jamaican merchant capital and advertised in international tourist brochures — including rafting trips to the river bridge at the eastern edge of Martha Brae.

A large number of Jamaica's tourists are from North America and Europe, and the industry (a significant part of which continues to be controlled by foreign interests) is especially vulnerable to fluctuations in the world economy and to bad publicity in the international press. In addition, Jamaican tourism is now experiencing substantial competition from within the Caribbean region itself — most recently from the burgeoning tourist industry of neighboring Cuba. In Trelawny, Falmouth is midway between the two major North Coast tourist resorts of Montego Bay in St. James and Ocho Rios in St. Ann. Large foreign-controlled resorts, such as the multinational Holiday Inn and locally owned Sandals Hotels on the outskirts of Montego Bay, are only a few miles from Falmouth and Martha Brae; Falmouth itself has recently been targeted by the private sector for heritage-tourist development based on its colonial Georgian architecture.[10] The Jamaican tourist industry, notably that of its world-famous North Coast, not only reinforces the land scarcity constraining the island's peasantry (especially in the immediate vicinity of resort areas — Martha Brae, for example, is only one and a half miles inland), but also inflates land prices. Whereas land was (and still is) measured in square chains in Trelawny's postemancipation villages, it is now measured in square meters in Martha Brae's squatter settlement of Zion, which is only about two miles from the coast.

Within these wider contexts of continuing and changing land monopoly in the island and the parish, Trelawny's free villages stand fast — hemmed in on marginal land by properties and plantations and by the escalating tourist industry. "Lawyer's" land sales from a part of Holland Estate to the villagers of Martha Brae in the late 1940s, and his subdivision of the Maxfield property among Granville villagers in the early 1960s,[11] enabled these two neighboring villages to fortify this foothold.

Multiple Tenures and Internal Differentiation

Martha Brae's peasant economy manifests the symptoms of land scarcity at the Trelawny peasant-plantation/tourist interface, as the villagers struggle to gain and retain "land of their own" (Farley 1964:52). These manifestations of the persisting land monopoly surrounding the village include miniscule house yards measured in square chains; insufficient land for cultivation, reflected in fragmented farms and the dichotomy of house yards and provision grounds; "penny capitalist" peasant marketing; occupational multiplicity; migration; and multiple small-scale legal and customary land tenures.

This land scarcity is also reflected in the internal differentiation of the peasant community based on the interrelated variables of genealogy, place of birth, and varying access to and tenure of village land, a differentiation that existed to some extent even in the postemancipation era among the former slaves. The villagers themselves classify their population into two main categories: "Born Ya" and "Strangers." Born Ya are those born in Martha Brae, whereas Strangers are immigrants, generally from other Trelawny peasant communities farther inland.[12] These two categories are further differentiated internally. Born Ya are divided into the Old Families, the unrestricted cognatic family lines descended (through males and females) from the ex-slaves who established the free village and who form the continuing core of the village population, and those who, though born in Martha Brae, are not descended from those ex-slaves but from more recent settlers. Strangers are distinguished according to whether they have recently arrived in Martha Brae or have lived there for many years, in which case (as the villagers put it) "they come almost like Martha Brae citizen."

The pattern of land tenure in Martha Brae both reflects and contributes

Holland Estate bordering Martha Brae in the late twentieth century. Photo by Jean Besson.

to this classification. Born Ya are holders of most of the village land, whereas Strangers tend to be landless tenants. Among Born Ya the core of village land is held as family land by the Old Families, which have inherited such rights from the ex-slave founders of the village who purchased land in Martha Brae. Other Born Ya hold family land of more recent origin, transmitted from immigrants who bought land in the peasant community or occasionally have individually inherited land. The majority of Strangers have no freehold land in Martha Brae, though some have rights to family land in other Trelawny villages. A few of the longer-settled Strangers have, however, managed to buy small plots in the village (such as land forfeited by Old Families to either the Parochial Board or the Parish Council) or at the edge of Martha Brae (from Lawyer in the 1940s), and this contributes to their classification as being "almost like Martha Brae citizen." In some cases such land is already being transformed to family land, a process paralleled among some members of Old Families who have recently managed to buy land of their own. Most Strangers, however, especially recent settlers, just "cotch" in the village as tenants of its landholding population, either renting a small "house-spot" in a yard for a chattel cottage or renting accommodations. The land-tenure pattern in Martha Brae is therefore complex: family land transmitted from the ex-slave settlers of the free village; more recently created family land; individually inherited land; purchased land,

A family-land house yard in Martha Brae. Photo by Jean Besson.

sometimes in the process of transformation to family land; house-spot cash tenancy; and landless tenants in rented rooms or tenant yards.

Yard tenures are further elaborated by the tenure of provision grounds beyond the village. Such ground tenures include family land, purchased land, cash tenancy (rental and longer leases), squatting, and "free land" on plantations.[13] There are also "landless farms" (Floyd 1979:87), created by grazing livestock (goats and cattle) on either plantation land or along the sides of the Granville-Falmouth road. Such landless farming, which is now sometimes a form of squatting, undoubtedly originates in the free pasturage that the masters permitted their protopeasant slaves (Patterson 1973:221; Higman 1998:202).[14] The problem of land scarcity or "land room" (as the villagers describe it) is generally most acute for immigrants to Martha Brae, whose escalating land crisis is manifested in the establishment and growth of Zion — the large satellite squatter settlement on land owned by the Trelawny Parish Council on neighboring Holland Plantation. Zion itself is now over-flowing through landless farming on other areas of Holland Estate, as evidenced in signs erected against such livestock "trespass."

Within this mosaic of multiple small-scale legal and customary tenures (which reflect continuity with the range of strategies used by protopeasants, maroons, and emancipated slaves to acquire land), two central and related themes can be identified: the strong desire for the acquisition of freehold land and the tendency for purchased land to be transformed into family land.

The Institution of Family Land

A complex of interrelated features defines family land in Martha Brae and other Trelawny free villages as a cultural or social structural system.[15] Family land is a customary transformation of freehold tenure, which contrasts in several ways with colonially derived freeholds in Jamaica's official legal code. Contrasting features include the size of landholdings, the nature of land rights, the modes of validating and acquiring land rights, intestacy rules, house tenure, and land use.

Legal freeholds, introduced to Jamaica by the colonial planter class and still pervasive in the national market economy, tend to be large-scale landholdings (but may also include small plots of purchased land) that are private property, alienable, marketable in the capitalist economy, validated by legal documents, and acquired through purchase, deed of gift, or testate inheritance. As elsewhere in the Commonwealth Caribbean, intestacy was traditionally defined on the basis of Eurocentric "legitimacy," male precedence, primogeniture, and legal marriage. Houses on legal freeholds are considered part of the real estate, and land use is governed by the capitalist values of maximizing profits and production in the world economy.

Customary family land contrasts with legal freeholds in all respects. Generally small in size and often only a few square chains, family land is regarded as the inalienable corporate estate of the purchaser's descending family line. Rights to family land are essentially validated through oral tradition and, though initially acquired through purchase, are primarily transmitted through intestacy. The definition of intestate heirs differs markedly from the traditional legal system: it is based on unrestricted cognatic descent, whereby all children and their descendants are considered heirs regardless of their gender, birth order, "legitimacy," or residence, and marriage is not regarded as a basis for inheritance. Houses, as distinguished from family land, are considered movable property that may be individually or jointly owned. Land use is not governed by the values of capitalist monoculture but reflects creole economic and symbolic values: family land is the spatial dimension of the family line, mirroring its identity and continuity; it provides freehold usufructuary rights, house sites, a spot for a kitchen garden, fruit trees from which to pick, and a place to visit or return to—especially in time of need. Before the introduction of the free-village cemetery in the early twentieth century by the Trelawny Parochial Board (drawing on "The Burial within Towns' Limits Act" of 1875), family land in Martha Brae also provided family burial grounds. This is still the case in some other Trelawny villages, including The Alps, Refuge, neighboring Granville, and parts of Kettering.

Family land is found not only in Trelawny's free villages, but also in peasant communities throughout Jamaica and the non-Hispanic Caribbean where it is sometimes known as "generation property," "children's property," or "succession ground." Explanations of the origins and persistence of these kin-based tenures are controversial and have conventionally been construed in terms of passive ancestral or colonial cultural retentions. In her pioneering studies Edith Clarke (1953, 1966),[16] in addition to suggesting that Jamaican family land resulted from the misinterpretation of land grants by former slaves, attributed it to African cultural survivals, namely, the principles of joint inheritance, equal rights of all the family, and the inalienability of land. More specifically, she argued that family land derived from the Ashanti kinship system, relating "the dictum that succession to family land was either 'through the blood' or 'by the name'" (Clarke 1966:48, see also 1953:112) to the Ashanti concepts of *abusua* (clan; blood; derived from the female parent; matrilineal descent) and *ntoro* (spirit; semen; derived from the male parent; patrilineally transmitted) respectively. However, this thesis does not stand up to closer scrutiny, for the Ashanti have a system of *unilineal* descent with "complementary filiation": they have primary *matrilineal* "corporate" descent groups (traced through women only), which hold and transmit land rights and in which men are prominent as mothers' brothers and sisters' sons, and secondary *patrilineal* "noncorporate" descent groups (traced through men only), which stress father-son spiritual ties but are not involved in landholding (Fox 1967:101–2, 132; Goody 1969). In contrast, family land throughout the Caribbean is based on *nonunilineal or cognatic* descent, traced through both women and men (i.e., "through the blood *and* by the name") within the *same* descent group, a system that typifies the Pacific region and some East African societies. Despite this difference, Charles Carnegie (1987) and Peter Espeut (1992) adopted Clarke's West African explanation of Jamaican family land; similar arguments have been used elsewhere in the Caribbean—for example, by Michael Craton (1987) for Bahamian customary tenures.

Caribbean kin-based tenures have also been variously attributed to survivals from English, French, and Roman-Dutch colonial legal codes. Sidney Greenfield (1960) accounted for Barbadian family land with reference to the English cultural heritage, namely, the legal technique of the "settlement" (positing that it was borrowed by the Barbadian planters, then by the peasantry, from the English aristocracy) and the associated "seed to seed" clause whereby land was entailed to all the "seed of the body" in perpetuity. Writers in the Francophone Caribbean have explained family land in terms of French cultural heritage. Michael Horowitz (1992:29–30), for instance, attributes family land in Martinique to the Napoleonic Code of equal inheritance by all children. In the same way, Herman Finkel (1971:299), D. C. Mathurin (1967:4), Carleen O'Loughlin (1968:102), and Janet Momsen (1972:103), commenting on the St. Lucian case, ascribed it to the legacy of the island's French occupation, and O'Loughlin (1968:102) made a similar point for family land in Dominica. The Afro-Guyanese tenure of "children's property" has been linked to the Roman-Dutch property code persisting from the period of Dutch colonization: specifically, to the Roman-Dutch principle of joint rights in undivided land (R. T. Smith 1971:245, 254–55, 1990). In addition, Peter Wilson (1995:56), citing Edith Clarke (1957), has attributed family land in Providencia to the island's Jamaican (and therefore "Ashanti") cultural heritage. Meanwhile, Michael Smith (1956b:138, 1960:42), from a nonretentionist perspective, explained family land in Carriacou as a functional adaptation to the island's social structure.

If one wished to pursue a cultural retention approach in the case of Martha Brae, family land could conceivably be attributed to the Celtic culture of the Scottish planters in Trelawny during slavery, as Scottish and Irish settlers abounded throughout Jamaica and elsewhere in the British West Indies (Sheridan 1977; Karras 1992; Dunn 2000). The traditional Scottish clan was a landholding kin group based on cognatic reckoning, and among the Tory islanders of the Celtic fringe a similar system of landholding cognatic descent groups still functions as a living fossil of the ancient Irish "rundale" system (Fox 1966, 1967, 1978).

Such explanations for cultural survival (African, English, Celtic, Roman-Dutch, and French), however, are piecemeal, inconsistent, and inadequate: they focus on specific territories only, whereas family land exists widely among Caribbean peasantries; they provide conflicting evidence; and (except for Michael Smith's), they do not consider the historical and contemporary socioeconomic contexts of the New World societies in which these tenures have evolved and persisted.

Instead, family land in Martha Brae and other Trelawny villages, as throughout Jamaica and the Caribbean region, is surely rooted in the dynamic *Caribbean* institution-building of both male and female protopeasant slaves who created customary cognatic descent-based systems for transmitting plantation house yards and provision grounds. In creating these cognatic systems, the slaves may well have drawn on the concept of landholding kin groups in West and Central Africa, but they transformed these groups from *restricted unilineal* to *unrestricted nonunilineal* descent in order to maximize scarce land rights and forbidden kinship lines, as they were now chattel slaves who were legally landless and kinless and property themselves. These creole tenures were then consolidated by emancipated slaves, who purchased land in the flight from the estates and stipulated that such property should not be sold but passed on to all of their descendants. The ex-slaves may also have drawn on African ideas about corporate kin-based landholding and on aspects of European legal systems to reinforce their Caribbean institution-building. Tiny family-land estates have been perpetuated, through both transmission and creation, by the descendants of chattel slaves to continue symbolizing their descent groups as well as maximizing such kinship lines and new freehold rights as bases of identity and security in light of persisting land monopoly and race-class stratification. The oral tradition of the Martha Brae peasantry and of other Trelawny free villagers highlights these central themes, and it is primarily through family land that these culturally distinctive peasant communities have endured to the present.

In Martha Brae (as elsewhere in Jamaica and the Caribbean region) this creole family-land institution, both rooted in and reflecting unrestricted cognatic descent, has overturned and reversed the principles of restricted colonial primogeniture on which the plantation system was based. The related Afro-creole use of the European surname of the founding slave/ex-slave ancestor who created the family land, as a title transmitted through both genders to designate the cognatic kin group (like the Minto, Thompson, Anderson, and Kelly Old Families considered in chapter 5), also represents the appropriation and reversal of a European institution, for the planters transmitted such surnames patrilineally and sometimes imposed them on their chattel slaves as a sign of ownership. Yet as Richard Burton (1999:46) notes in his illuminating but androcentric analysis of Afro-Caribbean names and naming as a form of creolization, taking "the name of the Other is less an obliteration or alienation, than it is a transmutation or renewal, of identity." In the case of Caribbean cognatic family land, European naming was appropriated and transformed to create *engendered* female as well as male identities.

Family land in Martha Brae (as elsewhere in Trelawny, Jamaica, and the Caribbean) may therefore be seen to represent especially clearly "*a mode of response* to the plantation system and its connotations, and *a mode of resistance* [or opposition] to imposed styles of life" — as Sidney Mintz (1989:132–33) portrayed Caribbean peasantries themselves. Cognatic family land is particularly "diagnostic" (Abu-Lughod 1990) of the dominance of colonial plantation primogeniture. The strength of Caribbean culture-building is most clearly manifested through the family-land institution and its oral traditions (chapters 3–5), and it is particularly around this creole institution that the Martha Brae villagers order their relationships and construct and perceive their world (chapters 4–8). Nevertheless, among the Martha Brae peasantry (as in other Jamaican villages), family land not only coexists with other forms of customary and legal tenures but also relates in complex ways to the island's agrarian legal code in the context of gaining and retaining access to land.

Family Land and the Legal Code

Sir Raymond Firth (1971), resolving the paradox of continuity and change or variation in society, distinguished between "social structure" and "social organization": "Structural forms set a precedent and provide a limitation to the range of alternatives possible. . . . In the aspect of social structure is to be found the continuity principle of society; in the aspect of [social] organization is to be found the variation or change principle — by allowing evaluation of situations and entry of individual choice" (40). In a discussion of the Hispanic Caribbean peasant institution of *compadrazgo* or Catholic ritual coparenthood, Mintz (1973) advanced a similar distinction between the "cultural" and the "social": "Culture and society — or better, the cultural and the social — are in some sense two sides of the same coin. They . . . should be considered different perspectives from which to view the same phenomenon or event. . . . *The social aspect of the peasant sector informs its culture — its historically-derived patterns of behaviour and its sets of values — with the element of manoeuvre*" (96, emphasis mine).

From these perspectives of distinguishing between structure and action, at least five variants of interplay between the customary family-land institution and the Jamaican legal-freehold system can be identified in Martha Brae: the imposition by the state of legal elements on family land; "crab antics," or the selection by individuals of aspects of the legal code to challenge the family-land system; individual selection of legal elements to reinforce, adjust, or create family land; the indirect reinforcement of family land by aspects of the legal code; and the transformation of areas of state law by customary family-land principles. Although the first two variants provide some support for Edith Clarke's (1953, 1966) interpretation of two totally conflicting systems of land tenure in Jamaica, the other three variants question this conclusion. In addition, the overall analysis contrasts with the plural society view that different "social sections" practice entirely different land-tenure systems in Caribbean societies (M. G. Smith 1956b, 1965a).[17] Such distinctions between structure and action provided the basis of my "intersystem" analysis of the relationship of family land to the Jamaican legal code, as well as my critique of the plural society theory regarding Caribbean tenurial systems and of Clarke's conflict-only approach, well before Carnegie (1987) and twenty years before Michaeline Crichlow (1994),[18] both of whom contended that I supported the plural society thesis. My claim was supported by Michel-Rolph Trouillot (1989). Long-term fieldwork in Martha Brae and comparative research in other Jamaican peasant communities, including free villages elsewhere in Trelawny, has consolidated and developed my perspective.[19]

Imposed Legal Elements

The state's imposition of elements from the Jamaican legal code on the Martha Brae villagers' customary family-land institution includes the requirement of obtaining a registered title for certain purposes, such as applying for a loan for house-building;[20] the registration of land for taxation; the alienation of land through forfeiture for nonpayment of taxes or as a result of registering on the Paupers' Roll of the Trelawny Parish Council (formerly the Parochial Board); and burial regulations. For example, William Tapper, a family-land trustee of the Thompson Old Family (chapter 5), had to obtain (with the consent of his absentee coheirs) a registered title for the family land created by his ex-slave paternal grandfather in order to borrow money from the Peoples' Cooperative Bank to build his "Farm House" on the land. Patrick Linton, the elderly trustee of the Love Old Family, told me that if he had not paid the taxes on his paternal family land it would have been confiscated, as the other coheirs were absent and paid no taxes. Likewise, some of the family lands created by emancipated slaves in Martha Brae's central family line (the Mintos) were reluctantly sold by the elderly female trustee to raise tax money to retain the most precious portions of the family estate. In a similar vein the Kelly family land, established by Rupert Bailey's great-great-grandfather, was forfeited to the Parochial Board when Rupert was a boy because his paternal grandmother died on the Paupers' Roll. Madeline Simmonds, another family-land trustee, had managed to save a plot of the Anderson family land from such a fate by paying back her pauper's child support to the Parish Council. The state regulation of family land is also reflected in the discontinuation of yard burial in Martha Brae, as well as more recently in parts of Kettering and, as some feel, imminently in neighboring Granville. Such changes result from the Burial within Towns' Limits Act, which enables Parish Councils to define the limits of, qualify, or discontinue burials in towns and villages.

"Crab Antics" and the Legal Code

Peter Wilson (1973), in his study of Providencia, coined the term "crab antics" to describe "behavior that resembles that of a number of crabs who, having been placed in a barrel, all try to climb out. But as one nears the top, the one below pulls him down in his own effort to climb. Only a particularly strong crab ever climbs out—the rest, in the long run, remain in the same place" (58). He argued that "crab antics manifest themselves in two attitudes toward land that islanders suggest are ingrained: covetousness and contentiousness" (58). Wilson based his analysis on a Providencian proverb: "You have a barrel of crab and they start to climb. The one that climbs highest, all the others are pulling him back. If he ever reached the top, he'd have to be a big, strong crab."[21] A similar proverb exists in Martha Brae, and a gendered concept of crab antics is useful in considering the land disputes that sometimes occur (among women as well as men) within unrestricted cognatic descent groups in the context of land scarcity. In that case, self-interested kin in a landholding corporation may draw on the legal system to challenge the unrestricted descent principle at the heart of family land. Such challenges aim to establish individual freehold rights to the corporate estate and thus to introduce exclusive restriction into the customary system. This may be attempted by obtaining a Squatter's Title (which may lead to sale of the land) based on long years of residence. Prior to 1976,[22] exclusive rights could also be established on the basis of "legitimacy." Though all children regardless of birth status have customary rights to family land, the Jamaican legal system traditionally included only legitimate children as intestate heirs.

The maternal family land of a woman I knew well provides a variation on the former strategy regarding residence. She asserted that a "craving" member of the kin group (her maternal aunt) had taken over the family-land estate. That elderly trustee had long been the only coheir of the senior generation residing on the land, and "she had papers drawn up" to obtain control. In discussions of this land with the trustee and her descendants, frequent references to this title were also made. The trustee sold part of the family estate to raise tax money to keep the remainder of the lands, and though the land retained continued to be regarded as family land by the entire descent group, this was now especially so in relation to one segment of the Old Family.

The case of Stella Senior illustrates an attempt to establish exclusion on the basis of legitimacy. Stella's father had two children: Stella, who was illegitimate, and her paternal half brother, who was legitimate. The father owned two plots in Martha Brae that, according to customary family-land principles, should have been inherited as a joint estate by his two children and their descendants. According to Stella, however, her brother wanted to inherit both plots and exclude her from the patrimony. His claim was based on the assertion that, as his father's only legitimate child, he was entitled to inherit his entire estate. The father, however, aware of his son's crab antics, himself drew on the legal code to ensure that both children would inherit in the usual way. He made a will designating both as his heirs, specifying that each should inherit a plot of land. Stella was now residing on her piece, while tenants lived on her brother's plot. Her father's strategy of making a will to reinforce customary principles also illustrates the next variant.

Selective Legal Reinforcement

Individuals may draw on the legal system not only to challenge the principles of customary tenure but also to reinforce, adjust, or create family land. The most widespread illustration of this variant is the recurring theme of creating family land from purchased land. This strategy was introduced by ex-slaves who bought land after emancipation and transformed it into family land for their descendants, thus reinforcing, by drawing on state law, the customary tenurial system created by the protopeasantry (which had itself transformed legal freehold). This appropriation of an aspect of the official legal system to create family land was conspicuous in the Baptist-founded free villages of Trelawny (such as The Alps, Refuge, Kettering, and Granville), where emancipated slaves bought land from the Baptist Church and then created customary freeholds. It also typified post-slavery Martha Brae, where ex-slaves bought land in the colonial town and created small family-land estates.

Contemporary Martha Brae villagers perpetuate the strategy of creating family land from purchased land. Victoria Robertson, a member of a central landholding Old Family, created her own family land for her children, several grandchildren, and great-grandchild from her small plot of purchased land at the edge of the village. Angela Armstrong, an immigrant to Martha Brae from the Trelawny village of Schawfield farther inland, transformed three acres of purchased land (bordering the cemetery) into family land for her eleven children, numerous grandchildren, and great-grandchildren. Keith Templar, a Stranger from another Trelawny village, managed to buy one-third of an acre in Martha Brae after living there for many years as a landless tenant. He, too, transformed this into family land for his nine children and other descendants. A variation on this theme is the practice of repurchasing family land forfeited to the Parish Council.

In addition to buying land and then transmitting it as family land, Martha Brae villagers (and their ancestors before them) have sometimes used the legal system to reinforce the customary family-land institution by creating such land from bought land through a written will, thereby adopting the legal element of testacy. In such cases a will may both ensure the life interest of a widowed spouse and limit the spouse's rights of inheritance to the land by stipulating its joint inheritance by the children. A will is also used in other ways to reinforce the customary system. For example, the customary rights of illegitimate children may be ensured through their inclusion in a will, or descendants' rights may be established by stipulating in a will that grandchildren, as well as children, should inherit.

The legal elements of surveying and subdividing of land may also be drawn on to ensure and adjust the customary principle of inheritance by all children; the subdivision of land may be accompanied by a proscription against alienation of the land so that it remains a variant of family land (which is usually undivided). The family land of Carl Vine (an elderly tenant-immigrant to Martha Brae who had spent most of his life as a casual laborer) in the parish of Westmoreland illustrates such a case. Carl's great-grandfather owned several acres that he stipulated in a will should be subdivided among his three sons. In the next generation Carl's paternal grandfather divided his share equally among his five children, three of whom were illegitimate. Carl's father, in turn, passed most of his share to his children, selling only a small portion. Carl himself and his siblings were planning a further subdivision and did not intend to sell the land. Their proscription against alienation applied especially to that part of their family land where their ancestors had been buried for generations.

Subdivision may also be used to adjust the customary system by combining the customary principle of inheritance by all children with the legal element of favoring a specific child. This is effected by giving one child an extra or larger piece of the land, as had occurred in the case of the family land of Joe Jackson (an immigrant to Martha Brae) in the parish of St. James. Joe's paternal grandparents' land was unequally divided among their four sons, according to their affection for each child, and their eldest son also received an extra portion. Other variations on this theme occur. For example, if an individual's estate comprises more than one parcel of land, one may be left to a particular child and the other jointly inherited by the remaining children. William Tapper's family estate in Martha Brae, created by his ex-slave paternal grandfather, is a case in point: one plot was inherited by the ex-slave's eldest granddaughter, and the other was jointly inherited by the rest of his grandchildren. Before the Status of Children Act of 1976, this variation could also be combined with the legal distinction between legitimate and illegitimate children by leaving one plot to each set of children. For instance, Frank Salmon, an immigrant to Martha Brae from another parish, had two plots of purchased land: one in his wife's natal village of Daniel Town, Trelawny, the other at the eastern edge of Martha Brae, purchased from Lawyer in the 1940s. Frank intended to leave his land in Daniel Town to his illegitimate son, whereas the Martha Brae land was for his six legitimate children. Another variation is for the land to be left as a joint estate for all the children, whereas the house (which may be movable property in the customary system) is allocated to a specific child.[23]

Indirect Legal Reinforcement

Aspects of the legal system also indirectly reinforce the customary family-land institution. The existence of a colonial and then a national land market, where land is surveyed and bought and sold through contract, has enabled the peasantry to buy land from which family land is constantly being created, as has occurred in Martha Brae and other Trelawny villages since emancipation. Purchases of land may also augment the total estate of a descent line and provide the basis for internal segmentation within the landholding family line. For example, in Martha Brae within the central family line, the Mintos, some members of the Old Family have bought land of their own. The concept of individual ownership promoted by the legal system is another factor that paradoxically reinforces the institution of family land, for it accelerates land purchase among the peasantry and contributes to the norm of neolocal residence (Mintz 1989:238–40; and chapter 6). It is thus a major element in the voluntary nonuse of family land by many coheirs, a factor that facilitates the functioning of the unrestricted cognatic descent system (chapter 8).

Joint ownership in undivided land has, however, long been a legal estate in Jamaica, and this aspect of the law may be drawn on to reinforce the family-land institution. In addition, the difficulties of conveying jointly held land when coheirs are scattered throughout the island and abroad provide a legal deterrent to the sale of family land, thus reinforcing the customary proscription against alienation. Likewise, any individual who wishes to take out a registered title for land (e.g., to sell property or to obtain a subsidy for a farmhouse or a loan to build a house) is first required by state law to advertise this intention to allow for possible objections from other claimants — as William Tapper of the Thompson Old Family had done. If there is proof of trusteeship, the law does not allow a resident coheir to claim exclusive possession of a piece of land, regardless of the length of residence. It is therefore difficult for a resident coheir of family land to claim a Squatter's Title against absent kin. This reinforces the customary system of unrestricted descent central to family land and acts as a brake against crab antics. For instance, closer inquiry into the case of the woman who had said that a "craving" resident trustee (her aunt) had "taken over" her maternal family land revealed that the trustee had, in fact, been supported in her actions by several nonresident members of the landholding kin group. Even her niece conceded that when the trustee applied for a title "nobody fight her," and she herself received a share of the proceeds from the sale of a portion of the family estate.

Other aspects of the legal system reinforce the customary unrestricted descent principle. In the eyes of the law a land-tax receipt is evidence of possession only, not of ownership. A resident member of the kin group paying taxes on family land cannot therefore establish exclusive rights. This is reflected in the frequently quoted saying among the Martha Brae villagers that "taxes can't mek you be owner" of family land. Regular picking from trees also provides legal evidence of land occupancy. Hence, the practice of nonresident coheirs picking from fruit trees on family land not only symbolizes their inalienable rights under the customary system, but furthermore is rooted in the law itself — thereby providing legal reinforcement of the unrestricted cognatic descent system.

The Transformation of State Law by Family Land

Finally, the customary principles of family land have transformed two aspects of the Jamaican legal code, and, like other reversals of the law, this reflects the dynamic opposition of the peasantry's culture-building to domination in capitalist class relations. First, Jamaica abolished the traditional principle of primogeniture — based on colonial law — in 1953 (retrospective to 1937), thus providing for the equal rights of all children regardless of gender or birth order (though not of legitimacy) in the case of intestacy. Second, the Status of Children Act of 1976 included illegitimate children as intestate heirs.

This process of transforming state law (which has occurred elsewhere in the Caribbean, such as in Barbados)[24] parallels the dynamic institution-building of the protopeasant slaves, who reversed the principles of legal freehold on which the plantation system was based to create customary land-tenure systems.[25] It also parallels the transformation, by emancipated slaves, of the colonial planter town of Martha Brae into a peasant village. Such reversal of colonially derived institutions as culture-building in opposition to capitalist class relations is currently reflected in the squatter settlement of Zion, established and consolidated especially by tenants from Martha Brae on a part of Holland Plantation owned by the Trelawny Parish Council during the period of my fieldwork (1968–2001). However, the council's current (1990s–2001) surveying of Zion for the purposes of land retrieval, sales, registration, and taxation, in turn, represents a further illustration of the imposition of state regulations on customary land tenure — as occurred, through the actions of the Trelawny planter vestry, when ex-slaves squatted in colonial Martha Brae following emancipation.

Martha Brae's Satellite Squatter Settlement of Zion

When I began my fieldwork in Martha Brae in 1968, there were no houses on the part of Holland Plantation owned by the Trelawny Parish Council, between the southern side of the Carib road (close to the site of Holland slave village) and the Maxfield road (near the sugar works ruins of Maxfield Estate), now known as "Zion." By the end of 1968, one chattel cottage stood there — on "captured land" — and two more followed in 1971. All three households were headed by established immigrants in Martha Brae, who had been tenants on the land of Born Ya or landed Strangers in the village. A few more chattel houses were moved to Zion in 1972, and by 1979 the area contained around thirty households. By 1995 Zion had become a vibrant squatter settlement of approximately seventy house yards, consolidated on about thirty acres of captured land as a satellite community of Martha Brae, and the Parish Council was surveying and subdividing the land with a view to retrieval, sales, registration, and taxation under the official legal system. Water and electricity had been installed and metered, though not all households had electricity or running water inside their houses. In 1999, although no land sales had yet been made, these were anticipated and Zion was being referred to as a "town." This was still the situation in 2001.

Tom and Mary Grant were the founders of Zion, having "captured" land there in 1968 — soon after I first met them as tenant-immigrants in Martha Brae. In 1995, when I interviewed them again, they had been together for nearly fifty years, since 1948, having arrived in Martha Brae as landless

Strangers in the 1950s. Around 1984 they were married legally by the Baptist minister at the William Knibb Memorial Church in Falmouth when Tom was seventy-two years old and Mary was sixty-seven.[26] Their wedding reception was held in a booth in their house yard at Zion, with a feast of goat, fowl, and cake. Tom was now retired from his job as a "worker in the cane" (Mintz 1974c). He had cut sugarcane on Holland Plantation and Hampden Estates, and had traveled many times to the United States to harvest cane in Florida under the Farm Work Scheme. Mary helped him cut cane at both Holland and Hampden and now worked in her house yard, but she still did a day's wage labor when she could — laundering clothes for another household at Zion.[27] In addition to her seven surviving children (two of whom, adult sons born in Martha Brae, lived in her household), she now had a "whole heap" of adult grandchildren and great-grandchildren, and three great-great-grandchildren. Mary was a member of the Falmouth Baptist Church but also became a Revival-Zionist: "Me did baptise in Baptist and join Baptist Church. But me can't tek de *one* man preach to me sit down and me can't seh anyt'ing. Me nuh like dat." So although she married in the Baptist Church, she attended Revival-Zion meetings in Martha Brae where she could stand up and fully participate (chapter 7).

From the 1950s to 1968 the Grants lived as tenants in Martha Brae in three different Born Ya yards: first in little rented houses on the family land of two Old Families, then in a two-room wooden chattel cottage of their own on a house-spot leased from a third Old Family — where I first met them in 1968. Shortly after, they decided to acquire land of their own: "Only little piece we capture here now fe weself." They first moved their chattel house by truck to the "bottom road" (the southern side of the Carib road, which now forms the northern boundary of Zion), but they explained that they had been evicted from that spot by the state police, the Parish Council, and a court in Falmouth. A partially successful legal defense resulted in a compromise whereby they were able to relocate (from an area where building had initially been planned) to their present house-spot, which was now the heart of Zion: "Twelve police [came] *one* time, you know. So after we go down the bottom and bring the house, the Parish Council *come*. They bring we up fe trespass. And afterward we go a *court*. . . . Well, anyway, they seh we's to leave and up to now we is here. But we move from down there and come up here." There was neither water nor electricity when they first captured land at Zion, but now there were both. They themselves had water in the yard but could not afford electricity.

Tom and Mary had created a house yard at Zion, a process that illuminates the parallel developments that occurred when emancipated slaves moved from Holland and Irving Tower Estates into the colonial planter town of Martha Brae and established house yards modeled on protopeasant adaptations in the slave plantation villages. At Zion, the Grants erected a fence, planted akee and breadfruit trees that now bore fruit, cultivated pumpkins and bananas, and kept chickens in a coop. The central focus of the yard was the house, moved a second time by truck within Zion itself. When they brought the cottage from Martha Brae it was just a two-room board house on pillars, but they had now added a third wooden room and a concrete verandah. The house had therefore become a firm fixture and part of the "real estate." There were also three outhouses: a kitchen, a shower, and a pit latrine. Tom and Mary appreciated that the Parish Council had now "run out" (surveyed and subdivided) the land at Zion and intended to sell "lots" but felt that their future was uncertain: "We nuh get i' yet still, we nuh know wha' goin' happen," and they worried about raising the cash for the potential purchase. If they were able to buy the land, they intended to leave it for those of their children who were landless, thereby creating family land for those in need. However, when Tom died in 1998 (at which time Revival wakes were held in his house yard at Zion, and he was buried in the Martha Brae cemetery), he was still a squatter-peasant.

One of Tom and Mary's resident sons, a fisherman, who grew up in Martha Brae and Zion (he was eight years old when they moved), clarified the naming of the new community. It was initially called Grant Town after their family, but during the first year "the younger guys say 'we going to Zion,' like it's *far away*: we living in Martha Brae, coming over." The "guys" were young boys and his friends, influenced by the Rastafarian dichotomy of Babylon (a place of exile) and Zion (a homeland), which in turn draws on the Revival-Zion worldview that derives from the Obeah-Myal slave religion.

The second house yard at Zion was established by Cynthia and Owen Rogers in 1971. Cynthia (by then in her sixties) was still there at the turn of the millennium, though her husband had died in 1994. I first interviewed Cynthia in 1968, when she and Owen were living in a two-room chattel cottage on a house-spot that they had leased in the yard of long-established Strangers who had purchased land in Martha Brae. She had moved to Martha Brae in 1951 from Duncans, adjoining Kettering, and Owen had come from neighboring Granville. They married legally in 1959. Owen was a mechanic at Hampden Estates, and Cynthia had been in domestic service. At Zion they extended their cottage, which they transported there by truck. By the 1990s Cynthia had electricity and running water inside the house. She and Owen had made a yard and planted bananas and breadfruit, avocado, mango, citrus, and akee trees. Cynthia was not sure of the size of her house yard (which was only a few square chains) but thought it might be the equivalent of two "lots" in terms of the Parish Council's subdivision: "Dem decide to sell us [the land] now. Dem seh dem 'lot' it out, but dem don't tell me is one lot me getting, or two lots, or whatever. But they are looking at it." Cynthia's adult daughter lived with her and was unemployed. Another daughter had migrated to the United States in 1993.

Cynthia, who like the Grants lived at the heart of Zion, described the establishment and growth of this squatter settlement:

> Mary Grant was living at the bottom. But after a while dem move her and tell her to come up here, 'cause the Mayor [of the Parish Council] never want any houses down on the bottom road. But after a while the people them were *flowing* on the land and they [the council] never want it like that, because them did want the land to sell. So them tell her to move come up here. And then after now, the people them *still* disobey and them go down there [to the bottom road]. . . . people still pass [disregard] them order and go on the land and *live*. She [Mary] came here '68. And I came here '71. And I were here t'ree months before this lady [Irene Morrison, her neighbor]. She came in November [1971]. I remember the date: 28th of November, she came after me. And then in '72 now Mr. Bates came up that house. But he die now. That house there came in '72. And then *dat* one, the same year too, in April.

I, too, remembered this handful of chattel houses "cotched" defiantly behind the Parish Council's "No Squatting" sign in 1972. Regarding the naming of Zion, Cynthia confirmed that "the *boys* them call it that way; the young people what live round here."

Irene and Peter Morrison established the third household in Zion, in 1971, and they too came from Martha Brae. Peter, a member of the Anderson Old Family (chapter 5), was a laborer at Holland papaw plantation. Irene had been a domestic servant but now cultivated her yard with dasheen (taro) and yams. In 1968, when I first interviewed her, she was living as a tenant in a one-room chattel cottage in the yard of established Strangers who had purchased land in Martha Brae. At that time she was in a visiting relationship with Peter, who was residing with another spouse on a three-square-chain plot of his family land. He retained his rights to this land and had left his house there, where one of their daughters now lived. They moved Irene's cottage by truck to Zion. and their new house-spot was sprinkled with rum as an offering to Revival-Zion spirits. Their youngest child and five of their grandchildren lived with them.

The Morrisons owned a Revival-Zion tabernacle that they also brought from Martha Brae, and the yard was marked by a tall Revival pole or "seal" to attract Revival-Zion spirits. Irene used to be a Pentecostalist but in the 1980s converted to Revivalism in Martha Brae. The Revival church that she attended at that time was established by a pastor from Upper Trelawny, on leased land in Martha Brae, and was subsequently taken over by a visiting pastor from Maroon Town in St. James. The church was, however, evicted by a village landlady, the tabernacle dismantled and rebuilt (from corrugated iron sheets on a concrete floor) around 1991 in the Morrisons' yard at Zion — on a spot where they had planted fruit trees and that was consecrated by the pastor from Maroon Town. Irene was a Revival-Zion deaconess, but her husband was not a member of the church and she described him as "a sinner-man."[28] Until recently a female Revival pastor who lived with them had conducted the services, but she had now moved to a new location in Zion (where I met her in 2000), and Irene was seeking another pastor for her church. Meanwhile, she sometimes held small meetings of her own and from time to time attended services at a Revival tabernacle in Martha Brae.

Irene had rights, which she regarded as inalienable, to three pieces of family land (including a family burial ground) in and around the postslavery village of Sherwood Content farther inland in Trelawny where she was born and raised. Together these three plots (five acres, four square chains, and three square chains) comprised the family estate of the Dawkins Old Family,[29] an unrestricted cognatic descent group to which Irene belonged on her paternal side. The largest plot of family land, located on a former plantation "mountain" where slaves cultivated provision grounds and where "the old, old ones" were buried, had been passed down from her late father's mother's father's father (her great-great-grandfather) to all of his descendants who comprised a partially dispersed cognatic landholding family line that had endured for seven generations. (The other two plots were more recently purchased lands, in Sherwood village itself, that had been transformed to family land within segments of the Old Family.) Several members of this landholding kin group had migrated from Sherwood to Martha Brae by 1968 and in 2001 either still resided there or had settled at Zion. Among these squatters was Irene's older sister, who was once a tenant in Martha Brae as well. Some of the younger members of the Dawkins Old Family in Martha Brae and Zion also had rights to family land in other overlapping Old Families. These included those of Irene's children fathered by her husband (who died in the late 1990s) who had rights through him to his maternal family land in Martha Brae and to his paternal family land in Granville.

All of these cases illuminate the process of the establishment and consolidation of Zion, and its relationship with the free village of Martha Brae and other Trelawny peasant communities, though discussion with the Parish Council and its surveyor in 1995 provided a complementary legal viewpoint on the squatter settlement. Since the 1950s the Parish Council has owned the part of Holland Plantation now appropriated as Zion, estimated at thirty acres. Its members confirmed that around seventy households had settled there "of their own volition" over the previous twenty-seven years and that more were anticipated. Zion had indeed been surveyed and subdivided into 146 lots. Any house yard considered too large had been subdivided into two or three lots ranging from around one-seventh to one-quarter of an acre, and the land is likely to be sold by the square meter. Unlike the period between 1968 and 1979, when households cotched defiantly behind the Parish Council's No Squatting sign, the council had now adopted a placatory position. Its aim was to resolve the "potentially explosive situation" by imposing a legal freehold land settlement (with reduced landholdings) on the squatter camp in order to register the squatters as legal titled occupiers on the Land Tax Roll—even though they did not apply to buy the land. Metered services had also been introduced or improved.

Martha Brae's satellite squatter settlement of Zion therefore highlights not only the persisting land scarcity in the free village, but also the imposition of legal elements by state regulations on the customary tenure of the squatter-peasantry. Paradoxically, however, the consolidation of Zion on plantation land owned by the state illustrates the continued transformation of colonially derived institutions and the related legal system by customary landholding.

The imminent formalization of Zion (still pending in 2001), established on the southern side of the Carib road (which had been recently been asphalted) on Holland Plantation, both compares and contrasts with the situation of those squatters who captured land on the northern side of the Carib road. That land is on Cave Island Pen or "Lyons Morass," an area of protected swamp owned by the Agricultural Development Corporation (ADC), which is controlled by the Jamaican government's Lands Commission. These squatters had been given notice of eviction on ecological grounds.[30] Pam Gilmore, of Martha Brae's central Minto Old Family (chapter 5), a seamstress-market woman in her sixties who had lived on ADC land since 1991, found herself in this predicament. Moreover, she faced eviction for the second time, as she had moved to squat on this land after reputed eviction from a rented yard in Martha Brae. One of her adult daughters (who sold with her in the Falmouth marketplace) was more secure, having previously established her house yard on the other side of the Carib road at

Zion—where she lived next to a Revival-Zion "balm-yard" or place of healing. Pam's adult Rastafarian son was also living on captured land belonging to the state—at Hague Pen, on the eastern edge of Martha Brae, where he too had found his "Zion" by acquiring (through customary tenure) land of his own.

The transformation of part of Holland Plantation into a peasant community, through squatting and anticipated land purchase at Zion, mirrors the postemancipation transformation of Martha Brae into a free village by ex-slaves who "captured" and then bought land in the planter town. Chapter 5 provides a further perspective on these events through extracts from the free village's oral tradition. These oral histories, which are contextualized within my anthropological and historical research, are presented through the lens of four Old Families who are central to Martha Brae's Afro-creole cultural history.

CHAPTER FIVE

Martha Brae's Free-Village Oral Tradition

Oral Tradition as Method, History, and Symbol

Although oral tradition cannot be assumed to be an entirely accurate account of past events, combined with historical and anthropological research it can illuminate the past, especially as written history may itself be biased and selective, as in the case of the Eurocentric history of Martha Brae as only a colonial planter town. Furthermore, as Ken Bilby (1984) contended in his anthropological study of the Jamaican Windward Maroons, oral history may contribute to a "more honest picture" of the past, "a picture alive with human emotions and attitudes rooted in the society of another time, yet belonging very much to the present as well" (4). In addition, as Richard Price (1990) has shown in his groundbreaking work among the Saramaka Maroons of Suriname, in the context of various "voices" oral history may reflect "the ongoing invention of culture" and a determination of the descendants of enslaved Africans "to create and preserve their own distinctly Afro-American lifeways" (xi, back cover).[1]

Barry Higman's (1998) study of the Jamaican plantation communities at Montpelier, St. James, in slavery and freedom (1739–1912) observes that historians are also recognizing the value of oral history: "Historians have become increasingly aware . . . that documentary sources suffer from a particular bias, being the selective creations of persons other than the oppressed majority of the plantation population. In order to overcome this limitation scholars have begun to exploit the evidence of oral history, ethnography and archaeology, all of which carry their own limitations but may be regarded as direct evidence from the mouths and hands of the people themselves" (4).[2]

Social scientist and novelist Erna Brodber (1983) argued for the role of oral history in replacing fiction at the interface of Euro-focused political and military history on the one hand and a new social history on the other in the so-called plural societies of the Caribbean. Brodber posited that oral history can replace fictional characters in incorporating emotions into historical analysis; she suggested that historians "enter the minds and hearts of the ancestors through the children and grandchildren and so extend the boundaries of the search for sources to include oral accounts" (7). Through a case study from her own extensive Jamaican oral history manuscript focused on the parish of St. James, which borders Trelawny, she demonstrated how the oral history of descendants of slaves and indentured laborers can not only corroborate events in existing historical accounts but also raise questions for historical analysis.

I have also shown the validity of such approaches in my use of oral traditions, combined with historical and anthropological research, in the social and cultural history of free villagers and Leeward Maroons in west-central Jamaica, and of descendants of Africans and Asians in Trinidad and Guyana (Besson 1984b, 1989a, 1992b, 1997). But unlike the static plural society framework used by Brodber, I have stressed the need to account for the dynamic process of creolization in the context of capitalist class relations. I have also suggested that oral tradition, even when historically inaccurate, may have a symbolic role that is valuable to both the narrator in portraying the past and the ethnographer in interpreting the present (Besson 1997:218–19). From these perspectives as method, history, and symbol, oral tradition in Martha Brae, when combined with historical and anthropological research, sheds light on the transformation of the settlement from a Euro-Caribbean planter town to an Afro-Caribbean peasant village and contributes to our understanding of the free villagers' Afro-creole culture-building.

The oral histories of Martha Brae's Old Families are an integral part of the oral tradition of the Trelawny peasantry generally and interweave with the oral histories of other peasant communities in the parish, especially the neighboring free village of Granville. Presented here are four case studies of oral tradition (contextualized and interpreted by my anthropological fieldwork and historical research) as narrated by the Old Families of Martha Brae in the Jamaican creole language created by their slave ancestors. As in the other Trelawny peasant communities studied, these Old Families are unrestricted cognatic descent groups (traced from ex-slaves of either gender, through both women and men, and including deceased and living kin and absent as well as resident descendants), with titles deriving from the surname of the founding ancestor or ancestress and generally transmitting rights to family land.

The four oral traditions are those of the Minto, Thompson, Anderson, and Kelly Old Families. At least some of these surnames were those of prominent slave-holding planter families or freeholders that may have been appropriated as descent group titles by ex-slaves.[3] The Mintos, Thompsons, and Andersons interweave with family lines in Granville, providing examples of unrestricted cognatic landholding corporations that overlap between the two free villages. In Martha Brae itself the Mintos, Kellys, and Andersons overlap, whereas the Mintos are further linked to the Fairclough Old Family.[4] The Andersons overlap with the Lindo Old Family in Martha Brae and with the Dawkins Family in the nearby village of Sherwood Content. Some members of the Dawkins Old Family lived in Martha Brae and Zion, and some of the Mintos and Andersons now also resided at Zion.

The forfeiture of the Kelly family land to the Trelawny Parochial Board (which succeeded the planter vestry) and the sale of part of the Minto family lands to raise tax money to retain the remainder of the small family estate (discussed later in this chapter) underline not only the precarious land base of the Martha Brae peasantry but also the continuing significance of their family-land institution that is rooted in the institution-building of the protopeasantry. These points are further highlighted by the successful struggle to save part of the Anderson family estate from forfeiture to the Parish Council (successor to the Parochial Board) and by the internal differentiation of the Minto Old Family, whose local house yards were held through a range of tenures (including insecure rental and squattage) despite their family lands. The Mintos also illustrate the internal differentiation among the Martha Brae villagers, for a few younger members of this Old Family achieved social mobility into the Jamaican transnational middle class. Yet, despite this mobility, the elderly founder of this segment of the Minto Family created new family land, from her own small plot of purchased land, for her descendants to identify with or return to in time of need.

The Minto Old Family

The Mintos comprise the central and most extensive Old Family in Martha Brae. They are descended from emancipated slaves on Irving Tower Plantation who acquired land of their own in the colonial town of Martha Brae and transmitted this as family land to their descendants. Members of this unrestricted cognatic landholding descent group, which now comprised eight postslavery generations traced through males and females, were during my fieldwork scattered in at least fourteen village households and were linked with other households in the community through affinity, bilateral kinship, and overlapping cognatic descent (chapter 8). In the later years of my fieldwork, some of the Mintos moved to Hague, the Carib road, and Zion — all bordering Martha Brae. Still others were dispersed beyond the village through migration to, for example, Falmouth, Montego Bay, Kingston, Canada, and the United States (chapter 6). The oral tradition of this Old Family was collected from several members of the descent group over the entire period of my fieldwork (1968–2001).

The Minto Old Family, which was mainly Baptist with a Revival-Zion worldview (chapter 7),[5] traced its ancestry to the parents (names unknown) of three brothers: George Finlayson Minto, John Jarvis Minto, and William Shakespeare Minto.[6] These three brothers and their parents are said to have been emancipated slaves from Irving Tower Plantation bordering Martha Brae who all settled in the planter town. The parents and two of their sons, John Jarvis and William Shakespeare, reportedly purchased five plots in the colonial town, four of which (those bought by the parents and William) subsequently became the Minto family lands (the fifth plot, purchased by John Jarvis, had been forfeited to the Parochial Board). Reinforcing this oral tradition are the names of two Mintos, against small plots in Martha Brae, in the 1876 land tax records for Trelawny.[7] In fact, these four pieces of Minto family land can be identified in Martha Brae today. On one of these plots (which has since been sold to raise the taxes needed to retain most of the family estate) is an old two-story house modeled on the Georgian architecture of the planter town. This house was built by the ex-slave William Minto, who migrated to the Hispanic Caribbean Coast of Central America after emancipation but returned to live in Martha Brae.

Many of the Mintos in Martha Brae lived neolocally (in independent households) on small plots of rented or purchased land. These included a retired returned migrant from England, Lloyd Nelson (aged seventy-nine in 2001), who was also a member of a central family line in Granville, where he had rights to family land as well. However, Lloyd had purchased two plots of his own on the eastern edge of Martha Brae. One of these (about an acre) he bought from "Lawyer," a former owner of Holland Plantation, when he subdivided the eastern part of Holland for "peppercorn" sales to Martha Brae villagers in the late 1940s,[8] an event that enabled the village to expand and was now enshrined in oral tradition. Lloyd purchased the second plot (also an acre), shortly after his retirement in Martha Brae in 1981, from a neighbor who bought the land from a man who had purchased it from Lawyer in the 1940s.

During my earlier fieldwork, the trustee for the Minto family lands was one of William Minto's daughters, Rhoda, who was born around 1897 and died in 1980 at the age of eighty-three. Until her death she was known as

"Miss Rhoda Minto," despite her legal marriage late in life to the father of her second set of children, Stephen Grimes. Her four sisters — Christine, Evadne, Edna, and Isobel Minto — had all predeceased her and she had long been the trustee for the family-land estate. This status was reinforced by her forceful personality, even in old age, which continued to be reflected after she died in her reputed spiritual activity.

Christine's two sets of children (including Lloyd Nelson), by two spouses from Granville Old Families, also had paternal family lands in Granville. They established their independence from their family lands in the two free villages while retaining rights in both. Evadne's daughter migrated to the United States and never returned. Isobel died young and childless. Edna's daughter, Victoria Robertson (aged eighty-six in 2001 and by then the oldest living Minto), with whom I lived during my fieldwork, had her own small plot of purchased land at the edge of Martha Brae, where she once kept a tiny rum shop and grocery store. Long before she retired, she transformed her bought land into family land for her descendants: two daughters and a son (who had entered the urban middle class in Kingston, Falmouth, and Montego Bay), seven grandchildren, and a great-grandchild. Her son, who resided with her during most of my fieldwork and still visited daily, now lived in Falmouth, and her daughters had recently migrated to the United States. Her grandchildren and great-grandchild lived elsewhere on the island or in "America." However, Victoria's family land has become a symbol of identity for this segment of the descent group who return there to visit. (In 2001 Victoria herself had been "sent for" to visit kin in the United States; this would be her first trip abroad, but she intended to go for "only two weeks.")

William Minto also had a son, who purchased land of his own elsewhere in Trelawny. His children migrated to England. William's brother John had two sons, John and Michael. Michael's daughter emigrated, and her five children lived in the United States. William's brother George remained in Martha Brae, as did some of his descendants.

After Rhoda's death the trusteeship for the Minto family lands devolved to Morgan McIntosh, one of her sons from her first set of children, who lived on his own small plot of purchased land at the western edge of Martha Brae across the road from Holland Plantation. He died in July 2001 and was buried in the Martha Brae cemetery. The following is an extract from his narrative, recorded shortly before his mother's death and his assumption of the trusteeship, outlining the site of the slave villages on Irving Tower and Holland Estates, the role of Martha Brae as Trelawny's first capital and its eclipse by Falmouth, the flight of ex-slaves into Martha Brae, and the transmission of oral history from these ex-slaves (later extracts recount the history of the Minto family lands and the architectural decline of the planter town):

As far as what I know, we had two villages where the slaves used to live. One was Irving Tower. The other one was down "John Ewen" section [a part of Holland Plantation],[9] which now they call it "Carib Road" where the factory is now and the School. The only thing that is down there now [from slavery] is the old breeze-mill [windmill], which is at the William Knibb Memorial High School yard. That's the old, old, breeze-mill; everything pull down save that.

Well now, after slavery, the people began to move from one place to the other. Well, Martha Brae was the first [parochial] capital. You have the soldiers, the police, the government buildings. All those was situated here. Well, in those [slavery] days the [Martha Brae] river was used as the shipping port. Small craft take the produce from down the wharf there, down to the ship in the harbor out there. By process of time Falmouth start to develop. So by process of time, people began to move from the [slave] villages into the township [of Martha Brae].

How did I learn all that? Well, look, I get to know them from the older people. Not even [just] me Mammy. Older than me Mammy. 'Cause there were a lot of old people that I know, you see. Because when I was a small boy, we have a lot of old people living here, which is even older than my [maternal] grandfather. And I know a lot of them, and they tell us what used to happen.

If they were people who'd moved in from the slave villages? Yes, yes; *plenty* of them. Because they was alive in slavery days. My mother's father come from Irving Tower; he was born there. . . . his forefathers was slaves; his parents. So you see, he was born there and he leave. That's where he leave from and come here and buy this place [the plot of land with the upstairs house, where Morgan rented premises for a rum shop, where we were sitting]."

The ruins of two windmills from slavery days could still be seen at the site of the William Knibb Memorial High School on Holland Estate. The ruins of Holland Great House had been directly across the road from Victoria's rum shop until the 1940s, when the cut-stone foundations were removed by then owner Lawyer to build a house in Georgian Falmouth. Part of Holland remained a sugar plantation (and cattle pen) until the early period of my fieldwork; since then it has been successively transformed by various owners into a maize, then aloe vera, and now a papaya (papaw) estate — all monocropping for the world economy. From the 1990s to 2001 Holland Farms (Trelawny), Ltd., were exporting papaws to supermarket chains in Canada and England, including London's "Safeway"; fruits and vegetables for internal markets and for export were grown on Irving Tower Estate, which still formed the southern boundary of Martha Brae.

Morgan explained that his maternal grandfather, ex-slave William Minto, purchased three plots in Martha Brae: one acre, three and a half square chains, and one square chain. His ex-slave great-grandmother, William's mother, obtained another plot of one square chain. This one square chain had the oldest ancestral history and was the house yard where Rhoda lived with her husband. Rhoda's account substantiated her son's; she added that *both* her paternal grandparents had owned the yard where she was living. She recalled them both residing there in a wattle and daub cottage, long since "mashed down." One of her paternal uncles, George Minto, had lived in another cottage in that yard, but that "blow down in a storm." Rhoda was uncertain as to exactly how her paternal grandparents obtained their land but said that she possessed a document passed down from her grandparents for this piece of land with the street number from the old town. This indicates a land purchase by the emancipated slaves in the colonial planter town.

Rhoda also knew the names of the people from whom her ex-slave father, William Minto, had purchased two of his three plots. In the case of the three and a half square chains bought from three siblings surnamed Kelly, their names can be identified in the 1876 land tax records for Martha Brae. One of these names also appears in the 1831–38 Falmouth Baptist Church records, registered as resident on Holland Estate. This indicates that at least one of these Kelly siblings was a slave on Holland Plantation, which, in turn, suggests that the plot in Martha Brae was purchased and resold by former slaves, a hypothesis strengthened by further evidence from the Kelly Old Family in Martha Brae. The Kelly family, which held another family estate in the village, traces its descent from an ex-slave surnamed Kelly from Holland Plantation who is said to have been one of several ex-slaves from Holland who purchased land in Martha Brae.

Two of the four plots bought by William and his parents after emancipation (Rhoda's paternal grandparents' one square chain, and her father's three and a half square chains) and a small portion of the third (her father's acre) remained in the Minto Old Family in 2001. Rhoda and her husband Stephen lived on the first of these three plots until her death in 1980. Stephen, who had only a life interest in the land, continued to live there until his death later in the 1980s. By 1995 three of their adult grandchildren were living in this yard with six of their own children (Rhoda's great-grandchildren), and some of these descendants were still there in 2001. One of Rhoda's sons (Morgan's maternal half brother) had long lived on the second, three-and-a-half-chain plot nearby, and he and his descendants were still there in 2001, though tenants who had been there in the 1980s had moved on. The portion of the third plot retained within the Old Family lay empty at the eastern edge of Martha Brae, near the river bridge and Irving Tower Estate. The rest of the Minto family lands (William Minto's one square chain with the upstairs house and the greater portion of his one-acre plot near the river bridge) had been sold, reluctantly, by Rhoda as trustee some years before her death to raise the tax money needed to retain the remainder of the family estate, with some surplus cash being shared among the coheirs.

The smaller (one-square chain) plot of alienated family land had been William Minto's house yard, where he lived in the two-story house and where his children (Rhoda and her siblings) were born. The house was repaired during my fieldwork, but the original stone walls, about eighteen inches thick,[10] remained. Morgan stressed the ancient postslavery origins of the house and the fruit trees growing in the yard: "This building, she [his mother, Rhoda] couldn't tell the age of it, because is plenty, plenty, older than she. These fruit trees out there: no-one around here [in Martha Brae] can tell you how long they is here. Nobody in the district can tell you when them plant here." Similar sentiments were expressed about the ancestral trees in the house yard of the Thompson Old Family. The idea that trees and land are symbols of the continuity of kin groups and communities is widespread among Jamaican and other Caribbean peasantries, and derives from the protopeasant past (Besson 1995d, 1997).

In old age Rhoda, whose house yard was a little farther down the street from William Minto's, often sat on the veranda of her wooden cottage gazing wistfully at that plot of alienated family land. She explained that, had she not needed to sell that land to raise the tax money to retain part of the family estate, the land "woulda still de deh"; that is, it would have remained as part of the Minto family lands. However, now that finances had improved, she planned to repurchase William's house yard; the person to whom she sold the land had promised her first option to buy. Meanwhile, Rhoda was acting as his agent for the land, as he was overseas. She died in 1980 without retrieving this land, and in 2001 William's house yard still remained alienated from the Minto Old Family. Yet the strength of sentiment among the members of the Minto family line surrounding this old house yard serves, with the remainder of their family lands, as a powerful symbol of Martha

Brae's Afro-creole cultural history. Moreover, Rhoda's sister's son Lloyd, the returned migrant from England, now proudly lived in a large refurbished house on his own plot of purchased land directly across the road from this house yard established by his ex-slave grandfather with earlier migrant remittances (chapter 6).

Both Rhoda and her son Morgan stressed that the rest of the Minto family estate should remain in the Minto Old Family as family land to "serve" successive generations. As Morgan explained: "She [Rhoda] said the land there musn't be sold. They must go down to family's family. That is what she tell me. Say they mustn't be sold. They must go from one family to the other family [from generation to generation]. That simply mean: sons, daughters, grandchildren, right down. Musn't be sold." This prohibition against the alienation of the family land applied most strongly to the one square chain on which Rhoda lived in later life, for this had the longest ancestral history. In addition, her paternal grandmother was buried in the yard, as was the custom in Martha Brae until the establishment of the village cemetery by the Parochial Board around the early twentieth century.[11] Of this postslavery house yard, Morgan observed: "That land, her [Rhoda's] father [William] tell her that she mustn't allow *anyone* [outside the Minto Old Family] to own it. She is maintaining her father's wish. And she asked me *hard* [earnestly] not to allow no-one [else] to own it; must be Family. So, it simply mean that it have to remain that way." Rhoda echoed these sentiments, and of the remaining Minto family land in general, said, "Me not selling it, lef' i' [I am leaving it] as 'family land.'" The latter she defined as land that derived "from generation, from old *creation*" (emphasis mine); that is, from the creative institution-building of former protopeasant ancestors.

Morgan also provided an eyewitness account of the last stages of the architectural decline of the Georgian town of Martha Brae. All that remained of the colonial town were the ruins of two houses, two old tombstones in village yards, and the Persian Wheel—together with the urban grid of streets. But Morgan recalled seeing a number of two-story Georgian houses from the former town, opposite his mother's yard, when he was a boy:

Right facing my mother's yard, the whole of that section was *heavy* [substantial, two-story] buildings. They was there when I was born. I know them. They was there when I was born. What I'm telling you, I not telling you about what I *hear* [but what I *see*]! They was there. High buildings with the big archway, with those large windows. Is stone building, you know. Now when you look at them building, you know, when you compare

167   Free-Village Oral Tradition

them, it's only all like St. Ann's Bay [capital of the neighboring parish of St. Ann] you would see them [similar architecture] and Falmouth. They was in Falmouth the same way. And is only one or two of them stand up in Falmouth today. They call them Georgian house. Those were the type of house. 'Cause sometimes even when we pass [those old houses] we run! 'Fraid, you know, to look at them. 'Cause it's like somebody [spirits] up there.

Morgan remembered eight such Georgian stone buildings from the planter town, including the old courthouse and prison. He explained that most of these buildings had been demolished (in his childhood and during World War II) so the owners could sell the old cut stone for buildings, including Hampden Estates' rum store in Falmouth and the chapel on the Mona Campus of the University of the West Indies in Kingston.

Morgan's narrative was reinforced by the oral history and eyewitness account of Georgian Martha Brae by his cousin Lloyd Nelson (the son of Rhoda's eldest sister Christine), the returned migrant born in 1922. Although as a boy he lived on his paternal family land in Granville, Lloyd often visited his maternal village. In 1943 he settled in Martha Brae, with his mother in her father William Minto's house, before making his first land purchase and migrating to England. In 1995 he recalled Georgian houses in four areas of the village, some of which had been occupied by members of Martha Brae's Old Families:

Originally, they say there was quite a few upstairs houses in Martha Brae, when I was a youngster. I remember them — some of them. There used to be one at the corner here facing where my old man [his maternal grandfather William Minto] was. . . . [There were] quite a few old, old houses . . . but nobody took proper maintenance of them. When I was younger, there used to be a big one right at this corner. When I came in 1943, that one was occupied . . . [by] Alice Bright [of the Bright Old Family], and she had some children. They was living upstairs when I came to Martha Brae. . . .

There used to be a big one down the hill there [River Hill] on the left hand side. Some people used to live there named Kerr. . . . I knew when it was occupied. When I was a youngster come to Martha Brae, come to river and learn to swim down there. I used to walk from Granville down there just to learn to swim.

And there used to be a few [other Georgian houses] down on the main [Granville-Falmouth] road, down the bottom where Hugh Shearer' mother used to live [the family land of the Lindo Old Family, the maternal family line of the former prime minister, the Hon. Hugh Shearer, "Son Lindo" of Martha Brae, next to the purchased land of my landlady, Victoria]. I used to go down to Mrs. Lindo, Grannie Jes Lindo [Mr. Shearer's maternal grandmother] when I was a boy. She and my Mom [Christine] used to be friendly and I used to go down there sometimes Friday after school, and there used to be an upstairs house. Is broken down now. . . .

But that house in particular [a Georgian ruin on the former Fairclough family land directly opposite his gate], the date that is there [1894] — I make some enquiry about it and somebody says that is *not* the date when the house was built. It's the date when one owner named Charles Fairclough — because it's marked C.F. — so that was when Charles Fairclough owned it. It's older than that. It's not recent. . . .

Originally here, if you notice this Martha Brae here, probably you wouldn't find another district in Jamaica like this. It divide up in blocks of streets like a town. You wouldn't find most any district in accurate blocks. Laid out. . . .

Another member of the Minto Old Family, Ruth Marshall (aged seventy-three in 2001), George Minto's great-granddaughter, lived with her husband on their own purchased land in Martha Brae and had seven surviving children, twenty-seven grandchildren, and six great-grandchildren scattered in Trelawny, St. James, and the United States. Ruth also belonged to the Kelly Old Family through her father. She illuminated the history of the Baptist Prayer House in the village: "My grandmother [George Minto's daughter, Rebecca] told me that she go to school at the Class House," as did William Minto's daughter, Rhoda. Ruth located her grandmother's birth in the 1870s and, as Rebecca's daughter (Ruth's mother, Thelma, who died in 1986 at the age of eighty-two) was born on December 31, 1903, this oral evidence is sound. Ruth explained that in those days the prayer house was an upstairs building, not just the one-story stone building of recent years: "They say the top [story] was a board [wooden] part. So she [Rebecca] tell us all that, and her teacher used to live upstairs. Her teacher was a Mr. Dan Roper; you couldn't hear anything but 'Teacher Roper'! Mr. Roper, they say he's the second person bury in this [Martha Brae] cemetery." This pattern of a class house (or chapel) serving as both a prayer house and a school typified Trelawny's Baptist villages.

Ruth's oral history, reinforced by other accounts, indicates that the protopeasant pattern of yard burial continued in the free village of Martha Brae after emancipation, until the Parochial Board instituted a cemetery there early in the twentieth century, an innovation stemming from the Burial within Towns' Limits Act of 1875. Postemancipation yard burial in Martha Brae also paralleled earlier yard burial in the planter town, before the Falmouth Anglican churchyard was used from 1783, prior to the establishment of the parish church in 1796 (Isaacs 1996:11); one of the old tombs, with an eighteenth-century inscription, was in Ruth's yard. The subsequent transformation of interment patterns in the free village of Martha Brae — from yard burial to interment in a community cemetery — parallels, in time, the change in burial patterns that occurred in both time and space in Knibb's free village of Kettering adjoining the town of Duncans. The reasons for this transformation in Martha Brae are likely to have been both the free village's proximity to the town of Falmouth and the intense land scarcity in the village, with its nucleated yards from the planter town on a small ridge surrounded by plantations. By the 1990s the Martha Brae cemetery had begun to serve other communities near Falmouth, such as Rock, Hague, and, most recently, the neighboring free village of Granville and the squatter settlement of Zion.

In 1991 one of the Minto households was reputedly evicted from rented land in Martha Brae. Its inhabitants consisted of some descendants of the ex-slave George Minto and his daughter Rebecca, including Rebecca's granddaughter Pam Gilmore (Ruth's maternal half sister, a seamstress and market woman, aged sixty-six in 2001), who was head of the household. Pam's household was now segmented. Pam herself, a daughter (who had recently migrated to the United States, but who sometimes returned home), and three grandchildren were squatting (in Pam's chattel cottage moved by truck from Martha Brae) on the northern side of the Carib road area of Holland Plantation, on swampy land owned by the Jamaican state. Pam's Rastafarian son was squatting on the border of the Hague government land settlement at the edge of Martha Brae.[12] Another of Pam's daughters, with her children, had established her own household at the squatter settlement of Zion in 1987, prior to the eviction. This predicament of the squatter-peasant descendants of the ex-slave George Minto highlights the continuing land scarcity faced by the free villagers of Martha Brae and the rationale of the family-land institution created by ex-slaves in the former planter town and rooted in protopeasant institution-building on Irving Tower and Holland Plantations. It also demonstrates the continuing emphasis on acquiring land of one's own, as have some of the Minto ex-slaves' descendants: such as by purchase (Ruth, Victoria, Morgan, and Lloyd); through rental, as in the case of Della Gilmore (Pam's full sibling and Ruth's maternal half sister, who lived in Martha Brae and died there in 1999, leaving six children); or by "capturing" land at the Carib Road, the Hague land settlement, or the Zion squatter camp.

The Thompson Old Family

Amy Bruce was the oldest living member of the Thompson family line, and of all Martha Brae's Old Families, in the earlier years of my research. Born in Martha Brae in 1892, she died there in 1982, at the age of ninety, and was buried in the village cemetery. By the time of my fieldwork she was widowed and lived alone on a quarter-acre plot that was part of a family-land estate created by her paternal grandfather, an ex-slave from Irving Tower Plantation. This emancipated slave is said to have purchased two pieces of land in Martha Brae, near the lands bought by the Minto ex-slaves and close to the border of Irving Tower Estate: the quarter-acre piece nearer to the center of the village and a one-acre plot (bought for £20) across the street but closer to the river bridge. His family-land estate, which remained in the Thompson Old Family, comprised both of these plots.

Throughout many of my years of fieldwork, Amy's brother William Tapper lived on the second (one-acre) piece of family land. One of the great oral historians of Martha Brae, he died in 1985 at the age of eighty-two. Both he and his wife, who was still alive in 2001, were members of the William Knibb Memorial Baptist Church in Falmouth, for, as he explained, "most of the people here are Baptists in Granville and Martha Brae." When he died he was "churched" by the Martha Brae burial society, whose secretary he had been in his younger days, and interred in the village cemetery. By the time of my research, Amy was ill and felt too old to recall much about the history of the village and the Thompson family line: "Me head can't retain nothing now." William, however, recounted in detail the evolution of Martha Brae as a free village and the history of the Thompson Old Family and its family lands.

William's description of Martha Brae's postslavery history points up the wider contexts of the Trelawny plantation heartlands, the flight of emancipated slaves from the estates, the free village movement in Jamaica and Trelawny, the role of the Baptist Prayer House (which is opposite the Thompson lands), and the significance of oral tradition for people without written history. His oral account also suggests the possibility of Baptist Church involvement in land purchase and resale of Martha Brae lands in the 1840s:

All the districts [villages] generally in Jamaica, they are excerpts from slavery; handing down from slavery. The slaves were here working on the farms [plantations], and when they get freedom, you see, you have little districts here, districts there: Granville, Martha Brae, Bounty Hall, Rock, Perth Town, Daniel Town [Trelawny villages]. So you have all the little districts around [and] those older slaves go there and they produce children. . . .

How did they get the land? The churches. The Baptist Church was foremost. William Knibb was a foremost preacher here, and Charles Mann and all those men. I think William Knibb even lose his life [*sic*] fighting to get freedom and lands for the slaves. And the first educational system in Jamaica was through the churches principally. Then the Government begin to form, then the people leave the churches and go on their own. But most of it through the churches.

After emancipation, the Baptists got the Martha Brae lands, in the 1840s. Most of the history of the black people don't come in big log-book. They keep it themselves, and grandparents told their children and grandchildren. And my grandparents [ex-slaves] told me that the Martha Brae lands were acquired by the church. The church got the land and then despatched it to their members. And this also happened in Martha Brae. The Baptist church — see the Prayer House there [across the road from his yard]. And it was a school and Prayer House. Many of the children went to school there, and Sunday school also.

Well, you see, [in the case of] Martha Brae, the slaves was occupying over Irving Tower. That's the property over there [the plantation bordering the village]; Irving Tower. Well, when they get their freedom now, they launch from there out here to Martha Brae. They were stationed over that side of the property. Because you had a little [sugar] mill over there; Irving Tower mill. There were several estates [in the area]. You have Green Park Estate, Gayles Valley Estate, Tilston Estate — all those estates right up. So the sugar estates occupy the slaves. Well, when they get their freedom, some remain in the barracks there, but some launch out in the little districts. That's why you see you have the districts. Holland is another one too. Holland Estate concern [borders] Irving Tower, [which also] go away down touching Southfield [Estate] and join on with the place they call Potosi [Plantation], and join on to Maxfield [Estate]. Irving Tower was the part where the sugar mill was. The old works was there.

William then commented on Martha Brae's pre-emancipation Euro-Caribbean history and on its eclipse by Falmouth before going on to outline how the ex-slaves moved into the colonial town, establishing their houses and yards in the face of intense land scarcity. He also spoke about the generational transmission of house yards and the ancient postslavery origins of the prayer house:

It [Martha Brae] was the first town [in Trelawny]. And Falmouth developed from Martha Brae for shipping purpose. Because they say they used to take boats come up the river to carry the produce out to ship. But now they develop the town [Falmouth] where they have their own wharves and so forth. So you see, Martha Brae becomes in the background now. But if you notice, Martha Brae develop the streets; see you have the streets right through and through. It was the first formation, you know. It was a little town. And if you notice how it situate, you have the streets running east-west, north-south. And every bit emerge on Irving Tower. All a them join onto Irving Tower.

If there were any buildings in Martha Brae when the ex-slaves moved in? They build it up. The slaves came in and build a little improvement. They start to build, and they start to build. Everybody come in, join. So if you notice, now, some a the people here in Martha Brae, is acquire them acquire [inherited land] from those who first got it. That's why you see some a the yards them so small. [For example] I get a block—I may get half-acre—and I give you a part of mine. And the other one come, give you a part of his. And then you find the whole place cut up small, small. Some a them don't even have a square [square chain].

The oldest [postslavery building] is the Prayer house. The old Prayer House there. The Baptist Prayer House. That one is one of the oldest buildings I think in Martha Brae. Not back to slavery, but near into slavery. Because, you know, the Baptist Society was during slavery. Because William Knibb was in slavery. He was doing the agitation for the freedom of the slaves.

William then recounted the creation and evolution of the Thompson family line and family lands in the context of the free village system and the transformation of Martha Brae. His account underlined the significance of protopeasant capital for land purchase after emancipation. His paternal grandfather, one of eleven sons scattered throughout Jamaica, had been a slave on Irving Tower Plantation. After emancipation, he settled in Martha Brae and bought two small plots. The grandfather stipulated that these lands should not be sold but should be retained as family land for his descendants in perpetuity:

He [the grandfather] was in the slave days. Him was an *old* man before him die, but him touch a little of the slavery. Because he said he was over

Irving Tower there, that him used to live there when him get the place [lands] to buy out here [in Martha Brae]. He bought it, you see, after the abolition of slavery—apprenticeship. There was an apprenticeship for the slaves. So they get allotted lands for them. That's why you find these little districts [free villages] all over Jamaica. The churches acquired land for the ex-slaves, so those who had a little accommodation [savings] bought land. That is how my grandfather come to get this piece. They had a little money, so they bought the land.

Well, my grandfather, he bought the piece of land that I am living on now, and the part where my sister is living. He make the house over the part where my sister is. Well, my grandfather said the land should not be sold. It is for his heritage going down. It must go from children to grandchildren, right down the line. Well, the grandfather, when his time is expired, he hand it [the lands] over to my father [the grandfather's only child]. Father said, "My time is ended"—he hand it to the children. Well, it was quite a few brethrens of us, but all died now, left only myself and me sister over there on the smaller plot, now. So she has that part—the same "lot" [two and a half square chains, i.e., a quarter acre].

As William's grandfather had two pieces of land, he made additional stipulations concerning the transmission of his estate. The smaller plot, where both the grandfather and his son (his only child) in turn made their home, was to be passed on to his first granddaughter; the larger piece was to be jointly held by his remaining grandchildren. There were five of them, but one died young leaving four—another granddaughter and three grandsons. These stipulations were set out in the grandfather's will: "Him [the grandfather] said that the first girl in the family as a lawful heir, they must get that [plot] where my sister [Amy] is. The first lawfully heir as a girl; he say is for a girl. Well, the first child that was born to my father was a boy, and the second was a boy, so they didn't get it. She [Amy, the third child] was fortunate to be the first lawful [female] heir and she has it until this day. So nobody don't fight her for it, because that is hers." Amy substantiated this point: "This place is me grandfather's. He bought it give me. This belonging to *me*. It will-out give me. It can't be sold." She explained that she intended to leave the land to her two children: a son in Kingston and a daughter in the United States. She had also inherited the old family home in this yard: a two-story wooden house that had been her father's and grandfather's, and where she and her full siblings had been born and raised. This house, however, had long since fallen into disrepair and was replaced by her present two-room wooden cottage. William and Amy's father had added one further stipulation to the will, namely, that his wife (William and Amy's mother) should have a life interest in the land; this would enable her to continue living on the Thompson family land until her death if she survived him, which she did.

"But the other piece, now," William continued, "he [the grandfather] said the others can occupy that. That was concerning four children [grand-children]. So all the others gone [died], lef' me alone. Well, my grandfather said the land should not be sold. It must go from children to grandchildren, right down the line. So well, my father had it. Him die leave it give my mother [the life interest]. My mother die lef' it give me. And see my children there now." This one-acre plot was, as stipulated by the ex-slave grandfather, jointly held among the coheirs and had never been subdivided since it was to be shared by William and his three designated siblings: "It just remain one block. Must live in peace." William, however, was the only one of the coheirs to have resided on the land, as all of the others had migrated and died abroad. His brothers settled in Cuba and New York, and his other sister, in Costa Rica. The children of these siblings were born abroad and did not intend to return to Jamaica. As a result of this voluntary nonuse of the family land by many of the coheirs, William and his children gained de facto control of the land. But, as he explained, this was subject to the right of his siblings' children to return: "They don't business with Jamaica! So I am actually free from them. But I'm just fortunate that way. But suppose they were interested now [in returning to the family land]: when they come, now, we'd have to share this one [this plot]." Migration and voluntary nonuse therefore served as a "fortuitous" or "pragmatic," rather than an "exclusive," restriction within an essentially unrestricted cognatic landholding corporation (chapter 8).[13]

William himself was a returned migrant and had only resided on this part of the family land since 1962 (by which time he was nearly sixty years old), following his return from Cuba and the United States where he worked as a migrant laborer for many years and several months respectively. On his return (from Cuba in 1938 and from America in 1945 and 1946), he first lived in a rented house in Falmouth. After returning from Cuba he cultivated food crops on a provision ground on one of the estates surrounding Martha Brae, producing surpluses that his sister Amy marketed for him. He went back to Martha Brae in 1959, initially living as a tenant elsewhere in the village while he built a house on the empty plot of family land. To obtain a "Farm House" loan for this house-building, he had to have a title for the land. This required the consent of his absent siblings, which they gave, enabling him to "administer" on the land.[14] On his return from migratory labor overseas, he first worked on the roads for the Public Works Department and then for the Parish Council. After settling on the family land he took up farming again and created a food forest in the yard through multicropping. Subsequently he also cultivated another provision ground, through intensive intercropping, on the outskirts of the village near the river bridge. This ground had been part of the Minto family estate, which was sold in 1975 to William's maternal half brother's daughter, who was from Trelawny but lived in London. William acted as caretaker for the land, cultivated it for household use, and paid the land taxes in his niece's name. He also became a village landlord, renting out two "spots" on the family land on which he lived: a house-spot for a tenant's chattel cottage and another piece for the tenant's cultivation.

Like Morgan McIntosh of the Minto Old Family, William remarked on the ancient postslavery history of the fruit trees on the one-acre plot of the Thompson family estate. He knew the origin of each tree brought as a sapling by his ex-slave grandfather, from the protopeasant adaptation on Irving Tower Plantation to this land in Martha Brae: "*This* naseberry tree — according to what my mother told me — this naseberry tree and that one there; the star-apple tree here; and these three naseberry tree along the road there; all of them came from Irving Tower. From the slave days they came out there. My grandfather bring it and plant here, and they catch [grow]. So there was quite a few tree here that really come from Irving Tower during the slave days. So we know of it."

As for the future, William stated that the Thompson family-land estate would remain in the Old Family as the inalienable property of the descendants of his grandfather, the emancipated slave. This included the descendants of those grandchildren (William's full siblings) who died abroad. After the deaths of Amy and William (in 1982 and 1985), these lands remained in the Thompson family. William died intestate, by design as his widow explained: "He never mek a will, he seh everybody mus' live [in unity]. If we want to kill one another over it, it up to we. But *him* seh everybody mus' live." In 1995, by which time the tenant household had gone, William's adult daughter and four sons had all established their households on the Thompson family estate. The daughter and her child lived in the farmhouse with her mother in the middle of the land. Two sons had made "board houses" at the top of the property, and a third son had built a concrete "block house" at the bottom. The fourth son had inherited his paternal aunt's (Amy's) wooden chattel cottage, where he now lived with his consensual spouse and their three children. Amy's daughter in the

United States was in charge of the second, smaller, piece of land but had assured her cousin that he could keep his cottage there until she returned. William's food forest had declined, but his daughter now cultivated his provision ground near the river bridge. In 2001 the four households (now all in concrete houses) still lived on the larger plot, where a fifth house-spot had been allocated for the remaining son, who presently lived in another Trelawny village.

William's mother, in addition to her six children from his father (her legal husband), had three older sons from two previous nonlegal unions. These three "outside" children were not considered heirs to the Thompson family lands. This was not due to their illegitimate status in the traditional Jamaican legal system but was simply because they were not the cognatic descendants of the ex-slave who established that family land. However, these maternal half brothers, as well as William's full siblings and himself, were all coheirs to their *maternal* family land held by the Samuels Old Family (which now comprised seven generations) in the neighboring free village of Granville. William provided a detailed account, substantiated by my later research in Granville, of the founding of the Samuels family line and family land by his great-grandfather (his mother's paternal grandfather), an ex-slave from Green Park sugar plantation. This emancipated slave is said to have purchased a "lot" of land (a quarter of an acre, or two and a half square chains) in Granville from the Baptist Church and transformed it into family land for his descendants:

> My mother's father's father, that is my mother's grandfather, he was Samuels, he acquired it [the land] from slavery. It was old time slavery land, from the apprenticeship in Jamaica. When the slavery abolish, he got a piece of the land. That was for Samuels, and also acquired by the churches and sold to them. The great-grandfather and most of them [who settled Granville] was living at Green Park [Plantation]. Some work [as slaves] at Irving Tower and some at Tilston [estates], so when slavery was abolished they scattered in the districts. He was at Green Park and he got it [the land] from the churches.

Unlike William's ex-slave paternal grandfather in Martha Brae, his great-grandfather in Granville died intestate, which was (and still is) more often the case in the free villages. However, the great-grandfather specified by word of mouth that his property should be retained as family land within his family line: "No will was left. He only handed down the land as heritage. Them never make any will. Those ancient people, they very few of them make any will. And most of them died 'intestate,' according to how the government put it." The great-grandfather had only one child, William's maternal grandfather, who first inherited the land and continued to reside there. He had four children: two daughters and two sons. The sons emigrated to Costa Rica and the United States and died abroad. The daughters, Eliza (William's mother) and Katrine, survived their father and the land was transmitted to them. Their mother, who had a life interest in the land, also continued living there until her death. Eliza, on her legal marriage to William's father, moved to Martha Brae, where she lived and died on the Thompson family land. Until this move she served as trustee for the Samuels family estate, but on leaving Granville she appointed her late sister's daughter Enid to oversee the Samuels land while still retaining her land rights there. Therefore (as with the Thompson family land in Martha Brae) pragmatic, rather than exclusive, restriction occurred within the essentially unrestricted landholding corporation. As William related: "My mother was fully in claim of it. But as we lived a united life, my mother simply said to the other lady up there, 'Well alright Enid, since I am married and get this piece here [her life interest in the Thompson family estate], you better hold on to that piece there. You take that piece, because you don't have anywhere yet; so you take it.' So she deliver that piece to her. So she have that piece. So the birth-place of her home up there fall to Enid."

When William first told me about this Granville family land, in the late 1960s, Enid was still living there and paying the land tax. She still, however, fully acknowledged the rights of the descendants of her (by then deceased) maternal aunt Eliza to the land. These absentee rights were both symbolized and maintained through picking from the fruit trees on the family land, as William explained: "Living together as a united family, if we go up there [to Granville] and they have star-apples or anything — guinep and so forth on the land — and we are passing there, they say 'Well alright boy, you want a bunch of guinep? Take it.' "

Through my fieldwork in Granville, I came to know this family land and some of the Samuels Old Family. By 1983 William's mother's sister's daughter Enid had died and Enid's daughter Shirley Kane (born in 1922) was trustee for the land. Shirley had worked as a cane cutter on Green Park Estate (since bought by a bauxite company) in the 1950s; she lived with her husband (who worked at the Carib Metal Factory near Martha Brae) and their foster child on a small plot of purchased land in Granville, across the street and farther up the hill, bordering Carrickfoyle Estate (which was now a chicken farm). She herself had bought this land (and constructed a concrete house), where she and her mother Enid had lived as tenants before moving to a one-room chattel cottage that she built on the Samuels family land. Although Shirley had left the Samuels family land, she still grazed her cows under the fruit trees at the bottom of the property. By then, Enid's sister's daughter's daughter, Tracey, who had been raised by Enid on the family land, continued to live there with her child who was in the seventh generation of the Samuels Old Family. In the 1990s the situation was much the same: Shirley (then in her seventies) had sold her cows because of drought, but she and her husband still lived on the bought land farther up the hill, while Tracey resided with her two children on the family land.

The Samuels family land lies on a rocky hillside bordering the Granville-Falmouth road, near the piece of land named — in the postslavery subdivision of the Granville lands — "Dispute." Just beyond the Samuels land is the bought land of another Granville family, purchased from Lawyer on Maxfield Estate. The Samuels family land is divided by the main road, with the house yard above and a burial ground below, as William had described: "The old father — the great-grandfather — he is buried under the guinep tree. The great-grandfather was a slave. He is buried against the slope, and it is a grave [unentombed]. The one that is tombed down the bottom is Enid's husband. The great-grandfather's grave is on the bottom piece. Sister [cousin] Shirley can show you the spot." Shirley, whose cows grazed peacefully among the family graves in 1983, did show me. By then Enid had been entombed in this family burial ground.

William, having described (through the oral histories of his paternal and maternal Old Families in Martha Brae and Granville) the transformation of protopeasant slaves to postslavery peasants, moved on to other themes of continuity with the protopeasant and postemancipation past. These themes included the persisting land scarcity constraining the peasantry, its continued dependence on plantations for wage labor and provision grounds, and the cultivation techniques evolving within these constraints and originating in the protopeasant adaptation:

It is such a state now, that the district [village] is surrounded by the properties [estates] *still*. So when the property want workers, they just notify the district and the workers come. The majority of the [provision] grounds that you have now, the land belong to the properties still. [For example] all over Hague there. All these people round here have ground there that belong to the Hague estate, Hague property.

The districts here, in process of time now, the population grow. And then we find that we are having trouble in Jamaica now: in large population and not enough lands for the smaller people, you see. *Many people here don't have a square of land. Lack of land space — the people is like you put a pig in a kraal. That's just how plenty a the poor people live. Just like a pig in a kraal* [emphasis mine].

Most of the people [ex-slaves] didn't get arable lands. Most of them is on the hillside. So they had to use picker [pickax] and fork. They didn't know anything about plough and all that. Moreso manual business; no mechanical equipment. You see, most of them [the ex-slaves] never get big amount of land that you can subdivide it. So they plant [a diversity of crops]: see I have a little bean, corn, coco, cassava, yam — right through, same as how you see it here [intercropping on his hillside provision ground, where we were talking].

William illustrated the continuity of the multicropping complex from the protopeasant past, referring to the food forest in his yard: "It being so small I trying to acquire everything: two coconuts [coconut trees], two plums, oranges, [avocado] pear, mango trees; everything there. But it so small now that the bigger trees crowd out the littler ones." Under this canopy of large and small trees, the yard had layers of shrubs (e.g., peppers and bananas) and root crops (such as yams) below ground. His technology on yard and ground was simple, like that of his ex-slave and protopeasant ancestors: only "a machete and old fork" for cultivation and "a machete me take weed the place." His cropping cycle was carefully controlled by the phases of the moon, as specified in the *MacDonald's Almanac* that William kept in his cottage library.

In concluding his oral history, William remarked that expansion of the free village of Martha Brae had been made possible in the late 1940s when the Trelawny lawyer-farmer nicknamed "Lawyer" by the peasantry made peppercorn sales of land from Holland Estate to several villagers on the eastern edge of Martha Brae:

You see all those lands down there [the eastern part of the village] belonged to him, you know. And the whole a that piece from where "Miss Hazel" live, going right back: Lawyer give the franchise [opportunity] to get it. So that was one of the best reformers in Trelawny. Because him give the people the privilege of owning somewhere. Every day I call his name and say he is a valuable white man ["Jamaica White"] in Jamaica. And if all the white men was of that nature, Jamaica would be a thousand per cent better than what it is now. If it had not been for him, many people here would never have *a square of land to call their own* [emphasis mine]. And he brings it down to the level that we can afford.

In the 1960s Lawyer made more extensive sales of land from Maxfield Estate to the Granville villagers. Lawyer sold this land in the face of continued planter resistance to peasantization; some members of the Trelawny plantocracy protested that he was "letting down the [planters'] side."[15] Lawyer's land sales are therefore regarded by the Trelawny peasantry as an exceptional event and, like the land purchases by ex-slaves from William Knibb, have been woven into oral tradition. William's account of these transactions was reiterated by other villagers in Martha Brae and Granville, and a Granville villager who bought land from Lawyer explained to me more fully the significance of these land sales at the persisting plantation-peasant interface:

Lawyer helped we, the poorer class, because the other big men them, dem only want to tek we to *slave*. But Lawyer mek most Trelawny man *own a piece of land*. Lawyer over the years mek me can give my children a better dinner. Everyday me and Frederick Duffy [another Granville villager] talk about how Lawyer help us. The others [other planters] gave us a piece of ["free"] land and we work it [as a provision ground] this year and next year them drive we off and say them want to raise cow and do all dem things. . . . [But because of Lawyer] today I have cow and can sell it to get money.

We all call Lawyer's name every day, as him was one of the best men come in Trelawny [from St. James] and help poor people. Lawyer trust us those lands and when we get money we pay him, and he don't run us down for the money. And he never took away our land [even though] sometimes we did not have the money. God's blessing must store on him, in Granville and all over. The others did not even give us a piece of land to work to buy bread, much more to sell us the land.

When Lawyer started selling land, most of the bigger men in Trelawny were against him, say the poorer people not going to work for them — and this is the truth. Me was working for a man and when him hear that me buy [land from Lawyer] him ask me how much acre me buy. Me tell him me no buy any land — me trust it from Lawyer and me no know if me can pay for it. And when I lef' him [that plantation owner] and buy the land [from Lawyer], him [the employer] did not want Lawyer to sell us the land, and they [the planters] did Lawyer bad [criticized him] round here.

Blessings will follow Lawyer. All who buy land pray every day [for him], including me and Frederick. If it was not for Lawyer, now that we are old, what would we do? Pick up weself and go between them boys now [laboring on the plantations] and say we working? But today, praise God, we put we hand to the plough [i.e., cultivate our own bought land] and anytime we go over there we can find something to eat.

Lawyer made the people know that there is something in this world for them. [Before] I work land [provision grounds] all about, and sometimes you should see what we have to destroy [to move off the land] — them turn cow in it. . . . The balance [of planters] you have to sign [papers] to plant grass and weed it up [on the plantations] and then you [are allowed to] cultivate a little piece on the "free land." Lawyer never did those things, and we could get any amount of land to cultivate without signing. Blessed Lawyer — him never follows the advice of the bigger men.

In 1990 — some time after these narratives were recorded, decades after the land sales, thirteen years after Lawyer had returned to St. James (having lived for forty years in Trelawny), and four years after his death in 1986 at the age of seventy-five — I stopped on the Trelawny road to Accompong (which peters out halfway, at Kinloss), several miles from Martha Brae and Granville, to talk to a Long Pond Plantation labor gang. Initially, when I was taken for a tourist, the reaction was suspicious. I therefore explained, by way of introduction, that my father had been a lawyer-farmer who worked in Falmouth and lived near Martha Brae and Granville. The atmosphere swiftly changed to one of welcome, as the comment "It's Lawyer's daughter, Lawyer who cut up land" swept through the gang. This filial tie with Lawyer was a major factor in my acceptance as a researcher among the Trelawny peasantry. In the early period of my research I was known in Martha Brae simply as "Lawyer's Daughter," only acquiring a reputation and title of my own ("Miss Jeanie") after many years of recurrent long-term fieldwork.[16]

The Anderson Old Family

Madeline Simmonds was the oldest living member of the Anderson Old Family and the trustee of its family lands until her death in the late 1990s; I had oral history interviews with her over a period of more than a quarter of a century (1969–95). Born in 1910, she was eighty-five years old and widowed in 1995.

Madeline traced the Anderson family line at least two ascending generations to the postemancipation period and slavery: to her father, Henry Anderson (who was a Baptist), and his brother and sister; and to their father, surnamed Anderson (first name unknown but possibly John), the grandfather's sister Christian Anderson, and the grandfather's spouse Nana Green. Nana

Green, who raised Madeline and died as a very old woman in 1922 when Madeline was twelve, is said to have been a slave girl who carried a lunch tray on her head to field slaves on Irving Tower Plantation bordering the southern edge of Martha Brae; Madeline recalled seeing a picture of her grandmother, in a group of other slaves, with the lunch tray on her head.[17] In addition to Madeline's generation, there were three further descending generations traced through men and women (including absentees). Thus the Old Family by then comprised at least six postslavery generations reckoned through unrestricted cognatic descent.

Madeline's father and his two siblings all had children. Her paternal uncle had one child: a son who migrated to the United States, lost touch, and never returned. Her paternal aunt, who married a man from the Trelawny village of Perth Town, also had one son, who migrated "to foreign" and remained overseas, where his mother joined him until her death. Madeline's father, Henry, had eight children by two spouses: three daughters (herself and two who died young and were buried in the yard of the Baptist Prayer House) and five sons. The five sons, now deceased, all migrated: four to other parts of the parish or the island and one abroad. Two of them are known to have had children and grandchildren in Jamaica, some of whom lived on bought land of their own.

Madeline had seven children, a daughter and six sons, by four spouses prior to her legal marriage in middle age, and now had numerous grandchildren and great-grandchildren. One of her childrens' fathers was from the Lindo Old Family, which had family land in Martha Brae; another "babyfather" was from the Kelly Old Family, and another was from a Granville landowning family line.[18] The Anderson Old Family therefore overlapped with other unrestricted cognatic landholding descent groups in both Martha Brae and Granville. Of Madeline's seven children, her oldest son lived in Martha Brae on part of the Anderson family estate. In 1995 her second son lived in England but was visiting and improving her house. The third son had worked in the Trelawny village of Duanvale but died in 1961. The fourth son used to live on the Anderson family lands in Martha Brae, but now resided with his wife in the squatter settlement of Zion, where he planned to purchase land of his own. Their children and grandchildren also had land rights in his wife's Dawkins Old Family in the Trelawny village of Sherwood. The fifth son migrated to England in 1961; helped to build his mother's present house with money sent from England; bought land of his own with remittances, near Merrywood Estate, that Madeline cultivated as a provision ground; and returned to live in Martha Brae in the early 1990s, taking over the cultivation of the "ground." He died in 1994 from a heart attack while digging corn holes. The sixth son died as a baby. The daughter (the seventh child) lived in the parish of Hanover on land bought for her by the fifth son with remittances.

The family estate of this unrestricted, dispersed, and ever-increasing Anderson landholding corporation comprised three small plots of land (½ acre, ¼ acre, and 3 square chains, totaling just over 1 acre), scattered throughout Martha Brae, that Madeline traced to the aftermath of emancipation. A fourth plot had been sold to raise money to pay the taxes on the remaining family lands. Madeline stated that the half-acre plot was "family land" left by her paternal grandfather for his three children: her father, her uncle, and her migrant aunt who paid the taxes that later lapsed. Madeline, who did not know precisely how her grandfather acquired this land, saved it from forfeiture to the government by paying the outstanding tax. This half-acre plot was where she had made her house yard since 1952: first in a one-room wooden cottage and then in a four-room concrete house, built with the help of her fifth son's migrant remittances. In the early years of my fieldwork, her legal husband lived there with her until his death in 1976. He was a carpenter who was a Stranger from St. James, but he became sufficiently accepted in Martha Brae to serve as chaplain for the village's friendly society (chapter 6), which later buried him. (Madeline belonged to a "burial society" in Granville.) Four of Madeline's grandchildren lived with them. At that time, her two maternal half siblings (a sister and a brother) also resided in this yard. Although they were not members of her paternal Anderson Old Family, she allowed them rent-free house-spots for their chattel cottages, cultivation, and small livestock, and permitted them to pick from the fruit trees on the land, where they lived until their deaths. Madeline herself cultivated a food forest in the yard, with root crops and banana shrubs canopied by fruit trees. She also kept a duck and fowls and had once raised white pigs. (In 1979, at the age of sixty-nine, she also cultivated her fifth son's provision ground.) In 1995 she still farmed her house yard, and an adult granddaughter and the granddaughter's son lived with her, while an adult grandson "moved" between Madeline's household and the squatter settlement of Zion: "he go and come." In addition, she had long had tenants on this land: first in her former wooden "one-room" and then in her late maternal half brother's cottage, which she purchased from his daughter. In 1968 two of her former tenants, Tom and Mary Grant, became the founders of Zion (chapter 4).

The quarter-acre plot, which adjoined the one-acre portion of the Thompson family lands near the border of Irving Tower Plantation, had long been a tenant yard. It initially included a house built by Madeline that "mash now" (had fallen into disrepair). There was also a concrete house constructed by her fifth son, the returned migrant who died in 1994, now occupied by his son. This quarter-acre plot is said to have come from Madeline's father Henry Anderson and his mother Nana Green, who had been a slave girl on Irving Tower Estate. Madeline was not sure how this land had been obtained and thought her father may have bought it; she stressed that "I [born] come see him 'pon it, he and his mother." That plot may therefore also have been transmitted from Madeline's paternal grandfather. This was where Madeline (whose own mother died soon after she was born) grew up, raised first by her paternal grandmother, Nana Green (until her death in 1922, when she was buried in the village cemetery), and then by a stepmother. After the death of Henry Anderson, Falmouth Baptist minister Parson Knight acted as caretaker for this piece of land until Madeline was able to assume the trustee-ship "long after." Combined with the burial of Madeline's two young sisters in the yard of the Martha Brae Baptist Prayer House, near the beginning of the twentieth century, this further indicates Baptist involvement in the trans-formation of Martha Brae. In addition, the transition from the yard burial of the two young sisters to Nana Green's interment in the village cemetery in 1922 locates the transformation of burial patterns in Martha Brae in the early decades of the twentieth century.[19]

In 1979 two of Madeline's sons (her first and fourth — maternal half siblings) and nine of her grandchildren lived on the three-square-chain plot of land in two houses: her former cottage and a house built by her eldest son. At that time Madeline also rented a house-spot to a tenant for his chattel cottage. In 1995 the eldest son remained there with his wife and some of his children and grandchildren; he was still there in 2000. By 1995 the fourth son had moved to live in his wife's house at Zion (where he died in the late 1990s) with one of their children and five of their grandchildren, while one of their daughters now lived with her children in the cottage on the family plot.

This three-square-chain piece of land is traced back to Madeline's pater-nal grandaunt, Christian Anderson, and to a John Anderson who appears to have been either Christian's brother (Madeline's paternal grandfather) or the father of these siblings (Madeline's great-grandfather). Complementing this account is the name of Christian Anderson in the 1876 Trelawny Land Tax Roll against a plot of land in Martha Brae. This three-square-chain plot, like the other two pieces of land, was part of the Anderson family estate, as Madeline explained:

That a generation [land]: Anderson, Anderson, Anderson, Anderson. Now mek I tell you something. Me father told me that he had an aunt, and the aunt told him that he [she] get the land from John Anderson. And John Anderson leave the land to Christian Anderson. And Christian Anderson give Henry Anderson, which is my father, the land. And Henry Anderson give it to me. So that land now, *not* to be sold; not to be sold. It must go from generation to generation. We call it the "family land," because it come from one straight to me, you know.

Madeline planned to leave the family estate for descendants of the Anderson Old Family, continuing this tradition of family-land transmission: "It [the land] not to be sold, it not to be sold. It has to leave for gran [grandchildren]: the daughter' and son' [daughters' and sons' children]. Everybody touch up [shares the land]. Me have 'nough [plenty descendants]. Me have twenty-seven grandchildren and, according to it, three [more] must be on the way. Them can partake anything. All of them [can] go over and pick [from the fruit-trees on the land]." This was the situation in 1969, when we first discussed the land. By the early 1980s Madeline had, in addition to her five living children, forty grandchildren and seventeen great-grandchildren, and at least all of those sixty-two descendants were considered coheirs to the family estate. Madeline insisted that all of these descendants (only a few of whom lived on the land) had inalienable rights to the family lands. By 1995 she had forty-seven great-grandchildren. Her ninety-two descendants (dispersed in Martha Brae and Zion, elsewhere in Jamaica, and in England) were among the coheirs to a family estate, just over one acre in size, that served primarily as a symbol of the fruitful family line and its status as a landowning corporation in the context of intense land scarcity.

The strength of sentiment surrounding this symbolic family land is reflected in the outcome of a court case, described by Madeline, that occurred around the late 1940s concerning one of these pieces of land (the three-square chains). Madeline had been living there with her second spouse, who subsequently died. After his death the Parish Council gave her an allowance to help support her children but later advised that, as she had this land, she did not qualify to be on the council's Paupers' Roll. She was therefore instructed to either return the money or forfeit the land: "After a while, now, Government seh [said] me have to pay back the money — seh me no Pauper! Me go all a court for it and them tell me seh that me have to pay back the money, or else, the land." Madeline repaid the money rather than forfeit the family land.

Since then Madeline had made the complex practical arrangements regarding the short-term economic use of the three portions of the family estate, and by 1995 she had specific plans for allocating future rights to these plots through her children in light of voluntary nonuse by other members of the Old Family. All of her descendants had been allocated usufructuary rights to the family estate. Her half-acre yard would be for the use of her migrant second son in England, who was visiting her at that time. Her daughter would have shared this land but was now established on land of her own in Hanover that Madeline's fifth son had bought for his sister with remittances before his death. The daughter of Madeline's third son, who died in 1961, lived with her on this house yard but planned to move to Zion (where she was building a house) when her grandmother died. However, this granddaughter was still at Madeline's yard, with her own son, in 2000. The fifth son, who helped to build his mother's concrete house, likewise lived there on his return from England until his death in 1994. But the ¼-acre plot was especially for him to use, and his son now lived there in the house his father built, while her son's daughter stayed in England. The three-square-chain piece was for Madeline's first and fourth sons and their descendants, and some of these coheirs were living on the land. In this way, Madeline's ninety-two descendants had all been allocated rights to a miniscule family-land estate of just over an acre in size, transmitted from emancipation to the new millennium. In August 2000 I learned that Madeline's second son had died in England and that his ashes were being interred in the Martha Brae cemetery, where his mother and four brothers were buried.

The Kelly Old Family

Rupert Bailey, born around 1905, was the oldest living member of the Kelly Old Family in Martha Brae throughout my fieldwork until his death in the late 1990s. In 1996, at the age of ninety-one, he was also the oldest living member of all of Martha Brae's Old Families. In 1990, at eighty-five, he had recently retired as president of the village's friendly society (chapter 6), an office he held for thirty-five years. He thus had long been a prominent person in the community. Like many Martha Brae villagers, he was a member of the William Knibb Memorial Baptist Church in Falmouth. Rupert explained the significance of the Baptist Church and Knibb: "What I know about the Baptist Church was that in time of slavery the parson at the [Falmouth] Baptist Church was a Reverend William Knibb. And he was the one, as I understand, who leave here and go to England for the liberation of slavery. That's why I was even wondering why he couldn't be one of those men — such like Manley and Busta [Norman

Manley and Sir Alexander Bustamante] — why he wasn't recognised as an Hero." (Shortly after this extract was recorded, in 1988, the 150th anniversary of emancipation, William Knibb was declared a National Hero by the Jamaican state.) However Rupert's oral history, unlike the oral traditions of the three other Old Families outlined in this chapter, does not highlight Baptist involvement in the transformation of Martha Brae, though it does reflect the significance of the Baptist Church in the community. Nor, as in those other cases, does it focus on ex-slave settlers from Irving Tower Plantation. Instead, it suggests a complementary perspective on land purchases in the colonial town, namely, peppercorn sales of land to emancipated slaves from Holland Plantation by the owner of Holland.

Rupert traced his ancestry in the Kelly Old Family through his father to a freed slave from Holland Plantation, Rupert's paternal grandmother's grandfather, who settled in Martha Brae after emancipation. As Rupert had children, grandchildren, great-grandchildren, and great-great-grandchildren, the Kelly Old Family comprised nine postslavery generations, including eight generations traced through cognatic descent from the emancipated slave. But the Kellys were no longer a landholding corporation due to the forfeiture of their family land (discussed below). Nevertheless, the Kelly family now overlapped with the Minto Old Family, Martha Brae's largest landholding descent group, for the mother of one of Rupert's daughters, Ruth Marshall, was the great-granddaughter of the ex-slave George Minto and the great-great-granddaughter of his emancipated parents, who all came from Irving Tower Estate. Ruth, her children, grandchildren, and great-grandchildren were therefore all members through unrestricted cognatic descent of both the Minto and the Kelly family lines. The Kellys also overlapped with the Anderson Old Family, and two contemporary generations of a segment of the Andersons were recognized as members of the Kelly family line. Meanwhile, Rupert had acquired land of his own in Martha Brae from which he re-created family land for his descendants.

Rupert, who was fostered by his paternal grandmother in the village, learned from her that her grandfather (his great-great-grandfather) was one of several freed slaves from Holland Plantation who bought land in Martha Brae. Rupert portrayed all the ex-slave land purchases in Martha Brae as peppercorn sales by the owner of Holland Estate. Yet the historical evidence of retrieval of plots from squatters by the vestry, the indications of Baptist involvement, and the presence of family lands and family lines originating from Irving Tower ex-slaves indicate a more complex process of transformation in Martha Brae. Moreover, Rupert's oral history itself subsequently indicated the historical significance of Irving Tower Estate to Martha Brae. In addition, the Thompson oral tradition states that a one-acre plot in Martha Brae was bought by an ex-slave ancestor from Irving Tower for twenty pounds (rather than through a peppercorn sale).

Nevertheless, Rupert's account, combined with the preceding evidence, adds further insight into the transformation of Martha Brae. His narrative also indicates that occupational stratification among former slaves (in addition to status within the Baptist Church and protopeasant savings) was a significant basis for differential access to land among ex-slaves:

> You see, I have learnt a lot from the older people, because what I'm saying here now, it is not what I see, but what I *learn*; [from] my grandmother and so on. I discover from my grandmother, my father's mother, because those were the people I grew with. . . . After Holland as an estate, and then after slavery, after the abolishment, they gave the people [ex-slaves] that was working on the estate, they gave them this plot of land — the whole of Martha Brae. . . . The estate owner, slave master from Holland [gave them]. I don't recall the name of the slave owner. So they had these places in plots and according to ability [occupational stratification] in the estate, you find that some of the people get more than some — bigger lots.

Rupert went on to explain that although the land was, in effect, "given" by the owner of Holland to his ex-slaves, the "gifts" of land were transacted through nominal purchase payments to establish and protect freehold land rights among the former slaves:

> When the land was really given to the slaves after emancipation, they gave them these lands with [for] a partial sum. That is to say that the land, it is *given*, but that one shilling [paid], as it was, is peppercorn [nominal purchase]. Just to show that they [the ex-slaves] are sole owners of the land. . . . The person who they [the estate owner] gave the land to pays that shilling or two shillings, whatever it might be, to show ownership of the land. . . . Just that amount and no more. Because you see, if something had not been paid, however small it is, it could be taken away. But something is paid for the land. . . . It is actually *bought*. But that was the little amount. Because they [the ex-slaves] couldn't have money. . . . You see, you [the estate owner] want to give them for nothing.

Reinforcing Rupert's oral account is the historical evidence of the names of three Kellys in the 1876 land tax records for Martha Brae, with one of these names also appearing in the 1831–38 Falmouth Baptist Church records kept by William Knibb, registered as resident on Holland Plantation. In addition, the oral history of the Minto Old Family states that its ex-slave ancestor William Minto purchased two of his three plots of land from three ex-slave siblings who were surnamed Kelly.

Rupert pointed out that the settlement of Martha Brae by ex-slaves occurred after the town's decline as Trelawny's capital. He also provided insight into the wharfing of sugar on the Martha Brae River, at the edge of the town, from both Irving Tower and Holland Estates, and remarked on the role and layout of the colonial town:

> Because it was the first town [in Trelawny]. But it must be after that it was given to the slaves. Because what I understand, the sugar that Irving Tower Estate made, just behind where I am living there now, I understand that they used to wharf it there. And then they move it [the wharf] from there and go down by the cane-field where a big oak tree was. That is down on Holland on the [Martha Brae] river; beside the river. They took it from down there and boat take the sugar down the river go out into the sea and they ship it. [So] when it [Martha Brae] give over [became transformed], we [our ancestors] didn't come and see the town. Because that time Falmouth was the town — after. So when there was a town we didn't know. It is from what we gather. And how we could really said "yes, it was a town" is because the streets were there, and they were with names.

Like William Tapper of the Thompson Old Family, Rupert observed that most of the buildings in the postemancipation village had been built by the ex-slaves and their descendants.

Rupert's ex-slave great-great-grandfather from Holland Plantation was, with the peppercorn purchase of a two-square-chain plot in Martha Brae, the originator of the Kelly family land. Freehold rights to this property (which is directly across the road from Holland Estate) were transmitted by the former slave to his descendants until the death of Rupert's paternal grandmother (a grandchild of the ex-slave), who lived and raised Rupert in that yard. Though intended to be retained by the Old Family, the land was forfeited to the Parochial Board following the grandmother's death: she was on the Paupers' Roll and "so the land was lost." (In 2000 Rupert's daughter Ruth remarked that her father should have later bought back his grandmother's land.) The land was sold by the Parochial Board and has since been sold again to an immigrant Stranger who built a concrete house. There were also two chattel cottages and a shop there. (By 2001 there were three chattel cottages and two shops.) One of these houses covered the Kelly family burial ground, with its earthen graves that Rupert recalled seeing as a boy. As he explained, "They used to bury dead in the land [yard] before they had a cemetery; all about, in nearly all the yards [in Martha Brae]."

After his grandmother's death, Rupert, who was then twelve years old, went to live with his mother, Beatrice Sneddon, who was from a Granville family line but lived at that time as a tenant in Martha Brae. His mother's maternal half sister, however, inherited half an acre from her father in Martha Brae, and Rupert inherited this land from his maternal aunt in return for his care and support in her old age. He now lived on this plot, across the street from the one-acre portion of the Thompson family land near the border of Irving Tower Estate, reinstated among the freeholders of Martha Brae.

During much of my fieldwork, Rupert's late wife (his fourth spouse) lived on this land with him, and they cultivated a kitchen garden and reared fowls in the yard. In addition, he became a landlord, with a tenant household on the land. In his younger days, he had also cultivated a provision ground on the backlands of Hague Estate as well as migrating for farmwork in Florida. I once trekked with him to his provision ground, which adjoined the hilly and rocky grounds of other villagers. Despite the distance from Martha Brae and the marginality of the land, these cool provision grounds with their spectacular sea views provide respite from the heat, a meeting place for villagers, and an autonomous sphere from the plantation lowlands. The economic, social, and symbolic role of these provision grounds therefore reflects a direct continuity from the protopeasant past.[20]

Rupert's oral history of the Kelly family land, and of the peppercorn land purchases by ex-slaves from their former owner on Holland Estate, parallels Edith Clarke's view that land grants to freed slaves were the origin of Jamaican family land in "its historical or primary sense" (1966:60). Clarke argued that such "grants made by the donor probably to individuals" were "interpreted by the recipient and the members of that family as including all the family in perpetuity" (60). However, the data from Martha Brae and other Trelawny villages indicate wider origins of the family-land institution, namely, roots in protopeasant institution-building and consolidation through various land purchases by emancipated slaves. These included purchases through the Baptist Church and among freed slaves themselves and, in the case of Martha Brae, probably peppercorn sales from the former slave owner of Holland Estate. Trelawny peasant oral traditions also highlight the rational strategy, by ex-slaves, of creating family land: to transmit freehold rights to all descendants in the context of plantation-engendered land scarcity and to root their family lines in free villages, rather than being a misinterpretation by the ex-slaves. Rupert's account of peppercorn land sales by the owner of Holland Estate to his former slaves has further significance, indicating an exception to the rule of Trelawny planter opposition to postslavery peasantization in the immediate postemancipation period. This exception would be paralleled more than a century later with Lawyer's peppercorn sales of land from Holland and Maxfield Estates to the descendants of ex-slaves in Martha Brae and Granville.

In the course of his narrative, Rupert observed that (as reflected in the Kelly Old Family itself) contemporary Martha Brae showed both continuity and change in relation to the postemancipation past. Continuity, he pointed out, could be seen in the presence of descendants of the ex-slave settlers — "I would be one, 'Miss Minto' would be one" — and in the lands still held by the Old Families. Change, however, had occurred as some of the Old Families had died out or their members had migrated permanently from the village, with Strangers buying their land: "You see, they change up. People came in. Some Families sold their lands. Then there are some people who leave the land alone. All Family goes from the land and leave the land. So you see, when somebody else comes in they bought these lands, probably from the Parochial Board at first, and then we had Parish Council. Then those lands is bought. So you see, [in those cases] the ancestors is directly die out from the land." Land sales in the village had also resulted from forfeiture of lands to the Parochial Board/Parish Council (as in the case of the Kelly family) and by the need to raise tax money for other plots of land. Also as Rupert noted, in addition to the ex-slaves from Holland (and Irving Tower), the ancestors of some Martha Brae villagers had arrived more recently from other Trelawny peasant communities such as New Cargen and Sawyers. He similarly highlighted the expansion of the free village of Martha Brae in the late 1940s through land purchases from Lawyer on Holland Estate.

In 1995 Rupert, at the age of ninety, again migrated to Florida. His son, who was a migrant there, had returned to Martha Brae to visit and had taken him back to the United States. After two of Rupert's daughters (Ruth and one of her half sisters) spoke to him on Ruth's recently installed telephone, they told me that he was undecided as to whether he would remain in Florida or return to Martha Brae. American city life did not seem to suit him, for, as he put it, "I don't know night from day." Meanwhile, the younger of these two daughters was residing in his house, and the older, Ruth (who also belonged to the Minto Old Family), lived with her husband and some of their children, grandchildren, and great-grandchildren on their own bought land in the village. By 1996 Rupert had returned to his own yard, where he died within a couple of years. He was buried in the Martha Brae cemetery, and his house yard passed on to his descendants. In

2001 Ruth herself had gone to visit some of her children in the United States but firmly intended to return home to Martha Brae.

In 2000 Ruth described how her father had transmitted his house yard, illuminating the contemporary creation of family land and illustrating a variation on this theme. Before his death, Rupert summoned Ruth, as his eldest child, to "share-out his yard" among his children, some of whom had children, grandchildren, and great-grandchildren of their own. Since Ruth was settled with her husband on their own bought land and also had Minto family land, and since one of her paternal half sisters lived on maternal Anderson family land, Ruth renounced her own share in her father's land and "shared-out" his yard among her other three paternal half siblings (a brother and two sisters, full siblings, all of whom were in the United States), and their descendants. One of these half sisters, who lived with Rupert in his declining years, was also given his house (where her brother's daughter's son lived in her absence), while one of the brother's sons lived with his children in a "one-room" chattel cottage on the land.

In the early years of my fieldwork, Rupert himself had a traditional wooden cottage. By the 1980s, however, the cottage had been replaced by a concrete house built with his son's migrant earnings. Such "concretization" of free-village land is an escalating feature of peasant villages in Trelawny and elsewhere in Jamaica, as overseas migrants send remittances to kin or return to retire, build, and reside on family land, or on other inherited land or purchased land—especially with the maturation, from the 1990s, of the pensions of many migrants who left for North America and Britain (chapter 6) during the peak migrations of the 1950s and 1960s. In the case of family land, such developments both reflect and test the dynamics of unrestricted cognatic descent (chapter 8). But gaining and retaining access to "land of their own" (Farley 1964:52)—not only through legal means but also by customary tenures, especially family land—in the context of persisting land scarcity has remained a central theme among the Martha Brae peasantry from emancipation to the present. Such land, in addition to its articulation with kinship, state law, religion, and oral tradition (chapters 4–5 and 7–8), provides a central basis for the peasant economy including house yards and provision grounds in and around the village (chapter 6).

CHAPTER SIX

Elaborations of the Peasant Economy

Caribbean peasantries have been Eurocentrically portrayed as inhibiting development, in contrast to the large-scale, monocropping, export-oriented plantation system based on legal freehold. They have been criticized for their "uneconomic" fragmented farms, "underproductive" customary land tenures, "chaotic" cultivation, and "wasteful" small-scale marketing systems.[1] Yet Martha Brae villagers, on their scarce, marginal land base, hemmed in by persisting plantations and escalating land monopoly in the tourist industry, have elaborated a peasant economy that represents "indigenous knowledge" (Purcell 1998) and Afro-creole development. Like the peasant village itself and its small-scale tenures, including family land and squatting, this economic system has been created by appropriating and transforming colonial institutions in a dynamic process of Caribbean culture-building.

This chapter explores this system of production, consumption, and exchange, which has evolved as a significant dimension of Martha Brae's Afro-creole cultural history. Like family land, some dimensions of the peasant economy are rooted in the culture-building of the protopeasant past and have been reinforced in the context of the island's postslavery agrarian relations; these include the house-yard complex, the internal marketing system, and some aspects of occupational multiplicity and mutual aid. Other dimensions of the village economy evolved after emancipation, such as wage labor, cash cropping, and migration. More recently, during the period of my fieldwork, river-rafting tourism and informal commercial importing have been incorporated. Considered first is the house-yard complex (including the dichotomy of "yard" and "ground"), which, based on multiple small-scale tenures, is the nucleus of the economic system.

The House-Yard Complex

The basic unit of Martha Brae's peasant economy is the domestic group or household,[2] located in the house yard. In his classic essay on "Houses and Yards among Caribbean Peasantries," Sidney Mintz (1989: 231–32) argued that "the house is far more than a fabrication of wood and thatch, the yard far more than a locale for the house. Together, house and yard form a nucleus within which the culture expresses itself, is perpetuated, changed, and reintegrated." In Martha Brae, the house-yard complex of the emancipated slaves and their descendants, originating in the protopeasant adaptation of enslaved Africans and Creoles on Holland and Irving Tower Plantations, also appropriated and transformed the planter town. The Martha Brae data further extend and modify Mintz's perspectives, and are illuminated by the recent excavations of slave villages in the parishes of St. Ann and St. James bordering Trelawny (Armstrong 1990; Higman 1998).

Peasant Adaptation and Settlement

Mintz (1989:234–36) emphasized the highland adaptation of Caribbean peasantries, in contrast to the monopoly of the coastal plains and intermontane valleys by plantations especially in Puerto Rico and Jamaica. However, many Trelawny free villages were established as reservoirs of labor for the surrounding plantations and were therefore founded on marginal land bordering estates. As a variation on this theme, the free village of Martha Brae evolved on a marginal ridge where Holland and Irving Tower Estates adjoin; it persists in the Trelawny plantation heartlands less than two miles from the tourist coast. Martha Brae's layout of house yards therefore differs from the dispersed highland settlement identified by Mintz, and Trelawny free villages reflect the "coherent patterning" of Jamaican church-founded communities that he cited as an important exception to this theme (238). In Martha Brae this nucleation is even more pronounced, as ex-slaves appropriated the site of a colonial town and retained its grid of streets. Within this setting land is extremely scarce, as reflected in the miniscule house yards that are usually only a few square chains.

Yard, Ground, and Mountain

The dichotomy of house yards and provision grounds identified by Mintz (1989:236–38), and by Douglas Armstrong (1990) and Barry Higman (1998) for Drax Hall Old Village in St. Ann and the Montpelier slave communities in St. James, is elaborated in Martha Brae. Here the distinction between yards and grounds originated in the highly developed Trelawny protopeasant adaptation, where slaves cultivated kitchen gardens in slave village yards and provision grounds on the hilly backlands of some plantations. But Trelawny was one of those Jamaican parishes where the slaves' provision grounds were often on separate estate "mountains" farther inland (Higman 1988:265–66), such as Holland Mountain. This trichotomy of yard, ground, and mountain persists in Martha Brae, where mountains are a source of timber and the location of some family land. The dichotomy of yard and ground on estate backlands closer to the village is, however, a central theme.

Land use on yards and grounds among the villagers varies according to land tenure and even differs within the tenure type of family land. Kitchen gardens are intercropped on purchased, leased, and rented land, and on some family land, and are the nucleus of peasant farms (Brierley 1991). Yards on family land also have ancestral fruit trees and multicropped "food forests" (Hills 1988) on some purchased and family land. In other cases clusters of houses on family land leave little room for cultivating, as in tenant yards. Poultry and small livestock (fowls, ducks, pigs, and goats) are often reared in yards, though miniscule size and insecure tenure may inhibit even this activity.

Despite the creativity of kitchen gardens, food forests, and family-land adaptations, Martha Brae is too confined on its scarce land base to enable sufficient cultivation in the yards. Villagers therefore acquire provision grounds on the backlands of properties and plantations, and it is this adaptation to land scarcity that generates fragmented farms. Many such grounds are insecurely held — as free land, or through squatting, lease, or short-term rental — though some are on purchased land. Insecure tenure further constrains cultivation: leasehold and rental inhibit long-term investment, squatting carries potential sanctions of eviction, and free land is open to exploitation by estate owners, as land may have to be relinquished unharvested. Despite these obstacles, Martha Brae villagers produce intensively on their provision grounds through intercropping and shifting cultivation, using unmechanized technology (machete, fork, spade, pickax, and hoe), a successful adaptation originating in the protopeasant past (Brierley 1987; Innes 1987).

The Caribbean cropping complex on yard and ground is likewise rooted in the ingenuity of protopeasant slaves, who synthesized food crops of New World, African, European, and Oceanic origin.[3] In Martha Brae, such crops include a range of economic trees (coconut, breadfruit, pimento, papaya, citrus, sweetsop, akee, and avocado); corn, plantains, and bananas; root crops (cocos, dasheen, Irish and sweet potatoes, cassava, and yams); vegetables (tomatoes, onions, callaloo, capsicums, scallions, and beans); and herbs and spices (peppers, peppermint, and thyme). The agricultural cycle is guided by local wisdom and linked with magical and pseudoscientific beliefs relating to phases of the moon.[4]

This small-scale diversified production dovetails with peasant consumption and exchange, as in the protopeasant past. Crops are produced mainly for household use, and cooking reflects creative creolization: both among crops grown (e.g., combining tomatoes, onions, herbs, and spices with coconut oil and yams) and between such crops and products bought in shops: like "salt-fish and akee" and "rice and peas," protopeasant culinary creations that now represent Jamaica's national cuisine.[5] In addition, small surpluses are grown to sell in the Falmouth marketplace. Some villagers also produce cash crops for the world economy, a pattern of production established in the "period of consolidation" of the Caribbean postslavery peasantry (Marshall 1985). In Martha Brae cash crops include pimento ("allspice"), bananas, and especially sugarcane, which is sold to Hampden Estates. Through this small-scale diversified cultivation on yards and grounds, the Martha Brae peasantry has reversed the pattern of large-scale, export-oriented plantation monocropping to maintain itself in the face of persisting land monopoly.

House Types and Internal Differentiation

In addition to tenures of yards and grounds, house types and tenures reflect and contribute to differentiation in Martha Brae's peasant community, as was the case with customary land rights and architectural variation in the Montpelier slave communities (Higman 1998:180, 193). Houses range in size from one-room chattel cottages to several rooms and, as in Jamaican slave plantation villages, the number of rooms is an index of prosperity and prestige.[6] Houses vary from the traditional wattle and daub, "Spanish wall," and board, as used in the slave communities, to more recent concrete structures. Roofs in the slave villages were of palm tree thatch or wooden shingles, and though some shingled roofs remain, others are now of corrugated iron. The presence or absence of electricity in the house is another differentiating variable.

The yard is an extension of the house; the hedge or fence around the yard is thus, in a sense, the outer boundary of the house itself. In my earlier fieldwork few houses had running water, though there was generally a stand-pipe in the yard. Pit latrines and outdoor bathing shelters typified most yards, and clothes were washed in pans outside and dried in the wind and sun. "Outside kitchens," with "coal-pots" or firesides, were another frequent feature, as in slave villages (Armstrong 1990:268; Higman 1998:177), but by 2001 more houses had indoor bathrooms and kitchens. The yard is also used for socializing and children's play, and there may be benches under shade trees. The area of the yard not used for buildings or cultivation is cleared of bush and swept daily with a broom. Some houses have verandas, which serve as a transitional space between the house and yard.

Yard tenure influences both the tenure and style of a house and its degree of permanence in the yard. Larger and more solid houses usually appear on purchased land and on some plots of family land, with smaller, flimsier structures on rented land or on house-spots in tenant yards. Migrant savings and remittances are increasingly affecting the size and type of house, and a growing number of newer, larger concrete houses are being built on bought or family land in Trelawny villages and other Jamaican peasant communities.

Mintz (1989:232–33) raised the question of the European or African architectural heritage of Caribbean peasant houses but noted that the evidence was inconclusive. Of Jamaican slave villages Orlando Patterson (1973:54) remarked, "The huts were built on the African pattern." Trelawny's slave communities reflected the general pattern of Jamaican slave villages, but, as Mintz (1989:233) cautioned, "we have no certain evidence that newly arrived Africans were ever able to build their houses according to their own traditions." In assessing "the sources of architectural style" in the Montpelier slave communities, Higman (1998:179–80) considered "the significance of cultural influences, the physical environment, the characteristics of available construction materials, and the economics of the slave system." However, his analysis of cultural influences was inconclusive. Armstrong (1990) identified West African influences for houses in Drax Hall Old Village but, consistent with his general view that enslaved persons at Drax "were participant creators of a new way of life and molders of Jamaican culture" (277), concluded that their "house remains suggest a local adaptation of the general Afro-Jamaican plantation pattern" and that such architectural creolization continued in free villages (101, 269). Green (1984) suggested that the "Jamaican vernacular" of small settler houses was a creative blend of Arawak, African, and European-Georgian traditions. This hypothesis could be usefully explored in the free village of Martha Brae, established on the site of a Georgian town. The ancestral home of the Minto

Old Family, Martha Brae's central family line, built with early migrant remittances, is an Afro-creole adaptation of the two-story architecture of the colonial town.

Daily Life and Divisions of Labor

The house and yard provide the basic setting for daily life and, to a large extent, define and reflect domestic divisions of labor. The house yard is essentially a female sphere, where women's most crucial work is done. Here children are brought up, clothes are washed, and food is cooked. Women also tend kitchen gardens and rear poultry and small livestock in the yard. Some women kept tiny grocery shops there, and two women had Revival-Zion churches in their yards (as did two more at Zion). The house yard is a focus of female social life, with much visiting of friends and kin. But female lives are not confined to the house and yard. Women play a central role in peasant marketing, which takes them to Falmouth and beyond. Some women also undertake wage labor in or outside the village. In addition, women are active in the Baptist Church in both Martha Brae and Falmouth. They are likewise central to Revival rituals with their village, parish, and island networking (chapter 7).

Most cultivation and the rearing of larger livestock, especially cattle, are pursued by men on provision grounds and landless farms at the edge of, or beyond, the village; wage labor may also take them outside Martha Brae. Men tend to socialize beyond the house yard, especially in rum shops, where they play dominoes and drink in peer groups.[7] (Dominoes are sometimes played in house yards as well.) In addition, men build houses and may butcher livestock in the yard.

These gender divisions of labor (and leisure) are, however, tendencies rather than rules. Several women cultivate or have cultivated provision grounds, especially when they have or had no resident spouse, and many participate in the labor market. During most of the period of my fieldwork the main rum shop in Martha Brae was kept by my landlady; some men have grocery stores. This gender flexibility is an adaptive strategy to the constraints of the peasant economy and is also a dimension of the creole conjugal system (chapter 8).

Age, as well as gender, provides a basis for divisions of labor in the peasant household. While small children play in the house yard with homemade toys, older children perform important economic roles. Older girls are socialized into adult female tasks, and boys soon learn to help with provision grounds and cattle raising. An early task for children of both genders is going to village stores, the age of children often being described as "old enough to go to shop." Thus children, as well as adults, are central to the peasant economy.

The Symbolism of the House Yard

In addition to being the nucleus of the economic system, the house yard has strong symbolic connotations. Mintz (1989:246–47) highlighted the significance of the yard as a symbol of independence from the plantations. Indeed, in Martha Brae, which is surrounded by plantations, the yard is an area of autonomy, as it was in Montpelier's slave communities (Higman 1998:144–45). Several households and houses may share a yard — for instance, households linked by kinship, as at Montpelier (136–37), especially on family land, and those in landlord-tenant relationships. In these contexts, the symbolism of the house is more pronounced, for, as among both Caribbean peasants and proletarians, "the rule of independent residence for cohabiting couples" ensures that conjugal couples live in a separate house (Mintz 1989:239). A couple that cannot, or does not wish to, establish a separate residence maintains an "extra-residential" or visiting relationship. The "neolocal" rule of independent conjugal residence, which is strongly adhered to in Martha Brae, therefore underlines the symbolism of the house as a basis of marital independence.

Mintz's (1989) discussion of the symbolic meaning of the house yard focused especially on family land (241–42, 246–47), which is at the heart of Martha Brae's new history. He observed that family-land yards expressed kin group continuity, identifying two features in addition to the links among the living: the burial of the afterbirth and interment in the yard "as is commonly the case in Haiti and as *was once the case in Jamaica*" (246, emphasis mine). In Martha Brae burial in the yard was replaced, in the early twentieth century, by interment in the village cemetery. However, yard burial persists in some other Trelawny villages, such as The Alps, Refuge, neighboring Granville, and parts of Kettering, as well as elsewhere in Jamaica — for example, Aberdeen in St. Elizabeth and Maroon Town in St. James. In addition, yard burial is now *emerging* in St. Elizabeth's Accompong Maroon community (Besson 1997, 2000, 2001a). In parts of Kettering, yard burial has been replaced by cemetery interment in the adjoining town of Duncans, which separates the dead not only from their family land but also from the free village. But in Martha Brae, burial in the village cemetery (which is now shared by Zion) has become a symbol of community identity and a basis for intercommunity Revival networking.

In Martha Brae, the custom of burying the afterbirth in the yard has been transformed by modern medicine. Trelawny has only one small hospital, in Falmouth, but this is less than two miles from Martha Brae. Despite their Revival-Zion worldview, with its magico-religious perception of causation, the villagers participate through the Falmouth hospital (and doctors' surgeries) in the scientific medical system, and nowadays the afterbirth is disposed of in the hospital. This transformation of birth from yard to ward reflects a widespread theme of change throughout Jamaica (MacCormack and Draper 1987:161–62).

Even yards that are not on family land have symbolic value, especially if they are established on freehold land. Yards on bought land symbolize economic independence, freedom, personhood, security, and prestige; individual land ownership is most highly prized. In addition, as among the emancipated slaves who bought land in the colonial town, purchased land is a legacy for descendants and tends to be transformed into family land. Tenant yards offer less status and independence than either legal or customary freehold but may represent a precarious independence, as in the case of some immigrant Strangers to Martha Brae who have rights to family land elsewhere. Even captured land may provide the basis of autonomous house yards, as in the appropriation of Holland Plantation land at Zion.

Cash Dependency

In addition to production on house yards and provision grounds for household use and export, Martha Brae villagers cultivate small surpluses for sale at the Falmouth marketplace in the island's internal marketing system. Like their export crop production, the villagers' market sales provide small quantities of cash with which to buy goods from shops in Falmouth and Martha Brae and from the Falmouth market. Money is also needed for land taxes and friendly society dues; for furniture, land purchases, house-building, and mortuary rituals; for employing some wage labor on yards and grounds; and for local transport and international airfares. Along with export crop production and sales in the peasant market, other sources of cash are wages, rotating savings and credit associations (ROSCAS), and migrant remittances. From the miniscule land base of their yards and grounds, the Martha Brae peasantry are enmeshed in the wider national and world economies and are therefore very cash dependent.[8]

The Peasant Marketing System

The Falmouth Marketplace

The Martha Brae villagers' marketing system, like their family-land institution and house-yard complex, originated in the protopeasant adaptation of the Trelawny plantation slaves who raised cash from marketing. This continuity is clearly seen in the persisting link between the Martha Brae peasantry and the Falmouth marketplace. From the late eighteenth century, when Falmouth began to eclipse the planter town of Martha Brae, Trelawny's protopeasant marketing focused on Falmouth, especially among the slaves in the plantation heartlands surrounding Martha Brae. On Sundays such protopeasants sold their surplus produce, from slave village yards and plantation provision grounds, on the streets of Falmouth and especially in the central square. So significant were these marketing activities that the main street and square in Falmouth came to be known as Market Street and Market Square (Ogilvie 1954:43; Concannon 1970:5). From about 1798 or 1799 the market was consolidated around the large stone water tank in Market Square, and in 1800 a shed for the Sunday market was built beside the square. In 1821 beef stalls were constructed in the market, and fish was sold (Ogilvie 1954:42–44). In 1830, four years before the abolition of slavery, Baptist missionary William Knibb commented on the vibrant weekly Falmouth Sunday market held by the protopeasant slaves (Wright 1973:56). Two years after emancipation, the classic lithograph from a daguerreotype by Adolphe Duperly of a "Jamaican Market around 1840, little changed from slavery days" (Craton 1978:284, cover) immortalized the Falmouth peasant market.

In 1896 the Albert George Market was constructed in Market Square (Ogilvie 1954:44); the Martha Brae villagers used it until 1982. By then, peasant marketing had so expanded that larger premises were built by the Trelawny Parish Council on the eastern edge of Falmouth. The market expanded further on this site, due to informal commercial importing, and its bustling activity on market days engrossed several street blocks beyond the marketplace, stretching to southern Tharp Street on the road to Martha Brae. As a result, the Parish Council ordered marketers to vacate the streets, an order that was only partially observed up to June 1999. At that time armed state police began patrolling the Falmouth market, which was closed soon after on health grounds. This attempt to contain informal marketing paralleled earlier efforts by the Jamaica Assembly and parish vestries to curb

The Albert George Market in Falmouth, founded in 1896. Photo by Jean Besson.

protopeasant marketing (Mintz 1989:197–98; Simmonds 1987:37–38). By the year 2000, however, the "new" marketplace was open once again. Bustling traders were overflowing to Tharp Street and beyond, music blared from a large sound system at the entrance to the market, and there was little sign of the police. The market continued to flourish in 2001.

On 9 December 1989 a local private company reopened the Albert George Market as a "historical and shopping center" in the tourist industry. In 2001 it remained a tourist attraction with souvenir, grocery, and dry goods shops and historical exhibits.[9] These exhibits included sugar-processing equipment and coins from the late eighteenth century. Among the coins was a large copper "cart-wheel," about two inches in diameter, which "the slaves hated" because it was so heavy to carry; a halfpenny; and "tokens given to the slaves" for collecting rat-bat manure from plantation mountain caves.[10] During slavery, such coins were part of the island's currency, at least 20 percent of which Edward Long estimated was controlled by protopeasants in 1774 (the zenith of Jamaican slavery) as a result of their marketing activities (Mintz 1989:199).[11] This market exchange has been both perpetuated and transformed by the slaves' descendants in Martha Brae, Falmouth, and elsewhere in Trelawny and Jamaica.

In 2001, after more than two hundred years of continuity and change, the Falmouth marketplace was Jamaica's most prominent rural market. It is part of an islandwide trading network, which links parochial capitals and smaller towns to the two most important urban marketplaces in the cities of Kingston and Montego Bay. This networking occurs through both the movement

A food stall at Falmouth's new market in the 1990s. Photo by Jean Besson.

of specialist market intermediaries, or "higglers," and the staggering of market days. In Trelawny, the Falmouth marketplace is linked to satellite markets in smaller towns such as Jackson Town near The Alps, Duncans adjoining Kettering, and Clarke's Town near Refuge. Throughout the 1990s–2001 period, I interviewed marketers in the Falmouth market from Trelawny (Albert Town, Ulster Spring, Stewart Town, Jackson Town, Bounty Hall, Deeside, Martha Brae, Zion, and Falmouth); from the parishes of Hanover, St. James, St. Ann, Westmoreland, St. Elizabeth, Manchester, Clarendon, St. Catherine, and St. Thomas; and from Kingston. The Parish Council's market clerk collects tax payments from such traders for the use of stalls.

As Paul Bohannan and George Dalton (1962) showed, the presence of the market *principle* and the market *place* vary inversely and this is reflected in the Falmouth marketplace. The location of the marketing system in a specific site underscores its smallness of scale. Transactions are miniscule when compared to those of the national and world economies, which are not confined to market sites. With the important exception of informal commercial importers (ICIs), who operate in the global economy, Falmouth marketers, including those from Martha Brae, are "penny-" (or dollar-) capitalists (Tax 1953) who straddle the interface between the national market economy and the village economies of the Jamaican countryside. They operate with small amounts of cash, small profit margins and market loads, small-scale purchases and sales, and large investments of time and labor. In this way thousands of individuals cooperate and compete throughout the island in the peasant marketing system. In this marketing network, stable and personalized channels of supply and demand may be established, consolidated, and symbolized through *brawta*: the giving, especially by higglers, of concessions of quantity, credit, or price to buyers to protect against scarcity and glut. The imposition of such personalized gift exchange (Mauss 1954) on the impersonal market principle typifies peasant markets throughout the Caribbean region.[12]

These features generate the vibrant, noisy, colorful markets that typify Falmouth on its market days: Wednesdays, Fridays, and Saturdays. The main food market is on Saturday, as has occurred throughout the island since emancipation with the shift from Sunday markets. Friday is also a major food market day. On these two days a wide variety of ground provisions, plantains and bananas, tree crops, vegetables, "red peas" (dried kidney beans), scallions, thyme, and other herbs and spices are bought and sold in and around the Falmouth marketplace. Meat, fish, cooked food, and drinks are also traded, as well as some dry goods.

Food marketing in Falmouth is mainly in the hands of women, as it is throughout Jamaica and the Caribbean.[13] This predominance of women correlates with tendencies in the gender divisions of labor in other dimensions of the peasant economy. In Martha Brae, and throughout the island and the region, female marketing activities complement the mainly male cultivator role. Women's marketing activities likewise dovetail with their commitments in the house and yard and may be scaled up or down as their domestic responsibilities diminish or increase. However, some women in Martha Brae cultivate provision grounds (as well as yards), and male food marketers and higglers were not as rare in the Falmouth market in the early 1990s as in the 1970s. By 1998 male food traders were much more noticeable due to larger-scale food higglering by van (especially in dasheen and yams for sale in Kingston and for licensed export) in some parts of Jamaica, including Upper Trelawny (Besson 1998b; Barker and Beckford 1998).

Wednesday has long been Falmouth's dry goods market day, and it is especially this market that has escalated since the 1980s, though the food markets are also flourishing. The Wednesday market is known as "Ben' Down Market," as many stalls are spread on the ground along the streets (as in protopeasant markets) so that buyers and sellers have to bend down to trade. Ben' Down Market stalls nearer the marketplace are laid out on

A clothes stall at Falmouth's Ben' Down Market in the 1980s. Photo by Jean Besson.

plastic sheets or barrows and covered by blue tarpaulins to protect them from the sun and rain.

The rapid expansion of Falmouth's Ben' Down Market has resulted from a new variant of small-scale marketing in Jamaica, namely, informal commercial importing, involving men as well as women (a central theme in *Higglers!*—Ginger Knight's Jamaican play that was also performed in London in 1995). In addition to representing a new dimension of the peasant marketing system, this development is a variation on the tradition of circulatory migration. Higglers of both genders now commute by air to Panama, Curaçao, Miami, and New York to buy goods retail and wholesale for resale in the Falmouth market and elsewhere in Jamaica. The main goods traded are clothes, bales of cloth, shoes, and vividly colored plastic pails and bowls, but other items include cosmetics, combs,[14] watches, jewelry, pots and pans, crockery, and small electrical appliances. Shoes are purchased especially in Miami and New York; clothes, in Curaçao and Panama (one higgler that I interviewed went to Panama five times a year); bales of cloth or "remnants," in Miami; and plastics, in Curaçao. The huge Ben' Down Christmas markets include tinsel decorations and exotic paper flowers. At Ben' Down from 1998 to 2001 large electric fans and brightly colored plastic laundry baskets were especially apparent, and marketers included ICIs and dry goods higglers (who may buy wholesale in Kingston) of both genders from Kingston in St. Andrew, Portmore and Spanish Town in St. Catherine, Montego Bay in St. James, Westmoreland Parish, Bounty Hall and Deeside near Granville in Trelawny, and Martha Brae's satellite squatter settlement of Zion. Such marketers include the higgler-daughter of the founders of Zion who in 2001 was still trading in laundry baskets, ironing boards, and electric fans bought from Kingston. The Ben' Down Markets that I attended in August 2000 and July 2001 were the largest I had seen during my long-term fieldwork, and ICIs included a female higgler who purchased cloth in California twice a year and a male higgler who flew to London several times each year to buy bales of cloth wholesale from Battersea and Brixton.

Despite high airfares, import taxes, and smallness of scale, such ICIs (and other dry goods higglers) maintain profitable retail market stalls. A similar transformation of the peasant marketing system, through overseas migratory higglering, is occurring elsewhere in the Caribbean,[15] though the Falmouth Ben' Down is probably the largest transnational market in the region and may have experienced the most significant change in gender identities and roles.

The Emancipation Anniversary Ben' Down Market held on Tuesday, 31 July 2001 (shifted from Wednesday, 1 August—Emancipation Day, a national holiday) was the largest market I have seen, despite downpours of rain. This market encapsulated both the symbol and the reality of the autonomy and freedom forged by protopeasant and ex-slave ancestors through the Afro-creole marketing system. This continuity with the culture-building begun in slavery was further indicated by the Emancipation Vigil held that evening, after the Ben' Down Market, in Falmouth's Market Square.

Marketers in Martha Brae

Martha Brae households with small food surpluses to sell usually send them by an adult female to the Falmouth marketplace. Some women have become specialists in this activity. Such higglers "buy and sell," that is, acting as intermediaries, they buy goods from other households or other higglers and resell them in the Falmouth market or from their house yards in Martha Brae. Sometimes goods are bought and sold at the village crossroads on River Hill. Variations on this intermediary role occur—for instance, a higgler may specialize in ground provisions, clothes, or fish. Some examples illustrate these variants of marketing in Martha Brae. These cases straddle the entire period of my fieldwork (1968–2001) as well as providing a perspective on peasant marketing throughout the twentieth century.

When I began my fieldwork in 1968, Jenny Hill, an established Stranger, was a retired higgler who formerly dealt in fish. Jenny was born in 1891 in the neighboring parish of St. James and started higglering there in 1903, when she was twelve years old, buying fish from fishermen and reselling at a marginal profit. After moving to Martha Brae early in the twentieth century, she purchased from fishermen at a beach near Falmouth. She resold the fish, usually on the streets of Falmouth but sometimes in Martha Brae, Granville, or the Falmouth marketplace, though she never had a regular stall. As her business became established, customers would also go to her house yard to buy fish. Jenny sometimes eked out her income with the resale of breadfruit, purchased at the market, to villagers in Martha Brae. Occasionally she sold small amounts of the bananas, coconuts, and limes that she grew in her tiny yard.

Early in my fieldwork Susan Soames worked as a small-scale ship chandler, taking orders for fruit and vegetables from ships docking in Falmouth Harbor. She had a monopoly on these orders and had pursued this business, from the mid-twentieth century, for over twenty years. Susan filled orders from one of two sources: either from vegetables grown in her kitchen garden, when finances and rain allowed (in which case, as she pointed out, this was "not higgling, but farming"), or from purchases at the Falmouth marketplace. She sometimes also sold her home-grown vegetables and fruit in either the market or her yard.

May Jackson was an established Stranger in Martha Brae, having moved from St. James with her spouse Joe to settle in the village in 1944. At first they lived as tenants, but by the late 1960s they resided on land of their own in a tiny cliff-side yard, which they bought through "lease-and-sale." Joe, who had rights to family land in St. James, cultivated a variety of food crops on a provision ground on captured land (now part of Zion) on Holland Plantation. They also grew some produce in their house yard. Their farming was mainly for household use, but May sold small surpluses in the Falmouth market, sometimes augmenting these with grapefruit, which she bought from another market woman and resold. She considered herself to be simply a "market woman" but was, in a limited sense, also a grapefruit higgler. By 1995, advanced in age, the Jacksons had given up their provision ground marketing activities (though they still cultivated the yard) and had become reliant on wage labor: he as a night watchman in Falmouth, she as a packer at the paw-paw factory on Holland Estate, jobs they were still doing in 1999 (though May retired in 2000). By the 1990s their roles as Revival Mother and Pastor had also become more central in their lives (chapter 7).

Throughout most of my fieldwork, Nora Hart was a food and dry goods higgler who built up her tiny business over several decades, starting with a capital investment equivalent to a few Jamaican dollars. She established a considerable reputation as a higgler in both Martha Brae and the Falmouth marketplace, where she had a regular stall that she moved from the Albert George Market to the new market in 1982. She resided with her sister on family land in Martha Brae and sometimes grew vegetables in her kitchen garden, as well as cultivating corn on her provision ground on free land beyond the village. However, she seldom grew enough to sell and therefore higglered in food produce, buying vegetables and ground provisions from other villagers and reselling them in the Falmouth market, which she attended three times a week. The food items in her tiny stall comprised miniscule amounts of vegetables and citrus, a slice of pumpkin, a few eggs, and herbs and "seasoning," such as scallions and thyme. In addition, she bought spices from Falmouth shops or other higglers, which she then decanted from their small containers and tied in minute parcels for resale. She would bring any unsold items back to sell in Martha Brae. In my later fieldwork, Nora expanded this dimension of her business, purchasing food (yams, cocos, bananas, and sweet potatoes) in the Falmouth market for resale in the village. She sold to six customers there weekly, but other villagers also went to her yard to buy these products.

Nora also higglered in dry goods on a tiny scale. At first she would ask another higgler in Falmouth to buy clothes for her in Kingston. But as her business became more established, she herself went to Kingston on Thursdays to buy clothes and other dry goods for her market stall. She also acquired a "colleague," a female cloth higgler from Granville who had the stall beside her and sometimes helped out by buying clothes for her in Kingston. At times they "watched" each others' stalls. As well as being higglers of reputation, both of these women played prominent roles in their village friendly societies. Later in my fieldwork, the colleague became ill and her niece took over her market stall. Nora continued higglering but, despite her large investments of time and labor, her profits remained small. By 1995 she had retired, in old age, on her family land, where she lived until her death about a year after. By 2000 Molly Sweeney had taken on part of Nora's role, buying produce from vans passing through the village and reselling in her yard.

Pam Gilmore, aged sixty-six in 2001, was a member of Martha Brae's central family line. After her eviction in 1991 from rented land in Martha Brae that she had inhabited for over forty years, she now resided with one of her daughters and three of her grandchildren on captured land on the Carib Road, adjoining Zion. In her former yard she had fruitful akee trees, but in her new yard she planted sugarcane, sweet potatoes, and bananas for household use. From time to time throughout my fieldwork she sewed clothes for sale in the Falmouth market. In 1995 she had just resumed this dry goods marketing and was buying cloth in Falmouth and Montego Bay, sewing underwear and children's clothes and selling them at her market stall on Saturdays and at the Wednesday Ben' Down Market. Her younger daughter, who lived with her, had recently begun to share the stall, buying cloth, rice, and cooking oil wholesale from Montego Bay, Saltmarsh, and Falmouth and selling retail in the Falmouth marketplace. Pam paid sixty Jamaican dollars a week for her stall but was often given credit. In 1999 she still sewed clothes and went to market, but her Rastafarian tailor-son, who lived on captured land at Hague, had taken over the sale of her homemade clothes in the Falmouth market. His move into marketing not only reflected the new trend of male ICIs and higglers throughout Jamaica, but was also a variant on a pattern of male Rastafarian marketing of clothes and crafts that emerged in the Falmouth marketplace around 1995. By 1999 this trend had developed further, with the resale of Rastafarian jewelry crafted and purchased in "the [Kingston] ghetto." In 2000 this male Rastafarian marketing had consolidated (and had expanded by 2001), but Pam had retired so her Rasta son just did tailoring at home. By then, too, Pam's younger higgler-daughter was working as a domestic in the United States. However, Pam's older daughter at Zion was now selling in the Falmouth market.

Although Martha Brae women (and some men) go to the marketplace mainly to buy and sell, "going to market" also provides the opportunity to see relatives and friends from Falmouth and other communities, and to enjoy a break from yard and village routine. The role of the market in disseminating information is likewise important in a context of limited literacy and access to television. The marketplace also reflects the subordinate position of the peasantry in capitalist class relations, and middle- and upper-class households obtain much of their food from peasant markets via domestic servants, whereas the power of the state is reflected through the Parish Council tax on market stalls and the policing of the market in 1999.

In his pioneering study of the Brown's Town marketplace in the parish of St. Ann (bordering Trelawny) in the 1950s, Mintz (1989:223–24) noted the need for further research on the relationship between marketing and production and on related gender divisions of labor. His hypothesis that peasant production and distribution "sustain one another" is substantiated by my study of cultivation and marketing among the Martha Brae villagers, whereas the long history of the Falmouth market and its continued expansion underline the small-scale marketing system as a mode of Afro-creole development. The role of marketing as a basis of some autonomy and prestige for peasant women, whose main alternative source of cash is domestic service (Katzin 1959b:439), is also seen in Martha Brae, where higglering provides some capital and independence and may also be a basis of reputation. Mintz's hypothesis of gender complementarity in male cultivation and female marketing is similarly substantiated to a significant degree. However, the increased recent involvement of men in dry goods marketing and even in food higglering reflects changing gender relations (Besson 1998b).

African Heritage and Caribbean Culture-Building

The predominance of female marketers and higglers in the contemporary Caribbean has been attributed to African influences (e.g., Herskovits 1937:260; Herskovits and Herskovits 1947:292). But in assessing the role of the African heritage, Mintz noted that, though women dominate Haitian and Jamaican postslavery markets as in West Africa, complementing a primarily male cultivator role, reports of protopeasant marketers provide no evidence that women outnumbered men and family groups; indeed, men probably outnumbered women. Moreover, the first marketplace in Jamaica was not African but English.[16] In a study including examination of the Trelawny slave-higglering system, Lorna Simmonds (1987:32) concluded that, although by the late eighteenth century gender division of labor in Jamaica was more marked among urban slaves than plantation slaves,[17] "the rural component [of trading] was at best shared between the sexes, with the possibility of the men being the principal cultivators, while urban marketing was dominated by females." She also suggested African influence on the marketing roles of urban female slaves (32), consistent with Higman's (1984:53–54) view that plantations rather than towns were the vanguard of creolization.

Nevertheless, Mintz's (1989:217) observation that in Jamaica "divorce among the slaves was consummated by tearing in two the *cotta*, or head-cloth" (used by Trelawny market women until the 1980s, when minivan transport replaced walking to market), and his "guess that this practice signified the breaking in two of a symmetrical economic relationship between male cultivator and female marketer," does suggest some gender differentiation among plantation slaves paralleling the female emphasis in urban trading. Moreover, urban and rural sectors were not isolated even during slavery, and the marketing network linked plantations and towns. Though Mintz (1989:216) had "no evidence that land use was ever afforded other than to male slaves," we now know that Afro-Caribbean women have obtained access to land and cultivated house yards and provision grounds since slavery days (Momsen 1988; Bush 1990:49; Besson 1992a, 1995d). A synthesis of the evidence therefore indicates some gender divisions of labor in relation to male cultivation and female marketing among the protopeasantry, but in a wider context of flexible gender roles and identities in these spheres, in contrast to more distinct gender ideologies among urban slaves.

After emancipation there was an increasing tendency toward male cultivation and female marketing in rural areas, as gender divisions of labor in agriculture replaced the age and health distinctions of the slave plantation fieldwork gangs (Patterson 1973:59–61; Momsen 1988:84, 92). From the classic lithograph of the Falmouth market around 1840, two years after emancipation, can be discerned both male and female marketers but a clear preponderance of women. Marketing and higglering provided women with opportunities for autonomy, mobility, flexible entrepreneurial roles, and an alternative source of cash to domestic service. Mintz and Price (1992:77) noted that in postslavery Haiti and Jamaica "women emerged as the overwhelming majority of marketers"; Mintz's (1960, 1989) research revealed the persisting predominance of female marketers and higglers in Haiti and Jamaica, complementing a male emphasis in cultivation. Mintz and Price (1992:80) therefore argued for active Caribbean culture-building in these gender roles, with African cognitive orientations regarding gender autonomy being "reinforced by the plantation experience," rather than for passive African retention.[18]

The data from Martha Brae and Falmouth advance this thesis of Caribbean institution-building by revealing not only continuing tendencies toward male cultivation and female food marketing, deriving from the protopeasant and postemancipation periods and reinforced by contemporary socioeconomic contexts, but also current change toward undifferentiated gender roles in dry goods trading and more flexibility even in food higglering. This trend toward gender flexibility in small-scale marketing is reminiscent of the protopeasantry, which appropriated the English institution of the marketplace (and in Falmouth took over the parish capital's central square) and whose descendants have continued to transform colonially derived large-scale export marketing through the creation and elaboration of a small-scale internal marketing system. The gender flexibility also complements the participation of both women and men in other areas of the peasant economy, for neither marketing nor cultivation are sufficient to sustain Martha Brae's peasant adaptation due to the scarcity of capital and land. Both genders thus reinforce their economic system by occupational multiplicity, migration, and mutual aid.

Occupational Multiplicity

In a comparative study of five Jamaican rural coastal communities, where fishing was combined with other productive activities such as cultivation and wage labor, Lambros Comitas (1973:162) argued that "no viable peasant subculture exists in Jamaica," as "poor, rural Jamaicans . . . cannot hope to maintain a subsistence level through agricultural production even with effective control of their limited land." Instead, he called such rural folk "occupational pluralists" due to the widespread phenomenon of "occupational multiplicity" (157, 169, 172).[19] Comitas's reasoning contrasted with Mintz's (1989:131–250) inclusion of Jamaican free villages in his analysis of Caribbean "reconstituted peasantries."

These differing views are encapsulated in the Trelawny free village of Kettering, which I studied as a reconstituted peasant community in relation to Martha Brae's new history but which is generally regarded as part of the adjoining town of Duncans, one of the communities in Comitas's study (1973:169–70). In Kettering (which Comitas did not distinguish from Duncans), as well as in Martha Brae and other rural communities of Trelawny, occupational multiplicity may be seen as a feature of the peasant economy and a dimension of the internal differentiation of the peasantry, reflecting the acute land scarcity that constrains the peasants' yard-ground-marketing complex.

Combining proletarian-type activities with small-scale cultivation has typified Caribbean peasantries since the protopeasant/protoproletarian adaptation (Mintz 1978; Craton 1994), when the cultivation of house yards and provision grounds and the marketing of surpluses took place in addition to plantation labor, which included the hiring out of slaves. In Martha Brae, this combination is now generally reversed: proletarian occupations of a wider range reinforce cultivation and marketing, though in some households cultivation supplements wage labor, reflecting not only the internal differentiation of the peasantry but also the "concealment" of proletarians in the peasant community (Mintz 1973, 1974a). The nature and extent of occupational multiplicity varies with an individual's or a household's access to land, and with the tenures of yard and ground. These variables affect cultivation, which may provide the primary means of livelihood or play a supplementary role. In addition, land may serve as the basis for security rather than production, enabling fuller involvement in nonagrarian roles. Occupational pluralism also varies to some extent with a person's gender, conjugal status, and age, as well as with the developmental cycle of the household. Overall, occupational multiplicity reflects both the struggle and the creativity of the villagers in maintaining their peasant economy.

Such occupational multiplicity is consistent with Dalton's (1967:265–67, 1971) characterization of peasantries in anthropology and history. Dalton defined "peasant" as a broad middle category between the two extremes of "tribal" (subsistence economy) and "post-peasant modern farmer," with socioeconomic organization typified by subsistence production combined with production for sale, the virtual absence of machine technology, a significant retention of traditional social organization and culture, and "incomplete" land and labor markets — that is, land and work are partly embedded in social relations. In Martha Brae, the partial land market permits the coexistence of legal and customary tenures, whereas the incomplete labor market combines the sale of labor with traditional production, thereby generating occupational multiplicity. Dalton's definition of peasantry encompassed various subtypes, including the "hybrid/composite peasantries" of Latin America and the Caribbean, and within this subtype Caribbean "reconstituted peasantries" may be identified.

Mintz's (1989:131–250) historical-anthropological approach to Caribbean peasantries, his emphasis on the significance of land for peasants in general (132, 141), and Dalton's comparative perspective on peasantries in time and space reinforce the validity of the concept of reconstituted peasantries in Martha Brae and other Trelawny free villages, particularly as they were established at the vanguard of the Caribbean ex-slaves' flight from the estates in a continuing quest for land of their own. This is especially so when the oral traditions of the villagers themselves emphasize freedom, kinship, community, and land. From these perspectives, Comitas's (1973) concept of occupational multiplicity may usefully be analyzed as a dimension of Martha Brae's peasant economy. Such plural occupations, like divisions of labor in marketing and cultivation, have complementary gender tendencies rather than exclusive male and female roles.

Men often combine cultivation with charcoal burning (for household use and sale), fishing (either in the Martha Brae River or on the coast near Falmouth), self-employment, or wage labor. Self-employment includes the butchering of livestock, carpentry, and shoemaking; wage labor may involve agricultural work on properties, pens, and plantations. Men also undertake roadwork for the Parish Council and the Public Works Department in Falmouth. Both types of wage employment may be casual or regular, casual labor including "day work" or "task work" on farms and estates. Task work dovetails with peasant agriculture, as it can be adapted to the cultivator's schedule. Most wage labor is unskilled, but a few men have skilled or super-visory jobs. In the past, some men worked as stevedores in Falmouth Harbor.

Women's work beyond the house yard and marketplace tends to be agri-cultural labor or domestic service. Agricultural labor takes place on planta-tions, properties, and pens; domestic service, either in middle- and upper-class households in Falmouth or on the estates surrounding Martha Brae. However, the increasing employment of domestic servants in village house yards, especially for laundering clothes, reflects growing internal differen-tiation that results mainly from migrant savings and remittances. Such dif-ferentiation is also reflected in the agricultural sphere, where some villagers (of either gender) employ others (mainly men) from the community to help on provision grounds, an arrangement that may parallel landlord-/landlady-tenant ties.

Self-employment for both women and men includes keeping small gro-ceries and rum shops in yards bordering village streets or crossroads and the Hampden-Falmouth main road. By 2001, there was a larger store in Martha Brae on the road from Falmouth to Rafters' Village on Southfield Estate. Women occasionally work at shops in Falmouth, and a few socially mobile villagers of both genders commute to clerical jobs in Falmouth, Montego Bay, and Kingston.

Over the years of my fieldwork, wage labor opportunities increased for both women and men. Male and female employment can now be obtained at the Fish Farm at Hague Pen and in the Carib Metal Factory on Holland Plantation, and women may work in the garment factory at Hague. The expanding North Coast tourist industry, including the Trelawny Beach Hotel near Falmouth, provides some jobs for bellhops, waiters, and domes-tics. But such work is highly competitive, largely seasonal, and dependent on fluctuations in global tourism.

Despite the dependent nature of the tourist industry, an expanding source of wage employment for the villagers is the rafting project estab-lished by the Jamaica Tourist Board (JTB) on the Martha Brae River shortly after my fieldwork began (1968). In 1969 Rafters' Village was set up by the JTB one-and-a-half miles upriver from Martha Brae, on a part of Southfield Estate purchased by the state, as the second major river-rafting project in Jamaica. Rafting begins at Southfield and finishes at a landing stage beneath the bridge at the eastern edge of Martha Brae. The training of "Captains" or raftsmen by the JTB began on 10 October 1969, and the first rafting licenses were issued on 15 December for the peak season in the Jamaican tourist industry (mid-December to the end of April). Raftsmen, who must make (and bear the cost of making) their own rafts,[20] are hired from Martha Brae and other nearby Trelawny communities such as Deeside, Sherwood, Wakefield, Falmouth, and Clarke's Town. Among the Martha Brae raftsmen are members of at least four Old Families — for example, Trevor Lindsey, who lives with other households in his Old Family on family land in Martha Brae, was the second raftsman to be awarded a license in 1969. In 2000, at the age of fifty-three, he had worked for thirty-one years at Rafters' Village.

In 1985 rafting was divested by the JTB to a private company, based in Montego Bay, which by 2000 owned Rafters' Village. From 1995 to 2001 the company employed ninety-two raftsmen and introduced T-shirts stamped with the project's name and captain's number.[21] Publicity has increased, and tourists, investing in package and combination tours,[22] arrive in Rafters' Village from hotels in North Coast resorts, including Ocho Rios and Montego Bay, and from Negril on the island's western tip. The recently refurbished luxury hotel on Good Hope Plantation, five miles inland from Martha Brae, advertises internationally the attractions of river rafting on the Martha Brae.[23] Cruise ships that dock at Ocho Rios and MoBay (especially from October to April) also provide tourists for rafting. As well as captains, Rafters' Village employs male and female staff in the gift shop, bar, and restaurant; some Martha Brae women sell cooked food at the river bridge.

In addition to cultivation, marketing, self-employment, local wage labor, and tourism, the occupational multiplicity of the Martha Brae peasantry has long involved migration.

Migration

In a pioneering essay on the establishment of the Caribbean overseas migration tradition after emancipation, through movements from the British West Indies to the Hispanic territories, Elizabeth Thomas-Hope (1978) initially concluded that "only through emigration could the former West Indian slaves attain the sense of freedom for which they yearned," as "the estates held the worst of past memories, and *even on smallholdings there was no deep-felt attachment to land*" (66, emphasis mine). However, such emigration (which occurred in the wider context of the flight from the estates) coexisted with the ex-slaves' acquisition, wherever possible, of land of their own (Farley 1964:52; Besson 1984a, 1992a). Migration and landholding were closely related: savings from migration provided capital for land purchase, and the unrestricted descent system at the heart of family land enabled return and circulatory migration (Besson 1979, 1987b, 1995d). In a subsequent analysis of Caribbean migration, Thomas-Hope (1980:36) noted a parallel between the slaves' "lack of freedom" and "their lack of land." She later highlighted the link between circulatory migration and the unrestricted cognatic descent system in family land that provided migrants with symbolic and economic security and the possibility of return (Thomas-Hope 1992:5, 1995:169) This dual role of land was paralleled by the symbolic as well as economic significance of migration among the emancipated slaves, for "freedom of movement" represented "an intrinsic part of the quest for a new identity," as well as a response to economic conditions (Thomas-Hope 1980:36).[24]

This twofold migratory rationale remains among the free villagers of Martha Brae, where overseas migration is both an avenue to autonomy and a strategy for reinforcing the peasant economy. Almost every household includes returned migrants or has migrant kin abroad. Such migration marks both adulthood and personhood, symbolizing independence, maturity, and prestige. The freedom of movement among the villagers since emancipation has also reversed the constraints of the slave plantation system; though migration parallels the flight of runaway slaves, the option to return contrasts with marronage (Thomas-Hope 1995). Migration is also interwoven with occupational multiplicity (Besson 1987a, 1988; Thomas-Hope 1995:168–69), and migrant savings and remittances have strengthened the peasant adaptation. Whereas some migrations are permanent or long-term, others are recurrent and some migrants have returned to settle. Such return is usually distinguished by social mobility, which may entail buying land or building a concrete house, especially on purchased land; rights to family land have facilitated return and circulatory migration. Overseas migration thus both reflects and contributes to internal differentiation in the peasant community.

Rural-urban migration is a significant aspect of occupational multiplicity and of the quest for identity and economic independence, as well as being a manifestation of land scarcity. Such internal movement has contributed to the rapid process of urbanization in Jamaica since World War II (C. G. Clarke 1973; Austin 1984; Hope 1989), and both men and women in Martha Brae have engaged in short-term, long-term, and recurrent rural-urban migration, especially to Kingston. Through these geographic shifts women may enter domestic service, while men may join the urban proletariat that has emerged with postwar diversification of the island's economy; a few migrants of both genders have entered clerical occupations. Many Martha Brae households have absent members in Kingston or Montego Bay who may send back earnings and return to live or visit. Less fortunate migrants swell the unemployed. Rural-urban migration has sometimes been a prelude to migrating overseas. Martha Brae is also characterized by immigration, generally from more rural parts of Trelawny, as a result of the village's proximity to plantations, farms, and Falmouth.

Four main overseas migrations typified the village in the twentieth century and into the new millennium. These reflected the main patterns of Jamaican emigration, which have varied with employment opportunities abroad and are mirrored in life histories. In addition, oral history highlights a nineteenth-century migration tradition among the emancipated slaves. Including such migration, five engendered overseas migratory trends have characterized postslavery Martha Brae. First, oral tradition tells of nineteenth-century migrations to Hispanic Central America by former slaves. This movement, shaped by labor demand for construction work in Panama on the trans-Isthmian railway and canal and on the Costa Rican banana plantation railroad, was mainly male. The second migratory trend was to Central America and Cuba in the early twentieth century. This generally involved older villagers, whose work histories I recorded early in my fieldwork, who are now deceased. Both genders participated, but this second wave of migrations still had a male emphasis due to labor demand for Panama canal construction, Costa Rican banana plantations, and Cuban sugar estates. Around this period, the third, chiefly male migration began — this time to the United States, first to work on the manpower projects of World War II and then on the subsequent postwar Farm Work Scheme. Some of these early migrants returned to the village, while others remained abroad.

The fourth movement, which followed the restrictive McCarran-Walter Act of 1952 passed by the U.S. Congress,[25] was the large-scale migration to Britain, especially to England, in the decade 1952–62. Both men and women took part, sent remittances home, and sometimes went back to visit; especially with maturing pensions, some migrants returned to settle in Martha Brae. The fifth and current trend has been further migration to North America, since Britain's exclusive 1962 Commonwealth Immigrants Act (reinforced by the 1968 Immigration Act and the Nationality Act of 1981), with the 1962 revision of immigration regulations in Canada and abolition of the U.S. quota system in 1965. Such migration (for farmwork and domestic service) continues to contribute to the peasant economy, transnational kinship, and the definition of gendered personhood. The following cases illustrate these trends, which overlap and interweave, as well as the articulation of occupational multiplicity and migration; they also demonstrate the relationship between migration and land.

Jenny Hill, the fish higgler who was born in 1891 in St. James and moved as a young woman to Martha Brae, emigrated from the village early in the twentieth century to Port Limon, Costa Rica,[26] where she continued higglering. She returned to settle permanently in Martha Brae on a tiny plot of purchased land. When she eventually retired, Jenny was supported by migrant remittances from her tailor son in England. He, too, returned to settle after many years abroad, having bought land of his own near Granville. When Jenny died in 1979 at age eighty-eight, the son hosted her large funeral at the Martha Brae cemetery and a Revival wake in her house yard, which was transmitted to her descendants.

Richard Hanson was born in 1892 and began his working life as an apprentice carpenter in Falmouth. In 1911, at the age of nineteen, Richard emigrated to Colon, Panama, where he lived for twenty-two years. He worked at a variety of occupations: railway switch tender, hotel waiter, bartender and porter, and taxi driver in the tourist industry. On returning to Martha Brae in 1933, Richard drove a taxi at a North Coast hotel. In addition, he cultivated and reared horses and cows on free land on "Lawyer's" Holland property, sold corn and milk, and occasionally did carpentry. He also worked as a district constable in Falmouth. By 1968 Richard lived on land of his own, purchased from the Parish Council, and rented rooms to tenants in his substantial but traditional cottage. He died around 1974. By 1995 his cottage had been replaced by a large concrete house built by his daughter who had migrated to Kingston.

By the late 1960s and early 1970s, Patrick Linton was elderly and lived on his half-acre plot of paternal family land in Martha Brae where he and his thirteen siblings were born. As a young man he had migrated to Cuba, where he worked as a carpenter and janitor. After a year he returned to Martha Brae but went back to Cuba the following year before returning permanently to Martha Brae. His main source of income on returning to the village was carpentry for estate owners and government departments in Falmouth. When Patrick retired, he leased house-spots in his yard to tenants. (One of these tenant households became the founder of Zion.) He supplemented the income from these rents with a small pension and the proceeds from the occasional sale of fruit. He also made a food forest in the yard, cultivating coffee and yams. Of his thirteen siblings, only two (and himself) survived their parents. These two siblings emigrated permanently: his sister to Panama and then to Kingston, and his brother, who had been abroad for over seventy years, to Costa Rica, Cuba, and the United States. Of

Patrick's two surviving children, his son migrated to Washington, D.C., and his daughter lived with her own household and now-widowed mother on the family land in a new concrete house, which replaced the Old Family's traditional cottage.

William Tapper, a trustee of the Thompson family land, was born in 1903 and died in 1985 (chapter 5). In 1921, at age eighteen, he migrated with an older brother (himself a returned migrant) to Cuba, where he remained for seventeen years planting cane on sugar estates. When William returned to his father's family land in Martha Brae in 1938, he cultivated a provision ground on a nearby estate. Toward the end of World War II he migrated to the United States on the manpower project. He worked there for fifteen months, first on a farm and then in a paper mill. William returned to Trelawny in 1945 but in 1946 spent another six months in the United States doing farm and factory work. Later that year he settled permanently in Jamaica. At this point he lived in a rented house in Falmouth, moving back to Martha Brae in 1959 to build on the family land. On his return to Trelawny in 1946, William did roadwork for the Public Works Department; after his retirement in 1970, he sometimes drove a steamroller for the Parish Council. He also multicropped a food forest on the family land and, when he stopped wage labor, intercropped a provision ground on the bought land of his niece who had migrated to London. Three of his siblings, who were coheirs to his paternal family land, migrated early in the twentieth century from Martha Brae to Costa Rica, Cuba, and New York where they died in the 1950s and 1960s.

North American Migrations

The next few cases illustrate mid- and later-twentieth century migrations from Martha Brae to North America (which continued in 2001), though the first example overlaps with the earlier movement to Central America. Adam Bayne was middle-aged in the early 1970s. He was born to a Jamaican mother in Barbados, where he had paternal family land. When Adam was three years old his parents took him to Falmouth. His adult migration history straddled that of the older and younger village men. Adam had been abroad three times as a migrant laborer, first for eighteen months during World War II to Panama, where he worked on the canal. He then made two trips to the United States on the Farm Work Scheme, the first of these during the war. On returning to Jamaica, he lived in Falmouth for many years and pursued various occupations including army instructor, special constable, flagman, and van driver. Adam and his wife Lucy, who was from a Martha Brae Old Family, first lived in Falmouth in a rented house and then built their own wooden chattel cottage. In 1966 they moved their house to Lucy's maternal family land in Martha Brae. Here Adam became a peasant cultivator, making a food forest in the yard.

The stories of Simon Quinn and Nick Yates exemplify the experience of younger men who engaged in recurrent migration to the United States on the Farm Work Scheme in the 1970s. Simon was a tenant in the house of another villager in Martha Brae, though he had recently purchased land elsewhere. He had already been twice to the United States for contract labor and was intending to go again. On both trips he worked as a cane cutter for a few months. Simon had no regular employment in Martha Brae, "just anything me reach," such as clearing pastures on a livestock pen. Nick, who lived in his own house on rented land in Martha Brae, had been to the United States for three six-month visits, working as a contract laborer harvesting cane in Florida. On his return he cultivated a provision ground and served as a foreman at the building site of the Trelawny Beach Hotel.

This male migratory trend was complemented by women who migrated to North America for domestic service from the 1970s to 2001, both to the United States and on the Canadian Household Helper Scheme. In the Minto Old Family, for example, Pam Gilmore's daughter traveled between Zion and Nantucket, Massachusetts, for household work. Two of Pam's nieces and a grandniece (Ruth Marshall's daughters and granddaughter) from Martha Brae were also in Nantucket as domestics, and one of Ruth's grandsons frequently went to Nantucket for six months on the Farm Work Scheme.

The Migrations to Britain

In the decade 1952–62 there was a flow of migrants to England from Martha Brae, providing an infusion of income into the village economy. Although some lost touch, others sent money home and went back to visit. From around 1979 still others returned to live in Martha Brae. Four such cases provide further insight into Martha Brae's transnational families and the significance of migration to the peasant economy. They also interweave with the earlier migrations to Central America and the United States, with later movements to the United States, and (through oral tradition) with the nineteenth-century migrations of emancipated slaves. Like the later movements to North America, the migrations to Britain involved many women as well as men, in contrast to the earlier mainly male migrations.

Vincent Bent, who was born around 1912 in the Trelawny village of Hammersmith, first migrated to two other villages in the parish: Bunker's Hill and Granville. In 1961 Vincent went to England, where he cleaned in a factory in Birmingham. He sent for his wife Janet in 1963, and she worked in a restaurant. They then moved to Luton, where he was still a cleaner and she a domestic. Vincent returned to Trelawny in 1973 and bought land in Martha Brae from the Lindo Old Family, which retained family land elsewhere in the village. Here he built a substantial concrete house and then went back to Luton. By 1979 he and Janet had both retired and returned to Martha Brae, where they were still living in the 1990s off their British pensions and on their own land that Vincent cultivated. They fostered a great-grandchild in their household, and a daughter in the United States had built a second concrete house in their yard. By 2001 Vincent had died but Janet was settled on their purchased land.

Across the street from the Bents was a yard with perhaps the largest and most modern concrete house in Martha Brae. This was the house yard of elderly Leah Wilkins, a member of an Old Family and a returned migrant from England and the United States. In 1995 Leah proudly told me that she had purchased this yard of one and a half square chains when she was seventeen years old, while living on her father's family land in Martha Brae where one of her brother's sons now lived. Leah then migrated to Kingston, where she worked to raise her fare to emigrate to Birmingham, sponsored by her brother in 1961. There she worked as a domestic. However, she did not "too like England" as it was cold and foggy. Therefore, in 1973 she migrated to the United States and continued to do domestic work. In 1990, due to failing health, Leah returned permanently to Martha Brae, where she had built a duplex house in the late 1980s. She lived in one side of the house and a tenant, who worked in Montego Bay, rented the other. This rental supplemented Leah's small pension from England and her more generous one from the United States. Throughout her migrations Leah had also been a village landlady, and her modern concrete house replaced her former tenant yard of three traditional houses of wattle and daub and wood.

In 1995 I finally met Frank Salmon, a migrant carpenter who had returned from England, of whom I had heard much from his late wife Paulette in the earlier years of my research. His overseas migration history, which followed one of internal migration, encompassed the earlier movements to Central America and the United States as well as the later exodus to Britain. Frank was born in 1906 in the parish of Hanover and was now "almost 89." As a young man he first migrated to the Trelawny village of Daniel Town, Paulette's natal village, where he purchased land of his own near her family land. In 1934, at age twenty-eight, Frank lived in Martha Brae while working at the Public Works Department in Falmouth. In 1939 he migrated from

Daniel Town to work in Panama, returning in 1940. In 1944 he emigrated again, this time on the manpower project, to the United States (where he worked in a paper factory), returning in 1945 after the end of World War II. On his return, Frank bought cheap "an acre and a perch" from Lawyer on Holland Estate, at the eastern edge of Martha Brae. Frank and Paulette created a house yard on this former plantation land, planting fruit trees and building. At first they constructed the core of their concrete house, which was later extended over many years, and erected a two-room wooden cottage to rent to tenants. This cottage was replaced by a second concrete house and a shop, both for rental, built with further migrant earnings.

In 1955 Frank migrated once more, this time to London, where he still maintained a resident address in the 1990s as he had not quite resettled in Martha Brae. In London, Frank moved from place to place (New Cross Gate, Peckham, Camberwell Green, and Brixton) seeking better work (as he often had to work outside in bad weather) and eventually secured a maintenance job with the Gas Board. One of his main reasons for migrating to Britain was to earn a pension. Initially Paulette joined him in England, working in a factory until 1961, when she returned to Martha Brae because she did not like the cold. She went back to England in 1976, living there much of the time until her death in 1991. By 1976 Frank had retired, and he and Paulette sometimes traveled to the United States to visit children, returning to "winter" in Martha Brae. Between 1961 and 1976, when Paulette lived in Martha Brae, he sent her remittances from England. These remittances and the savings from his earlier migrations financed his entire property in the village: "All that is here, what you' feet is on [we were sitting in the yard]: the land is when I came back from *America*, I bought this. Then I start to do [build] bit, by bit, by bit . . . always adding." Frank was still extending his concrete house in the 1990s with his savings from migratory wage labor in England. He was also finalizing his decision to settle permanently in Martha Brae with a daughter and some of his grandchildren. He was, however, first planning to return to Brixton to sort out his affairs and was hoping that he could adjust to the Jamaican Welfare System.

Lloyd Nelson, born in 1922 (aged seventy-nine in 2001), was a member of Martha Brae's largest Old Family, the Mintos, through his late mother Christine (chapter 5). She was the eldest child of emancipated slave William Shakespeare Minto, who with his ex-slave parents from Irving Tower Estate acquired land in Martha Brae. William Minto had himself been an early migrant from the free village after emancipation, emigrating to Port Limon, Costa Rica, and then returning. His daughter Christine, who moved to Granville, had two sets of children by two spouses from two Granville family lines. Her first husband emigrated to Guatemala and remained there until his death. Her second spouse, Lloyd's father, emigrated when Lloyd was a boy to Port Limon to join several relatives and never returned.

Following in the migration tradition of the two previous generations, Lloyd first emigrated from Granville to the United States on the manpower scheme in the early 1940s. Shortly after his return, in 1943 at age twenty-one, he and his mother moved from Granville to her paternal family land in Martha Brae after a hurricane destroyed their cottage on his father's family land. In Martha Brae, Lloyd first lived with his mother in the large two-story house that had belonged to his grandfather, William Minto. In 1946 Lloyd bought an acre of land cheap from Lawyer at Holland Estate on the eastern edge of Martha Brae, financed by his savings from wage labor in the United States. He then built a small "stone-knob" house on this purchased land.

In 1954 Lloyd (a cooper by trade) migrated again, this time to Birmingham. At first he could not find a job, as he did not belong to the "selective" Coopers' Union, but was then befriended by an Englishman who gave him a brewery job. Lloyd later found other employment with car manufacturers British Leyland, for which he worked for seventeen years. In 1965–66 Lloyd returned to Martha Brae to visit and to build a second, better concrete house on his purchased land, to which he returned in 1981: "It came to a time — I lived in England for 27 years and I never feel like I'm an Englishman. Never feel like a European. It was alright, nobody ever bother me. . . . But I never feel like a European. And that's why I came here in '65 and have that place built. And I say 'One of these days I'll come back. And if I do come back, I want to be a little more comfortable than when I left.' Because that was the idea of leaving."

Lloyd lived in that second house on his first piece of purchased land for eighteen months and cultivated the yard. However, within six months of his return he had bought another plot farther up the street that had changed hands once before since it had been bought from Lawyer. This land was directly opposite the upstairs house of William Minto, Lloyd's ex-slave maternal grandfather. Lloyd purchased the land from a middle-class fair-colored family with a business in Falmouth after its large house was damaged in a fire. He restored the house and refurbished it with furnishings from England. He was still living there in 2001, retired and content, and selling mangoes from the fruit trees on his land. Lloyd continued to be a landlord, renting out the houses on his other plot of purchased land. He had also negotiated the sale of an adjoining piece of land to his sister's son, a migrant in England who returned to visit, and supervised the building of this nephew's concrete house next door.

In addition to owning two pieces of land in Martha Brae, Lloyd was the trustee for his paternal family land in Granville. This land was transmitted to his father and four paternal aunts from the "older ones," and it "is for family and not to be sold, but passed on" to descendants. No will was made, but a title had been transmitted down the generations. Lloyd now had this title and paid the taxes on the land. There were family tombs there, but no houses anymore. Nevertheless, the dispersed transnational Old Family (which included his siblings, cousins, and three adult children in England and the United States) retained inalienable rights to this family land, which they could use in time of need.

As a returned migrant, then, Lloyd did not go back to live on his empty paternal family land in Granville for which he was trustee and where he could have built a house. Nor did he activate his rights to his maternal family land in Martha Brae. Instead, he consolidated the independence that he had achieved through migration by purchasing landholdings of his own in Martha Brae. Moreover, he was not only continuing the migratory traditions of his father and mother's father but was also consolidating a pattern of land purchase through migration that had been established by his ex-slave maternal grandfather. Lloyd explained that this grandfather had acquired his own landholdings (three small plots, which became part of the Minto family lands), in postslavery Martha Brae, directly through migration. For, according to Lloyd's late mother Christine, her father had acted as a usurer to other ex-slave migrants from the free village: "Lend them the money to go, and when some of them never return, the property that they [owned] — because that was the surety" was forfeited to Lloyd's maternal grandfather, William Minto, the emancipated slave.

Mutual Aid: Labor Exchange and "Partners"

Like occupational multiplicity and migration, mutual-aid institutions elaborate Martha Brae's peasant economy. Such reciprocity includes agricultural labor exchange and the rotating savings and credit association known as "partners."

Agricultural Labor Exchange

Labor exchange is a significant, but changing dimension of the peasant economy. There have been two variants in Martha Brae: "day fe day" and "digging," both relating to provision-ground cultivation. Day fe day is the direct exchange of labor between two people or among a small group of people, each of whom takes it in turn to provide a day's work for heavy tasks like clearing bush. This form of reciprocity, which I observed, involves mainly men, but some women with provision grounds participate. Digging is an indirect work exchange, on a much larger scale, that is now dying out. Elderly villagers enthusiastically recalled their digging days and recounted how men from the entire community, and sometimes from nearby villages such as Granville, would help with major tasks such as digging yam holes. Participants were summoned at dawn, by the blowing of a conch shell,[27] and work was accompanied by digging songs and rum. A feast or "second breakfast," cooked by women, was provided at midday by the "ground-master" on whose provision ground the work was being done. In addition to this direct reciprocation of work by food and rum, delayed reciprocity (Sahlins 1972) typified this variant, the ground-master being obliged to return such labor in diggings at a later date. Diggings were sometimes held by women, who reciprocated by helping with household tasks such as laundering clothes.

In addition to being observed elsewhere in Jamaica (M. G. Smith 1956a), such labor exchange has been widely reported throughout the Caribbean — for example, in Trinidad, Barbados, Martinique, and Haiti.[28] However, its cultural origin is controversial. Whereas Melville and Frances Herskovits (Herskovits 1990:160–61; Herskovits and Herskovits 1947:290–91) argued for African derivation, Michael Smith (1960:44) posited that no clear evidence of an African connection could be found, concluding that African/Caribbean parallels can exist without causal connection. Mintz (1989:210–11) was also reluctant to attribute Jamaican agricultural practices, originating in the protopeasant adaptation and perpetuated in the postslavery context, to African traditions. During my fieldwork digging was being replaced by wage labor on provision grounds, enabled by social mobility, new sources of employment, and migrant remittances, a transformation that strengthens the argument for the primacy of Caribbean contexts.

Partners

The rotating savings and credit association known as "partners" is widespread in Martha Brae as well as linking villagers to partners in neighboring villages and Falmouth. Partners has also been identified in other rural and urban areas of Jamaica.[29] Similar ROSCAS have been reported throughout the Caribbean region and among Caribbean migrants in Britain and the United States (Besson 1995g).[30] Like the relationship of the village economy with national land and labor markets, and with internal and global marketing and migration, the partners institution underscores the cash-dependent nature of the peasantry.

Partners in Martha Brae fits the basic model of the structure, organization, and function of the ROSCAS identified by Margaret Katzin (1959b), though the associations are now larger. Katzin described partners as consisting of a "banker" and from ten to twenty "throwers," called a "round" in Martha Brae. The banker initiated and organized the partners, which lasted for the same number of weeks as there were throwers. Contributions to the fund varied among groups, ranging from a few shillings to a pound sterling or more per week at the time of Katzin's study but were consistent within a given group. (Early in my fieldwork, the usual weekly contribution in Martha Brae was one pound [Besson 1974, 1:209].) The banker consulted each thrower as to his or her position for receiving the "draw." The banker, who usually received a gratuity from throwers, was also responsible for ensuring that each thrower met his or her obligations. Throwers who drew late in the rotation were prevented from defaulting by the fact that they could not retrieve the contributions already paid. Sanctions for those who drew early were the knowledge that their default would become widely known and prevent them from being admitted to other partners and the fear of court prosecution or physical reprisals. All but the last to draw received credit.

The function of partners, according to Katzin, was to raise capital for large financial outlays such as school fees, payments on houses or land, and in the case of petty traders purchasing goods for stalls. The main reasons for participating in the informal partners institution, rather than formal banks, were that the ROSCA provided a personalized context for raising capital and a means of forced saving, and it did not carry the danger of government taxation (Katzin 1959b:439). In Martha Brae, the purpose and rationale of partners is similar: to provide a controlled mode of acquiring savings, capital, and credit through mutual aid.

In the new millennium, partners is still a thriving institution in Martha Brae. One ROSCA was run by Daisy Desmond, who observed that "partners is a good t'ing [thing]; very, very good t'ing; helps a lot, especially for poor people." Daisy was born in the neighboring parish of St. Ann but had lived for many years in Martha Brae on her sister's late husband's land that was bought from the purchaser of the Kelly family land. There were three houses in this yard (a third sister also lived there), including Daisy's little wooden cottage that she built with capital saved through the ROSCA. In 2000 Daisy also had a one-room chattel shop on the property that she had financed through her savings in partners: "When I throw my hand, I tek it and build the shop." By 2001 she had built a second chattel shop; she now used this newer shop for selling groceries and the older one for selling meat.

Daisy had been the banker for many partners, starting "a long time ago" when "it's two shillings" a throw. In 2000 she explained that there were "thirty-five somebody" in the "partners running now" who paid "two hundred Jamaican dollars per hand" (about three pounds and sixty pence sterling or five American dollars) weekly.[31] Each participant received Ja $7,000 (approximately £127 or US $184) about twice a year. Sometimes the partners was smaller, with draws three times a year. Both genders participated, but in her present partners "the majority is women" — from Martha Brae, Granville, and the nearby village of Bounty Hall near Hampden Estates. Daisy was known in the area for running "a good partners," so people were eager to join. Due to her sound reputation, she was confident that she could raise her throws to Ja $300, Ja $400, or Ja $500 if she wished.[32]

The reputation of participants in Daisy's partners was also important. She said that members must be reliable and that she had to be "confident" that they could contribute before she accepted them: "If I don't feel to tek her, I don't tek her," because "some a dem don't throw the partners good." As banker, she dealt directly with her members, who paid their weekly contribution on Fridays or Saturdays at her yard. She distributed the money almost immediately: "As soon as you gather the partners, you pay it out," generally on Wednesdays, so someone drew every week. To determine when members received their draw, she wrote numbers and "drop it in a little bag and everybody come and pick up a number"; that is, the order of rotation was determined by lot. When everyone had drawn, the ROSCA started again and the membership might change. Some members might throw two or three hands and thus receive more than one draw. Participants saved to acquire materials to build a house,[33] to buy furniture or domestic appliances ("a stove, a fridge, a bed"), to pay their children's school expenses, and to engage in higglering. Daisy's husband, who worked as a porter in Falmouth, belonged to a different partners with his friends. Though he had been a member for many years before his wife began to run her ROSCAs, he was not a banker and so Daisy's reputation in partners was more significant than his.

Her neighbor, Victoria Robertson, had two "hands" in Daisy's ROSCA and therefore contributed Ja $400 per week and received the rotating fund about four times a year: "I throw those two 'hands' from my business [her grocery and rum shops]. And whenever I draw it now, I always take one hand and throw in the business and one hand and put in the bank." May Jackson, another member who lived across the street, put her draw toward her expenditures for Revival rituals. Victoria's cousin, Pam Gilmore, the seamstress-higgler who lived for over forty years in Martha Brae before moving to captured land on the Carib road at Holland in 1991, would from time to time "throw partners" (in 1995, Ja $100 per week) in a ROSCA with about forty-five men and women for which her daughter at Zion was the banker. Pam used her draw (Ja $4,500) to repair her cottage, assist another daughter and grandchildren, and raise capital for her seamstress-higglering business. However, as the throw had now been raised to Ja $200 weekly and her finances were tight, she did not rejoin the ROSCA. By 2000 Pam had retired but her banker-daughter now had a market stall.

Katzin (1959b) observed that a traditional role of partners was investment in peasant marketing. Such ROSCAs are widespread in the Falmouth market-place, and both their scale and role has escalated since the 1990s and into the twenty-first century, especially in the Ben' Down Market, where male as well as female ICIs and higglers use partners to raise much larger sums of capital for goods and travel. Such marketers were throwing hands of up to Ja $500–$1,000 a week and even Ja $2,000 a day; others spoke of throwing Ja $5,000–$7,000 per hand and making draws of Ja $10,800, Ja $23,400, and Ja $30,000 (about £545 or US $789). Today partners can also be transnational: for example, a banker in the Falmouth market ran a ROSCA with members from Linstead, Montego Bay, Kingston, and the United States (Connecticut).

The derivation of Caribbean ROSCAs is controversial. Herskovits and Herskovits (1947:76–77, 292) maintained that the Trinidadian *susu* was a retention of the Yoruba *esusu*. Olive Senior (1991:146) likewise argued for the Yoruba derivation of ROSCAs "known variously as 'meeting turn,' 'credit turn,' 'partner,' 'throwing box' and 'sou sou'" in the English-speaking Caribbean.[34] Though Yoruba survivals could account for the retention of the susu in some parts of the Caribbean such as Trinidad, this would not explain the widespread distribution of ROSCAs throughout the anglophone, francophone, and Hispanic Caribbean, whose populations derive from many African societies (Besson 1995g). Although it could then be argued that ROSCAs are widely found in Africa (Ardener 1964:204–8), the cultural survival thesis would not sufficiently account for the role of ROSCAs in the Caribbean today. Moreover, as Shirley Ardener's cross-cultural review of ROSCAs showed, such associations were found not only in Africa and the New World (including Indo-America), but also in Europe and Asia (202–4, 208); moreover, they appeared to be absent among Americans of African descent in the United States (208; Light 1972:36, quoted in Foner 1977: 132). A worldwide analysis of women's use of ROSCAs (Ardener and Burman 1995) reinforces and extends Ardener's earlier cross-cultural study.

A more meaningful explanation of the widespread existence and escalation of ROSCAS among contemporary Caribbean peoples (especially marketers and migrants, both of whom now use these associations to raise money for return airfares) is the appropriation and transformation of colonially derived banking institutions through Caribbean institution-building rooted in the protopeasant economy (Besson 1995g). Higman (1998:244), in addressing the scarcity of capital among slaves at Montpelier and throughout Jamaica, notes: "One writer at the end of the eighteenth century, stated that when slaves wanted 'to lay by a sum to purchase any thing extraordinary' they gave their money to another person to hold it for them for a period. This was done reciprocally in a manner similar to the rotating credit systems of West Africa and modern Jamaica. Some slaves were said to 'deposit what they can spare in little boxes, which have no other opening than a slit for the admittance of the money.' "

In addition to parallels with West Africa, this suggests Afro-Caribbean cultural creativity. A culture-building perspective likewise illuminates the creation, which I encountered in Trinidad and Tobago in 1992, of "*susu* land" — whereby the acquisition of freehold land rights through installment payments to the state is represented by an African symbol but is a new type of Caribbean land settlement (Besson 1995g).[35] The escalation of Caribbean ROSCAS (which are now used by some members of the middle class) in the articulation of the informal sector with the national and world economies, including the growth of trading and investment among the peasantry, supports Ardener's challenge to "the assertion by Clifford Geertz (1962) that ROSCAS, though useful in an intermediate stage of development, would necessarily fade away as more developed financial institutions replaced them" (1995:1–2).[36]

Mutual Aid: The Friendly Society

History, Structure, and Organization

The most prominent mutual-aid institution in the village is the Martha Brae Come To-Gather [*sic*] Society (CTS), a friendly society that provides secular and ritual assistance for illness and death. The CTS was founded shortly after World War II, in 1948, by Martha Brae villagers now deceased, one of whom, Patrick Linton (who named the society), I knew in the early years of my research. By 2001 the CTS had played a central role in village life for over fifty years. Unlike many other friendly societies in Jamaica, the CTS was not founded as a branch of a wider island organization such as the Jamaica Burial Scheme Society or the Royal Reliance. Instead, it originated as an independent institution. Over the years the CTS has expanded: whereas in the 1970s there were approximately 125 paid-up members with 75 more "floaters," totaling about 200 persons, in 2001 there were around 300. When the CTS was first established, its meetings were held in the Baptist Class House, but in 1963 the society purchased two square chains of land near the Class House on which to erect its own building. The construction of the society hall began around 1967 and was almost completed when I started fieldwork in 1968. The hall is a concrete structure, like a church, with a large meeting room furnished with wooden benches and a dais. In 1995 the hall was being "piecened" or extended, and by 2001 its exterior had been painted.

The CTS has an elaborate structure of offices and committees. Officers include the president, the first and second vice presidents, the treasurer, a secretary, an assistant secretary, a presiding daughter, and a male chaplain. Except for the last two offices, which are complementary, none of these is gender-specific. In addition to the secular roles of other officers, the gendered statuses of chaplain and presiding daughter have ritual significance. The chaplain leads the "Devotion" at meetings, modeled on the Baptist Church service. If there is no minister to conduct a member's burial, the chaplain officiates. The presiding daughter marches with the chaplain in front of the society's banner, which leads the funeral procession. The Old Families play a major role in the CTS, and its officers tend to be members of such family lines. But Old Families do not monopolize these positions, nor are all officers from Martha Brae. Men's and Women's Sick Committees are elected to represent each gender in Martha Brae and, when CTS membership outside the village warrants it, to represent other member communities. These committees receive reports from members who are ill and those who require sickness maintenance grants and contributions to doctor's bills. Like the devotion at meetings, visitation of the sick derives from the Baptist mission church.[37] Four members of the CTS are chosen to represent the Four Apostles and are in charge of collecting money for the annual fund-raising anniversary.

In 2001 it cost Ja $350 (about £6 or US $9) to join the CTS; annual subscriptions and the death tax were Ja $100 and Ja $30 respectively, and death grants were Ja $8,310 (approximately £150 or US $219). The death tax was paid following a member's death, not to finance the deceased's funeral but to fund the rituals of the next member to die. The treasurer banked all monies with the Trelawny Building Society in Falmouth and, with the president and secretary, authorized withdrawals for death grants and sickness benefits, which included both a grant and the payment of doctor's fees. By the 1990s only a portion of these fees could be paid by the society. The secretary signed the doctor's certificates presented by the Sick Committee.

Anyone between the ages of twenty-one and fifty could join the CTS if her or his application was approved.[38] The majority of members were from Martha Brae, though not all villagers belonged. The CTS also drew its membership from beyond the village, particularly from Falmouth, Daniel Town, and Rock, but also from neighboring Granville and Hague. Granville had two other friendly societies, one of which predated the CTS. Some Martha Brae villagers belonged to friendly societies elsewhere, especially to the two friendly societies in Granville (the Granville Benefit Society and the Social and Beneficiary Society) and to the Royal Reliance in Wakefield, a village a few miles farther inland. Membership of Martha Brae residents in societies outside the village and of people from outside the village in the CTS links Martha Brae with other Trelawny communities, as becomes apparent at funerals and anniversaries. In addition, friendly societies from beyond the parish (including urban centers such as Montego Bay, Port Antonio, and Kingston) participate in the anniversaries of Trelawny friendly societies, which reciprocate. In this way an islandwide network, which overlaps with Revival networking, is forged, paralleling the Obeah-Myal networks of the protopeasant and postemancipation past.

Secular and Ritual Activities

The CTS is responsible for secular and ritual activities relating to illness and death. Secular activities include CTS and Sick Committee meetings, commemoration of anniversaries, visitations of the sick, allocation of grants at sickness and death, and collection of the death tax. Ritual occurs especially at funerals, though meetings and anniversaries also have ritual aspects. All Jamaican friendly societies hold annual anniversary celebrations to commemorate their founding. The CTS, founded in September 1948, celebrates in September. Anniversaries involve fund-raising and issuing invitations to other friendly societies to participate. Funds are raised through collections by individual members and at the anniversary church service concert that takes place after a ritual parade, where each friendly society marches behind its banner, in uniform and regalia, with the host society in front.

An anniversary procession setting out from Martha Brae. Photo by Jean Besson.

CTS anniversary uniforms consist of mauve skirts, white blouses, and white turbans for women and, in the early years of my fieldwork, suits of any color for men. By the 1990s men wore mauve bush jackets with trousers, a variation on the national trend. The presiding daughter and chaplain parade in mauve gowns and berets, and the chaplain also wears a white surplice. Ordinary members wear a green sash, with the society's initials embroidered in yellow. Officers' regalia includes an elaborate red sash with initials in gold. The CTS anniversary banner is mauve, with "Martha Brae Come To-Gather Society" embroidered in green. CTS anniversaries are often held at the William Knibb Memorial Baptist Church in Falmouth after a parade through the streets of the town. However, one anniversary that I attended was held at the Falmouth Methodist Church, and another took place at the William Knibb Memorial High School on Holland Estate, processing through the plantation.

In contrast to the excitement of anniversary rallies is the routine of visiting and financing the care of the sick. Despite Revivalist theories on the supernatural causation of misfortune or illness, the Martha Brae peasantry draws on the scientific medical system in Falmouth. Villagers visit either the Falmouth Hospital doctor for a minimum charge or the same or another doctor privately.

Grave digging in the Martha Brae free-village cemetery. Photo by Jean Besson.

When a CTS member dies, a death grant is made to the bereaved to help with funeral expenses. Funerals are costly, generally including an expensive coffin and wreaths and refreshments for Revival mortuary rituals. The beneficiaries arrange the funeral, at which the society officiates, and most of the community attends. Grave digging (in the Martha Brae cemetery) for any villager is provided by voluntary labor, but the status of the deceased is reflected in the number of men who assist. In the case of deceased CTS members, society men are among the grave diggers. Though no cash payment is made, breakfast is cooked by the bereaved and carried to the diggers at the grave. Rum is also served, especially as this is believed to keep the as-yet unplaced *duppy* and *shadow* at bay (chapters 1 and 7). Prior to the funeral of a CTS member, the body is "churched" or laid in state in the society hall. The "churching" is often preceded by Revival "set-ups," which traditionally include the lyke-wake or watch over the dead on the night before the burial. The society then escorts the coffin to Falmouth, where most funeral services are held — usually in the Baptist church. Following the service, the corpse is returned to Martha Brae in either a hired or makeshift hearse. Society members then accompany the hearse to the village cemetery, parading two abreast. If the deceased is not a church member, the CTS chaplain conducts a service in the society hall and the mourners process directly to the grave.

A funeral procession by the "burial society" at the Martha Brae cemetery. Photo by Jean Besson.

CTS funeral dress is somber: white dresses and turbans for women, white bush jackets, black trousers, and berets for men; the presiding daughter wears a white gown. Members' reversible sashes are black, with the society's initials embroidered in white. Officers' regalia are a more elaborate variation on this theme. Male officers carry swords at the front of the procession behind the banner, which is reversed to a black background with "Martha Brae Come To-Gather Society" embroidered in white. Friendly societies from neighboring villages join in the funeral ritual, and in the case of deceased villagers who belonged to another friendly society, that society officiates.

In addition to providing mutual aid and linking kinship and community, the CTS integrates the Baptist Church and the Revival-Zion worldview (chapter 7). This is reflected in the burial ritual itself. The service in the cemetery is usually conducted by the Baptist minister, but after the parson leaves mourning turns to rejoicing as Revivalists sing and wave their society regalia while dancing on the grave. This custom is perceived to assist the duppy on its journey to join the ancestors; it is also thought to help settle the shadow in the grave. These beliefs are rooted in the Obeah-Myal slave religion and reinforced by Revival wakes, which are believed to further place the dual soul. Such rituals, regarded as linking dead and living generations of kin, reinforce the cognatic descent system (chapter 8).

Institution-Building

The CTS is part of an islandwide and Caribbean regional tradition. Woodville Marshall (1985:11) noted that after emancipation various cooperatives, including friendly and benefit societies, emerged among the British West Indian peasantry. In addition to being widespread in Jamaica, and reported in Trinidad and the Bahamas (Herskovits and Herskovits 1947:314; Johnson 1991b), these societies have also been described for French Martinique (Horowitz 1992:87).

In establishing a friendly society, the Martha Brae villagers drew on their protopeasant and postslavery traditions to create a creole institution that has appropriated and transformed the European institutions of the building society, masonic lodge, scientific medicine, and mission religion, as well as the English model of friendly societies. The CTS serves the economic functions of savings and investment that typify the Trelawny Benefit Building Society; provides similar social solidarity and ritual mutual aid to the Masonic Lodge, which is now in Montego Bay (the island's first "exclusive" Scottish lodge having been founded in Falmouth in 1798 [Sibley and Ogilvie 1975a]); relates to both Baptist Christianity and the medical system in Falmouth; and mirrors "the virtues of sobriety, good conduct and thrift," which were the goals of English friendly societies (Johnson 1991b:185). Unlike the Building Society, however, the CTS is embedded in the community. It is also based on Revival-Zion ideology, with its beliefs in a spirit pantheon and supernatural causation, deriving from Obeah and Myal (which appropriated Baptist Christianity). The CTS likewise reinforces Revival mortuary rituals in house yards and the free-village cemetery; in some other Trelawny villages, such as Granville, friendly societies officiate at family-land burials. In addition, the CTS symbolizes Afro-creole and community identities as well as interweaving with the internal differentiation and status system of the peasant community. By including both genders as "sisters" and "brothers," the society has overturned the patriarchal masonic solidarity of "brotherhood," a transformation that parallels the reversal of colonial primogeniture by the creole cognatic descent system.[39]

In his analysis of friendly societies in the Bahamas from 1834 to 1910, Howard Johnson (1991b) provides insight into the reason why ex-slaves and their descendants established such societies:

Historians who have studied the process of adjustment to emancipation in the British Caribbean have usually concentrated on the economic aspects, especially the transition to free labour. Comparatively little interest has been shown in the ex-slaves' adjustment to a free society in which they assumed the responsibility for their own maintenance during periods of sickness and in old age. . . . The establishment of friendly or benefit societies in the post-emancipation years was one of the strategies employed by the former slaves for dealing collectively with this new responsibility. . . . The main objective of these societies was to provide, by mutual assistance, for periods of sickness, old age, and burial expenses. (183)

As Johnson further indicates, the ex-slaves may have drawn on African cultural values — such as West African title associations and secret societies — to transform the English structure of the friendly society (184).

Yet the dynamic in creating a friendly society in postemancipation Martha Brae was neither European acculturation nor African cultural retention, but rather Caribbean culture-building rooted in the protopeasantry. Both mutual aid and Obeah-Myal mortuary ritual were highly developed among Jamaican slaves in their own plantation communities and among slave villages on different estates (J. Stewart 1823:267, quoted in Mintz 1989:187; Schuler 1979a:128; D. Hall 1989:185–86).[40] Although Johnson provides no information on slave cosmology and ritual, and focuses on the "practical" reasons for friendly societies in the postslavery Bahamas, his suggestion that mutual aid among the slaves was the basis of these friendly societies and his emphasis on the Bahamian context reinforce this culture-building perspective: "Although English and African organisations were important influences on the formation of friendly societies, this collective action was *primarily a local response to practical necessity*. The prompt formation of friendly societies after the abolition of slavery suggests that an organisation of that type, on a more informal basis, might have existed during the slavery era, especially in the final three decades when slaves exercised extensive control over their own lives" (Johnson 1991b:184–85, emphasis mine). Moreover, "such an organisation existed in British Guiana during slavery" (196 [n. 12]). In addition, Mary Karasch (1979:139) showed that slaves in urban Brazil manipulated the institution of the Catholic lay brotherhood to serve their own ends, the most significant transformation being "as burial and mutual aid societies," an appropriation in which the slaves hid their own religion behind the masters' symbols — as has occurred among the Revivalists of postslavery Martha Brae. The next chapter explores this Revival ideology, and its relationship to the Baptist Church and Rastafarian movement, among the contemporary descendants of the Obeah-Myal-Baptist ex-slaves who appropriated the colonial planter town.

CHAPTER SEVEN

The Baptist Church, Revival Ideology, and Rastafarian Movement

The Baptist Church

The significance of the Baptist Church in Martha Brae's Afro-Caribbean cultural history reaches back to the late eighteenth and early nineteenth centuries, with Baptist missionizing among the Jamaican slaves — especially in St. James and Trelawny — and the antislavery critique by Baptists such as William Knibb. After emancipation, the alliance between Baptists and ex-slaves continued in the church-founded free-village system, which was especially pronounced in Trelawny under Knibb's sponsorship. The planter town of Martha Brae was appropriated by ex-slaves in this wider context.

As touched on in chapters 4 to 6, the Martha Brae villagers are still Baptist in formal faith and regularly attend the William Knibb Memorial Baptist Church in Falmouth. There is an old Baptist Class House in Martha Brae that the oldest villagers remember as always being there. This prayer house, which represents Class 5 of the Falmouth Baptist Circuit, symbolizes the free village. Throughout most of the lifetime of the oldest villagers weekly prayer meetings and Sunday school and a monthly church service have been held in this class house. Elderly villagers also attended school there. During my early fieldwork the prayer house was in disrepair, but the village continued to have a Baptist class leader chosen from either the Old Families or the established Strangers.

In July 1984 the minister of the William Knibb Memorial Baptist Church started to plan the rebuilding of the Martha Brae Class House, and this was completed two years later. On 27 November 1986 the prayer house was reopened at a large village function by the Honorable Hugh L. Shearer, a former Jamaican prime minister and then deputy prime minister and minister of foreign affairs and trade. Shearer, known in his native Martha Brae as the Lindo Old Family's "Son Lindo," had generously supported the rebuilding of the prayer house with donations of cash and paint. The three-hour dedication service, which was well supported by the villagers, was also attended by ministers from the Falmouth Baptist Church and the Jamaica Baptist Union in Kingston. In his sermon the vice president of the Jamaica Baptist Union rejoiced at the reopening of the class house as the center of Martha Brae's religious life and envisioned that the prayer house would evolve into the Martha Brae Baptist Church (as occurred in Granville in the 1940s), thereby consolidating the history of the village as a Baptist community. To mark the reopening of the class house, a week of nightly services was planned from 1 December 1986, and it was anticipated that this would be followed by a return to weekly prayer meetings and Sunday school and a monthly service.

The class house was destroyed by Hurricane Gilbert two years later, in 1988, but the Martha Brae villagers continued to attend the William Knibb Memorial Baptist Church and to represent Class 5 of the Falmouth Baptist Circuit. From 1993 to 1995 the Martha Brae prayer house was again rebuilt and refurbished by the Falmouth Baptist Church. In the new millennium it still functions as the formal focus of free-village religious life, in contrast to the elite Anglican planter church in Falmouth.

In 1975–76 the William Knibb Memorial High School was built on a part of Holland Plantation acquired by the Jamaica Baptist Union, next to the ruins of the sugar works and the site of the slave village, directly across the road from Martha Brae. This school, which still serves Falmouth, Martha Brae, and nearby Baptist free villages, has since expanded.

In 2001 the small Riverside Baptist Church (built and accidentally burned down in the 1990s) was reestablished by white American Baptist missionaries from Montego Bay on River Hill, at the eastern edge of Martha Brae, near the Persian Wheel.

The Coexistence of the Baptist Church and Revival Ideology

In the 1970s Barry Chevannes (1978) concluded that Revivalism was "a disappearing religion" in Jamaica, "virtually dead" and "buried under the forces of change" (16), and that "as far as the peasantry is concerned, it is no longer a force" (15).[1] But even then his conclusion did not apply to Martha Brae and other Trelawny "Baptist" villages (Besson 1974, 1987a, 1993, 1995c, 1995f), where Revivalism remains a vibrant

A Revival church in Martha Brae. Photo by Jean Besson.

force in the twenty-first century. My argument has been reinforced by Chevannes's recent research on the resurgence of Revivalism in urban Kingston (1995c, 1995d, 1995h), while his study, in turn, is strengthened by data from Martha Brae (Besson and Chevannes 1996).

During my fieldwork in Martha Brae (1968–2001), there were three Revival tabernacles or "mission houses" and a "balm-yard" or place of healing in village house yards.[2] Although the balm-yard healer emigrated overseas early in my research and two of the tabernacles had declined by the 1990s due to factionalism, one of the mission houses (the oldest and most prominent) has endured. Revival tabernacles also coexist with the Baptist Church in other Trelawny villages, such as Refuge and Granville. In addition, Revivalism has taken root in Martha Brae's satellite squatter settlement of Zion, where several Revival yards have been established on captured land; one tabernacle was literally transported there from Martha Brae.

From the viewpoint of the Baptist Church, Revivalism and Baptist Christianity are still "competing faiths," as they were in Sturge Town, St. Ann, in the aftermath of emancipation (Mintz 1989:168). However, from the perspective of Martha Brae's Afro-creole cultural history, Baptist Christianity and Revival ideology have long been complementary,[3] with the Baptist Church providing the formal framework for free-village religious life and Revivalism negotiating with, appropriating, and transforming Baptist Christianity. During slavery, the roots of Revivalism were forged in Obeah-Myal ideology, created through Caribbean culture-building and consolidated by the mid-eighteenth century. "Obeah" originally referred most often to morally neutral magical/spiritual power that could be accessed through spirit possession, or "Myal," and used for protection and healing (Schuler 1979b; Bilby 1993; Handler 2000; Handler and Bilby 2001). With Baptist missionizing in the later slavery period, the Trelawny slaves (who were at the center of both the Obeah-Myal complex and Baptist proselytizing) attended the Baptist chapel in Falmouth, while on the Trelawny slave plantations Obeah and Myal controlled Baptist Christianity in the Native Baptist variant.

The Obeah-Myal complex has persisted among the Accompong Maroons in St. Elizabeth, where it was preserved and elaborated in marronage, and where it presently coexists with the United (formerly Presbyterian) Church and is ascendant at the annual "Myal Play" (Besson 1995c, 1997, and fieldwork 2000). However, ethnography from Martha Brae and other Trelawny villages, combined with sources such as Schuler (1979a, 1979b, 1980), Bilby (1993), and Alleyne (1996), suggests that whereas Obeah-Myal ideology has been retained at one level among Baptist free villagers, it was transformed at another level in the later slavery and postemancipation eras through the frequent interaction between slaves/free villagers and Baptist missionaries.

In Baptist villages in the immediate aftermath of emancipation in 1838, Orthodox Baptist faith provided the formal religious focus of these freed communities as well as a means for acquiring land. At the same time, the Native Baptist variant, reinforced by a Myalist Revival from the 1820s to the 1850s (when Trelawny, with St. James, was the vanguard of the Myal movement), formed "the core of a strong, self-confident counter-culture" against the persisting plantation system (Schuler 1980:44). In the context of this Myalist Revival, the relationship between Obeah and Myal became more complex — especially in the Baptist villages from around 1841. Myal shifted closer to Baptist Christianity, recognized "three grades of membership — Archangels, Angels, and Ministering Angelics," and rejected Obeah as sorcery, as did the Baptist Church (Schuler 1979b:72). This development paralleled the anti-Obeah view and legislation of the colonial state from the later eighteenth century, which is still evident in postcolonial Jamaica. From this new stance, the Myal movement evolved as an ideology aimed at eradicating the sorcery of postemancipation hardships that were acute in Trelawny and St. James, including various epidemics and inequitable agrarian relations that the Baptist missionaries could not dispel (Schuler 1979b:70–74). This antisorcery activity was manifested in "clearing the land for Jesus Christ [which] meant eradicating obeah through special public rituals which only Myalists could perform" (72). This contrast between Myal and Obeah was consolidated around 1860 as one dimension of the Revival-Zion cult and persists today within this cult at the peasant-plantation/tourism interface in St. James and Trelawny — including Martha Brae, where similar public rituals continue to be held.

In 1860 an intense evangelical revival, known as the Great Revival, started in Ireland, swept through the anglophone world, and arrived in Jamaica, where it began in the Moravian Church, spread "rapidly to Baptist and Wesleyan congregations" (Schuler 1980:104), and "received overwhelming support from all the clergy, including the Anglican bishop" (Chevannes 1994:20). Together, this Euro-Christian revival and the Myalist Revival generated a new Afro-Protestant religion, called "Revival," which both controlled the Baptist faith and incorporated more elements of Baptist Christianity in opposition to Obeah as sorcery (Beckwith 1929:158; Schuler 1980:104–5, Alleyne 1996:96, 99–101). In 1861, however, the Great Revival "turned African" (P. Curtin 1970:171); that is, it was appropriated by the original Obeah-Myal ideology. In this way, two variants of Revivalism were distinguished: Revival-Zion (seen as nearer to Baptist Christianity and as opposing Obeah) and Pukumina (closer to the original Obeah-Myal complex and regarded as practicing Obeah). Mervyn Alleyn (1996:96) describes these two forms as "important points in the continuum of religious differentiation created by the meeting of Myalism and Christianity." These two variants, also known respectively as "the '60" and "the '61," persisted in the twentieth century. However, since the 1990s Revival-Zion has become ascendant, with Pukumina being attributed by free villagers and urban folk to either other practitioners or another time and place (Besson and Chevannes 1996).

Through this continued negotiation with, and transformation of Baptist Christianity, Obeah, in the sense of sorcery as portrayed by the Baptist Church and representing material hardship,[4] is still explicitly opposed and "eradicated" in Martha Brae by Revival-Zion meetings said to "cut and clear destruction" — as in the Myal movement. But simultaneously, Obeah, in the original sense of a morally neutral magical/spiritual power that may be used for protection and healing, is still believed to be accessible through the "spirit-possession" (the original meaning of Myal) that is regularly enacted in this same Revival-Zion cult. Therefore, despite the distinction between the two variants of Revivalism and the apparent disappearance of Pukumina in the 1990s, the belief in the morally neutral magical/spiritual power of Obeah is retained and cocooned at the heart of Revival-Zion ideology. It is not only hidden behind the postcolonial symbol of the Baptist Church, but also kept from view even at some Revival-Zion meetings.

In their recent study, *Come Shouting to Zion: African American Protestantism in the American South and British Caribbean to 1830*, Sylvia Frey and Betty Wood (1998) show, as Randall Miller (1999:128) states, that "Afro-Protestantism . . . evolved as a reciprocal process wherein whites and blacks negotiated and exchanged religious forms and social space and together developed a revival culture, especially in the American South. For them [Frey and Wood], too, that process did not spell 'the death of the [African] gods,' " but rather the continuity of "African religions as the basic stock on and from which African Americans grafted evangelical Protestantism in British America." Miller further notes that Frey and Wood "draw on a large comparative and conceptual canvas," but "in so broad a sweep, the authors forego close examinations of *particular African/African-American peoples shaping a particular religious community, culture, or place. They do not get down to cases*" (128, emphasis mine). The case of Martha Brae provides a detailed local study of such Afro-Protestant culture-building, at the heart of the former British Caribbean, still ongoing in the twenty-first century.

Revival Ideology and Ritual

The Spirit Pantheon

Revival ideology in Martha Brae closely resembles that reported to exist elsewhere in Jamaica (Seaga 1982:10; Chevannes 1978:5). In Martha Brae, Revivalism is essentially a spirit-possession cult based on the perception of an integrated world of living persons and spiritual beings, which include God (especially the Holy Spirit) and the dead. Though the unseen portion of this world includes the Christian Trinity, the total spirit pantheon is Africa-derived.[5] As Edward Seaga noted, the Revival spirit pantheon has three dimensions: "Heavenly" spirits, "Earthbound" spirits, and "Ground" spirits: "The first category consists of the Triune Christian God, Archangels, Angels, and Saints. In the category of 'Earthbound' spirits, are the satanic powers (Fallen Angels), Biblical Prophets and Apostles. The third group consists of all the human dead except those mentioned in the Bible" (1982:10). Variations on this theme differentiated Revival-Zion and Pukumina, each of which focused to some extent on different categories of spirits:

The Triune Christian God is considered the leading power of the pantheon by both groups, and although appealed to in prayer, it is the spirits of the lesser orders who are propitiated, exorcised, remunerated, and contacted for advice and protection, for all specific purposes. *Zionists* deal primarily with Heavenly spirits and with Apostles and Prophets of the "Earthbound" group. They believe in the existence of the other powers of the pantheon, but consider them evil, and therefore useful only for evil purposes. . . . On the other hand, *Pukkumina* [*sic*] followers work primarily with "Ground" spirits and "Fallen Angels," who in their value system are not considered evil. They maintain that these spirits are more useful than those used by Zion, since they are nearer to them and more easily contacted. (10–11)

This distinction between the variants of Revival is explicit in Martha Brae and in the neighboring settlements of Granville and Zion. In these communities Revivalists regard themselves as Zionists adhering to the '60 variant of Revival, in contrast to followers of Pukumina who are said to practice the '61; six Revival leaders whom I interviewed in these communities in the 1990s emphasized this distinction. Moreover, Zionism is thought to be able to overpower "Obeah," which is said to be used by Pukumina followers.

Pastor Roberts, from Lime Hall in St. Ann, who in 1983 and 1995 visited and supported Revival mother May Jackson in Martha Brae, expounded on these themes to me in May's Revival tabernacle in 1995:

Sometime some people are spellbound and they need to be delivered. Spellbound by evil forces, witchcraft or sorcery. Then they need a deliverance. And sometime by taking them and waving the banners around them, free it up. I mean you have the Obeahman and you have spiritual people, deal with spirits. You have '60 Revival and you have '61. We are '60. '61 mostly deal with a different type of spirit: like occult spirit, like invocation, like demons. But the '60 doesn't really go in that. Sometimes the '60 really go there, but it doesn't dive too long in that. But sometimes the '60 really go *over* the '61; when they are travailing and jumping, but it doesn't really dive too long. They try to come back out. It can create a different feeling.

Roberts went on to outline the focus of the "'60 Revival" on the Holy Spirit and the prophets: "Is just the Holy Spirit. You have various types of Messengers. You have to be spiritual, divine, to understand these things. Message for Miriam in blue. These are the old people that the bible really speak about. Miriam, Moses and Joshua." He explained that this differs from the emphasis in Pukumina on Fallen Angels: "Fallen Angels — fallen from Heaven — those are spirits that people use as witchcraft. But the spiritual person [Zionist] can despatch them away. . . . That's why Obeahman doesn't like the '60 Revival. They [Obeahmen] are part of '61. Like Pukumina." Roberts elaborated on the relationship of Revival-Zion with Pukumina, including the diagnosis and defeat of Obeah, and on the biblical origin of Zionism:

But sometime Zion-Revival go into '61, when they are triumphant. Sometimes you have to go over within their '61 world [by a different dance movement]. But we try not to go, because '60 Revival is the strongest. We are coming off St. John 11, where Jesus *groan* in the spirit. One of the reasons Jesus groan in the spirit was because Lazarus was dead. He had something [evil] to remove. He *groan* in the spirit before He go there and He went to the grave and He *groan* in the spirit. And He cry with a loud voice and say "Lazarus come forth from the dead" and Lazarus came forth from the dead. That's why Revival is from then work to righteousness. Sometime when you groaning in the spirit, sometimes destruction [Obeah] is in the "city," and sometime you know somebody is sick. And you *groan* in the spirit. There always been destruction passing, which the spiritual person [Zionist] can diagnose.

In 1995 May's husband, Pastor Joe Jackson, likewise asserted this distinction between the two Revival variants, pointing out that "'60 Revival is the leading one." Joe went on to explain the different kinds of spirits in Revival-Zion, underlining the perception of Pukumina spirits as evil:

You see, Satan can come in the midst. Remember Satan have his own angels. And Satan' angels can come teach you different things. . . . So sometimes Fallen Angels can come in the midst to deprive you of the Spirit of God. Fallen Angels is those angels that Christ cast out of Heaven. They come out of Heaven with Satan; that is their friend. But the true Angels remain in Heaven taking *orders*, taking message, which is the Archangels. You have Gabriel. Satan was the highest Angel in Heaven, you know . . . but through he rebel now, Christ gave Gabriel stronger power over him. And Michael and Joshua, but Gabriel is the highest one.

The spirits of the dead, Joe stated, "is like the natural man that bury came up"; that is, the shadow believed to be buried with the corpse. Discussing practitioners of Pukumina calling up the dead, he asserted that "when they invoke, they sprinkle rum at the spot and they use rice and all those things, *paying* that spirit; *paying* them for what they want them to do." (This observation regarding market exchange between the living and the dead in Pukumina, in contrast to gift exchange in Revival-Zion spirit possession, recurs in Pastor Brown's account below.) In response to my query as to whether Joe had ever seen anyone working with the spirits of the dead, he assured me that he had—at Pastor Currie's church in Upper Trelawny: "And dats nuh [that is not] supposed to be. Because even the Scriptures tell you that the living have no dealing with the dead. Because [if] them move with the dead, you must do [be practicing] witchcraft." This account paralleled gossip in Martha Brae in the early 1990s that Currie, who briefly set up a rival Revival faction there, was forced to leave the village because of Pukumina practices. There had been similar rumors in 1983 to account for the defection of Pastor Brown's congregation from Granville to the Jacksons in Martha Brae (Besson 1993).

In 1995, however, Pastor Brown of Granville (having partially retrieved his congregation and participated in Revival-Zion services in Martha Brae) asserted his allegiance to Zionism: "I am more of the '60, the '60 Revival—there was a time when the power of God break through. So we came up and we find that Spirit going on, people carrying on the work. It was going on fine. But now many of the older people who were *grounded* in the work, they die out. . . . The Revival work, it is a *gift*. You get the Spirit as a gift. But you have people that *discerning*, you have the gift of healing, you have people that can interpret things. The '61 is as the Poco [Pukumina]." Nevertheless, he too provided an eyewitness account of Pukumina, drawn from his youth in the neighboring parish of St. Ann around the 1930s and reinforced by his travels around Jamaica:

Pukumina, what I know, they are people that don't work with divine spirit. They work with the dead. They work at grave-place. They work from cemetery. They keep their meeting, set up them business what them want to set up and jump, jump whole night and going almost like Zion is. But there the jumping is different. And at that time them have a man at the grave waiting there so till certain hours, whether midnight or such, when them want to carry on them business. They chiefly go places where people invite them to do a work, to do a job. Some a them help sick, people with demons. But not all. And so dem carry on and that man will be there until certain hours and they say "Clear the way, Hunter-Man deh come!" So him come from the grave with the other spirits there.

They call him "Hunter-Man." He jump around and go a the grave and wait fe de spirit. Is "*shadow*," but people call it "*duppy*" still. Is "*shadow*," evil spirit. They can get on people, if them put it to it. Can knock people out of their proper senses and all them t'ing. Can make people go sick and all those things. Is a good and bad thing. Good and evil. You can get better if you get good treatment. You'd have to get people who have the divine power [Zionists], who do by the power of God, that can counteract them.

Asked whether he had ever witnessed such events, Brown replied: "I never see him [Hunter-Man] at graveside, but I see it *proform* [perform] away in St. Ann's, when I was a youth. And I travel Clarendon and I hear about it. And all around. I go to Kingston and hear about it. . . . . They call it *dry bone*, those that work with the dead. I see it perform once in my district, Stephney. That's where I was born." In her visits to Jamaica between 1919 and 1924, Martha Beckwith (1929:181–82) recorded a song used by the "Pukku-merians" for "calling up the spirits" that included repeated references to "dry bone," such as "Dry bone come down the gully road." During my own fieldwork an incident occurred in Martha Brae that was attributed to dry bone activity.

Leaders, Healers, and Evangelists

In Martha Brae and neighboring communities, Revival leaders, healers, and evangelists are perceived as manifesting the activity of the spirit pantheon and carrying out the orders of spirit Messengers. During my fieldwork, Joe and May Jackson (aged seventy-three and seventy-one in 2001) were the main Revival leaders in Martha Brae. They came from the parish of St. James in 1944 and became well-established Strangers. Although Joe was trustee for three family-land estates in St. James, in Martha Brae he and May first lived as tenants in a rented house in the yard of other Strangers (who had bought the forfeited Kelly family land) and attended a Revival church in Falmouth led by Brother Jones. They established their first Revival tabernacle in the tenant yard around 1948 and later married legally while still residing there. They now had five adult children (and grandchildren), one of whom, in 1995, resided in Negril, where he had bought two square chains of land. In 1967, the year before I began my fieldwork, the Jacksons moved to their present cliff-top yard of one square chain that they purchased through "lease-and-sale" and cultivated. Joe used to plant a ground on captured land at Zion, while May higglered at Falmouth market. Joe was now a night watchman in Falmouth, and May became a packer at the paw-paw factory on Holland Plantation.

Reflecting in 1995 on his career as a Revival leader, Joe described to me his conversion to Revivalism in Martha Brae around 1948 following bodily symptoms that he first assumed were due to physical illness. But the Scottish-trained doctor in Falmouth told him that he was well and Revivalist Brother Jones diagnosed the symptoms as resulting from beneficial spirit contact. Joe explained that the Archangel Gabriel then appeared to him in a vision and instructed him to build a church on the rented land. He constructed a church of sticks and coconut branches with the assistance of an "old-time Revivalist" who miraculously appeared and advised him to place a basin of water on a table in the middle of the church for the spirit-messenger Gabriel to visit. Gabriel soon sent him his first *bands* or congregation from Leysham in St. James.

When the Jacksons began to buy their present yard, they built a more substantial tabernacle on this land. Joe became pastor of this church follow-ing his ordination by a "Bishop" in the parish of Westmoreland, while May, who "received the Spirit" soon after Joe's conversion, became its "Mother" or "Leadress." Following initial links with Revival bishops in Westmore-land, Clarendon, and Kingston (who had tenuous ties with churches in the United States), Joe and May were in 1995 switching their clientship to Brother Jones, who had become a bishop in Falmouth and who continued as their patron. May used to do "physician work" but no longer practiced such spiritual/magical healing, though she continued to diagnose and re-fer. Pastor Roberts (from Lime Hall) asserted that were May to stop her Revival work, she would either drop dead or become a cripple. Similarly, Joe said that he could not leave his tabernacle as "is me who get the order to build it."

Whereas the Jacksons were of African descent, like the majority of people in Martha Brae and other Trelawny villages, Lily Rasheed was an Afro-Chinese Revival-Zion healer who had lived at Zion since 1986. She too believed that she must carry out her Revival work, which was a "gift," or else fall sick and die. Indeed, even if she removed her red Revival headdress she immediately felt ill. Like Joe, Lily had had a dramatic conversion through "spiritual sickness" in 1976, while living at the Hague land settlement ad-joining Martha Brae, that (as she informed me in 1995) she initially mistook for a medical illness. She therefore "reluctantly" became a Revival healer, recovered within a week, and had now been "practising" for nineteen years (and was still doing so in 2001). From Zion she had attended Revival meet-ings at the tabernacle of Pastor Currie, who briefly settled in Martha Brae but who had now moved to Upper Trelawny—beyond The Alps to Free-man's Hall and Warsop.[6]

Lily perceived herself as healing by undoing the work of Obeah and

Pukumina. Her clients came "from Martha Brae [and] different places" to her "balm-yard" at Zion. She healed in the front room of her cottage, which had a "treatment couch," a Revival Table with fruit and bottles of consecrated water, and red cloth banners that "cut and clear destruction: destruction like anyone would try to set evil on you." She healed through "the Holy Spirit of the Lord. I don't deal in any other spirits. Those spirits are some demonic, satanic powers." In 1995 she told me that she had healed someone the previous week who "blow up from some evil hands. They set those things on them. Some dead spirits." Such spirits, "set" by someone with a "grudge" against the victim, "cause weakness, loss of appetite, things like those." Lily diagnosed with the Bible, wrote up and drew "the cases" in an exercise book, and healed by anointing the patient with perfumed oils as advised by the Holy Spirit. She also used an "all-purpose rod — if the person sick, you can move it over the person in any form."

Pastor Brown of Granville also performed Revival-Zion diagnosis and healing: "It is in the Spirit. Can do it in the church [Revival tabernacle], whenever I having service — anywhere, because I heal people on the wayside the same. Because when I in the Spirit, I *feel* — the Spirit give me a feeling that if you have any ailment or pain anywhere, I can spot it out and tell you." For example, he had healed his wife's skin complaint that doctors, medical X ray, and biopsy had been unable to diagnose or cure. Pastor Roberts claimed to heal "when the Holy Spirit operates in me." He explained that his preaching could also make evildoers sick, as it did in Martha Brae in 1983, when an Obeahman attending May's Revival service became ill inside her church as Roberts was preaching: "I was the one who came and deliver Mother Jackson out of the Obeahman' hands."[7]

As well as Revival leaders and healers, there are evangelists who are believed to convey messages from the spiritual Messengers (such as the Archangel Gabriel or the prophet Jeremiah) and who are sometimes referred to as messengers themselves. Joe's account of his conversion, when an "old-time Revivalist" brought a message from Gabriel, provides one illustration. I was told that I had witnessed another such example at May's Revival convention in 1995. Talking with her and Pastor Roberts following one of the convention meetings, I asked why a visiting female evangelist from Duanvale had been groaning in a pronounced fashion. Roberts explained that she had been conveying a message from the Messenger or prophet Jeremiah, who wished to drink some holy water. In addition, he commented, "Revival is based on different types of movements" representing "different types of spirits." On a number of occasions following my participation, through singing and dancing, in Revival meetings, I was told that I had been in the initial stages of possession. For example, in our discussion in 1995, May remarked: "You get a flash [of the spirit]. You was starting to *move* Sunday night!" It is thought that spiritual Messengers may also convey their messages by instructing Revivalists to tie their turbans in different styles. This belief accounted for the wide range of turban knots that I observed at Revival meetings.

Evangelists may also pass on their messages by traveling around Jamaica. In 1995 Pastor Roberts clarified that when I first met him visiting Martha Brae in 1983, he was an evangelist or messenger, not a pastor, and had been sent to deliver a message to Mother Jackson (who was unknown to him at that time) as her "church was down and it needed a spiritual awakening, a spiritual reviving." Such evangelizing may serve as an apprenticeship or prelude to becoming a mother or pastor. For example, in 1995 Pastor Brown in Granville outlined how he had started his Revival work as an evangelist or "Pilgrim" traveling around the island until he was sent to Granville, where he settled as a tenant in 1959 and subsequently established his own Revival yard on land that he purchased in 1962. Similarly, Joe explained that his patron Brother Jones, who became a pastor and then a bishop, had been an evangelist just traveling around preaching as a messenger when they first met in Falmouth around 1945, having been sent there by a Messenger to "an old *band seal*" or Revival yard of an elderly leadress whom he later succeeded. Fifty years later, in 1995, Bishop Jones was himself concerned with the issue of succession and was said to regard Joe as his successor. In addition to such patron-client relations, kinship provides a basis for advancement in Revival. For instance, one of the Jacksons' sons was a prominent Revivalist in Negril who played a leading role in his parents' convention in Martha Brae in 1995 and who, by 1999, had returned to live in their Revival yard to assist more fully with their rituals. Pastor Roberts was the son of Revivalists of reputation in Lime Hall, St. Ann.

Meetings and Ritual Symbols

In Martha Brae and neighboring settlements, Revival ideology is not confined to those who go to Revival tabernacles and balm-yards but pervades the worldview of these communities.[8] However, Revival ideology is crystallized in certain ritual symbols used in tabernacles and by healers; it is most apparent in Revival meetings and mortuary rituals. As in George Simpson's (1956) pioneering study of Jamaican Revival cults referred to by Barry Chevannes (1978), the Jacksons' house yard, which was the center of Revivalism in Martha Brae, was marked by the "seal, or pole, or

A Revival meeting in Martha Brae. Photo by Jean Besson.

station, or centre" (Simpson 1956:6) — that is, by a tall pole and flag believed to attract and symbolize Revival spirits. Similar *bands seals* (flagpoles) distinguished other Revival yards that arose and declined in Martha Brae, as well as in Granville and Zion. Some of these house yards had tabernacles, like the mission houses of Pastor Brown in Granville and Deaconess Morrison at Zion. In other cases, like that of Zion's Lily Rasheed, the pole indicated a balm-yard or place of healing. The ritual symbols in mission houses in Granville and Zion were similar to those described below for Joe and May Jackson's tabernacle in Martha Brae.

The Jacksons' tabernacle was made of "zinc" (corrugated iron sheets) with a concrete floor and wooden benches. Around 1990 the "church" received a coat of turquoise paint and in 1995 the benches were also painted. The congregation faced central and subsidiary altars. In the early years of my fieldwork, the two altars were covered in brightly patterned cloth, but by 1995 this had been replaced by cloths of white and red symbolizing the power and the danger of spirit contact.[9] As with Lily, the Revival healer at Zion, there were also red banners "to cut and clear destruction" said to be caused by Obeah. On the altars were other ritual symbols: bottles and a basin of holy water, believed to aid mediation with the spirit Messengers, and vases of croton leaves representing the spirit world.[10] Doves, kept in the yard, were also believed to aid communication with Revival spirits.

Hanging from the rafters were four goatskin drums made by Joe that, when played, were believed to induce possession by the spirits. Drums are also symbols of Africa and of Caribbean slave opposition to enslavement (Campbell 1985:25); they still serve as a mode of communication among Revivalists today. Pastor Roberts touched on these themes, including the original Obeah-Myal complex as a source of protection against the sorcery of slavery, when he discussed the drums with me and May:

> Revival is based upon a slavery movement. When the Africans were in slavery, and the master—what they would call "Buckie-Master" [*bukra* or white]—is on [oppressing] them, they would go into their corner and clap their hands. Because they [the slave masters] say they [the slaves] musn't keep no service or anything like that. And they will chant their rituals . . . and the Buckie-Master would hear them and then it mashed-up [deflected] them, Buckie-Master them, because they were coming on them and they [the slaves] were chanting. And anywhere the other rest [of slaves] are, the drum beat . . . 'cause the drum can send message like a telegram.

> There are different ways of sounding the drum. When visitors is here or bands come een [in], they can sound the drum and the whole district understand that a bands is here. When is sound fe dem, deh know that it sound fe dem 'cause a de different sound dat it give. So de drum carry a message.

> Now, when I knock the drum like this—listen to the different sound [he demonstrated]—the whole district can know there is a visitor. . . . Or when I go to the cross-road and knock like this [he demonstrated again] they know that it's some destruction [evil] passing t'rough. But they got to understand the different sounds of the drum, what it is all about.

Roberts said that drums can also communicate with "Indian spirits"; that is, with the Hindu spirits of the postslavery East Indian indentured laborers that are still significant among their descendants (some of whom continue to work on plantations) today: "[The drums] is part Indian. Because when the Indian Messengers come into the church sometimes, they [Revivalists] have to really entertain the Indian Messengers. Indians love rice and all those feasts and goat [curried goat] and all those things, [so] sometimes you have to make feasts. And sometimes they make 'Table.'"

Such "Tables" are a central feature of Revivalism (Simpson 1956:371–76; Chevannes 1978:11–12; Seaga 1982:9). Chevannes defines a Table as "a feast held in honour of an event or a person, but involving a long drawn out ritual perhaps reminiscent of the combined Eucharist and feasting of the primitive Christians during their early practice of primitive communism.

Tables may be held to raise money, to give thanks, to mourn the dead, and, in the case of Pocomania, to destroy" (1978:11). Tables were held by Revival healer Lily (who was married to an East Indian) both at Zion and on her travels throughout western Jamaica; they were apparent in a Revival street meeting in Martha Brae in 1983 and were discussed by May, as well as Pastor Roberts, in Martha Brae in 1995. May described the Tables that she makes, demonstrating both how the Christian ritual has been creolized and how it serves the purpose of fund-raising:

> Well, anytime I going to have a Candle Table, I get a table put right there and so I make it up and I might put three dozen candle and some fruits, like orange, pine and syrup and all those things that I can afford: grapefruit, mangos, ripe bananas, naseberry, and put them on it. So when the service start and reach a time, then everybody go an' light a candle. And I tell them, "Light *dis* [this] candle, 50 dollars, or dis candle 20 dollars." Or you light for a 30 dollars, or you light for a 40 dollars to *gain* something. So when we put the candle on the table we consecrate it, such as read and pray over it, before we light it.

These various ritual symbols—altars, bottles and basins of holy water, vases of crotons, Tables, and drums—were integrated in the Revival meetings held by May in her tabernacle three nights a week on Wednesdays, Saturdays, and Sundays and during occasional week-long conventions that drew visitors from other communities. Revival meetings, attended by both genders but especially by women, lasted for several hours, a pattern reinforced by unemployment. The meetings started with drumming, which called *bands* members together from throughout the village, followed by the singing of Revival hymns or "sankeys" and dancing to the drums.[11] The drummers were both male and female, but the lead drummer was a woman. The dancing and singing were interpreted as a manifestation of the early stages of spirit possession. Interspersed with the drumming, singing, and dancing were the presentation of the minutes by the secretary; the reading of the biblical text and the sermon by Joe or May; testimony from the congregation (which included Revival deacons); "trumping" with various dance movements and overbreathing around the basin of holy water, which was believed to be visited by spirit Messengers; and, finally, the portrayal through dance and trance of what was perceived to be full possession by Revival spirits.

Such spirit possession, which may culminate in glossolalia or speaking in tongues (which I recorded in Martha Brae in 1983), was thought to enable communication with the spirit pantheon for protection, prophecy, and healing—a clear parallel with the original Myal-Obeah complex (whereby the morally neutral spiritual/magical power of Obeah was accessible through Myal or spirit possession) during slavery. Individual members of the congregation manifested different stages of possession (which was a mark of status), the most intense being demonstrated by the charismatic May. Contact with the Revival spirit world (which, it was believed, may also be revealed to individuals through visions in dreams) was perceived to be a source of both power and danger, reflected in the symbolic colors of white and red in altar cloths and banners. This symbolic color coding was appropriated by members of the congregation, especially by women, who often dressed for meetings in red and white. Revival turbans, tied in different styles to symbolize spirit messages and worn by both men and women but especially by women, likewise tended to be white or red.

Other ritual symbols, encountered in Pastor Brown's tabernacle in Granville and discussed by Pastor Roberts in May's mission house in Martha Brae, are a machete and sugarcane. Chopping a piece of sugarcane is, like the red cloth banners in the tabernacles and in Lily's balm-yard, believed to "cut and clear destruction." Brown explained that "sometime you have destruction. Can use a cane, people will see it, you use a cane and chop it up. It cut the destruction." Roberts recounted in 1995 that, when he had been sent as a messenger from Lime Hall to Martha Brae in 1983, he had been instructed to first use these symbols at a meeting in the Falmouth marketplace:

> When I was down in Lime Hall, in the Spirit, I went down in the Spirit for seven days. And the Spirit said to me—at that time I was an evangelist, I wasn't a Pastor—"Arise, and go to Falmout', take a C-A-N-E with you." And I said "I'm not going to carry it with me, because it is too big to carry on the bus." The Spirit told someone to go and get one [a piece of sugarcane] come give me. So I said, "Lord 'ave mercy, I'm going to have to take it with me." When I came to Falmout' wid it in my hand, the Spirit said to me seh I must go in Falmout' into the *broad* street, keep a service in Falmout' first, at the market, chop the cane in *seven* pieces. When I chop the cane in seven pieces, I was preaching the message.

Roberts stated that simultaneous with those events the state police shot a wanted man seven times at the same spot by the marketplace. These alleged happenings are said to have converted a Rastafarian onlooker to Revivalism,[12] to have resulted in a bus being chartered to take Pastor Roberts and his six supporters to meet May, and to have drawn a crowd to receive Roberts's message in Martha Brae.

The symbolism of the machete and sugarcane for "cutting and clearing destruction," that is, for eradicating hardship and evil, clearly derives from the Caribbean context. It reflects the process of culture-building in Revival (which has evolved as a continuing challenge to colonially derived society and culture, including both the plantation system and Baptist mission Christianity), here manifested in the appropriation and reversal of the main representations of plantation labor to become symbols of the Afro-creole spirit world. The incorporation of East Indian spirit Messengers into Afro-Christian Revival, which was also practiced by Afro-Chinese Lily Rasheed, who lived with her East Indian husband, likewise underlines the significance of the Caribbean context — in which cultures from Europe, Africa, and Asia have been transformed.

Mortuary Ritual and Belief

In addition to ritual symbols and meetings, Revival ideology in Martha Brae is reflected in elaborate mortuary ritual (originating in the African past and Jamaican slave society) in which Revival-Zion plays a complementary role to Baptist Christianity. Though the Baptist minister from Falmouth generally conducts village funerals, Revival-Zionism is especially manifested in the "set-ups" or wakes whereby members of the community visit and keep company with the household of the deceased.

The lykewake (generally preceded by other set-ups) the night before the burial is a major component of this ritual, which is undergoing change. The traditional lykewake, whereby the corpse was laid out in the house (with a saucer of salt placed on the body to keep the dual soul at bay) and the household and community kept watch over the deceased,[13] sometimes occurred during my earlier fieldwork. But even at that time, in the late 1960s and 1970s, this custom was beginning to change, with the corpse sometimes being held in the "drift"; that is, in the Falmouth hospital morgue, especially if the death occurred in hospital.[14] However, villagers explained that there were only five drawers in the morgue, one of which was reserved "fe dem what squash out a road"; that is, for car accident victims. When the morgue was full, the corpse was "iced" (preserved with ice) in the house yard by the village's male mortician, nicknamed "Sam Isaacs" after one of Jamaica's leading undertakers in Kingston and Montego Bay. By 1995 there had been further change: the deceased was now routinely removed from Martha Brae, either to the recently established "dead-house" at Hague or to a funeral parlor in Falmouth. Regardless of whether or not the corpse is present the night before the burial, merrymaking and sankey singing in the house yard are aspects of the lykewake, which has parallels with the lykewakes of the Scots and Irish societies from which Jamaica's Celtic planters and indentured servants came (Patterson 1973:48; Karras 1992; Dunn 2000:161), as well as African continuities among the slaves.

In addition to the lykewake and other set-ups before the funeral, and the funeral itself, Revival mortuary ritual in Martha Brae during my early field-work included a wake on the night of the burial, a "Nine Night" wake approximately nine nights after death, and sometimes a "Forty Night" wake. All of these rituals were believed to both mark and effect the transition of the *duppy* to join the ancestral spirits. But, like the lykewake, these rituals are changing. In the earlier years of my research, the Nine Night was considered to be the most important wake, marking the night when the duppy was believed to briefly return to his or her house yard before finally crossing to the spirit world. Like other set-ups, the Nine Night in Martha Brae — as elsewhere in Jamaica — was therefore observed at the yard of the deceased nine nights after death. However, even by the late 1960s Nine Nights in Martha Brae were being rescheduled to the nearest Saturday to accommodate wage labor, which is becoming an increasing dimension of the peasant economy. At such Nine Night rituals, a feast of rum,[15] coffee, and bread was held; sankeys were sung; and merrymaking including domino playing set the scene. At midnight, the living members of the community would "brave-up" themselves and sing more vigorously as the duppy reputedly made its transit. A Forty Night might also be held, approximately forty nights after death, to further assist the duppy's journey.

By the 1990s these rituals had changed even more. Nine Night and Forty Night wakes were dying out, while, simultaneously, there was an increasing emphasis on the lykewake, now known as "Singing Night." May Jackson explained this change: "They generally have singing. Like they goin' bury tomorrow, they have singing tonight. For the whole night. And sometimes some of them they make tea and eat bread — and sing. The Nine Night is after they bury. Bury this week and Nine Night next week. But nobody really do that again. From they bury, they just stop so. Things is so expensive that you really can't [afford it] and the person bury. So after they bury you just stop." This was the plan for the burial that year, 1995, of Leah Wilkins's elderly sister, from an Old Family, who had been the Baptist class leader. The bereaved household (comprising three generations of descendants living on land purchased from "Lawyer") was simultaneously being set apart from the rest of the village, by the "dead-yard" banner displayed on their house by the Come To-Gather Society (CTS), and integrated into the community as the Singing Night and funeral were being planned. The deceased's sister, Leah (a returned migrant living elsewhere in Martha Brae), explained that there would only be a Singing Night and the funeral due to the high cost of such rituals. But the rising cost of mortuary rituals, while undoubtedly a factor in the decline of Nine Night and in the increasing significance of Singing Night, seems an insufficient explanation for this change. The escalating practice of immediate entombing or vaulting at the funeral and the logistics of the return of rural-urban and overseas migrant relatives to attend the mortuary ritual may also be contributing to this transformation — not only in Martha Brae and other rural communities such as Granville, but also in urban Kingston (Besson and Chevannes 1996).

In Martha Brae and Granville, as elsewhere in Jamaica, it is believed that entombing completes the placing of the dead. Entombing was traditionally undertaken a year after interment and was comparable to the "second burial" (Hertz 1960). The new Jamaican fashion of the earlier, final, sealing of the grave through concrete vaulting (as was occurring in Martha Brae and Granville by the 1990s), which is replacing older tombs and cairns and is completed at the burial, may therefore be transforming the perception of the duppy's journey to the spirit world — hastening this transit. Such a transformation may be contributing to the decline of Nine Night and complementing the increasing emphasis on Singing Night, as migrant kin and friends gather for the funeral the next day.[16]

During my fieldwork, the significance of entombing was underlined by the case of an unentombed burial and a reputed unplaced female soul in Granville who was said to have caused a baby's death in Martha Brae. But the case was controversial among Revivalists. One perspective, in both communities, was that the wandering duppy had caused the death. Another view, expressed by the dead woman's sister, maintained that the soul could not have wandered after burial, as the kin of the deceased had stuck pins in the soles of the corpse's feet and planted corn on her unentombed grave.[17] However, such Revival practices are designed to secure the shadow (rather than the duppy), namely, that dimension of the dual soul believed to be buried with the corpse. These precautions would therefore have been generally considered insufficient to place the duppy among the ancestors. The differing views can thus be accounted for in Revival ideology itself. The illness and death of the woman, whose unsettled soul was reputedly roaming between Granville and Martha Brae, was in turn said to have been caused by Obeah resulting from a conjugal triangle including the deceased. This theory of supernatural causation coexisted with, and transcended, a medical diagnosis of the deceased's illness by a doctor in Falmouth.

Even with proper entombing, it is believed that the shadow may be invoked by Obeah to cause misfortune (as is said to be practiced in Pukumina). In the 1980s such a case reputedly occurred among Zionists in Martha Brae. After the death of a family-land trustee, entombed in the village cemetery, conflict arose between her descendants (the customary coheirs) and her widower, whose position in the dispute was weak. The trustee had legally married her now-widowed husband late in life; he was the father of only some of her children, and, as a spouse, he had only a life interest in the land. He was suffering terrible back pain and sleepless nights, which he attributed to the shadow of his late wife who was reputedly being manipulated by living kin. Her shadow was said to be manifested at night by the repeated tweaking of her widower's bed socks and the snuffing out of his bedside candles. Although his back pain had been medically diagnosed in Falmouth ("Doctor tell me I have gastritis in my back"), there seemed to be little improvement until the tormented widower sought Revival-Zion healing. There was then a slight decrease in the pain, but the widower believed that the spiritual battle continued to be waged, as manifested by the persistent stifling of his candle flames. The principle of cognatic land transmission was thus upheld. In the early 1990s, on revisiting this yard, which had devolved to the trustee's descendants, I was told that the widower had died in a house fire there.

It is believed that, even with proper burial and without invocation, a shadow may cause misfortune and death of its own volition. In 1995 I was advised that another death in Martha Brae (that of a middle-aged woman whom I knew well) had been caused in this way. Following rumors throughout the village to this effect, I cautiously raised the matter with the deceased's mother, whom I had also known for many years. The mother, a keen Revival-Zionist, immediately confirmed the gossip I had heard. She indignantly explained that her daughter's death in the early 1990s had indeed been spiritually caused and stated angrily, "is her own fault"; had the daughter listened to her mother's warnings, she would still be alive. But despite maternal cautions, the daughter had touched the hand of an elderly woman's corpse in a house yard elsewhere in the village. To confound the situation, the daughter had then reputedly established an extraresidential conjugal relationship with the elderly widower,[18] who was the legally married spouse of the deceased, thus reversing the usual pattern of conjugal relations whereby visiting and consensual unions precede legal marriage (chapter 8). According to the mother, the vexed shadow of the dead wife subsequently came from the entombed grave in the village cemetery and dispatched the daughter with a glance: "Look 'pon her, is her [shadow] kill her."

In addition to sanctioning institutionalized conjugal relations and cognatic descent, Revival mortuary ritual comforts the bereaved and symbol-izes community solidarity. Like Obeah-Myal rituals surrounding death and burial during slavery, Revival mortuary ritual also provides a basis for inter-community networking as villagers attend funerals and wakes in other com-munities,[19] either as individuals or through their friendly societies. Revival is also now the basis of transnational networking, as overseas migrants return home for burial rites (Besson and Chevannes 1996). In August 2000 a new variant of transnational ritual occurred with interment of the ashes of a migrant member of a Martha Brae Old Family brought from England for burial in the free-village cemetery.

The Dynamics of Revival

In addition to mortuary ritual, other aspects of Revivalism promote intercommunity solidarity, as did Obeah-Myal, Native Baptism, and the Great Revival in the slavery and postemancipation pasts. Histor-ically, the Baptist War and the emergence of a black ethnicity (Robotham 1988) are examples of this theme, another being the way in which this shared body of belief and ritual "drew semi-autonomous plantation slave villages or free villages together" (Schuler 1979a:128). In Martha Brae, Revival links the village with bands in other communities in Trelawny and beyond, such as in the neighboring parishes of St. Ann and St. James. Such networking includes the travel of Martha Brae Revivalists by hired van to St. James's Granville and to Lethe on the Great River (on the boundary of St. James and Hanover) to participate in river baptisms.[20] These visits are re-ciprocated; for example, in the summer of 1983 Zionists from Lethe spent a week in Martha Brae, a Revival mother from Sav-la-Mar in Westmoreland stayed several days, a bands from Lime Hall in St. Ann (including Pastor Roberts, who was then an evangelist) made a Sunday visit, and on a week-night Mother Chisolm traveled to Martha Brae from Watt Town, a Revival stronghold in St. Ann. Such visitors joined rituals in the tabernacles and held meetings at village yards and crossroads. There were similar visits in subsequent years, including 1995 and 1999.

A significant dimension of Revival is competition among leaders and factions—as I observed especially from 1983 to 2000. During the years 1983–90 three Revival bands competed in Martha Brae. Two of these were Zionist and led by women: Harriet Best and May Jackson, who had become more prominent than her pastor husband Joe. Harriet, who led the smaller bands, had left May's larger group to create a rival faction, as envisioned in a dream. However, Harriet was unable to maintain a credible congregation or to maintain her bamboo booth, as she lacked the oral skills, reputation, and resources of charismatic May, including Joe's support. In addition, May's congregation had been augmented by the defection of Pastor Brown's Revival bands from neighboring Granville to her tabernacle; this not only strengthened May's reputation, but also temporarily left Brown without a congregation. Moreover, gossip implied that the Granville bands had been shifting from Revival-Zion to Pukumina (Besson 1993). Around 1985 a male-led bands was established in Martha Brae to become the third rival faction. Its leader was Pastor Currie, from Upper Trelawny, who had visited the village in 1983 to participate in Revival rituals. By 1990 his Martha Brae congregation had dissolved due to a reputed shift from Revival-Zion to Pukumina, though he reestablished his reputation at Freeman's Hall and Warsop. Meanwhile, May Jackson stood fast in Martha Brae.

The visitors to Martha Brae in 1983 contributed to the dynamics of Revival in the community and reflected parallels with the public meetings of the Myal movement. May convened one widely attended meeting for villagers and visiting Revivalists at a female drummer's house yard. At this assembly Mother McNeil, from Sav-la-Mar in Westmoreland, "cast out destruction" from the village, smashing bottles as she whirled around in dance; she also spoke in tongues. The success of this gathering reinforced the reputation of May, McNeil's sponsor. At an even larger crossroads meeting, which May supported, Mother Chisolm from Watt Town in St. Ann (wearing a long white robe with a red sash and a white turban) asserted the presence of Obeah in the village, repeatedly pronouncing "Obeah deh in Mart'a Brae." She prophesied the evil that would come to pass and strove to protect the village through Revival-Zion ritual. With such a specific prediction she put her reputation on the line, and it was both challenged and validated by whispered words among the crossroads congregation.[21] Whatever the pros and cons, Mother Chisolm so excelled in oral skill that she held the crowd spellbound for many hours, while her dramatic performance further bolstered May's reputation. Meanwhile, Harriet Best (who had defected from May's congregation), in her losing battle for reputation, volunteered to serve as Mother Chisolm's assistant at her crossroads Revival Table. Harriet also convened a week of nightly meetings led by Pastor Currie, who briefly patronized her tabernacle. After an initial plan to boycott Harriet's rituals, May attended them through noblesse oblige. There her verbal skills triumphed, and Harriet's congregation subsequently melted away. By the early 1990s Harriet's bamboo booth had completely disintegrated, leaving May and her tabernacle unrivaled in Martha Brae.

Around 1993, however, a reputed rift developed between May and Joe that, by 1995, had detracted from their reputations, and their congregation began to fall away. Meanwhile, Pastor Brown in Granville had reaffirmed his commitment to Zionism and retrieved some of his supporters. In addition, Pastor Currie's dismantled tabernacle had been rebuilt by a former follower, Deaconess Irene Morrison, at Zion under the patronage of a Revival bishop in Maroon Town, St. James. At Zion a further struggle for reputation occurred between Irene and her female tenant, Pastor Berry. By 1995 Berry had left Irene's mission house and yard to live elsewhere in Zion and to lead her own congregation under a tree. By this time, too, Revival healer Lily Rasheed had established her balm-yard at Zion.

In 1995 I found May battling to retrieve her reputation. She was planning a week's convention, but according to gossip these plans were precarious and Joe (who was now residing in Falmouth) would undermine the convention. May concentrated on mobilizing her Revival-Zion network, sending several letters of invitation to bands in other communities. Although she received no written replies, she told me that she felt she could count on support from Duanvale in Trelawny and Lime Hall in St. Ann. On the opening Sunday of the convention, about fifty Revivalists (many in turbans and dressed in red and white) flocked to May's tabernacle. They came from throughout Martha Brae; from Granville, Zion, and Duanvale in Trelawny; and from Lime Hall in St. Ann. Mr. Roberts from Lime Hall (who had supported her as an evangelist in 1983) once again threw his weight behind her, this time as an established pastor, and their combined oral skills salvaged her rocky reputation. He stayed in Martha Brae for several days, returned briefly to Lime Hall midweek, then brought twenty more supporters to Martha Brae. May hosted nightly meetings throughout the week, and the Friday night service was patronized by Bishop Jones from Falmouth.

May's convention culminated in two large concluding meetings on the following Sunday, and after the midday service she and her adult daughter hosted a "breakfast." At 4:00 P.M. the final service began and lasted for six hours. About sixty Revivalists attended from several communities and parishes: Granville and Zion in Trelawny, Lime Hall in St. Ann, Tower Isle in St. Mary, Negril on the border of Hanover and Westmoreland, and many from Martha Brae. Moreover, Joe Jackson (who greeted me warmly beforehand and asked to see me for another interview) swept into the tabernacle from Falmouth and "pulled together" with May. This familial support was reinforced by the presence of their eldest son, a leading Revivalist in Negril. The service, through singing and drumming, progressed swiftly into "trumping," with the first seven people to feel possessed moving and groaning around the central basin of holy water. Many more members of the congregation joined in the trumping, and "spirit-possession" soon swept through the "church" — as had Myal on the slave plantations.

After the convention, May took a few days' leave to rest before returning to work on Holland Plantation. During that time Joe came up from Falmouth for the interview (on a roadside) he had requested. He explained that, contrary to rumor, he had never left "his" church. But he outlined his increasing involvement with aging Bishop Jones, in Falmouth, whose health was failing, and his own role as designated successor. Joe was therefore committed to advancement in the Revival hierarchy beyond Martha Brae. By 1999 Jones had died, but his wife — not Joe — succeeded him, while May was confidently preparing for another convention, which would draw invited guests from beyond the village. May now had the full-time assistance of her Revivalist son from Negril, a cabinetmaker, who had returned to reside in her house yard.

By August 2000 May was frail. Her cabinetmaker son was taking over her Revival rituals, with the tabernacle doubling as his workshop; her daughter was keeping a shop and bar on their terraced cliff face; May, her son, and daughter were planning a convention for November; and Joe now lived at Zion. Elsewhere at Zion, Irene Morrison's tabernacle was dormant, but her former tenant Pastor Berry was escalating her Revival rituals, traveling around Trelawny between Duanvale, Kinloss, Zion, and Granville where she supported her cousin Pastor Brown. Lily Rasheed likewise continued to "travel out" and to perform Revival healing, and there was another Revival yard at Zion. In Granville, Pastor Brown still defined himself as a Zionist and was building a more substantial, concrete Revival-Zion church. By 2001 May was ill, Joe visited her often, their son had returned to Negril, and their resident daughter was taking over May's Revival role, while Lily was said (in the Falmouth market) to be "hotting up" her Revival practice at Zion. The higgler daughter of Tom and Mary Grant, the founders of Zion, was also getting "heated" through Revival and sometimes had to put cold water on her head.

It remains to be seen how the dynamics of Revival will further unfold among these "men- [and women-]-of-words" in and around Martha Brae in the new millennium.[22] Meanwhile, it is in Revival ideology, rooted in the Obeah-Myal slave religion, that the African cultural heritage of the Martha Brae villagers can be most clearly identified. However, this African legacy has not persisted passively but has been dynamically transformed — through negotiation with, appropriation, and reversal of Baptist Christianity — in new social contexts, including "Baptist" free villages, to create an Afro-Protestant religion forged through three centuries of Caribbean culture-building.

The Rastafarian Movement

Rastafarians do not acknowledge death, which they either deny or suffocate with taboo. They also reject the elaborate mortuary rituals of Baptists and Revivalists, looking instead to a symbolic return to Ethiopia. Nevertheless, the Rastafarian movement coexists with the Baptist Church and Revival ideology in Martha Brae and other Trelawny villages where, rather than being deviant or criminal (L. E. Barrett 1988:84–89), it elaborates the Afro-creole culture-building that opposes Euro-American lifestyles and land monopoly.

The Origins of Rastafari in Jamaica and Trelawny

The roots of the Rastafarian movement, like those of the Revival cult and the Baptist Church, reach back to the Jamaican and Trelawny protopeasant past. The origins of Rastafari lie partly in eighteenth-century Jamaican slave religion, with the emergence of the ideology of Ethiopianism among the plantation slaves (L. E. Barrett 1988:68). Leonard Barrett argued that "by the time of the emergence of the Black churches" in antebellum America, "Africa (as a geographical entity) was just about obliterated from their [the slaves'] minds. Their only vision of a homeland was the biblical Ethiopia. It was the vision of a golden past — and the promise that Ethiopia should once more stretch forth its hands to God — that revitalized the hope of an oppressed people. Ethiopia to the Blacks in America was like Zion or Jerusalem to the Jews" (75). Barrett pointed out that Ethiopianism developed even earlier in Jamaica and highlighted its link with the Baptist Church and with the subsequent development of the Native Baptist variant: "Long before Ethiopianism came to America, the term had been adopted in Jamaica by George Liele, the American Baptist slave preacher who founded the first Baptist church in the island in 1784 — which he named the Ethiopian Baptist Church. This church . . . grafted itself onto the African religion of Jamaican slaves and developed outside of the Christian missions, exhibiting a pure native flavour. . . . From it came the grass-roots resistance to oppression" (76).

The link between the ideology of Ethiopianism and the Baptist Church during slavery can be clearly seen for the parish of Trelawny. In the Falmouth Baptist Church, whose congregation during slavery consisted mainly of slaves from surrounding plantations, a plaque commemorating emancipation was erected by "The Sons of Africa." This plaque can still be seen in the William Knibb Memorial Baptist Church with this inscription (reflecting

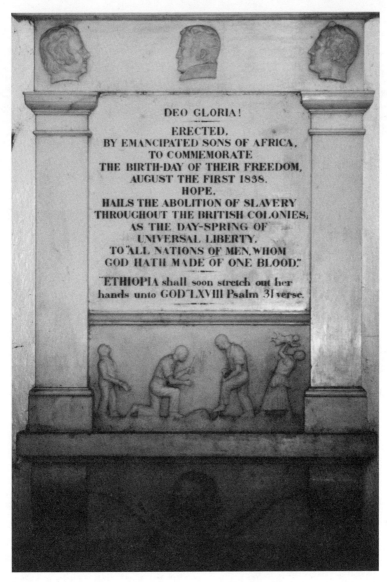

DEO GLORIA!

ERECTED,
BY EMANCIPATED SONS OF AFRICA,
TO COMMEMORATE
THE BIRTH-DAY OF THEIR FREEDOM,
AUGUST THE FIRST 1838.
HOPE,
HAILS THE ABOLITION OF SLAVERY
THROUGHOUT THE BRITISH COLONIES,
AS THE DAY-SPRING OF
UNIVERSAL LIBERTY,
TO "ALL NATIONS OF MEN, WHOM
GOD HATH MADE OF ONE BLOOD."

"ETHIOPIA shall soon stretch out her
hands unto GOD" LXVIII Psalm 31 verse.

The emancipation plaque in the William Knibb Memorial Baptist Church, Falmouth. Photo by Jean Besson.

an Ethiopian theme): "Deo Gloria! Erected, by emancipated Sons of Africa, to commemorate the birth-day of their freedom, August The First 1838. Hope hails the abolition of slavery throughout the British colonies as the day-spring of universal liberty. To 'All nations of men, whom God hath made of one blood.' 'ETHIOPIA shall soon stretch out her hands unto GOD' LXVIII Psalm, 31 verse." Below the inscription is the profile of Baptist missionary, William Knibb, who championed the emancipation cause and would lead Jamaica's postslavery village movement, especially in Trelawny. In Trelawny's free villages, including Martha Brae, would flower the rich complex of religious forms—the Baptist Church, Revival worldview, and Rastafarian movement—that coexist today. This coexistence is rooted in the interweaving of Obeah-Myal ideology, Nonconformist Baptist mission Christianity, Ethiopianism, and the Native Baptist variant, all of which were modes of opposition among the Trelawny protopeasantry to colonial plantation slavery and the planters' Established Anglican Church.

The Rastafarian Movement in the Twentieth Century

Ethiopianism burgeoned into the Rastafarian movement in the twentieth century. Ethiopian ideology was reinforced by the teachings of Marcus Garvey (born in 1887 in St. Ann, bordering Trelawny, and known to the author's father, Lawyer) in Jamaica during 1914–16 and 1927–35.[23] Garvey portrayed blackness and African culture as a symbol of greatness and promised repatriation of African Americans to Africa. The Rastafarian movement itself crystallized with the crowning of Ras Tafari as Haile Selassie, emperor of Ethiopia, in 1930; the preaching of the Howellites from the 1930s to the 1950s; and the innovations of the Youth Black Faith, founded in 1949. In the 1950s young activists introduced the dreadlocks or matted hair complex, which symbolized both the construction of a greater social distance from Jamaican colonial society and the perception of Rastas by that society as derelicts and outcasts. Dreadlocks also denoted the male focus of the movement (Chevannes 1995f, 1995g). Leonard Barrett (1988:86) emphasized the link between the first Rastafarian commune at Pinnacle, established by Leonard Howell around 1940 "deep in the hills of St. Catherine overlooking the city of Kingston," and "the Maroon communities of Jamaica." He could also have drawn a parallel with nearby Sligoville, Jamaica's first Baptist free village, founded in the St. Catherine hills in 1835–38 (Paget 1964:46).

Following the academic report on the Rastafarian movement in Kingston by M. G. Smith, Roy Augier, and Rex Nettleford in 1961, the anthropological literature on Rastafari burgeoned. The movement itself became "routinized" in Jamaica; it has spread throughout the Caribbean region and diaspora, has influenced youth cultures and the music industry on a global scale, and provides the basis of an international nongovernmental organization (NGO), the International Rastafarian Development Society, approved by the United Nations in 1996.[24] The Rastafarian movement remains decentralized, with variation and internal sects (including the Twelve Tribes of Israel and the late Prince Emmanuel Edwards's Bobo Dread or Ethiopian International Congress) and open membership of the House of Nyabinghi with its Assembly of Elders. However, the principal ideology, symbols, and rituals have endured, with Rastafari representing not only a new religious movement but also a new morality opposing colonial and neocolonial society. Central to the movement is the symbolic dichotomy of Babylon (exile in Jamaica or oppression) and Zion (the African homeland or indigenous culture). Other major themes are the symbolization of the dreadlocks (though the Bobo are turbaned) and of a black God/Messiah (Ras Tafari/Haile Selassie/Jah, despite his death in 1975), and the identification of Rastafarians with this God as "I and I." Also featured are rituals with drumming, singing, and dancing followed by Bible reading and preaching; an emphasis on oral expression through symbolic speech and ritually aggressive argument or "reasoning"; belief in magical power (accessed through dancing and inherent in the dreadlocks) and in Bible divination, the sacred significance of marijuana as the "holy herb," herbal healing, female contamination, and visions; and *I-tal* natural, salt-free food with dietary taboos (L. E. Barrett 1988; Chevannes 1995e; Homiak 1995). Although there have been some changes in gender and class relations within the movement, including the increasing involvement of women and the middle class, Rastafari remains essentially patriarchal and subaltern.

The Rastafarian Movement in Trelawny

The destruction of Pinnacle by the colonial state police in 1954 dispersed the Howellites to Kingston and other parts of Jamaica, and the movement grew in the rural parishes including Trelawny, where it has taken root within free villages such as The Alps, Kettering, Sherwood, Schawfield, Deeside, Reserve, Granville, and Martha Brae as well as urban Falmouth. Rastafarian arts and crafts — displayed in stalls along the Falmouth–Montego Bay North Coast road and in the Falmouth marketplace — are now important in the tourist industry. In 2001 house yards with Rastafarian symbols and a Rasta museum were also noticeable along the Falmouth-MoBay tourist route.

In Martha Brae and other Trelawny villages, the coexistence of Rastafari with the Baptist Church and Revival ideology sometimes occurs in the same house yard or household. For example, in Martha Brae a woman who was both Baptist and Revivalist had a dreadlocked Rastafarian son-in-law living in her yard. In Granville, two Rastafarians (father and son) lived in separate houses on family land with the father's maternal aunt who was a Baptist-Revivalist, and Granville's Revival pastor had a Rasta son in his household. In The Alps, Sylvester Bonner, a stalwart of the Baptist Church and a member of several overlapping Old Families (including the central Campbell family line) with Revival-based burial grounds, also had a Rasta son residing in his yard. This "Dread" was well versed in the Rastafarian faith and (in 1983) was associated with Prince Emmanuel. Originally situated in "Back-o-Wall" in the slums of Kingston (destroyed by the Jamaican postcolonial state in 1966), the prince's commune had moved to Bull Bay in St. Thomas on "seven or eight acres of 'captured lands'" (L. E. Barrett 1988:182). Sylvester's son was part of this organization and regarded his name, including his Old Family's title, as his "slave name in 'Babylon.'"

Such islandwide networks have enmeshed Rastafarians in other Trelawny villages. In Granville in the 1980s, a Rastafarian "crew" often met under a shade tree in the yard where two members of the group lived with other kin on family land (Besson 1995f:66–69). The focus of the crew was a dice-and-board game reflecting the Rastafarian faith. The board was brightly painted in Rastafarian colors: red, green, gold, and black—a combination (as the Dread in Alps explained) of the red, gold, and green of the Ethiopian and Israel Covenant and the red, black, and green of the Marcus Garvey Covenant. The route around the board— "Jamaica, Ethiopia, Adis Abbaba, Home"— reflected the Rastafarian repatriation theme. Three different styles of dreadlocks adorned the Rastas' heads; on one occasion when I visited, a member of the crew had just prepared some I-tal food. The crew—four young men and an "Older Dread" (who was still there, aged seventy-five, in 2000, though one of the younger Rastas had migrated)—explained that there were not many Rastas in Granville, but that they were part of a wider Rastafarian network spreading from Granville to other parts of Trelawny, Montego Bay in St. James, Kingston, and Prince Emmanuel in St. Thomas.

In 2001 this Rastafarian network still weaved through Martha Brae and had spread to its satellite squatter settlement of Zion. By the 1990s there were about twenty Rastas in Martha Brae, all young or middle-aged males. They sometimes met to "reason" at the village crossroads or at the Rastafarian tabernacle in Reserve. They were scattered in house yards of various tenures in Martha Brae and embedded in Baptist and Revival families and households. For example, in addition to the woman with the Rasta son-in-law in her (inherited) yard, another Baptist-Revival "church lady," who was a long-established Stranger in Martha Brae with family land in Duanvale, had three middle-aged dreadlocked sons living in her leased yard. These Rastas earned their livelihood in various ways: the eldest was a raftsman, the second

Trelawny Rastafarians in a family-land house yard. Photo by Jean Besson.

was a fisherman, and the youngest kept a cook shop (selling fried fish and chicken) in the yard. As one of them explained, they "have seen the light of Rastafari": they ate no "red-meat," drank no alcohol, and observed strict mortuary taboos: "Rastafari don't mix up in the dead-business, the dead-business don't fe I."

Alec Seaton (aged forty-one in 2001) was another Rastafarian, with dreadlocks grown "by nature" for twenty years and a Rasta nickname. He was in the sixth descending generation, on his maternal side, of Martha Brae's central family line (many of whom were Baptist-Revivalists) traced from plantation slaves on Irving Tower Estate. He grew up with his mother, Pam Gilmore, and maternal grandmother on family land in Martha Brae but moved in 1990 to live on one square chain of captured land bordering the village. A self-employed tailor, he had recently worked as a carpenter on a hotel construction site in Montego Bay. He had his own chattel cottage and once cultivated his unfenced yard, but roaming cattle destroyed his crops. He now bought food in the Falmouth market, where he used to sell Pam's homemade clothes, and fished in the river. He ate vegetables, fruit, and fish and avoided meat and alcohol. Unlike most Rastas he took a little salt, as "the blood want a little salt."[25]

Alec declared that Haile Selassie was "the King, . . . we recognise Haile Selassie as Rastafari God." When I asked in the late 1990s for his views on Haile Selassie's death in 1975, he observed that "the God could never dead." He also explained the taboos surrounding death. Like other rules governing the Rastafarian way of life, these taboos were biblically derived — from the Old Testament and Nazarites:

> It's in the Bible, in Numbers chapter 6, where it shows the rules of the Rastafari. Where it seh we should come at no dead body, neither for you' mother, father, sister or brother. Because the moment you come at a dead body, then you are unclean. And you are supposed to shave you' head within seven days. . . . Rastafari should not come at no dead body. So then [if a Rastafari dies, those] who are not Rastafari maybe will bury them. Somebody always help. I wouldn't look at the body. Because I don't want to be unclean. Is like, as it in the Bible seh we should never come at the dead, so we just have nothing to do with the dead. I would have to cut the *locks* off my head, because I see the dead. Because it seh we should not come at no dead body.

He showed me the relevant passage in the Bible on his table and asserted that Rastafarian ritual attitudes were therefore "different from Revival, completely different" (though see later in this chapter).[26]

Alec also explained that anyone could become a Rastafarian, though some Rastafari view white people as originating from the Fallen Angel Lucifer: "'Cause in the olden days, it was just black people. And the white come off Lucifer. And God cast Lucifer out from Heaven and say 'Go and you will be white like a pillar of salt.' So the white people come off Lucifer, 'cause Lucifer make nations . . . Cain, Adam [etc]." Alec, who met with other Rastafarians at the tabernacle in Reserve, asserted that "Rastafari is all over [Trelawny], every community you went you is supposed to find Rasta." For instance, he knew quite a few Rastas in Deeside, where he visited his two daughters and their mother.

I met one of Alec's Rastafarian friends (young, black, and male), Sean McDonald from Deeside, in the Falmouth marketplace in 1995; he was dreadlocked and wearing a vest of red, green, and gold. Sean, whom I kept in touch with through the market until 2001, was also known by his Rasta nickname (for, as he remarked, "Who ever heard of an African named 'McDonald' or 'Sean'?"). With another Rasta, he knited Rastafarian tams, belts, and vests to sell in their market stall. Nearby a third Rasta, from Sherwood, had a stall in which he sold men's clothes and shoes, purchased from higglers "who go to foreign"; that is, to Miami in the United States. (He sold on Saturdays and in the Wednesday Ben' Down Market and cultivated a provision ground on family land on Mondays.) In August 2000 Sean was also selling jewelry, buying chains and beads wholesale in Ocho Rios and Falmouth, and crafting necklaces for sale. In the 1990s he sold in the Falmouth marketplace on Wednesdays and Saturdays, but in 2000 he was selling every weekday except Wednesday on the Montego Bay Parade. By 2001 Sean was only trading in MoBay on Mondays, Tuesdays, and Thursdays and was back in the Falmouth market on Wednesdays, Fridays, and Saturdays.

Sean grew up in a Baptist household in Deeside. He observed, however, that he now expected to meet his God " 'Haile Selassie/Jah' " during his own lifetime, not after death as Baptists hoped for. At our first meeting, in 1995, Sean reasoned with me at length in the marketplace, expounding Rastafarian perspectives, and underlined his views by sparring with a Baptist higgler (a retired nurse — mulatto, mature, and female) in the neighboring stall, who incensed him by asserting that "God is white and sin is black." Using her as an illustration, Sean argued that, even in the 1990s, "one hundred percent of Jamaicans are European" in outlook and the few who were not (Rastafari) were still "under the eyeballs of the oppressors." (In June 1999 another Rastafarian trader told me that "white people" and their "black allies" in Jamaica were responsible for the state police "pressuring the poor in the market" — a reference to the policing of the marketplace at that time and a statement that generated great debate among other marketers.) In contrast to the brown Baptist higgler-nurse, who felt that humanity could only hope for "three score years and ten" and that funeral rites were important so that others would repent, Sean asserted that there was no need for death, which was only caused by disease or accident. Disease was triggered by a "European diet, if you eat red meat you *must* die"; this was also true of rice, white flour, and salt. By contrast, vital I-tal food was the healthy Rastafarian diet. In Sean's view, Rastafarians did not need to repent, for, unlike Europeans, they "have not enslaved anyone nor taken anybody's land"; neither were they concerned about the decomposing dead and did not need to "commercialize death." (Nor were they interested in placing the dead in the Revival spirit pantheon.) Moreover, he contended, no one had yet proved that either Haile Selassie or Moses had died. As seen from

Alec's similar denial of Haile Selassie's death, this represents a wider viewpoint among Trelawny Rastas.[27] Should a Rastafarian die, either "the Christians will come in and bury him" or (I was told) if there were no Christians around, other Rastafari would bury the body quickly without ritual.

In 1991 in the Falmouth marketplace there had been intense interest in the Gulf War, and in 1995 Sean suggested that Babylon (a place of sin and exile) was now Iraq. His symbolic shifting of Babylon from Jamaica to Iraq is consistent with the rooting of Rastafarians in Caribbean land, despite the ideology of return to Africa/Ethiopia or "Zion." Rastafarians in Martha Brae and elsewhere in Trelawny are either settling on leased, inherited, purchased, and family land or are "capturing" land — as in Martha Brae's satellite squatter settlement of Zion, which is located on Holland Plantation at the very heart of Babylon (where Rastas had an "Uprising Notice-Board" at the center of the camp). In the Accompong Maroon community in St. Elizabeth, common land is providing the foundation for a Rastafarian-Maroon peasantry. Elsewhere in Jamaica, the cry for gaining access to land has become a significant aspect of the routinization of Rastafari (L. E. Barrett 1988; Homiak 1995:129, 144), while captured lands have been important in the spread of the movement to the Eastern Caribbean (de Albuquerque 1980:238, 241), underlining the theme of Rastafari as an emergent variant of Caribbean squatter peasantries (Besson 1995c, 1995f). Similarly, in 1995 Sean lived on leased land in Deeside but by August 2000 had moved to the nearby village of Schawfield, where he had more secure land rights to two acres of family land purchased and transmitted by his paternal grandfather. The other members of the McDonald descent group had been dispersed through migration, but Sean was cultivating some of this land, was planning to build a house there, and, in three weeks' time, would visit his migrant father in Wembley, London. In 2001 Sean said that his trip to England had gone well, that he was now residing in his own house on the family land, and that he intended to visit Wembley again that year. Meanwhile, on the eve of the anniversary of Emancipation Day (31 July 2001), he would play his Rastafarian drums at Nyabinghi in St. James after the Falmouth Ben' Down Market.

Rastafari, Revival, and Baptist Christianity

In his groundbreaking work on Rastafari, Chevannes (1990, 1994, 1995e) argues that the Rastafarian movement must be seen as both a new departure from, and a continuity with, the traditional Afro-Jamaican peasant "worldview," Revival, which he initially concluded was disappearing in Jamaica due to the growth of Rastafari and "American-derived evangelical sects" (1978:1). Chevannes (1995e:31–38) identifies continuities and transformations of Revival in Rastafari, including parallels in their acephalous organization. "Direct traces" include the structure of rituals (drumming, singing, and dancing followed by Bible reading and preaching), the use of drums and the transformation of Revival songs, and a belief in magical power (e.g., accessed through dance), Bible divination, herbal healing, and communication through visions in dreams. "Indirect traces" are the beliefs in the power of the word, contamination by death and women, and fusion between the human and spirit world.

Chevannes (1995e:38–39) draws four related conclusions from these arguments. First, Rastafari is an African-derived religion with direct continuity from Myal (but seen as anti-Obeah from the mid-eighteenth century [Chevannes 1995c:6–7]), Native Baptism, and Revival. Here Chevannes goes beyond Mervyn Alleyne (1996:83–84), who, in the search for African continuities in Jamaican religion, finds such continuities in Myal (interpreted as overlapping with Obeah), Native Baptism, and Revival but argues that "whereas Africa remains very high among Rastafarians at the level of ideological consciousness, there isn't very much of African continuity in the system of religious belief and religious behaviour" (103). Second, Rastafari may be regarded as the fulfillment of Revival, though this is seen as fulfillment through rejection, Rastafari being anti-Revival and patriarchal. Third, Rastafari represents a worldview movement rooted in Myal and Revival. And fourth, Rastafari is a cultural movement that is constructing a new reality rather than being political and millenarian.

Chevannes (1995f) also establishes, through new evidence based on oral sources, that the Rastafari matted hair complex was the innovation of the Youth Black Faith in the 1950s, rather than originating earlier in Howell's Rastafarian camp at Pinnacle (M. G. Smith, Augier, Nettleford 1961). He also concludes that the Youth Black Faith "represented a reform trend of younger converts bent on purging the movement of Revivalist beliefs and practices" (Chevannes 1995f:77). He further argues "that the dreadlocks phenomenon symbolized both a rejection of social control . . . [and] a triumph of male power over the female" (Chevannes 1995g:97). In this process, "the Dreadlocks sought to overthrow the religion of the peasant, Revival" and "attempted to . . . isolate the negative ideas about women, which were abroad in the culture, ritualize them, and by so doing establish ritual distance from the contaminating source of their confinement in Jamaican society, in Babylon" (104, 120).

Though providing a new approach to Rastafari, aspects of Chevannes's perspective find support in other analyses of the movement. For instance, Leonard Barrett (1988), despite advancing the view of Rastafari as a "messianic-millenarian" movement, saw its roots in Jamaican slave religion. Horace Campbell (1980), in contrast to Chevannes, highlighted the political aspect of Rastafari but, like Chevannes, questioned the centrality of millenarianism to the Rastafarian movement and saw Rastafari as a culture of resistance.

Support for Chevannes's new approach to Rastafari can be found in the cultural history of Martha Brae and other Trelawny villages. Here, at the heart of Babylon or Jamaican plantation/tourism society, the continuity between the religious forms of Myal (both the Obeah-Myal complex and the later Myal movement), Native Baptism, and Revival can be clearly seen. However, this chapter suggests a revaluation of Revival in the context of Revival-Rastafari continuity, one that accentuates Revivalism itself as oppositional to Euro-American hegemony. The Rastafarian movement has made an impact in Trelawny only since the 1950s, whereas Revival and its precursors, Obeah and Myal, have been modes of opposition for three centuries of Afro-creole life. This underscores the strength of Revival ideology as Caribbean culture-building, rather than as simply a traditional worldview reaching fulfillment only through male-dominated Rastafari.

Martha Brae's new history also shows the significance of women in such culture-building. Moreover, it may be that the future reality of Rastafari partly lies in Caribbean peasant cultures of opposition, where Revival has long had a central place. This rooting of Rastafari in peasant adaptations, along with the now early removal of corpses from house yards by Revivalists, may account for the recent participation by Rastas in some Revival rituals, as in the wakes reported by Huon Wardle (personal communication 1995; 2001), and for the presence of a Rastafarian in May Jackson's 1995 Revival convention in Martha Brae. It also illuminates the Revival set-ups held on twelve successive nights in Granville preceding the Baptist funeral of the Older Dread's maternal aunt in 1994. The set-ups were held by her daughter in the dead-yard on their family land (after the deceased's removal to a funeral parlor in Falmouth), despite the presence of her Rastafarian cousin — who still lived there in 2000, notwithstanding the Revival family-land cemetery in the yard rooted in the Obeah-Myal past.

Chevannes has modified his conclusions in the light of my preliminary analysis of Revival and Rastafari in Trelawny (Besson 1995f). In an afterword, he stated that "by adopting a continuity approach, Jean Besson . . . has elevated Revival from a simple African retention to cultural resistance on par with the Baptist and Rastafarian religions. This suggests underlying values at work and she makes it quite clear that the role of women and the role of land are central. Whether or not these are some of the 'grammatical principles' (Mintz and Price 1976) we should be looking for, she has convincingly demonstrated the fruitfulness of the approach" (Chevannes 1995a:253–54).

My argument that the Baptist Church, Revival ideology, and Rastafarian movement coexist in Martha Brae and other Trelawny villages as variants of cultural opposition to Euro-American hegemony is further strengthened by Malcolm Cross's (1979:96–100) interpretation of Afro-Caribbean religions. Cross argued that Nonconformist sects, Afro-Christian cults, and the Rastafarian movement are all points on a continuum of rejection of colonial orthodoxy. He asserted that although the Nonconformist sects, such as the Baptists in Jamaica, are "hardly a very radical rejection of orthodox Christianity," they are nevertheless "of great importance" in challenging the colonial orthodox churches (97). The Nonconformists are therefore the opening point of his continuum. At midpoint are the Afro-Christian cults such as Jamaican Revival, whereas Rastafari represents the most radical rejection of colonially derived Christianity.

My conclusions modify Cross's interpretation in some respects. His thesis was set within an analysis of Caribbean urbanization, and he asserted that Nonconformist sects are found in both rural and urban areas, whereas Afro-Christian cults typify rural communities and Rastafari exists (in Kingston) "on the rim of a major Caribbean city" (1979:100).[28] However, Alleyne (1996:96) contends that Revival is largely urban. Leonard Barrett (1988: 84–89, 146, 160–61) noted that, although Rastafari's early incubation period was in the slums of Kingston, the first Rastafarian settlement was the rural community of Pinnacle, with the movement subsequently spreading to both urban and rural areas of Jamaica. My research not only reveals the coexistence of all three religious variants as modes of cultural opposition in Trelawny peasant communities, suggesting a more complex situation than Cross's continuum of distinct religious forms in different social contexts, but also resolves the contradictions among Cross and other authors regarding the rural-urban contexts of Afro-Jamaican religions. In addition, my interpretation highlights the relationship of these variants of oppositional African American Protestantism (the Baptist Church, Revival ideology, and Rastafarian movement) with gender, land, and kinship (chapter 8), elaborating central themes in Martha Brae's new history.

CHAPTER EIGHT

Households, Marriage, Kinship, and Descent

Consanguinity, conjugality, and affinity, or blood, marital, and in-law relationships, are (like the peasant economy and the villagers' cosmology and ritual) crucial to maintaining Martha Brae's reconstituted peasant community. This family system is likewise rooted in the Caribbean institution-building of the protopeasant and postslavery past. As with the peasant economy and religion, the family system also interrelates with land, including the family-land institution at the heart of Martha Brae's new history.

Domestic Groups and the "Problem" of Explanation

Domestic groups or households are not only the basic units of Martha Brae's peasant economy, but also the residential nuclei of the peasant community. Such households (ranging from one to twelve inhabitants) manifest features that have been widely identified as typifying the African American family. These features include varying conjugal statuses: "extra-residential" or duolocal visiting relations, "consensual cohabitation" or coresidence, and legal marriage.[1] Other characteristics are sequential conjugal unions (which I refer to as "serial polygamy"); male or female household headship; large numbers of children; a high incidence of half siblingship, "outside children," and so-called illegitimacy; a high rate of fostering, most frequently with the maternal grandmother; a range of household forms (single, nuclear, female-headed, and extended); and sometimes a cluster of related households in a common yard.

Throughout African America such domestic groups have tended to be regarded as evidence of a "disorganized" family structure, which has been generally attributed to either anachronistic African survivals or deviations from European norms. This has been especially true of Jamaica — at the very heart of African America—which in 1980 was reported as having the world's highest rate of "bastardy" or "illegitimacy" (Hartley 1980; Laslett 1980:xi).[2] Moreover, a colonial mass marriage movement in the mid-twentieth century failed to significantly increase the incidence of legal marriage in Jamaica (M. G. Smith 1966:iv–v).

Although colonial authorities and churches condemned the so-called immorality and promiscuity of Caribbean family life (M. G. Smith 1966:iv; Olwig 1981b:59–60; Horowitz 1992:57), early anthropological explanations of the Afro-American family provided a different perspective. Melville Herskovits (1990:64) asserted the retention and reinterpretation of West African polygyny as "accounting for some of the aberrant types of family organization,"[3] whereas Franklin Frazier (1966) argued that the destruction of African family structure by colonial plantation slavery was responsible, opposing views that generated the classic Herskovits-Frazier debate.[4]

Other explanations of the so-called matrifocal or mother-centered African Caribbean family have included economic deprivation in the Jamaican color-class system, generating a failure to achieve European legal marriage and the nuclear family (Henriques 1968); the marginal occupational status of Afro-Guyanese men, resulting in "matrifocality" in the later stage of the development cycle of domestic groups (R. T. Smith 1956) —a model derived from the matrilineal Ashanti (Fortes 1949); and the socioeconomic ethos of Jamaican rural communities, such as the variable of land tenure and whether or not the economic prerequisites of European marriage could be achieved (E. Clarke 1953, 1966). These economic explanations were concerned with the distinction between legal and nonlegal coresidential unions ("marriage" and "concubinage"),[5] and overlooked extraresidential conjugal relations. Keith Otterbein's (1965:77) economic-demographic explication of Caribbean domestic organization in terms of "opportunities to earn and save money and the sex ratio," which focused on a "house-building requirement" for legal marriage and the significance of migrant wage labor, was a further variation on this economic-determinist theme.

In a comparative study of Jamaica, Grenada, and Carriacou, Michael Smith (1962b) recognized the extraresidential or visiting relationship, in addition to consensual cohabitation or coresidence and marriage, but his explanation of West Indian family structure in terms of the so-called mating system was tautologous (Horowitz 1971:484). In addition (as discussed later in this chapter), he oversimplified Caribbean conjugal relations. Nevertheless, he showed that an ordered progression from extraresidential to consensual to legal mating forms typified rural Jamaica and Grenada, in contrast to the absence of such a sequence in the urban areas of these societies and the rarity of consensual unions in Carriacou.[6] In a study of the Martinican peasant village of "Morne-Paysan" (Morne-Vert), Michael Horowitz (1971, 1992) sought to explain this contrast by a "decision model" of conjugal patterns in Martinique. In an androcentric analysis, he related the ordered progression of conjugal forms in the peasant community to decisions made by men of varying ages to maximize the values of the peasant economy. He contended that young men cultivated their parents' land, resided in their parental household, and engaged in extraresidential relations, whereas middle-aged men tended to acquire land of their own and, as they needed access to female marketing, established consensual unions. Old men married legally to legitimize their children, consolidate their children's inheritance, and gain respectability in the eyes of the Catholic Church. Horowitz therefore concluded that landholding accounted for ordered conjugal patterns among Caribbean peasantries, in contrast to disordered patterns in urban and plantation communities where such productive property did not exist.

Horowitz's analysis was complemented by arguments asserting that the plantation system had resulted in weak communities and unstable families in plantation America and Third World plantation societies (Wagley 1960:8–9; Beckford 1999:76–77). Sidney Mintz (1971a:38–39) similarly posited "the weakness of community organization in the Caribbean area," "sexual unions [that] are 'fragile,' and frequently terminated," "individualization" in "kinship, mating and domestic forms," "kinship systems of a noticeably shallow sort," and the virtual absence of kin groups resulting from colonialism, slavery, and plantations.[7]

Meanwhile, the interpretation of the African American family in the United States had become interwoven with postwar race relations policy and issues. Daniel Moynihan's (1965) U.S. government report argued that the so-called black problem in the urban areas was due to a disorganized Negro family system, rooted in the absence of a kinship system during slavery (MacDonald and MacDonald 1978:3). A similar view was advanced by William Goode (1960, 1961, 1966), who regarded the nuclear family and the "Principle of Legitimacy" as "universally necessary for the preservation of social order," and who considered "black family forms in the United States and the Caribbean to be deviant and disorganized" (MacDonald and MacDonald 1978:4).

In contrast, Carol Stack (1970, 1974) critiqued application of the concept of matrifocality to the urban "black family" in the United States as unhelpful and unclear. In considering the African American family in midwestern cities in the 1960s in the context of the massive circulation of migratory wage labor provided by rural southern blacks to urban centers, Stack argued that the noncorporate ego-focused kindred or an individual's relatives (especially sibling ties) generated, as adaptive strategies, changing residence, cooperation, and mutual aid. Eugene Genovese (1974) also concluded that marital instability and the isolation of the mother-child unit had been exaggerated in the case of African American families in the southern United States. He contended that the self-interested paternalism of slave masters had given the slaves some scope to create their own world, including nuclear families. Barry Higman (1973, 1975, 1998) has made a similar argument, in the Caribbean context, for the existence of nuclear and extended families among the Jamaican slaves.

Opposing Genovese, as well as Frazier and Moynihan, Herbert Gutman (1976a, 1987) argued against a "reactive model," in which slaves in the southern United States were seen as culturally dependent on the masters' world.[8] Instead, Gutman (1987:358) suggested that there was a "profound misperception of the historical development of the slave family, and especially the enlarged slave kin group." For Gutman, the slave family was "the medium in which an oppositional culture took shape," and "intergenerational ties allowed slave culture to develop over time" (Berlin 1987:57–58). Such agency and culture, based on kinship, was the basis of some power or autonomy among the slaves and their descendants (58; Gutman 1987). These themes find many parallels with my analysis of Afro-Caribbean kinship in this chapter and with the wider thesis of Afro-creole culture-building, which is the central focus of this book.

Meanwhile, in the Caribbean attention had begun to focus on ego-oriented bilateral kinship, beginning with William Davenport's (1961a) classic study of the Jamaican family system. In their review of the literature on the black family in the Americas, the MacDonalds argued that Davenport's analysis of the bilateral kindred summed up Caribbean kinship organization: "Davenport's (1961) description of the lower-class black kinship system in Jamaica is, in the main, still applicable to the entire Caribbean. The system is characterized by bilateral kindred organization of the noncorporate type" (MacDonald and MacDonald 1978:7). Arnaud Marks's (1976:12–13) study of the Afro-Curaçaoan household had likewise emphasized, in relation to Caribbean kinship studies, "the general lack of integration of domestic groups in wider corporative kinship contexts." Later analyses by Karen Olwig (1981a, 1981b, 1985) on St. John, Hymie Rubenstein (1987a) on St. Vincent, and Raymond Smith (1988, 1996) on Guyana and Jamaica also focused on noncorporate bilateral kinship.[9]

Such studies, however, failed to recognize the significance of intergenerational ancestor-focused unrestricted cognatic descent lines and landholding corporations, enduring over time, while nevertheless providing rich data on this dimension of the family system.[10] Other analyses have acknowledged the importance of cognatic landholding kin groups, but they have asserted either that such groups must necessarily be restricted or that they are restricted in Jamaica (Solien 1959; Otterbein 1964; Espeut 1992). Davenport's (1961b) view that the groups associated with Jamaican family land are only residential joint families is a variation on this theme. Edith Clarke's (1953, 1966) pioneering study of Jamaican family land (republished in 1999) identified the unrestricted and dispersed nature of the ancestor-oriented landholding kin group but inaccurately described this as the "kindred" — a concept denoting a noncorporate ego-focused category of relatives (Goodenough 1955; Besson 1987a:106–7). In addition, Clarke attributed cognatic family land to the heritage of the Ashanti who hold land matrilineally, while her analysis was situated in a study of the mother-centered family that overemphasized economic determinism and overlooked extraresidential conjugal relations.

Explanations of matrifocality or of an aberrant, disorganized, or weak family system in terms of African survivals, economic variables, and an all-encompassing impact of slavery and plantations do not, however, explain the structure and dynamics of domestic groups in Martha Brae, where neither the nuclear family nor the household are the basis of kinship and marriage in the village. Nor does a focus on either male decision-making or bilateral kinship adequately illuminate the underlying family system, while analyses of restricted cognatic descent obscure kin-based landholding.

Instead, in Martha Brae domestic groups are generated, transformed, dissolved, and integrated by an ordered three-dimensional family system rooted in protopeasant and postslavery Caribbean institution-building in which both genders fully participate. This creole family system comprises three related features: a dynamic "complex" or open system of marriage and affinity, linked both to serial polygamy and to a progression through increasingly enduring marital forms; ego-focused bilateral kinship networks with no specific boundaries, rather than formal kindreds; and an ancestor-focused unrestricted cognatic descent system that forges overlapping and ever-increasing family lines that are most fully developed in dispersed family-land corporations.

Together these three dimensions of marriage, kinship, and descent not only result in the varying and changing domestic groups that typify the village, but also maximize the villagers' ties of conjugality, consanguinity, and affinity. Whereas the households generated through this family system provide the immediate framework of daily life, the wider family ties create bases of identity and mutual aid throughout the community; link Martha Brae with other free villages, urban centers, and transnational migrant networks; and, especially in the case of the unrestricted cognatic descent system, perpetuate the peasant community. A previously unrecognized "Hawaiianized Eskimo" kinship terminology reflects this intricate system of marriage, kinship, and descent forged through Caribbean culture-building from the atom of the fictive kinship shipmate bond — the first African American institution, created on the slave ships and maintained in the slave plantation villages.[11]

The "Complex" Marriage System

As Robin Fox (1967:27) stated, "kinship and marriage are about the basic facts of life": birth, "mating," parenthood, and death, which reproduce all human societies; what varies is the cultural elaboration of these biological facts. In this cross-cultural context, anthropologists (e.g., Gough 1959; Goodenough 1970) have sought to provide a universal definition of marriage, and this has been an even wider source of controversy than the debate on the African American family system. Of great utility has been Sir Edmund Leach's (1961) view that marriage is "a bundle of rights" and hence all universal definitions of marriage are vain. Leach showed that marital institutions may take various forms and serve varying functions in different societies and cultures, and they should therefore be analyzed in a social and cultural context. Drawing on his own Sinhalese data, he demonstrated that different forms of marriage may coexist within the same society. These perspectives may be usefully applied to Martha Brae to show not only that the villagers' conjugal system should be considered in its own right (as a Caribbean creation, rather than as an African survival or a deviation from European norms), but also that each institutionalized conjugal form may be regarded as a type of "marriage" from an Afro-creole point of view.

Claude Lévi-Strauss's (1969) cross-cultural analysis of marriage systems as modes of alliance and gift exchange is also helpful for illuminating marriage in Martha Brae; the Martha Brae data, in turn, both develop and modify his approach. Lévi-Strauss distinguished two types of exogamous or outmarrying systems: "elementary" and "complex."[12] Elementary systems stipulate prescribed or preferred classes of cousin-spouses from a man's perspective, such as his father's sister's daughter or his mother's brother's daughter, thereby perpetuating marital and affinal alliances among kin. Complex marriage systems have no such prescribed or preferential rules, specifying only which relatives a man may not marry. Complex systems therefore have no recurrent marital patterns and affinal alliances but forge them in numerous directions.

From this viewpoint Martha Brae villagers can be seen to have exogamous proscriptions, indicating who they should not marry (cousins are regarded as "too close"),[13] but no prescriptive form of marriage. This absence of prescriptive marriage rules results in proliferating patterns of marital exchange and affinal alliance. This "complex" marriage system is elaborated by three coexisting and interrelated types of marriage: extraresidential relations, consensual cohabitation, and legal marriage. These marital forms, in turn, are further elaborated through sequential unions or serial polygamy, that is, a series of monogamous relationships on the part of both husbands (serial polygyny) and wives (serial polyandry).[14] In addition, a single relationship may move through two or three marital forms. The combination of these features results in a nonprescriptive, unrestricted system of exchange and alliance, maximizing marital and affinal ties, more complex than even Lévi-Strauss envisioned. Moreover, both genders equally participate in this system of exchange, initiating and terminating conjugal relations, in contrast to Lévi-Strauss's androcentric model of groups of men exchanging women. This dynamic complex marriage system in Martha Brae originated in the culture-building of male and female chattel slaves, who elaborated the incest taboo of the fictive kinship shipmate bond to create an intricate creole marriage system asserting their humanity.[15]

Within the wider framework of this dynamic and engendered complex marriage system in Martha Brae, each of the three marital forms provides an institutionalized context for conjugality and procreation; all three forms are distinguished from casual sexual unions, which are described by villagers as either "we never in friendship" or "teef pass" (a fleeting, thieved, or stolen liaison). The institutionalized extraresidential relationship crosscuts household boundaries and is based on duolocal residence and visiting; as such villagers say, "we go and come." In contrast, both consensual cohabitation ("living together") and legal marriage ("we is married") involve a shared household based on neolocal residence. These two coresident forms of marriage are distinguished by different rights and obligations, which also differ from those of an extraresidential union. All three marital institutions vary in commitment and are ranked by the villagers in terms of both stability and prestige.

The least stable and prestigious form of marriage is the extraresidential relationship. This typifies young adults in the early stages of their "conjugal careers" (a term I use to denote the overall pattern of serial polygamy) who are not yet committed to establishing a common household. This type of marriage may, however, also mark the early stages of any new conjugal union. An extraresidential marriage, despite its minimal conjugal commitment, entails expectations of mutual fidelity and common responsibility to any children resulting from the relationship. Children born in such unions are regarded in the village as socially legitimate, and their recognized paternity is underlined by the giving of the father's surname, by the "baby-father," to the child. This paternal naming contrasts with "teef pass" liaisons, which may result in the denial of paternity and the giving of the mother's surname. Extraresidential marriages are generally short-lived, either dissolving (in which case each person usually moves on to another extraresidential union) or becoming transformed into consensual cohabitation. The typical duration of extraresidential relationships in Martha Brae ranges from a few months to a few years.

Consensual cohabitation is a more enduring form of marriage, entailing greater mutual commitment and resulting in more prestige. Entry into a consensual marriage is generated by various factors, such as the birth of children in an extraresidential union, increasing conjugal commitment, and the accumulation of sufficient economic resources to enable the partners to establish a household independent of another married pair. Such coresidence may involve acquiring a separate house, but a consensually cohabiting couple may live with an elderly parent or in a rented room. Consensual cohabitation may therefore be associated with either the increasing stability of a particular conjugal relationship or, in a more general sense, the middle stage of the conjugal career. Expectations of fidelity and shared responsibilities are stronger than in extraresidential unions. A consensual marriage also reinforces the gender emphases in the division of labor that typify the peasant household. Consensual relationships range in duration from a few years to several years, and I encountered such unions that had endured for up to thirty years. Marriages based on consensual cohabitation may become transformed to legal marriage or may dissolve. In the case of dissolution, each individual usually moves on to either another consensual union or an extraresidential marriage.

Legal marriage is the most enduring and prestigious form of marriage and, in the context of the wider creole conjugal system, is a transformation (not a mirror) of European marriage. Typically, legal marriage in Martha Brae is embarked on late in life and symbolizes a long and proven conjugal relationship that may have progressed through both extraresidential and consensual marital forms. Legal marriage may also mark a new relationship between an older couple, since legal marriage is regarded as the appropriate marital status for persons of advanced age. Further, legal marriage may be associated with improved economic resources, reflected, for example, in acquiring a new house or making improvements to an old one. However, neither house nor land ownership is regarded as a prerequisite for legal marriage. The fact that some couples continue to consensually cohabit despite the ownership of house and land underlines the independent dynamic of the overall marriage system, which is based on a combination of the variable of conjugal commitment and the values of a village status system based on increasing conjugal stability and age.

Legal marriage in Martha Brae (which may take place in the Falmouth Baptist Church) entails legally sanctioned shared responsibilities and an expectation of enduring conjugal commitment. This is why it is usually deferred until late in life; for, in contrast to the Baptist Church (which baptizes "illegitimate" children on special days), the villagers' Revival ideology does not require early "Christian" marriage as a basis for conjugality and procreation. Young adults therefore seldom marry legally, legal divorce among the villagers is rare, and their legal marriages tend to endure. I recorded such legal marriages varying from a few years to thirty years, in the context of conjugal relationships (which had often moved through two or three marital forms) that had lasted from a few years to around sixty years.

From the viewpoint of the colonially derived Jamaican legal code, legal marriage was the only marital form that legitimized children. However, the 1976 Status of Children Act—which reflects the reversal of state law by creole values, such as those of family land—de facto abolished the status of illegitimacy by de jure recognizing the rights of children born out of legal wedlock to inherit in intestacy. Along with the abolition of primogeniture in 1953 (retrospective to 1937), this change indicates the significance of Caribbean institution-building in transforming imposed Eurocentric culture in Jamaica.

The creole cultural values regulating the various coexisting forms of marriage in Martha Brae result in serial polygamy typifying many conjugal careers. Although the overall progression through the marital forms of extraresidential unions, consensual cohabitation, and legal marriage reflects increasing conjugal stability, this progression is typically elaborated through several relationships—some of which may themselves be marked by either a progression or a temporary "regression" (typically, a movement from consensual cohabitation to an extraresidential union) of marital form. Within this pattern of serial polygamy, conjugal unions tend to reflect increasing stability. This is expressed not only through the variable of marital status, but also by the increasing duration of each relationship. Extraresidential and consensual marriages therefore characterize not only the earlier stages of conjugal unions, but also the earlier unions of conjugal careers. Similarly, though legal marriage typifies the final stage of an enduring conjugal relationship, it also marks the later period of the conjugal career. Whereas some villagers enter only one institutionalized relationship, many others have had between two and four conjugal unions, and I recorded up to seven sequential marriages.

Whereas legal marriage reflects conjugal stability and extraresidential marriage indicates relative instability, consensual cohabitation combines both dimensions and is essentially transitional. In an early conjugal relationship, consensual cohabitation may indicate only slightly more stability than an extraresidential marriage if the consensual stage has been brief. Likewise, short-lived consensual marriages may typify the earlier period of the conjugal career. At such a time there may be oscillation between consensual and extraresidential unions and a temporary "regression" from consensual cohabitation to extraresidential marriage. In contrast, if a consensual marriage has lasted for several years, it may reflect the conjugal commitment that leads to legal marriage. The recognition of this dual and dynamic aspect of the consensual status resolves the classic controversy regarding the interpretation of such unions in the Caribbean family system, for whereas Judith Blake (1961) viewed consensual cohabitation as an unstable status, George Roberts (1955) and Fernando Henriques (1968) focused on its stability.

The Martha Brae data also suggest a more complex model of conjugality than that advanced by Michael Smith (1962a) and Michael Horowitz (1971, 1992) for Caribbean peasantries. Smith (whose analysis provided the basis for Horowitz's decision model of conjugal patterns in Martinique) regarded the statuses of extraresidential "mating," consensual cohabitation, and legal marriage as "irreversible" among the Jamaican and Grenadian peasantry. He asserted that "each of the three alternative mating forms has its proper place in the individual life cycle, and couples may ideally move from extraresidential mating into consensual cohabitation and so to [legal] marriage," referring to "the irreversibility of this mating order" (1962b:143–44).

In Martha Brae, by contrast, though the "irreversibility" of such marital forms occurs when an individual has only one conjugal relationship that progresses through each marital form, the situation is usually more complex due to serial polygamy. In this context there may be oscillation between extraresidential and consensual marriages in the early stages of the conjugal career, and each consecutive relationship preceding legal marriage may begin with an extraresidential union. The Martha Brae data thus do not support Smith's conclusion that a consensual union is "much more likely to develop into [legal] marriage than to dissolve, in rural Jamaica" (1962b:130). My data also indicate that his observation that "alternatively persons whose consensual unions have broken down re-enter others shortly after" (130) was an oversimplification, as such persons may then enter extraresidential marriages.[16] Nevertheless, the data from Martha Brae are closer to those reported by Michael Smith and Horowitz for peasant communities elsewhere in the island and the region than to Raymond Smith's (1956) thesis of increasing conjugal instability in the Afro-Guyanese domestic group due to the occupational marginality of the lower-class male, an economic-determinist analysis he later revised, while retaining an emphasis on a "matrifocal" family system (now combined, in his analysis, with a focus on bilateral kinship) in Guyana and Jamaica (R. T. Smith 1978, 1988, 1996). But male bias is a further weakness in Horowitz's decision model of conjugality.

The dynamic and engendered complex marriage system of the Martha Brae peasantry is a major variable in generating varying and changing domestic groups in the village. It can now be seen why such households may be headed by either women or men of varying conjugal status; how domestic groups may comprise single, nuclear, matrifocal, or extended groupings; and how these groupings may become transformed. Matrifocality itself can also be reinterpreted. Rather than being the major feature of the family system, matrifocality reflects different situations in varying contexts: a household headed by a woman in an extraresidential marriage, an interstitial status between marriages (extraresidential, consensual, or legal) in a woman's conjugal career, or a consequence of widowhood, including a stage after legal marriage.

"Outside" children and half siblingship are other features of domestic groups reflecting the underlying marriage system in Martha Brae — factors, when combined with the positive evaluation of female fertility and male virility, that also contribute to large household size. Fostering children likewise relates to the dynamics of the creole marriage system, in addition to facilitating migratory wage labor, in which both genders now participate, and reflecting the significance to grandparents of grandchildren. Bilateral kinship networks may also be drawn on for fostering children.

Moreover, illegitimacy may be reinterpreted. The status of outside child bears no stigma in Martha Brae — a situation predating the 1976 Status of Children Act (Besson 1974) — denoting only that the child was born outside the parents' current marriage. Extraresidential relations, consensual cohabitation, and legal marriage all confer social legitimacy on children, and this has long been reflected in the institution of family land. The family-land institution, in turn, based on unrestricted cognatic descent, may generate clusters of related households in a common yard.

Bilateral Kinship Networks

The complex conjugal system in Martha Brae not only results in widespread marriage exchange and affinal alliance, as well as varying and changing domestic groups, but also generates extensive personal kinship ties around each engendered "ego" or individual on both parental sides.[17] These ego-focused categories of bilateral kin endlessly overlap and both differentiate and integrate the village community and its component households. Such bilateral relations typically reflect the "amity of kinship" (Fortes 1969) and the ethos of exchange (Mauss 1954; Lévi-Strauss 1969), and provide bases of identity and mutual aid. Bilateral kinship may also serve as a basis for household recruitment and for establishing households in a common yard. Such relationships stretch beyond the village, linking the Martha Brae peasantry with other communities and with migrants overseas.

Bilateral kinship in Martha Brae recognizes an individual's parents, parents' children (full siblings and half siblings), parents' siblings and half siblings, parents' parents and other ascending kin, parents' siblings' children (first cousins) and more distant cousins, and eventually children and descending kin. The tracing of bilateral kinship has no specific boundary but reflects each person's knowledge and interest—generally to about third-cousin range. Even beyond that, relatives may be recognized as being (as the villagers say) "some family to me."

As there are no restrictive boundaries and no formalized rights and duties, these circles of relatives are more accurately described as interlocking, unrestricted, bilateral kinship networks rather than formal bilateral kindreds as Davenport (1961a) and others contend (e.g. MacDonald and MacDonald 1978:7; R. T. Smith 1996:27–28).[18] The usual observation that no two personal kindreds or kinship networks are the same, except those of siblings, applies with some qualification in Martha Brae. There siblings' networks are not identical—not only because all such networks have different egos, but also because the differentiation of siblings' networks is pronounced due to the high incidence of half siblingship generated by serial polygamy.

Bilateral kinship is the basis both of incest prohibitions and of exogamy in Martha Brae, that is, it defines negative rules for sex and marriage.[19] Individuals should neither have sexual relations with ("teef pass") nor marry (extraresidentially, coresidentially, or legally) their primary kin (parents, siblings, half siblings, children) or close relatives (grandparents, parents' siblings, first cousins) on either parental side; in Martha Brae and the other Trelawny free villages that I studied, I never encountered cousin conjugality of any kind.[20] This free-village cousin exogamy contrasts with the Accompong Maroons, where cousin conjugality is favored in the context of community endogamy (Besson 1995b).

The bilateral kinship organization of the Martha Brae villagers, like their dynamic complex marriage system, is rooted in the institution-building of the Trelawny slaves whose protopeasant marriage system generated extensive kinship networks on both parental sides. There was undoubtedly a continuity of meaning between these bilateral networks and the significance of kinship in African societies, but the process of Caribbean culture-building was reflected in the new role of these networks on Jamaican slave plantations. Such kinship networks provided an important basis for identity, exchange, and mutual aid among the chattel slaves and were crucial in forging the protopeasant communities that underlined the slaves' humanity. In addition, bilateral kinship networks had, literally, to be rebuilt within the framework of slavery, for the African slaves imported to Jamaica had usually been torn from all their kin. The fictive kinship shipmate bond was central to this process of re-creating ego-focused kinship, as well as to the creation of the creole conjugal system.[21]

Unrestricted Cognatic Descent

In the comparative study of kinship, nonunilineal or cognatic descent was long neglected due to the focus, first by specialists in family law,[22] then by anthropologists,[23] on unilineal descent systems that were widely identified in kin-based societies.[24] Emerging evidence of cognatic descent systems was initially dismissed as only reflecting unilineal systems in the process of change (Fox 1967:162). Therefore, as Ladislav Holy (1996:115) emphasizes, "That societies can be organised not only in terms of patrilineal or matrilineal descent but also on the basis of cognatic descent was discovered comparatively late in the development of kinship studies." Robert Parkin (1997:143) observes that "cognatic descent, largely disregarded in earlier anthropology, had to wait a century before receiving much in the way of theoretical attention."

The perceived advantage of unilineal descent is that it creates discrete descent groups that provide the foundation of an ongoing social structure.[25] Thus from a structural-functional perspective, Alfred Radcliffe-Brown (1950:43) asserted that unilineal descent was a necessity for an ordered social system. Societies lacking unilineal descent groups were therefore regarded as rare and placed in a residual category (Keesing 1975:91). The basic features of these societies were seen as the absence of ancestor-focused corporate descent groups and the presence of ego-focused bilateral kindreds. This view undoubtedly resulted in the neglect of cognatic descent systems in the Caribbean region. It was also reflected in Edith Clarke's misuse of the concept of the "kindred" to refer to the ancestor-focused descent groups in Jamaica that transmitted family land (1953:83, 1966:68).

Ward Goodenough's (1955) groundbreaking analysis of Malayo-Polynesian social organization revolutionized this perspective by identifying nonunilineal descent groups associated with various functions, including landholding, and by distinguishing these groups from ego-focused kindreds. He also showed that discrete descent groups can be recruited through the nonunilineal principle combined with restricting factors, such as parental residence or the individual's own residential choice. This led to a new dogma, namely, that cognatic descent systems must necessarily be restricted (e.g., Leach 1960:117). This dogma influenced early analyses of cognatic descent groups in the Caribbean region as being necessarily localized, discrete, and restricted (Solien 1959; Davenport 1961a).

On the other hand, Sir Raymond Firth (1963a) showed that unrestricted, overlapping dispersed descent groups can operate in relation to a "specific situation," such as a "specific occasion" (e.g., Scottish clan reunions) or a "specific resource," such as land. The nonexclusive ancestral ritual groups among the plantation slaves of the Para region of Suriname, identified by Sidney Mintz and Richard Price (1992:68), provide further illustration of unrestricted cognation in the context of a "specific occasion." However, Mintz and Price conclude that such nonexclusive kin groups "would not function efficiently" for landholding in the postslavery Caribbean (70). Firth (1963a) himself asserted that cases of unrestricted descent groups operating in relation to a "specific resource" were rare, the classic example being the Sagada Igorots of the Philippines, who had unrestricted descent groups associated with hillside grazing land and pine tree groves.

Goodenough (1970:52–53) subsequently acknowledged that "property-holding groups can readily overlap, just as someone in our society can easily be a shareholder and member of the board of several corporations." Studies in Tory Island, East Africa, and Polynesia identified other examples of unrestricted landholding (Fox 1966, 1978; Caplan 1969; Hoben 1973; Hanson 1971; Webster 1975). In these analyses, the focus shifted from the search to identify regular restricting mechanisms, resulting in discrete descent groups, to the more gradual process of controlling the progressive increase in descent group size (such as "genealogical amnesia"). Fox (1967:156) also pointed out that unrestricted descent groups can have nonexclusive "pragmatically restricted" residential cores, which differ from exclusive restricted cognatic lineages.

My reinterpretation, from these perspectives, of Clarke's (1953, 1966) pioneering Jamaican study showed strong evidence of unrestricted cognatic descent in the institution of family land (Besson 1974, 1979, 1987b). My own work shows that such unrestricted cognatic descent groups were forged through Caribbean institution-building among the Jamaican protopeasantry, especially for customary landholding, and were consolidated in postslavery peasant communities like Trelawny's free villages, including Martha Brae (Besson 1984b, 1987a, 1992a, 1995b; and chapters 1, 3–5). Today unrestricted cognatic family lines, rooted in the protopeasant and postemancipation past, are the most enduring dimension of the Martha Brae villagers' kinship system, and wherever possible these family lines are mirrored and anchored in landholding through the creole institution of family land. The so-called cognatic descent problem envisioned by anthropologists on paper (Hoben 1973:17–22; Keesing 1975:92) is resolved among the Martha Brae villagers in a number of creative ways in the family-land institution, which also reflects paradoxical — or apparently contradictory but in fact quite realistic — attitudes toward land.

Paradoxical Attitudes toward Land

In Martha Brae and other free villages in Trelawny, the creation and transmission of family land through unrestricted cognatic descent reflects a paradox in attitudes toward land (Besson 1987b, 1988). Whereas family land represents a response to strongly perceived land scarcity in the context of land monopoly at the peasant-plantation/tourist interface, family land itself is portrayed as an unlimited resource within the landholding descent group. The description by William Tapper (of the Thompson Old Family) that the land-hungry Martha Brae villagers are "like a pig in a kraal" is widely reiterated throughout the peasant community, which is chronically and explicitly concerned with the problem of "land room." Yet the miniscule family-land estates of the unrestricted Old Families are referred to as "serving" ever-increasing numbers of descendants "forever." William himself stated that the Thompson Old Family's estate of one and a quarter acres was for his ex-slave paternal grandfather's "heritage going down": "it must go from children to grandchildren right down the line," as should his even smaller piece of maternal family land in Granville. In a similar vein, Morgan McIntosh explained that the Minto family estate of less than an acre "must go down to family's family . . . that simply means sons, daughters, grandchildren, right down." Madeline Simmonds stated that the Anderson family lands of just over an acre "must go from generation to generation," there being, at that time, at least ninety-two coheirs to the land (chapter 5).

Family Land as a "Specific Resource"

The emphasis on discrete unilineal and restricted cognatic descent groups emerged in the study of so-called primitive, or tribal, societies with "embedded" subsistence economies. In such precapitalist societies, all land rights are allocated according to either kin-based "reciprocity" or political and/or religious "redistribution" (Polanyi 1957; Dalton 1967), rather than through market exchange, and serve as the basis of both residence and production, while religious and political organization may also be embedded in descent. Discrete descent groups can therefore serve as the multifunctional building blocks of the social structure. Even in such societies, overlapping groups may have the advantage of flexibility, as among the Maori of New Zealand and on the Polynesian island of Rapa (I. M. Lewis 1976:266–67; Hanson 1971).

Post-Conquest Caribbean societies are not, however, indigenous precapitalist societies, having been forged at the vanguard of Western European colonial capitalist expansion. Therefore in Martha Brae and other Trelawny villages ancestor-focused kin groups, created in peasant adaptations during and after colonial plantation slavery, do not form the basis of either the social structure or of an entirely embedded economy; nor are all land rights allocated through nonmarket exchange. Instead, family land exists within the peasant economy in a wider context of multiple small-scale legal and customary tenures linked to the national market economy and corresponds with circulatory migration in the capitalist world system. In these contexts the unrestricted cognatic descent corporations crystallize in a "specific situation" only (Firth 1963a), namely, in relation to the "specific resource" of family land. Such ad hoc overlapping landholding corporations present no structural problems and have the advantage of flexibility in relation to land scarcity and circulatory migration.[26] Overlapping membership also integrates Old Families within and among free villages, while the augmentation and continuing expansion of unrestricted cognatic descent groups maximize, in light of persisting land scarcity, scarce freehold land rights as bases of security and identity.

Immortal Land and Enduring Family Lines

The unlimited quality of family land is perceived as relating to its permanence and immortality, rather than to its productive capacity or size.[27] It is this immortal quality of the land that symbolizes the perpetuity of the enduring descent line. Providing this symbol of identity for the kin group is a primary function of the family-land institution among descendants of plantation slaves, whose humanity and kinship were legally denied; the unrestricted mode of cognatic descent maximizes formerly forbidden family lines. Family land can thus be seen to be the spatial dimension of the kinship line.[28]

This symbolism is a recurring theme in the creole language of the oral traditions associated with family land in Martha Brae. It is constructed through two interrelated contrasts: the opposition between the immortality of land and the mortality of humanity, and between the mortality of the kin group's individual members and the enduring nature of the landholding descent line. Humans and specific trustees or trusteeships of family land are referred to as "expiring," "dying," "ending," whereas the land "carries continuously," "serving generations," and the landholding descent corporation persists "forever." These contrasts are further reflected in statements indicating the timelessness of the land, such as "I born come see the land," and the absence of precise genealogical knowledge that sometimes results from this situation — as in the case of Madeline Simmonds in relation to the exact origin of the Anderson family lands. The tradition of intestacy associated with family land is also often seen as reflecting its undying, timeless quality.

The examples of William Tapper of the Thompson Old Family and Annie Fergus of the Williams descent group demonstrate these underlying contrasts. When William spoke of his paternal family land in Martha Brae (chapter 5), he noted: "Well, my grandfather said the land should not be sold. It is for his heritage going down. It must go from children to grandchildren, right down the line. Well, the grandfather, when his time is expired, he hand it over to my father [the grandfather's only child]. Father said, 'My time is ended' — he hand it to the children. Well, it was quite a few brethrens of us, but all died now, left only myself and me sister." After the deaths of William and his sister Amy in Martha Brae and their siblings overseas, the Thompson family lands were "carried continuously" to the next descending generation.

Near the Thompson family lands is the half-acre family estate of the Williams Old Family. In the earlier years of my fieldwork, Annie Fergus, a member of this landholding corporation and trustee for the family land, lived elsewhere in Martha Brae with her legally married husband and three of their adult daughters and five grandchildren in a wooden house on their purchased land. One of her sisters, Lucy Bayne, lived with her own husband and two grandchildren on one square chain of the family land in their chattel cottage that had been transported from rented land in Falmouth after an absence of twenty-two years from Martha Brae, while Annie rented out a deceased brother's cottage also on the family land. One of Lucy's several children lived elsewhere in Martha Brae in a rented room with nine of her eleven children.

Annie's discussion of the family land (which she still referred to as "my yard"), inherited through her mother and maternal aunt, reflected similar contrasts to those highlighted by William Tapper. She explained that the Williams family land "leave for everyone of us. As one die it come to the other, and the other, come right round. Is only three of us [the two sisters and a brother who migrated] alive now [in the senior generation]. All the rest [two other brothers and a sister who migrated to Costa Rica fifty-seven years previously] die." The brother who migrated to another parish and bought land of his own "did want to leave out" of the family land, that is, he voluntarily did not use the land as he did not need to, though he still retained inalienable rights to it. Annie stipulated that after the death of the three remaining siblings, the family land would pass to the next generation (which included children of the absent and dead siblings as well as children of the two sisters in Martha Brae): "Just the same like how we get up [were born] and see that it [the land] has been passed through the family, the same way it carries continuously. Old ones dead, and young ones tek it. And children dead and grandchild tek it. And it go right over till great grand-children have it. Mustn't sell." Some years later Annie's sister and brother-in-law died, she herself was widowed, and her wooden house burned down. In the face of this adversity she returned to her immortal family land (which she had left in 1936), where she lived and died in the 1990s.

Family land in Martha Brae is perceived as providing inalienable freehold land rights for the enduring family line. These freehold rights are of crucial significance to the descendants of landless chattel slaves who were once property themselves, symbolizing freedom, personhood, security, and prestige.

The short-term dimension of family land as a scarce economic resource among living kin is therefore subordinated to its long-term symbolic role of "serving generations." In the peasant economy, family land is thus given a residual economic function as an insurance policy: it is a place to go "in time of need."[29] This strategy is explicit in the proverb often quoted by Martha Brae villagers when discussing family land: "Mother have, father have, but blessed the child who has its own." That is, even with rights to family land through overlapping unrestricted parental family lines, it is best to be economically independent from such land, ideally by purchasing land of one's own. However, only a minority of villagers are able to buy their own property, and many resort to less secure bases of independence. Their alternatives include obtaining space for residence or cultivation through cash tenancy, acquiring "free land," "capturing" land or squatting, "landless farms," or renting rooms. Occupational multiplicity and migration promote this quest for self-reliance. Many immigrants to Martha Brae desired independence from family land elsewhere in the parish or the island, such as the various members of the Dawkins Old Family in Martha Brae and Zion who had inalienable rights to family land in the Trelawny village of Sherwood. Similarly, a large proportion of the members of Martha Brae's Old Families (and of new landholding family lines) emigrated from the village to other parts of Jamaica or overseas to seek an independent livelihood. A few managed to establish their independence in Martha Brae itself by purchasing small plots of their own, such as my landlady Victoria Robertson, Morgan McIntosh, Ruth Marshall, and the returned migrant Lloyd Nelson — all of the Minto Old Family (chapters 4–6).

The main pattern of land use associated with family land is therefore nonresidence: the coheirs form an unrestricted, dispersed corporation holding inalienable rights to their family estate, rather than a localized restricted group residing on their land. The individuals who live on family land are thus regarded as caretakers for a larger nonresident kinship corporation, including generations still unborn, rather than exclusive owners of the land. Resident kin represent only a "pragmatically restricted" core of a much wider unrestricted landholding descent group.[30] The inalienable rights of dispersed kin are recognized by residents and absentees alike and are often symbolized by gifts of food or by the freedom to pick from the fruit trees on the land. From time to time these rights are activated by absentees "in need" who return to take up residence on the land. Various cases from among both Born Ya and Strangers in Martha Brae typify this experience.

The first case concerns the Anderson family estate in Martha Brae. Madeline Simmonds was the trustee for the three small plots of family land, totaling just over an acre, of the Anderson Old Family, which comprised at least six generations and ninety-two living coheirs. Of this vast number, only a few coheirs resided on the family lands. The others were dispersed elsewhere in the village, the island, and overseas. But Madeline emphasized the inalienable rights of all the absentees to the family land: "Everybody touchup [shares joint rights to the land] . . . them can partake anything. All of them [could] go over and pick" from the fruit trees on the land. The resident kin did not have exclusive rights to this family estate. Likewise, William Tapper, who lived on the Thompson family land transmitted within his paternal family line, retained rights to his maternal family land in Granville that were symbolized by his picking from the star apple and guinep trees on the property.

Loretta Tait, who in the early years of my research was an elderly woman and a Stranger to Martha Brae, lived with her husband on land of their own that they had bought there. Loretta also had rights, in the Trelawny village of Carey Park, to family land that originated at least as far back as her paternal grandparents. One coheir resided there "unmolested," but both Loretta and an absent sister — neither of whom had ever lived on the family land — retained inalienable rights that were symbolized by gifts of fruit and "picking." In addition, though the payment of the land tax by the resident coheir validated her use of the land, it did not mark exclusive ownership: "We was occupying it. No we weren't living there. We go and come and pick. Is a fruitful place: coffee, breadfruit and coconut. So we go and come and pick, each of us. . . . And every now and then them bring things from there come give me: breadfruit, coconut and all. We don't trouble one another. If they bring anything come give me, me tek it. The child [woman] what live on it paying the taxes; so me no molest her. And as everybody goes and comes [gets on well] together it isn't such a ticklish time." In other words, the "cognatic descent problem," which poses a theoretical puzzle for anthropologists, is "solved" on the ground through the give-and-take of amicable kinship relations.

The case of Cynthia Rogers illustrates the extremes of the pattern of nonresidence typifying family land and underlines the land's residual economic role. At the beginning of my fieldwork Cynthia was a middle-aged landless immigrant who lived with her husband Owen in a chattel cottage on a house-spot leased from a villager with purchased land. Owen and Cynthia subsequently moved their house to "captured land" on the part of Holland Estate owned by the Parish Council and thus were among the earliest residents of Martha Brae's satellite squatter settlement of Zion. Cynthia chose this precarious independence in both Martha Brae and Zion rather than reside on family land in the Trelawny village of Crawle. The Crawle property derived from her great-grandparents (her father's paternal grandparents). After they died the land passed to their children — Cynthia's paternal grandfather and his siblings — and it remained the corporate estate of all of their descendants. This landholding corporation comprised at least five generations, as it also included Cynthia's children and other members of her generation: "For it's not me alone have children, you know, is plenty family." This large unrestricted corporation was entirely dispersed ("them scattered all about"), for none of the living coheirs had exercised the option of residing on the land. The property thus functioned only in its long-term role of symbolizing the family line and providing inalienable freehold rights to all descendants. Cynthia, whose husband died in 1994, was now hoping to buy land of her own at Zion.

As the next three cases show, absentees may indeed activate their rights to family land and return in time of need. William Tapper, of the Thompson Old Family, left Martha Brae in 1921 as an eighteen-year-old and spent many years abroad as a migrant laborer, returning to the village from time to time to visit. On his return in 1945 and 1946, he lived in a rented house in Falmouth until 1959. By then he had four children and wished to give them and their mother more security. He therefore decided to settle in Martha Brae and reactivate his rights to the family estate. His elder sister, Amy, was living on the smaller of the two plots of family land, but the second plot was uninhabited and overgrown with bush. At first William and his household lived as tenants in Martha Brae while they cleared the larger plot of family land and built a house; this was completed in 1962, by which time he was nearly sixty. He remained there until his death in 1985 at age eighty-two. In 2001 his widow, most of their children, and one of their grandchildren were still living on the family land.

Like William Tapper, Annie Fergus moved to family land when circumstances required it. One of the coheirs and trustee of the Williams family land in Martha Brae, Annie had lived with her husband on purchased land elsewhere in the village while one of her sisters resided with her household on the family land. But after the death of her sister, brother-in-law, and husband, and the burning down of her house, Annie returned to the family land to live in her old age.

Whereas William Tapper and Annie Fergus came back to empty plots of family land where no one else was living, Maud Lindsey returned (early in my fieldwork), in middle age, to a tiny cluttered yard that had been left by her maternal grandmother for her descendants. Though most of these numerous coheirs were dispersed elsewhere in Martha Brae, Jamaica, and overseas, three households of descendants resided on the land. Maud herself had been living for many years with her husband in another parish. When this marriage broke up, she returned with her children to Martha Brae, where her chattel cottage joined the other three as the resident core of the dispersed landholding corporation. In 2001, in her old age, she was still living on this family land, as were two of her adult sons.

A Joint Estate

The custom of keeping family land undivided both ensures and symbolizes that the land is the jointly held estate of a landholding corporation. In the earlier years of my fieldwork, Angela Armstrong, who lived into her nineties, followed this tradition. She was an immigrant to Martha Brae from the Trelawny village of Schawfield farther inland, where, along with "plenty" siblings, she had rights that she regarded as inalienable to one acre of jointly held undivided family land. Her parents had verbally created that family land from purchased land, and "it can't sell, not selling, for is there mother and father bury." Although only one of their children (one of Angela's sisters, who lived in the parents' house) used the land, "all of we can go in and come out same like this land." However, she did not intend to use that parental family land in Schawfield because she has "this land" of her own in Martha Brae.

The land that Angela referred to was three acres at the southern edge of Martha Brae, bordering the cemetery, purchased by her ex-consensual spouse who had fathered eleven of her twelve children. She now controlled this land and had transformed it into family land for their eleven children, numerous grandchildren, and great-grandchildren. She had stipulated that the land should not be sold: "Not to be sold, *not* to be sold; *not* selling it. If me even *dead* it can't sell. Not selling. It's fe the children; all the children" and her descendants in perpetuity. Only a small core of this unrestricted corporation lived on the land: Angela herself with four of her grandchildren and one great-grandchild whom she fostered in her household, and one of her middle-aged sons with his consensual spouse and their ten children in another house. This son, who like his mother cultivated part of the land (which had a variety of crops and fruit trees), helped her pay the taxes. But these payments gave him no priority over absent kin (some of whom returned to visit), who were scattered elsewhere in the parish, the island, and abroad in England and the United States, for, as the villagers say, "taxes can't mek you be owner" of family land, it only validates land use. Angela had also stipulated that the land should remain undivided among her descendants. She explained the rationale behind her strategy: "Them go and come and anything them want, them get. . . . Nobody can stop one another from go and come. Me no measure nothing give them. For you know when you measure things [survey and subdivide] give them, any amount of fuss: this one don't want people to come over here, and that one don't want other to come over here." Undivided as the land remained, she insisted that it would "serve generations" of her descendants even if they could only find standing room on the property: "If they even want stan' up under tree, is for them."[31] Her house would also remain unallocated so that "anyone want to come, them come."

By 1995 Angela, her resident son, and one of his sons had died and been buried side by side just over the fence at the edge of the adjoining village cemetery. From this location, which closely resembled yard burial, she was said to "watch her land," where a pragmatically restricted core of her descendants resided. Nonresident coheirs still retained rights to the land; these included a son (now aged eighty-three, with twelve children, more than twenty grandchildren, and five great-grandchildren), who lived and ran a business on his wife's half acre of inherited land in Falmouth but who kept a pigpen on his family land in Martha Brae.

A similar theme regarding jointly held undivided land was expressed by Keith Templar, who, like Angela, was an older immigrant to Martha Brae in the early period of my fieldwork and was in his seventies in the 1980s. After living for many years as a landless tenant, Keith managed to buy one-third of an acre in the village. He then transformed this into family land so that his nine children and their descendants would have inalienable freehold land rights providing a foothold in the peasant community. Like Angela, he had stipulated that this land should not be sold and that it should remain an undivided joint estate so that no one individual could exclude the others or sell any part of it:

My land already turned into family land. I give away my land to my seed [children] them — all nine. No one can molest [exclude] each other. Is just like this: I told them this land is not to sell. It serve generation, generation, generation. Suppose you lef' it for a certain one [individual freehold], that one can dish-out [exclude] other rest. But I leave down there say is for *nine*. I give them this now that any part of the world they go and come, they have just where they were born. Anywhere they are, they can go and come. And *no one* out the nine can sell it. So I told them it cannot be sold. They call it "family land." It cannot be sold. *So* I told them. Now being these children of today they have a lot of children. So grandchildren, and grandchildren, and grandchildren, they will inherit.

Keith's nine children had all migrated, but their undivided family land in Martha Brae provided a symbol of identity for the family line and a foothold to return to in time of need. By 1995 Keith had died, but the estate remained as family land for his migrant descendants.

A Burial Ground

Family land may also serve as the burial ground of the landholding corporation. Here the Martha Brae villagers draw on a wider parish and island tradition, for the custom of burial in the yard has been discontinued in Martha Brae itself due to the imposition of the village cemetery by the Trelawny Parochial Board early in the twentieth century. But yard burial still persists in many other Jamaican villages, including Trelawny free villages like Refuge and neighboring Granville, and many Martha Brae villagers have rights to family lands and burial grounds in these peasant communities. In addition, as yard burial existed in Martha Brae until this century, members of some Old Families (such as the Mintos and the Kellys) were strongly aware of the interment of ancestral kin in house yards in the village. Burial on family land, generally followed by "tombing," places an individual in the wider context of the ancestors of the family line and fuses this enduring line with the immortal land. It also consolidates the status of the deceased as a freeholder.

Adaptive Land Use and the "Amity of Kinship"

The Martha Brae villagers' paradoxical perception of family land as an unlimited resource "serving" an ever-increasing number of descendants in the context of land scarcity is reinforced by several features that permit the unrestricted cognatic descent system to function. Together these features generate a system of land use that diverges from that in the national capitalist economy. Peter Espeut (1992:80) has asserted for Jamaica that "the existence of family land is a hindrance to rural development in general and to agricultural development in particular" and that "if development planners do not take steps to deal with the problem of family land, then the scandal of land scarcity in the midst of idle land will remain a feature of rural Jamaica." Family land has also been condemned throughout the Caribbean region as "under-productive," "wasteful," "disastrously inefficient," and an obstacle to modernization.[32]

Family land among the Martha Brae and other Trelawny villagers generates at least five variants of land use, resulting from the unrestricted cognatic descent system, all of which could be regarded as underproductive from a Eurocentric capitalist point of view. From the creole perspective (and the "substantivist" viewpoint), however, family land may be seen as an adaptive system of land use in the case of land scarcity produced by colonial and postcolonial land monopoly.[33]

The first variant, which is the most "uneconomical" from a Eurocentric perspective, are those plots of family land, especially in other Trelawny free villages where yard burial persists, engrossed by graves and tombs of family lines. Even unmarked graves are sacred and inhibit cultivation, while stone and concrete cairns and tombs render this impossible. Moreover, their presence is regarded in the national economy as lowering the market value of the land. William Tapper's maternal family land in Granville is a case in point, as is the paternal family land there of some of Madeline Simmonds's children from Martha Brae's Anderson Old Family. Both of these plots have ancestral graves and are either uncultivated or "underutilized," though there are fruit trees growing on the land. An uncultivated burial ground of some fourteen ancestral graves in Kettering and a plot with thirty-four cairns and tombs in The Alps are more extreme illustrations of this practice. This mode of "uneconomical" land use occurs widely on the marginal land of Trelawny's peasant communities and may overlap with some of the other variants of "underproduction."

A second variant are those plots lying empty and uncultivated due to migration, such as Cynthia Rogers's family land in Crawle, Trelawny. William Tapper's paternal family land in Martha Brae, which was overgrown by bush when he returned to Jamaica, is another example of this variant. Representing the third variant are the cluttered yards, such as Maud Lindsey's in Martha Brae, where the presence of several houses leaves little space for cultivation. A fourth variant are those cases where land use by resident kin is "hampered" by the inalienable rights of absentees, especially when symbolized by their practice of picking from the fruit trees on the land—for instance, in the case of Madeline Simmonds's family land in Martha Brae and Loretta Tait's in Carey Park.

The fifth and final variant concerns cases such as William Tapper's paternal family land in Martha Brae where, following his circulatory migration, the likelihood of other migrant-absentees returning was so remote that he practised intensive cultivation on the land. Similarly, Madeline Simmonds maintained a "food forest" (as well as raising livestock and renting tenant houses) on her half-acre family yard, despite its numerous coheirs. However, such cultivation is for household use and sale in peasant markets and is based on multicropping, land use strategies rooted in the protopeasant past that are considered underproductive from the standpoint of capitalist monoculture.

For each of these variants, the so-called uneconomical land use is a function of a wider complex of values governing family land as a symbolic as well as an economic resource, for the central purpose of family land is its long-term role of "serving generations." In this context such land may also be used as an economic resource in limited ways by living kin. It can provide a residential site for those most in need, fruit for residents and absentees, and a burial plot; it can even allow intensive peasant cultivation, including food forests that reflect "ecological artistry" rather than "random chaos" (Hills 1988). The strategy of voluntary nonuse by independent members of the kin group is the crucial mechanism regulating access to family land as a scarce economic resource in the short-term and resolving the paradox of family land itself as both limited and unlimited.

The uneconomical pattern of land use associated with the unrestricted cognatic descent system in family land can therefore be reassessed as an adaptive strategy to the constraints of land monopoly, because the long-term role of family land can only be fully understood against the background of Caribbean agrarian relations.[34] The Martha Brae villagers' perception of family land as unlimited within the unrestricted descent group in the long term does not ignore land scarcity at the peasant-plantation / tourism interface; on the contrary, it is a creative response to this very situation.

These adaptive forms of land use, positively sanctioned and governed by the "amity of kinship" (Fortes 1969), are not the only ones that are applied to family land among the Martha Brae peasantry. Constrained by persisting land scarcity, self-interested individuals may challenge the unrestricted cognatic descent system and attempt to establish exclusive restricted rights to corporate family-land estates, sometimes by drawing on the legal code. Such "crab antics" (Wilson 1973:58, 1995) are negatively sanctioned in the customary unrestricted descent system, but it is precisely because descent is unrestricted that crab antics occur (see also chapter 4).

Unrestricted Cognation and Crab Antics

When crab antics take place, the long-term symbolic role of family land as an unlimited resource serving an unrestricted descent corporation is subordinated to the perception of the land as a scarce economic resource among living members of the kin group, and an individual member or segment of the family line attempts to establish exclusive rights to the corporate estate. In the face of intense land scarcity, the Martha Brae villagers are acutely aware of this possibility. This awareness, as well as the negative sanctioning of such behavior (underlining the principle of unrestricted descent), is often reflected in the discussion of family land. The morality of kinship relations, which regulates the customary use of family land, is frequently contrasted with the disharmony, trickery, and mistrust typifying crab antics. Harmonious kinship relations in family-land affairs are referred to by phrases such as "everybody goes and comes together," "moves together," "lives loving," or "lives in unity," whereas the behavior of crab antics is designated by concepts such as "depriving," "robbing," "selling-out," "fighting," "molesting," or "dishing-out" other kin. Those who participate in crab antics are "craving" and "contentious," while crab antics themselves are referred to as "fuss."

The case of Madeline Simmonds illustrates the contrast between family unity and crab antics. In her account of the three plots that comprised her Old Family's estate of just over an acre in Martha Brae, with its ninety-two coheirs, she indicated that two of the plots were governed by harmonious kin relations. The third plot, however, had a history of "trickery" and "contention." In 1995 I was told of a court case resulting from ill-feeling among nonresident coheirs in regard to use of the family land created by elderly Angela Armstrong before her death. (Despite this, Angela's undivided family land endured as she had planned.)

Another elderly villager, independent on her own purchased land in Martha Brae (which she had transformed to family land for her children, grandchildren, and great-grandchild), mentioned the "fuss" surrounding her Old Family's land elsewhere in the village (chapter 4). As a result, she claimed to have no interest in this land, though when we passed it on a stroll she wistfully remarked, "That's where I was born." According to her, one "craving" member of the kin group had taken over the family land deriving from her maternal ancestors: "She crave for everything, and she taken it over, and nobody fight her; she just keep it. The reason? Just to crave. You know some people want everything." On closer inquiry this case was more complex, involving voluntary nonuse by coheirs who then supported the actions of the trustee and shared in the proceeds from the sale of some of the land. But the elderly villager saw the situation as a reflection of a more widespread contentious attitude toward land that typified "some people" in Jamaica: "Is the land, that's why some people kill some. People chop-up [with machetes] you know, for land. Chop-up and go to court. That's what happen you know, all about. In Jamaica here you always find land killing people. People kill one another for land. Just chop them up or shoot them for land." One such case reputedly occurred in Martha Brae itself. A villager remarked of the murdered man: "A man cut out his belly and it was over some land business."

Contention, violence, and controlled ill-feeling are not the only character-istics of crab antics. Conflict over family land may also be reflected in the be-lief that illness has been supernaturally caused, as occurred within a segment of Martha Brae's central landholding family line. This belief results from the combination of Revival ideology, with its perception of an active spirit world, and the significance of the ancestors of the landholding kin group.

Concretization and Circulatory Migration

The unrestricted cognatic descent system in family land has long enabled circulatory migration. Such migration is now resulting in an architectural transformation in Jamaican peasant communities, from the construction of wooden cottages (which were often movable) to the build-ing of concrete houses (i.e., concretization) with migrant savings and remit-tances — as occurred in the case of Rupert Bailey, of the Kelly Old Family in Martha Brae, whose traditional wooden cottage on his inherited land was replaced in the 1980s by a concrete house built by his migrant son's remit-tances. In the 1990s–2001 this trend escalated due to the maturing of the pensions of many Jamaicans who migrated overseas (especially to England) in the 1950s and 1960s, combined with the continuing devaluation of the Jamaican dollar, resulting in a favorable rate of exchange in the contexts of return and circulatory migration and remittances.

So far concretization in Martha Brae has mainly involved purchased land, which itself has sometimes been bought with remittances or individually inherited land, as in Rupert Bailey's case. However, in other Trelawny vil-lages (such as Refuge and Granville) concretization is occurring on some family land, and this begs the question of the future of family lands in Martha Brae. Several developments seem possible. One is an escalation of crab antics.[35] A second possibility is the continued strategy of voluntary nonuse, which lies at the heart of the unrestricted cognatic descent system. This happened in the case of the late Patrick Linton, whose migrant son remained in the United States while Patrick's widow and daughter's household now lived in the new concrete house on the family land in Martha Brae. A third option is suggested by the Wallace Old Family's land in Granville, where two large concrete houses (in effect, family-land hotels) were built to accommodate visiting migrant kin. Madeline of the Anderson Old Family in Martha Brae had arranged a variation on this theme: her concrete house, constructed in her family-land yard with a son's remittances, was used by various kin including returned migrants. This option is one dimension of family land as an undivided joint estate, as expressed, for example, by Angela Armstrong regarding the family land that she created in Martha Brae.

At the start of the twenty-first century, family land retained its symbolic as well as economic role among Jamaican and other Caribbean migrants overseas. This symbolism was reflected not only in return and circulatory migration to peasant communities and family lands, but also in the custom of migrants to London treasuring a small box or bag of soil from family land, signifying inalienable roots.

Hawaiianized Eskimo Kinship Terminology

The three dimensions of the Martha Brae villagers' family system — a dynamic complex marriage system, ego-focused bilateral kinship networks, and ancestor-oriented unrestricted cognatic descent groups — are manifested in the kinship terms used by the villagers. This is a modified "Eskimo" terminology, reflecting bilateral kinship and serial polygamy (rather than the nuclear family), combined with a "Hawaiianizing tendency" highlighting the cognatic descent principle.[36] This modified and Hawaiianized Eskimo kinship terminology has not previously been recognized in the Caribbean region. For instance, George Murdock (1960:6), in his cross-cultural review of cognatic forms of social organization, described the Jamaican kinship system as simply "bilateral . . . of the Eskimo type," one criterion of this type being the "absence of any functionally important descent groups, unilineal or ambilineal [cognatic]." Murdock's view coincides with many analyses that portray Afro-Caribbean kinship as being simply bilateral noncorporate kindred organization.[37]

In Martha Brae, some aspects of the kinship terminology do reflect ego-focused bilateral kinship organization and its unrestricted range. Primary kin are referred to by specific terms — "mother," "father," "sister," "brother," "daughter," and "son" — that are not used beyond these primary contexts. Half siblings are referred to as "brother" and "sister," but with the added descriptors "same mother's children" or "same father's children" to denote maternal and paternal half siblings respectively, in contrast to full siblings, who are described as having the "same mother" and "same father." Parents' siblings on either side are "aunt" and "uncle," reciprocated by "niece" and "nephew." First cousins on both parental sides are designated in terms of the parental relationship: "two sisters' children" and "two brothers' children" for matrilateral and patrilateral parallel cousins respectively and "sister's and brother's children" for cross-cousins. More distant cousinships may be described as "cousin" or by elaborating on the first-cousin tie if the specific relationship is known; for example, second cousins might explain that "our mothers are two sisters' children" or variations on this theme. Grandparents and ascending generations are called "grandmother," "grandfather," "great grandmother," "great grandfather," and so forth on both parental sides, with grandchildren and great-grandchildren being referred to as "gran" and "great gran" respectively.

These terms reflect the principles of Eskimo kinship terminology, for, as Fox (1967:258) explained, although this mode of classifying kin is named after the Eskimo kinship system, "it is, in fact, quite a common scheme amongst peoples lacking unilineal descent-groups or elementary forms of [marriage] exchange." Fox further noted that "what it seems to do is carve out the nuclear family for special emphasis, and then to stress the equal balance between the two kindreds united by marriage — the matrilateral and patrilateral kin of ego" (258). In Martha Brae, however, the elaborations that distinguish half siblings from full siblings stress the role of the dynamic complex marriage system of serial polygamy in generating bilateral kinship ties, rather than emphasizing the nuclear family.

In addition to this modification of Eskimo terminology, a "Hawaiianizing tendency" (Fox 1967:259) of the Eskimo terminology itself can be identified. Hawaiian kinship classification "stresses . . . the separation of generations, but . . . makes no concessions to lineality or to systematic [marriage] exchange" (256). It is "a great respecter of generations," in contrast to the Eskimo system, which "plays havoc with the generation principle" by applying the "rogue term 'cousin' . . . promiscuously to relatives outside a narrowly-defined group" (259). In Martha Brae, the Hawaiianizing tendency is reflected, for example, in the extension of the terms "aunt" and "uncle" to refer to parents' cousins. The terms "old parents" and "older heads," which especially in family-land corporations are employed to refer to ascending generations, are also variations on this Hawaiian generational theme. Fox observed that "in most societies having a Hawaiian terminology there is a tendency to some form of *extended* family or cognatic descent group" (259). The identification of a Hawaiianizing tendency in Martha Brae thus reinforces the analysis of the kinship system as being typified not only by bilateral kinship networks, but also by cognatic descent groups.

The kinship terminology of the Martha Brae villagers therefore reflects all the dimensions of their system of kinship, marriage, and descent: unrestricted bilateral kinship networks, a dynamic complex conjugal system (generating unrestricted marriage exchange and affinal alliance, including serial polygamy), and unrestricted cognatic descent lines and landholding corporations. Together these various unrestricted dimensions of the family system maximize relations of conjugality, affinity, kinship, and descent as bases of identity, alliance, procreation, perpetuity, and mutual aid among the descendants of chattel slaves, a family system created, through the process of culture-building, from the atom of the fictive kinship shipmate bond.

This analysis of Martha Brae's family system as a Caribbean creation moves beyond interpretations of the African American family in terms of either African survivals or deviations from European norms. It also departs from views of "fragile" conjugal relations and "shallow" kinship systems in the Caribbean region, even among those pioneering a creolization approach (Mintz 1971a:39, 1989:xviii; R. T. Smith 1996:27–28). In addition, the focus on cultural creativity in the family system of a Jamaican peasant community contrasts with the Eurocentric view of Jamaica as distinguished by the world's highest rate of "bastardy" or "illegitimacy" (Hartley 1980; Laslett 1980:xi). It seems fitting that such elaborate institution-building should be identified in Martha Brae at the very heart of the Caribbean region, which is characterized by the most pronounced experience of cultural re-creation in modernity (Mintz 1996a; Trouillot 1998; Price 2001). Moreover, my analysis of Martha Brae's family system and its kinship terminology resolves the issue of the nature of Caribbean landholding kin groups raised by Mintz and Price (1992:75).

Unrestricted Cognatic Descent and Caribbean Customary Tenures

In their groundbreaking work on *The Birth of African-American Culture*, which focuses on the core Caribbean region, Mintz and Price (1992:75) argue that in some parts of postrevolutionary Haiti "following the [ex-]slaves' acquisition of land in the early nineteenth century . . . groups of patrikin — co-residential units called *lakou* — grew up around parcels of land, each of which contained an ancestral shrine and was inhabited by particular deities associated with the group." By contrast, in the vast forested interior of Suriname, which was the main slave plantation colony of the Netherlands, the largest post-treaty maroon societies in African America, including the Saramaka, consolidated communities, ancestral rituals, and landholding systems based on matriliny. Simultaneously, in the Para coastal region of Suriname, slaves on the plantations had formed overlapping unrestricted groups, comprising all descendants of each original enslaved African, for ancestral ritual (68–70). After emancipation Para ex-slaves communally purchased former plantations where they had lived, as in neighboring Guyana. However, Mintz and Price contend that, after emancipation, "the nonexclusive (cognatic) kin-groups of these people (1) would not function efficiently to hold land in common, and (2) by this time were so strongly institutionalized that a switch to a Saramaka-like unilineal system was out of the question." Therefore, "the plantation communities themselves became the land-holding corporations, with individuals gaining rights to land use through their genealogical connections to ancestors who had lived there" (70).

Despite Mintz and Price's (1992:70) strictures on nonexclusive cognatic landholding groups, they identify, based on studies by Edith Clarke (1953) and William Davenport (1961a, 1961b), "late-emerging nonunilineal kinship groups . . . centered on 'family land' " in postemancipation Jamaica, resembling "in certain ways those of the Para region of Suriname, with a ritual association between ancestors and land on which they were buried" (1992:75). Drawing on Rémy Bastien's (1961) work, Mintz and Price highlight similarities with the "patrilineal" Haitian *lakou* but observe that "a good deal remains obscure about the precise nature of the kin groups involved in both the Haitian and Jamaican cases" (1992:75). Elsewhere Price (1967:47–48) referred to the "mysteries" of Caribbean land-tenure systems, and Mintz (1989:242) remarked that "the problems of land tenure and the transmission of land rights among Caribbean peasantries remain largely unsolved."

Of Mintz and Price's sources on Jamaica, neither Clarke (1953) nor Davenport (1961a, 1961b) explicitly discussed nonunilineal landholding descent groups. Clarke, writing before Goodenough (1955) had identified the ancestor-oriented nonunilineal descent group and distinguished it from the ego-focused bilateral kindred, used the concept of the "kindred" in the family-land context.[38] Nevertheless, her rich data suggested the ancestral focus of this kin group and the unrestricted cognatic nature of its descent system. Clarke interpreted this system as a survival from the Ashanti heritage, an explanation adopted by Charles Carnegie (1987) and Peter Espeut (1992). But the Ashanti transmit land matrilineally (Besson 1984a, 1987a, 1992a). Davenport explicitly rejected the existence of an unrestricted landholding system in Jamaica on the grounds that such systems must necessarily be restricted, a conclusion derived from Goodenough (1955), who later revised his opinion (Goodenough 1970). Davenport searched unsuccessfully for the restricting mechanism in Jamaica but, hypothesizing what this might be,[39] concluded that the Jamaican landholding kin group is only a residentially restricted "joint-family" system (1961a:449–50, 1961b:384).[40] Similarly, Nancie Solien (1959), discussing her Black Carib study and Clarke's Jamaican data, argued that nonunilineal systems must be restricted. Her interpretation was inconsistent with Clarke's conclusion that nonresident kin and their heirs retain inalienable rights to family land, as Solien herself conceded (581), whereas Charles Gullick (1976:252, 1985:18) showed that Black Carib nonunilineal descent groups are dispersed and unrestricted.

In a comparative discussion of family land in the Bahamas, Barbados, and Jamaica, Keith Otterbein (1964) regarded both unrestricted and restricted nonunilineal descent as workable.[41] Nevertheless, his reinterpretation of Clarke's Jamaican data closely resembled those of Davenport and Solien. He asserted that Jamaican landholding kin groups were discrete, restricted, and residential, with regular exclusion of some descendants occurring each generation through parental residential choice and an exclusive residence rule. His analysis rested on the hypothesis that increasing land scarcity results in greater restriction and that such scarcity had shifted the Jamaican system from an unrestricted status in the postslavery era to restricted nonunilineal descent, while the Bahamaian and Barbadian systems remained unrestricted. However, Otterbein's conclusion was inconsistent with his interpretation of Barbadian landholding kin groups, which, he argued, were unrestricted due to extreme land scarcity.[42] It was also at odds with the fact that the dynamics of the Jamaican descent system described by Clarke are identical to those of the Bahamas and Barbados, both of which Otterbein rightly interpreted as unrestricted.

By the time of Mintz and Price's 1992 study, my research had begun to show that Jamaican landholding kin groups are based on unrestricted cognatic descent.[43] Moreover, in his second edition of *Caribbean Transformations*, Mintz (1989:xxvii) noted that the Trelawny case had "begun to unravel the mysteries of so-called 'family land' and kinship in Jamaica." In addition to Jamaica, unrestricted descent groups, rooted in protopeasant institution-building, function widely among Caribbean postslavery peasantries in the contexts of "generation property," "children's property," "family land," and "succession-ground." Such unrestricted landholding corporations have burgeoned especially in the non-Hispanic Antilles, at the heart of the postslavery plantation-peasant interface and where tourism and bauxite mining have exacerbated land monopoly.[44] This unrestricted system typifies Trinidad and Tobago; the Windward Islands of St. Lucia, Grenada, St. Vincent, and Dominica; the Leeward Islands of Antigua, Nevis, and now-erupting Montserrat; French Martinique; Danish/American St. John; Dutch St. Eustatius; the British Virgin Islands;[45] Providencia; Barbados; and Bequia in the St. Vincent Grenadines.[46]

From this regional perspective, Mintz and Price's (1992:75) conclusion that Haiti is characterized by patrilineal landholding kin groups may be revised. Serge Larose (1975:486–90) has shown that in Léogane, a "sugar-plain" penetrated by American neocolonial plantations, the Haitian *lakou* (with its inalienable *démembré* or family-land burial ground and sacred ancestral trees) is an unrestricted cognatic descent group. The lakou may therefore be seen to be a Caribbean creation, originating in protopeasant adaptation and consolidated after the revolution and during American occupation (Mintz 1960, 1979, 1995), rather than being either a French survival or an African retention (Mintz 1989:242, 274). This reinterpretation clarifies the nature of Haitian landholding kin groups, as called for by Mintz and Price (1992:75).

The argument that unrestricted descent typifies the Antilles may be taken even further. Mintz and Price (1992:71), following Michael Smith (1962a), note that Carriacou (in the Grenadian Grenadines) manifests "the most fully articulated system of unilineal descent (other than that of the Suriname Maroons) in all of Afro-America, replete with a complex ancestral cult and functioning localized patrilineages." However, Michael Smith's data on family land in Carriacou clearly indicate a cognatic system of customary tenure and transmission (1956b, 1962a:74, 296–98, 1965a:221–61). Smith (1962a:296) stated that in Carriacou " 'family land' is the principal form of common property held by lineage members," "purchased land reverts rapidly to this customary system of family tenure," and "since most islanders die intestate, most of the locally owned land is inherited and held by 'family tenure.' " Though Smith argued that "agnatic elements within such [family-land] groups tend to dominate the others and to administer the common holding *if* the original owner was a man," he observed that "if they are more than two generations deep, groups sharing family land, partitioned or other [jointly held undivided land], include *many who are not agnatic kin"* (296, emphasis mine). Moreover, *"inheritance cumulatively trans-fers the majority of lineage held or purchased land to this category of family land* and simultaneously vests the control of the land in the agnatic core of *cognatic groups"* (296, emphasis mine). Likewise, "the *cognatic idiom of inheritance* prevents exclusive transmission of corporate [agnatic] lineage property"; "the blood [patrilineage] as a whole is thus unlikely to have land in common," and such property "vests in a *cognatic group* for which agnates exercise control" (297–98, emphases mine). Writing of "family land" in Carriacou, Smith also noted that "people inherit land from *either parent* and consequently have rights in scattered plots" (74, emphasis mine), thereby indicating a system of overlapping unrestricted cognatic landholding kin groups.

The contradiction in Smith's analysis (and perhaps evidence of the coexistence of agnatic and cognatic descent principles in Carriacou) is encapsulated in his observation that such cognatically transmitted family land perpetuates the identity of the patrilineage (1962a:297). He similarly concluded that patrilineal ancestral rituals are conducted in a cognatic idiom: "At rituals the spirits of the principal's paternal and maternal kin are invoked and all other spirits are invited. These are the old parents — the collectivity of local dead. The *cognatic reference* and invocation of other dead express community values in a form consistent with the lineage principle" (298, emphasis mine). Despite his stress on an agnatic core and on the primacy of legitimate heirs, Smith identified both a female emphasis and the inclusion of illegitimate children in customary tenure and transmission: "A woman's unlawful issue inherit freely from her, and since women are the principal occupants of Carriacou land, they are quite likely to receive a larger portion from their mother than the lawful children do from their father. In addition, outside-children generally have usufructuary rights on their father's land" (296).

The pioneering studies of family land by Edith Clarke (1953, 1966) in Jamaica and Michael Smith (1956b, 1962a, 1965a) in Carriacou both clearly indicate landholding systems rooted in unrestricted cognatic descent, rather than in either bilateral kindreds (Clarke) or agnatic lineages (Smith), a conclusion that Clarke and Smith may have been unable to draw at the time due to the overemphasis, in cross-cultural kinship studies, on unilineal descent and the related confusion over the concept of the kindred.

In addition to the widespread occurrence of unrestricted landholding kin groups in the context of family-land institutions throughout the Antillean heartlands of the Caribbean, such nonexclusive cognatic descent systems interweave with common land (reflecting the even wider principle of community) elsewhere in the region.[47] This is true in Barbuda, the Bahamas, among the Black Caribs of Belize, and on the Carib reservations of Dominica and St. Vincent, at the margins of the region; and on the Caribbean frontiers of coastal Guyana. It is evident even in the corporate landholding communities in the Para area of Suriname—for, as the ancestral genealogical connections among the Para ex-slaves were not unilineal (Mintz and Price 1992:70), they could only have been cognatic. Moreover, in Para social organization, "the principles of descent and ancestry" are still "richly particularized and anchored in the land" (70). This indicates that unrestricted cognatic landholding kin groups consolidated and continue in Para postslavery peasant communities, rooted in a similar protopeasant tenurial system. During slavery the "collective ancestors . . . were buried locally"; this shows a close relationship between the unrestricted ancestral ritual groups, "each with strong attachments to a particular locality," and customary tenure and transmission of ancestral land (68). A similar interweaving of unrestricted cognatic descent and common land exists on the marginal mountainous reservation of the Jamaican Accompong Maroons, where external governments have sought to undermine maroon landholding, as well as among the Windward Maroons in the eastern mountains of Jamaica (Besson 1995b, 1997; Bilby 1996).

Only among the maroons in the vast forested interiors of mainland Suriname and French Guiana have African American slaves and their descendants had the relative autonomy and available land to retain, or forge anew, restricted African-type unilineal (matrilineal) landholding systems.[48] Elsewhere, in varying degrees, the unrestricted cognatic descent principle has evolved among Caribbean reconstituted peasantries as a mode of adaptive opposition to land monopoly, maximizing rights to the precious, but scarce, resource of land. The creation of such nonexclusive landholding systems, which anthropologists (including Mintz and Price) once regarded as unworkable and even now consider rare,[49] reflects the strength of African American institution-building among chattel slaves and their descendants in the core Caribbean region, Europe's oldest colonial sphere.

CHAPTER NINE

Conclusion

In addition to contributing to Caribbean controversies, including the interpretation of Afro-creole kinship, the two histories of Martha Brae have wider relevance for theoretical issues in social anthropology, which marginalized the Caribbean region. Such issues include the cross-cultural study of kinship, ecology, and land; the analysis of economy, development, and dependency; the anthropology of law; the study of gender; the anthropology of death and the regeneration of life; the cultural construction of identities; the analysis of power, opposition, and resistance; the understanding and siting of culture; and the reconfiguration of ethnography.

For comparative kinship theory, which lies at the heart of anthropology (Holy 1996; Parkin 1997; Schweitzer 2000), Martha Brae's two histories reveal the evolution, over three centuries, of unrestricted cognatic descent groups throughout the Caribbean *oikoumenê*, especially in the context of landholding, as a mode of opposition to European expansion and Euro-American land monopoly. Such unrestricted descent systems were traditionally thought to be unworkable and are even now considered rare, with examples drawn from Oceania and a few East African societies.[1] Martha Brae's new history also identifies a marriage system more complex than even Claude Lévi-Strauss (1969) envisioned and uncovers a variant of Hawaiianized Eskimo kinship terminology that has not been recognized before.

Linked with the comparative study of cognatic and unilineal descent has been a long and unresolved controversy on kinship and ecology, which has likewise focused on Africa and the Pacific.[2] As Michael Allen (1971:23) noted: "The relationship between the availability of land and descent-group structure has been a subject of considerable debate amongst anthropologists. While Goodenough has argued that cognatic systems may be regarded as functionally advantageous in situations of land scarcity, Forde, Worsley, and Meggitt have put forward equally convincing arguments in favour of land scarcity as a necessary precondition for the emergence of corporate [unilineal] lineages." Allen attempted to resolve this controversy on the link between the variable of land availability and the type of descent system by asserting, based on his study of the Nduindui of New Hebrides, that in societies with shifting cultivation "a necessary precondition for the existence of corporate lineages is a sufficient scarcity of productive land to result in a restriction of rights to unilineal kin," but this correlation breaks down "once the scarcity increases beyond a certain level" (23), resulting in cognatic descent. However, though Ladislav Holy (1996:120) concludes that Allen "reconciles Meggitt's and Goodenough's hypotheses," Allen in fact reinforced Goodenough's argument by linking cognatic descent to intense land scarcity.

Meanwhile, in the study of such nonunilineal or cognatic descent systems, William Davenport (1959:569) undermined Goodenough's perspective, that greater land scarcity resulted in a more flexible descent system, by arguing that the restricted variant is linked to extreme scarcity of land. In a comparative analysis of family land and generation property in three Caribbean societies — based on Edith Clarke's (1953, 1957) work on Jamaica, Sidney Greenfield's (1960) data on Barbados, and his own Bahamian study — Keith Otterbein (1964) attempted to provide a diachronic view of Davenport's hypothesis by showing that "scarcity of resources can shift a system from bilateral to ambilineal descent" (40),[3] that is, from unrestricted to restricted cognatic descent groups, as he argued had occurred in postslavery Jamaica.[4] But Otterbein's conclusion was invalidated by Clarke's Jamaican data, which portrayed an unrestricted descent system, and by the case of Barbados where, as Greenfield (1960) showed and Otterbein (1964) acknowledged, an unrestricted system persisted in the context of the highest population density of any Caribbean society (Besson 1979, 1987b).[5]

The comparative data synthesized from throughout the Caribbean region in relation to Martha Brae's new history are suggestive in relation to both the variable of land availability and the role of culture in shaping landholding systems anchored in, and reflecting, kin groups and communities. This synthesis reveals unrestricted cognatic descent groups in the Antilles and matriliny in the forested interiors of Suriname and French Guiana. These variations initially suggest that the intense land scarcity constraining the peasantries in the Antillean heartlands generates flexible and inclusive modes of customary landholding based on unrestricted cognatic descent, in contrast to the restricted unilineal systems of the more expansive mainland Guianese interiors. Thus far, this argument coincides with Goodenough (1955, 1956) regarding the advantageous flexibility of cognatic descent

314   Conclusion

systems in the face of extreme land scarcity. However, this hypothesis is complicated by the existence of the most flexible and inclusive tenures of common land, interrelating with unrestricted cognatic descent groups, at the margins and frontiers of the Caribbean region (such as Barbuda, the marginal reservation of the Jamaican Accompong Maroons, and the coast-lands of Guyana), where land is not as scarce as in the plantation-tourism Antilles.

These Caribbean data therefore also highlight the role of *culture*, and of kinship itself, in shaping the structure of landholding systems mirroring descent groups and communities.[6] The important symbolism of the unre-stricted descent groups themselves, as well as of land in Caribbean slave and postslavery societies, is especially manifested in the family-land institutions of the Antilles. Here the unrestricted cognatic descent systems created by the slaves and their descendants, at the heart of Caribbean societies, have maximized family lines as bases of Caribbean cultural identity and have projected these ever-increasing family lines onto miniscule landholdings, thereby also maximizing scarce and precious rights to land.

In contrast, the stronger emphasis on African cultural principles in the largest maroon societies, such as the Saramaka in the Suriname interior, mirrored in matriliny, symbolizes the greater autonomy of these maroons as well as reflecting their more extensive territories. Common tenures were forged at the margins and frontiers of the region, where they reflect the significance of reconstituted Caribbean peasant communities in smaller and less autonomous maroon adaptations (the Leeward and Windward Maroons of Jamaica) than on the mainland and among less constrained protopeasants and postslavery peasantries (as in Barbuda and the Bahamas and on the coastlands of Guyana) than in the Antillean plantation heart-lands. However, the existence of unrestricted cognatic descent systems in the wider context of such common tenures and the increasing emphasis on cognation in these contexts underline the role of cognatic descent in max-imizing family lines and freehold rights in situations of ethnogenesis and escalating land monopoly — as in the Accompong Maroon wilderness reser-vation in Jamaica and in Barbuda, where postcolonial governments have attempted to undermine common land as a result of bauxite mining and tourism.[7]

The Caribbean institutions of family land, generation property, and chil-dren's property also highlight paradoxical perceptions of land as both a scarce economic good and a symbolic resource unlimited through its per-manence and immortality, thereby illuminating the cross-cultural study of land-tenure systems. This theme of paradoxical attitudes toward land as both economic and symbolic, scarce and unlimited, finds parallels, for example, among Native Americans (Feher-Elston 1988), Australian Aborigines (Strang 1997, 2000), the Maori and Tikopia of Polynesia (Firth 1963b:331), the Merina of Madagascar (Bloch 1971), and the Greek mountain peasantry (Du Boulay and Williams 1987). Indeed, it may universally exist at the interface of "Lands of Law" and the immortal "Lands of Myth" (Besson 2000).

In addition, analysis of these paradoxical attitudes toward land in the Caribbean region contributes to the comparative study of symbols of the regeneration of life in contexts of death and mortuary ritual (Bloch and Parry 1982). For instance, in Martha Brae's free-village oral tradition, the immortality of unrestricted descent groups and their family lands is contrasted with the mortality of individuals and humankind. Whereas specific kin and trusteeships in these descent groups are referred to as "expiring," "dying," and "ending," family land is said to "carry continuously, serving [ever-increasing] generations," and the related family lines are regarded as lasting "forever." The sacred fruit trees, which are part of the corporate estates of both Caribbean family land and common land, are variations on this regeneration theme, symbolizing the continuity and spirituality of kin groups and communities.[8] When these corporate estates are further typified by generational or community burial grounds (as was the custom among Jamaican, St. Johnian, Martinican, Barbadian, and Surinamese protopeasantries and mainland and Antillean Maroon societies, and as still is the case in Haiti, the Virgin Islands, Barbuda, the Guianas, and Jamaica), the regeneration of kinship and community by Caribbean chattel slaves, rebel slaves, and postslavery peasants is most clearly symbolized.[9]

The elaborate mortuary ritual of Revivalists in Martha Brae and other Jamaican free villages, perceived as placing the dual soul in both the eternal land and an active spirit world, similarly reinforces the regeneration theme — as does the Myal Play among the Accompong Maroons (Besson 1997). In addition, the creation by Caribbean slaves and their descendants of corporate burial grounds based on kinship and community and linked to elaborate Myal and Revival rituals reveals a significant contrast to Robert Hertz's (1960) point that "the death of a stranger, a *slave*, or a child will go almost unnoticed; it will arouse no emotion, occasion no ritual" (76, quoted in Bloch and Parry 1982:4, emphasis mine).[10] Likewise, the symbolic denial of death by Rastafarians, who are also setting down roots in Caribbean land, provides an unusual perspective on immortality.[11]

The analysis of Caribbean attitudes toward land encapsulated in Martha Brae's two histories, including the relationship of land with colonialism and its aftermath, and with slavery, kinship, gender, religion, and migration also contributes to the comparative study of the cultural construction of identities. This includes the anthropology of the engendered person and the self, the understanding of transnational ethnicities, and the analysis of ethnogenesis in the Americas from the conquest to the new millennium.[12]

The exploration of Caribbean customary tenures based on kinship and community and the interrelation of these tenures with the peasant, national, and world economies reveal the local wisdom of so-called Third World peoples in the context of "indigenous" development.[13] Moreover, the analysis of the symbolic aspects of family land, constraining the maximization of production from a capitalist point of view, advances comparative perspectives on the reinterpretation of "underproduction" and on culturally "embedded" or partially embedded economies, reinforcing an alternative, non-Galbraithian, view of "affluence" (Dalton 1967; Sahlins 1972). The evolution of the Falmouth marketplace from a protopeasant market to the most important rural market in Jamaica, including its links to informal commercial dry goods importing and export food higglering, highlights the developmental role of the Jamaican peasantry and adds to the comparative study of "peripheral" and "peasant" markets in anthropology and history (Bohannan and Dalton 1962; Dilley 1992; Larson and Harris 1995), especially as the Falmouth market is rooted in an Afro-creole marketing system originating in the seventeenth century. The analysis of partners in Martha Brae and Zion, and among Falmouth marketers, contributes to the cross-cultural understanding of rotating savings and credit associations (ROSCAs) in engendered development (Ardener and Burman 1995; Purcell 1998).

My interpretation of peasant land tenure in Martha Brae has questioned the plural society thesis of Caribbean tenurial systems, revealing instead the complex interplay between customary family land and the Jamaican legal code. This interaction includes not only conflict between legal and customary systems, such as the imposition of state law on customary landholding and crab antics or land disputes (which sometimes occur within the family-land institution itself), but also the coincidence of customary and legal elements, the reinforcement of customary tenure by aspects of state law, and the transformation or reversal of the law by the ethos of customary landholding and thereby the creation and shaping of state law itself. These findings are significant for the anthropology of law, especially the cross-cultural analysis of "legal pluralism" and "unofficial law," underscoring the dynamic interaction that may occur at the interface of so-called plural legal systems, the variations of this interplay, and the cultural creativity of indigenous and creole populations in colonized and postcolonial societies, where "folk law" may affect the shaping of state law and the official process of nation-building.[14]

The Martha Brae findings, including the analysis of land disputes both within the peasant community and at the peasant-plantation / tourism interface, are also significant for understanding disputes through historical contextualization, interpretation of meaning, and use of ethnography, areas that have been marginal within anthropology itself and are now moving to center stage (Caplan 1995). This is especially so as the essential dynamic of the post-Conquest Caribbean, as the oldest colonial sphere, has been a dispute over land between the powerful and the powerless, an "argument" that continues in a neocolonial context and is central to Martha Brae's two histories.

The critique, arising from Martha Brae's new history, of Peter Wilson's (1969, 1973, 1995) androcentric thesis of reputation, respectability, and crab antics, and of Richard Burton's (1999) related male-focused analysis of Afro-Caribbean naming, has wider implications for the anthropology of gender. Henrietta Moore (1988:10) observed that feminist anthropology needed to confront more fully "the question of how gender is constructed and experienced through race," in addition to understanding the structuring of gender through colonialism, neoimperialism, and capitalism. My critique of Wilson and Burton shows that Afro-Caribbean peasant women, as well as men, have been fundamental to opposition, resistance, culture-building, and development in the colonial and neoimperial race-class stratified Caribbean region since slavery days.

These conclusions, in turn, contribute to the study of Third World peasant communities and their histories (Wolf 1982; Keesing and Strathern 1998:401), while postslavery Martha Brae itself reflects a hidden history at the center of a region depicted as the "Third World's third world" (Naipaul 1973) but reinterpreted as the First World's first annex (Mintz 1996a: 304). In addition, Martha Brae's two histories advance the world-historical-political-economy approach to the ethnography of local communities and their cultural symbols (Marcus and Fischer 1986; Miles 1992), especially by exploring the symbolic as well as economic significance of land in peasant communities at the heart of the Third World's peasant-plantation / tourism interface.

The two histories of Martha Brae, reflecting European expansion and Caribbean culture-building, also correct the overemphasis in dependency and world systems theories on metropolitan-satellite and core-periphery relations (Frank 1969; Wallerstein 1974, 1980; Beckford 1999). Martha Brae's two histories highlight the internal class dynamic at the very core of the so-called periphery, revealing that independent thought and action by the powerless are only constrained, not destroyed, by dependency and hegemony.[15] This perspective underscores the significance of agency (Giddens 1976:75) or cultural creativity (Wulff 1995:8–14) and contributes to the comparative analysis of power, opposition, and resistance.[16]

Empowering and engendering Martha Brae's Afro-creole history, with its principal theme of culture-building, is also relevant to the analysis of cultural retention and change, thereby illuminating the central focus of anthropology. Martha Brae's new history reveals that the African cultural heritage has not been passively retained in the core area of African America, nor has European culture been successfully imposed at the gateway to Europe's New World. Instead, African and European institutions have been transformed by chattel slaves and their descendants in a dynamic process of *Caribbean* institution-building. The case of Martha Brae also suggests that this creativity has been neither totally dependent on the dominant culture, as Franklin Frazier (1966), Eugene Genovese (1974), Richard Burton (1999), and others have contended, nor entirely "*separate from* the masters' institutions," as Sidney Mintz and Richard Price (1992:39) and Monica Schuler (1979a:121) have argued. Rather, it has entailed *engagement with, and appropriation, overturning, and reversal of* colonial culture in the oldest colonial sphere. This Caribbean saga, encapsulated in the family-land institution and in the related transformation of Martha Brae from planter town to peasant village, not only reflects the most pronounced example of culture-building in modernity, but also exemplifies "the encounter of the entire non–Western world with the West" (Mintz 1996a:305).

My analysis of the unrestricted, transnational fields of relations in Caribbean landholding kin groups, linked to the symbolic importance of family land and emerging from global and regional perspectives on Martha Brae's two histories, also continues to inform the study of "place" and "cultural sites" in "the siting of culture" (Olwig and Hastrup 1997) "in a world of movement" at the turn of the millennium (Rapport and Dawson 1998; Besson 2002).[17]

Finally, my interpretation of Martha Brae's two histories, contextualized within a "positioned (and repositioned)" subjectivity (Rosaldo 1993:7) and underlining the significance of "anthropology at home" (Caputo 2000), including homelands in the so-called periphery, in contrast to the colonial study of "other cultures," contributes to the reconfiguration of ethnography for the twenty-first century.

NOTES

Preface

1. The title of this book perhaps begs the question of its relation to Philip Curtin's 1970 classic, *Two Jamaicas: The Role of Ideas in a Tropical Colony, 1830–1865*. My title is coincident with, rather than derived from, Curtin's, and I focus (without either the expertise or caution of a historian and with the preoccupations of an anthropologist, including the process of culture-building) both on a longer period of the past and on the present: from around 1754 (the date of the first known arrival of slave ships at the site of Martha Brae) to 2001, including my fieldwork during 1968–2001. Nevertheless, from time to time my analysis is indebted to Curtin.

2. For an assessment of the role of oral history in my research, see chapter 5.

3. My anthropological use of "peasant" is discussed in chapters 1, 3, and 6.

4. Mintz's use of the concept of *oikoumenê*—a modification and elaboration of Alfred Kroeber's (1946) use of the ancient Greek term denoting their known inhabited world—was crystallized in his 1994 Huxley Lecture but is rooted in his earlier delineation of the Caribbean region as a societal area.

5. For the dual naming system in some Jamaican free villages, see chapters 1 and 3 and Besson (1984b). Martha Brae also had two names, being originally called "Lyttleton" (chapter 2).

6. Cf. Ortiz (1972), Ngubane (1977), Rosaldo (1993:45), Purcell (1998:268), and Agbasiere (2000).

7. Cf. Karras (1992:53). During my research I discovered that the Aberdeen peasant community that I studied in St. Elizabeth was consolidated on Island Estate, the plantation established by Alexander McFarlane of Scotland prior to his death in Jamaica in 1755. A preliminary account of the McFarlane family in Jamaica is given in Besson and McFarlane (1995). I am grateful to Robert B. Barker for drawing my attention to the urban dimension of Alexander McFarlane's life as the initiator of postal services on the island and the first postmaster general of Jamaica, in 1735, and as the owner of a Georgian townhouse in Kingston—see Cundall (1937:158), including Michael Hay's illustration.

8. See Higman (1998).

9. "The End of an Era" (1986).

10. Fernando Henriques (1968:185 [n. 1]) states that "the office of *custos* of a

Jamaican parish is analogous to that of a lord lieutenant of an English county." For the creolization of this role, see ibid., 60, 173.

11. Cf. Burton (1997) and Abu-Lughod (1990).

12. I refer to two different Top Hills in this preface: a plantation in Trelawny and a peasant village in St. Elizabeth.

13. *Colonial Standard*, 27 August 1870. I am grateful to Pat Hepburn of the Myers family for drawing my attention to this obituary.

14. Some of the information on Albert Myers's ancestry is drawn from his letter of 24 February 1932 to his eldest daughter, Editha Myers.

15. I am grateful to my maternal aunt, Editha Hearn (née Myers), for this information from the unpublished Philpott Papers researched and compiled by Mrs. Hearn in 1986.

16. I am indebted to Professor Dorothea Baxter (personal communication, 1991) for some of this information on the Baxters. See also Ivy Baxter (1970).

17. Cf. Chevannes (1994:50–51).

18. My use of "new" history for Martha Brae's African Caribbean cultural history draws on Mintz (1971b:331), who noted that "Afro-American History is not a substitute for other kinds of history, but represents instead a 'new' way — new only in its having been so thoroughly forgotten, once before — of looking at the New World and African past".

19. Here I use the villagers' mode of address for women of status or "reputation" (see chapter 1).

20. Cf. Horowitz (1992).

Chapter One

1. See also Trouillot (1998).

2. Mintz (1996a) develops this theme.

3. In unilineal systems, descent is traced through one gender only. The unilineal systems of West and Central Africa include patrilineal and matrilineal landholding groups, traced through men and women respectively. However, as Robin Fox (1967) pointed out, men (in their roles of mother's brother and sister's son) tend to hold the power even in matrilineal systems, whereas cognatic descent systems are characterized by more equal gender relations.

4. See, e.g., Maurer (1997a) and Austin (1998).

5. Thus my view that plantations have underdeveloped the Caribbean region, though to some extent drawing on and advancing Beckford's (1999) thesis on "persistent poverty" (cf. Besson 1995e), does not reflect an uncritical "allegiance" to Beckford's framework as Michaeline Crichlow (1995:307 [n. 3]) asserts. See also Besson (1995a:301) for clarification on this point, overlooked by Crichlow.

6. Cf. Henriques (1968).

7. The Providencian proverb (comparing such behavior to that of crabs in a barrel) cited by Wilson (1973, back cover) and discussed in chapter 4 is male-

oriented. As my own analysis makes clear, the Martha Brae villagers do not have an androcentric view of crab antics.

8. See, e.g., Beckles (1988, 1989), Bush (1985, 1990), Dadzie (1990), and Gaspar and Hine (1996).

9. Those women particularly concerned with this aspect of the Christian Church interpret "sinful living" literally, confining nonlegal childbearing to extraresidential relations rather than entering consensual cohabitation.

10. "Science" is the modern form of Obeah, perceived as a magical power for healing, harming, or protecting.

11. The Afro-Jamaican Myal religion is discussed more fully later in this chapter.

12. That is, a leader in the Pukumina/Kumina cult.

13. An English-based African American language, passed on by English-owned to Dutch-held slaves, developed in Suriname within twenty years of the colony's settlement. A creole religion already existed on the slave plantations in the early decades of marronage and was transported into the forest by maroons (Mintz and Price 1992:48–50).

14. The shipmate bond was a dyadic social relationship of fictive kinship forged among slaves who were transported on the Middle Passage in the same ship. In the case of slaves of opposite gender, such fictive kinship included the incest taboo, which was maintained and extended to children and descendants on the plantations. The shipmate relationship was therefore the atom of African American institution-building. In addition to Jamaica, it was found in Haiti, Trinidad, Suriname, and Brazil (Mintz and Price 1992:43–44).

15. Cf. Gutman (1987:360).

16. Cf. Greenfield (1960).

17. See also Craton and Saunders (1991) and Besson (1984a:58–59).

18. Lévi-Strauss (1969) distinguished two types of exogamous or outmarrying systems: "elementary" and "complex" (see also Fox 1967:175–239). In contrast to the prescribed or preferential rules of elementary systems, complex systems specify only which relatives one may not marry. The slaves' complex marriage system was elaborated by conjugal forms, including extraresidential relations and consensual cohabitation (and legal marriage in the later slavery period), and by sequential relationships.

19. Patterson (1973:162–70) identified "unstable unions," "stable unions," "multiple associations," and "stable monogamous and legal marriages" among the Jamaican slaves.

20. See also Momsen (1988:84) and Bush (1990:49).

21. Cf. Gaspar (1992:135).

22. Higman (whose data are based on one day only) is inconclusive on the nature of these patterns, both for the anthropologically well-studied African systems from which the slaves originated and at Montpelier. Yet his data do not contradict an emergent pattern of cognatic descent.

23. Bilby's (1993) conclusions are based on a sound range of historical sources in

addition to his ethnographic research in the Caribbean region, including the Jamaican Windward Maroons. I am grateful to Dr. Bilby for permission to cite his unpublished paper.

24. This conclusion is based on Maurer's *own* assumption that "Jean Besson's discussion of family land turns on a conception of *Caribbean societies as composed of loosely organized descent groups*, each of which is imagined as spreading down from a supposedly common ancestor; *the argument depends thus on a weak notion of 'family'*" (1997b:203, emphases mine). I have pointed to the unrestricted/overlapping nature of Afro-Caribbean cognatic descent systems and the ad hoc crystallization of related landholding kin groups that occur in relation to family land (in the wider contexts of multiple small-scale tenures in peasant communities and national market economies), in contrast to structural-functionalist models of restricted descent groups as building blocks of "tribal" societies with subsistence economies (Besson 1979). But this does not mean that I see such Caribbean kin groups as either "loosely organized" or "weak." Instead, as developed in chapter 8, I have identified a highly creative system of consanguinity and affinity rooted in creole institution-building and combining an elaborate "complex" marriage system, bilateral kinship networks, and strong overlapping unrestricted cognatic descent lines and landholding kin groups—a combination reflected in the Hawaiianized Eskimo kinship terminology that has not previously been recognized for the Caribbean region (cf. Besson 1987a:122, 1995b).

25. See, e.g., Besson (1974:chap. 7, 1984a, 1987a, 1987b, 1988, 1992a, 1995a, 1995d, 1999a, 2000) and chapter 4.

26. Cf. Otterbein (1964).

27. See Fox (1967:256–61) and chapter 8.

Chapter Two

1. Frank (1969, 1973); Wallerstein (1974, 1980); Wolf (1982); Greenfield (1979, 2000); Eltis (2000).

2. See, e.g., "Agricultural Report," *Falmouth Post*, 5 June 1839, which refers to "the prosperous and pleasing state of [estate] agriculture in Trelawny," where numerous plantations including Good Hope are reported as doing well. Holland Estate (bordering Martha Brae), among others such as adjoining Maxfield and Greenside, "are thriving admirably," and "a better crop than that of last year when one hundred hogsheads were made, is expected" at Irving Tower Estate, also bordering Martha Brae.

3. Jamaica is divided into three counties, whose names reflect English colonization: Cornwall in the west, Middlesex in the middle, and Surrey in the east. I use Shore and Stewart's (1952) term "old St. James" to refer to the original parish of St. James (in Cornwall), out of which Trelawny was created, in contrast to the present parish of St. James.

4. Goodwin (1946:13) wrote that there was an "Indian Village" situated here, along an Arawak trail between the northern and southwestern coasts, whereas Shore and Stewart (1952:15) asserted that Martha Brae was "the Spanish Melilla," thought to be one of the two oldest Spanish towns (and possibly the first) in Jamaica (cf. Goodwin 1946:85). Goodwin (81, 89), however, identified Melilla with present-day Annotto Bay, located much farther east along the island's North Coast. Nevertheless, he argued that there was a later Spanish town on the site of Martha Brae, established at "a point on the south trail inland where the early Spaniards must have taken refuge directly after the abandonment of Sevilla d'Oro," the first Spanish capital near present-day St. Ann's Bay (82; see also pp. 13, 85, 87, 146). Initially, Fremmer (1967) also believed that there had been a Spanish settlement at Martha Brae, but he subsequently concluded that "there never was a Spanish town where Martha Brae now stands" (Fremmer 1968).

5. Island Record Office, Jamaica, Grantors Old Series 4, Lib. 165, f. 11. I am grateful to Jackie Ranston for the archival assistance that uncovered this information. I also thank Helen Nedham, a descendant of the Irvings in England, for drawing my attention to the extensive Irving family history, including John Beaufin Irving of Bonshaw's (1907) account of the establishment of Irving Tower Plantation.

6. Dan Ogilvie's *History of the Parish of Trelawny* (1954) contrasts with Craton's more thoroughly researched information in that Ogilvie states that "the eastern section [of old St. James] . . . had 88 Sugar estates while the western section possessed just about half that number" (1). However Ogilvie, like Craton, notes that the eastern part of old St. James (from which Trelawny was created) produced more sugar: "It was then obvious that greater wealth was centred in the eastern section of the parish" (1).

7. Jacobs (1970:15) cited these figures for exports shipped from the wharves at Falmouth Harbor (possibly including the Rock) from the 1804 *Jamaica Almanack*. On Trelawny's sugar estates, see Craton (1978:39).

8. Jacobs (1970:15) adeptly illuminated this paradox: "Napoleon was busy laying the foundations of a long period of prosperity for Falmouth. His invasion of Spain . . . increased the chances of trade with Spanish America, and the Continental System, with the retaliatory British blockade, tended to put a premium on sugar, so that development of western Trelawny must have been rapid." More generally, Eric Williams (1964:150–52) observed that soil exhaustion contributed to the collapse of the plantation slave economy in the British West Indies.

9. See n. 2 above.

10. See, e.g., the letters "to Scottish Emigrants," written by a "Scotchman" with the opening phrase "My Countrymen," in the *Falmouth Post*, 1, 29 June, 10, 17 August 1836. See also "New Song of the West: Cain's Address to His Sons in Jamaica," to the Air "Scots wha hae wi Wallace bled," by "MacLeod," *Falmouth Post*, 20 July 1836.

11. In the late twentieth century Hampden was again managed by a Grant of Scottish descent.

12. Cf. Long (1774, 2:404–16), Patterson (1973:145–52), and Higman (1998).

13. However, in 2001 Hampden was reputedly enmeshed in debt and government receivership.

14. Although my information on Charles Gordon's Georgia Plantation is mainly drawn from Alan Karras (1992), I am indebted to Ms. Gordon of Aberdeen (personal communication, 1970s) for my initial information on Georgia Estate, based on her research on the Gordon of Buthlaw and Cairness Papers in the Library Archives at the University of Aberdeen. For more on Charles Gordon's Georgia Estate in the 1780s, see McDonald (1993:21, 43–44, 120, 287).

15. I am grateful to the late Ivy Baxter (personal communication) for the archival information on the Martha Brae Burns Supper.

16. Ogilvie (1954:6, 32); Fremmer (1967, 1968); Wright and White (1969:46); Jacobs (1970:14); Black (1979).

17. Writers have generally claimed that Falmouth (in Trelawny Parish, Cornwall County) was named after the birthplace (Falmouth in the county of Cornwall, England) of Sir William Trelawny, governor of Jamaica at the time that Trelawny Parish was created and after whom the parish was named (Ogilvie 1954:31; Jacobs 1970:14; Wright and White 1969:206). But Inez Sibley and Jasper Ogilvie (1975b) dispute this. Robert Barrett (2000:8) suggests that Falmouth and Cornwall in Jamaica may have been named after the Barrett family's "English place of origin."

18. In 1840, two years after emancipation, a cast-iron bridge was imported from Glasgow, Scotland (Sibley and Ogilvie 1975c), an event reported in the *Illustrated London News*, 8 November 1851 (M. Curtin 1991:29).

19. Wright and White (1969:215); Tenison (1971:11); Georgian Society of Jamaica (1970:22–23); cf. Hart (1994:58).

20. See, e.g., the wide range "of NEW GOODS from the latest arrival from London, *via* Kingston" advertised by Robert J. Virgo of Water Square in the *Falmouth Post* on 14 December 1836.

21. These figures are based on my one hundred percent census of the village in 1979. The population of Martha Brae has increased since that time.

Chapter Three

1. For more on the Dominican case in the context of the debate, see Trouillot (1984, 1988, 1992b), Marshall (1991a), and later in this chapter.

2. An attenuated domestic economy did emerge among plantation slaves in Cuba in the mid-nineteenth century, with customary land rights related to kinship and community (Scott 1985:15–19).

3. An exception to the encompassing influence of the Hispanic plantation system was Cuba's hilly and mountainous eastern province of Santiago de Cuba, where "large-scale plantations did not yet have a monopoly of the land" (Scott 1985:259). There protopeasants evolved into postemancipation peasantries, and "slaves and their descendants had the greatest opportunity to obtain access to small plots of land

by ownership, rental, or de facto occupation" (259), that is, through legal and customary tenures. The Cuban Revolution of 1959 would further constrain the peasantry by continuing the plantation system through state control and by inhibiting peasant marketing and landholding (Hagelberg 1985; Mintz 1985; Pollitt 1985).

4. Barry Higman (1998:290–305) shows that, despite recent critical assessment of the concept of slave community, this concept remains viable for the analysis of slave communities on large plantations, such as Montpelier in Jamaica, which were rooted in locality, kinship, and values surrounding land (including house yards and provision grounds as the basis of some autonomy and internal differentiation within the slave community), as well as in creole language and reciprocity.

5. Kevin Smith also cites Mary Turner (1988) on the significance of customary land rights among the Jamaican slaves: "Turner, who focused on the development of wage labour and work norms before emancipation, stressed the sense of customary land rights among slaves engendered by the provision ground system and the slaves' early participation in Jamaica's internal commerce and export trade" (Smith 1995:129 [n. 28]). However, Turner's later essay (1995:12) underplays the role of land access (in favor of wages as a symbol of free status) in the flight of ex-slaves from Jamaican estates (cf. Sheller 1998:97).

6. The Haitian peasants would again be constrained by plantations as a result of neocolonial occupation by the United States in 1915 (Larose 1975:487–88; Hagelberg 1985:96; cf. Mintz 1995:84).

7. A circular, "The Apprenticeship — Crown Lands" from Downing Street, 30 January 1836, which appeared under the section "Colonial Affairs" in the *Falmouth Post* of 8 June 1836, favorably assessed apprenticeship but warned against "the incautious distribution" of Crown lands to the ex-slaves. In contrast, an article entitled "Death Extraordinary" in the *Post* of 1 August 1838 (the date of emancipation), critiqued apprenticeship, opening with the statement "DIED, after a very short illness the monster, APPRENTICESHIP; he was the eldest born of SLAVERY."

8. As Douglas Hall (N.d.:6) observes of the early end of apprenticeship: "The original plan called for the complete freedom of the non-praedial labourers in 1838, and the praedial labourers in 1840; but by the former year the discontent was general, and full freedom was granted to all apprentices."

9. Reports by Rev. William Knibb and Rev. Benjamin Dexter on the "Working Classes" connected with the Baptist Church in Trelawny, in the *Falmouth Post* of 27 March and 3 April 1839, reflect this concern regarding the withdrawal of labor. They list the number of men, women, and children "At Work" and "Not at Work" on sugar estates in the parish and defend the Baptists against charges by the "Trelawny Committee Report" of influencing the ex-slaves against the plantations. For an assessment of the reasons for the withdrawal of female ex-slave labor from the estates in the British Caribbean after 1838, see Bridget Brereton (1999). Brereton concludes that "ex-slave men and women were not blindly obeying hegemonic gender ideologies nor seeking to transform freedwomen into dependent housewives confined

to the home. They were pursuing rational family strategies aimed at securing the survival and welfare of their kin groups, in the face of appalling odds" (107; cf. Sheller 1998).

10. See D. Hall (1959:19–23), Paget (1964:39), Marshall (1972:31), Wright (1973:167), and Knox (1977). An article on "The Crops!" in the *Falmouth Post* of 13 February 1839 discusses a belated increase in wages for the peasant laborers on plantations, combined with rent charged for houses and provision grounds on estates, and refers to the earlier issuing by planters to ex-slaves of "hundreds and thousands of 'Notices to Quit.' "

11. In Antigua, where emancipation occurred in 1834, some ex-slaves created the first (nonmaroon) villages in the British West Indies by 1835. Sligoville, Jamaica's first Baptist-founded free village, was also established around this time.

12. Momsen showed how the Nevisian peasantry transformed the externally imposed solution of land settlement into a customary system with similarities to family land and common land, stating that the Nevisian peasantry "recreated its traditional attitudes to land within the formal structure of the land settlement" (1987:65). Some Nevisian migrants were also retaining their settlement land.

13. Such migration was later to the Dutch Leeward Islands.

14. Thomas Little (1995) explores the skillful way in which Lisle consolidated his ministry, including negotiating with the planters.

15. The Baptist class-leader system was adopted from the Methodists and further appropriated by the slaves: "An invention of John Wesley, the ticket-and-class-leader system involved establishing small groups of converts and giving a lay leader responsibility for their spiritual and moral well-being. In the hands of the Baptists, 'the leaders, commonly called "daddies," were responsible for weeknight prayer meetings in class-houses on estates or in the villages, for the day-to-day spiritual oversight of class members. . . . It was a common occurrence for the people to form their own classes, select their own leaders, and have them accepted by the missionary, a procedure never followed by the Wesleyans' (Stewart 1992:8)" (Besson and Chevannes 1996:224 [n. 1]).

16. Class leaders among the slaves in the Baptist Church, or "daddies," perpetuated Myalism. For details on the role of Daddy Sam Sharpe (or "Father Tharpe") in the 1831–32 Jamaican slave rebellion, see Turner (1982:152–55).

17. During the period of my fieldwork, a sculpture of Sam Sharpe was erected at this spot and the square was renamed (from Charles Square) Sam Sharpe Square.

18. See Wright (1973:112–33), for an account of Knibb and the abolition movement, and Sibley (1965:10–11). The forces contributing to the British antislavery campaign were economic as well as humanitarian. Mary Turner (1982) argued that the missionaries in Jamaica became abolitionists only when they realized "that the future of mission work depended on the destruction of the slave system" (170). Prior to this, the missionary societies "did everything they could to preserve a political distinction between themselves and the antislavery movement," as "they regarded slavery as a manifestation of the mysterious workings of God" (9, 8), though

"at a practical level . . . the missionary societies and the antislavery movement shared a common conviction: that the most important single benefit to bestow upon the slaves within the framework of the slave system was Christianity" (9).

19. In a useful article exploring the link between the Jamaican free-village system and the construction of English identities, Catherine Hall (1992–93) describes Phillippo's aims in founding Sligoville as a model for free villages and notes the discrepancy between "Phillippo's fantasy of his all seeing, all regulating, all supervising hand and eye" and the "Afro-Jamaican way of life" of the villagers (129). Hall's "White Visions, Black Lives" draws on my earlier outline of culture-building in postslavery Martha Brae (Besson 1987a). However, I maintain that the involvement of the Baptist Church in the establishment of Martha Brae as a free village was not as systematic as in other Trelawny villages such as The Alps, Refuge, Kettering, and Granville, which were founded through Baptist land settlements (Besson 1984b). Moreover, in her discussion of New Birmingham, Hall (1992–93:112–13) does not recognize that this is the contemporary village of The Alps. And although she refers to the founding of Kettering and Wilberforce/Refuge (114–17), she does not explore their evolution to the present.

20. Sturge Town in St. Ann, established on 126 acres in 1839–40 by John Clark with the assistance of Joseph Sturge, was also known as Angwin Crawl and Birmingham (Mintz 1989:160–64, 168). As in the case of New Birmingham/The Alps in Trelawny, the free village of Angwin Crawl took the name of the estate on which it was established (162). See also n. 21 below.

21. R. Greenwood and S. Hamber (1980:86) mistakenly equated Knibb's Trelawny New Birmingham with Birmingham in St. Ann, stating that "in 1838 William Knibb obtained £1,000 from the parent Church in England to buy 200 hectares in St. Ann [sic] on which to build Sturge Town, 'our little Birmingham' as he called it." The naming of both of these free villages, in neighboring parishes, after Sturge's hometown may have contributed to the adoption of alternate names in both cases. See also n. 20 above. In addition, there are two free villages named Sturge Town: one in St. Ann and one near Sligoville in St. Catherine (Sibley 1965:14).

22. Another article, "The Baptists and the Falmouth Post," published later that year in the *Post* on 25 September 1839, refers to the general belief "in this and other parishes, that the present Editor of the *Falmouth Post*, was the paid Agent of the Baptist Missionaries in Jamaica." Though refuting this assumption, the article acknowledges the pro-Baptist sympathies of this newspaper, in which Knibb often published.

23. Knibb died later that year, 1845, at Kettering, Trelawny.

24. As Wright (1973:168) noted, "under the existing law a £10 freehold conferred the right to vote." Swithin Wilmot (1992) shows how Trelawny ex-slaves used their newly acquired freeholds in Baptist free villages to curtail the power of the planter class and the Established Anglican Church in a by-election for a seat in the Jamaica Assembly in 1852, though this advantage was short-lived.

25. Rev. Henderson (pastor of the Brown's Town Baptist Church in St. Ann from

1876 to 1926) described the role of these prayer houses in his history of the establishment of Baptist free villages in the parish of St. Ann (adjoining Trelawny) under the leadership of Rev. John Clark (Henderson 1967:81).

26. See also "What Wages Can the Planters Afford?," *Falmouth Post*, 28 August 1839.

27. The Cockpit Country, with its outstanding wilderness limestone karst topography of poljes and sinkholes (resembling cock-fighting pits) and rich flora and fauna, has long been regarded as a world-class geomorphical and biological environment. It has been under consideration as a National Park since 1970 and has more recently been proposed as a World Heritage Site, especially in view of its ecology, "natural beauty," and Leeward Maroon history (Barker and Miller 1995; Eyre 1995; cf. Besson 1995b, 1995c, 1997).

28. The traditional mode of transporting ground provisions, by donkey with market hampers, continued into the early years of my fieldwork and is still occasionally seen in rural Jamaica.

29. A "long shirt" was part of the typical clothing of male slaves, including those in Trelawny and St. James (McDonald 1993:125–26; Higman 1998:236).

30. The two Archibald Campbells are hereafter distinguished as Archibald/Archie Campbell I and II. It is likely that, in addition to namesaking, this name was appropriated from Major General Archibald Campbell, lieutenant governor of Jamaica in 1781 (Ford and Cundall 1910:54). The Robert Campbell of the land deed may have been a son, brother, or father of Archibald Campbell I.

31. Egbert Edwards also provided details on the early Baptist ministers of New Birmingham, and on the history of the Baptist mission house and church, that are substantiated by documentary sources. Rev. Dexter was said to have remained in Stewart Town; Pastor O'Meally and then Pastor Webb (who built the manse or mission house above the church) were the ministers for the New Birmingham Baptist Church (cf. Underhill 1862:360, 363). This first church and school were built on the foundations of the Great House of the slave master, whose tomb I was shown. The early church and school also served surrounding communities such as Warsop (said to be the village of "Mocca" studied by Edith Clarke 1953, 1966), Troy, and Ulster Spring. In 1939, as the date on the present church at The Alps confirmed, a new church was built on the foundations of the first. Egbert worked as a carpenter in the rebuilding of this church.

32. In 1997 I met in London one of the diaspora members of the Ferguson Old Family who had been born in the United States. She had never been to The Alps but had long been planning to go there and had treasured the oral tradition of this Old Family that had been passed on to her in the diaspora by older members of the descent group. She was also able to extend the oral tradition back to Africa. See Besson (1999b, 2001c).

33. Cf. Handler and Lange (1978:203).

34. Illustration 4 in the appendix to the *Speech of the Rev. William Knibb* (1842)

shows the first chapel at Refuge. This wooden structure is much smaller than the later cut-stone Baptist church.

35. See also "Agricultural Report," *Falmouth Post*, 5 June 1839. According to oral tradition, the site of the village also provided a hiding place for Knibb during the reprisals by the planters' Colonial Church Union following the slave rebellion of 1831–32, and that it was from this refuge that Knibb sailed to England to argue the abolitionist cause.

36. The church at Wilberforce/Refuge was originally the "Mother Church" of what later became the Kettering circuit of Baptist churches. Even after this circuit was established, the Refuge church continued to draw its congregation from outside the village — specifically, from the nearby free village of Daniel Town, which had no church of its own until the 1960s.

37. The title of the Lyon Old Family may have been an appropriation of the surname of a colonial landholding family in Trelawny. Edmund B. Lyon was a special justice of Trelawny around the time of emancipation who seems to have recognized the potential of the peasantry (see *Falmouth Post*, 10 July 1839, and Paget 1964:42). "Lyon" was also one of the names listed in the *Falmouth Post* of 13 February 1839 as a "friend of Freedom" in relation to the naming of streets in New Birmingham. Moreover, there was a ship *David Lyon*, in which Samuel Moulton Barrett owned shares in the 1830s (R. A. Barrett 2000:94, 100–101). In the mid-twentieth century, "Lawyer" (my late father, Ken McFarlane) purchased Holland Plantation from the Lyon family.

38. The "Bell" title may have derived from the English Bell family, who had close ties with the Barrett family at Oxford Plantation. Surveyor Robert Bell appraised slaves at Oxford and witnessed a Barrett will in 1798, and Sam Goodin Barrett married into the Bell family around the time of emancipation (see R. A. Barrett 2000:40, 44, 96, 127, 129, 146).

39. Long Pond exports sugar, as part of the Jamaican sugar industry, mainly to Tate and Lyle at Sugar Quay in London's East End. Up to the year 2000 most of the rum from Long Pond Estates was purchased through National Rums by Seagrams's sole remaining employee in Jamaica, based in Falmouth, who exported it from Kingston to bottling plants in Scotland (Renfrew), Canada, and the United States (Baltimore). These rums are sold as the world-famous Captain Morgan's Rum, Myers' Rum, and Trelawny Gold. The distillery is still owned by the Jamaican state. I am grateful to the late "Bill" Ive of Seagrams for this information.

40. Cf. Mullin (1994:28–29) on scarification and ethnicity among enslaved Africans in Jamaica and elsewhere in the Americas, including reference to " 'A Negro mark.' "

41. It is possible that the cholera outbreak referred to in the oral traditions of The Alps and Refuge was the postslavery epidemic of 1850–51 (see, e.g., Sibley 1965:v), and that the timescale has been "telescoped" through oral history.

42. See Jacoby (1994:90) for an analysis of the "recurring parallel between the

status of domestic animals and of slaves," perceived by both masters and slaves in African America in terms of relations of domination and the use of force and control by the master in the institution of slavery.

43. Ann Knibb, a daughter of William and Mary, "married Ellis Fray, a graduate of the Calabar training college who became pastor of the congregations at Kettering and Refuge. And so, in the grandchildren of the man who had called the apprentices bone of his bone and flesh of his flesh, the strain of poor but noble-minded English nonconformists was united with that of enslaved Africans" (Wright 1973:244). A Fray granddaughter, Knibb's great-granddaughter, the late Inez Knibb Sibley, whom I interviewed in Mandeville in 1983, was a valuable source of information in my research.

44. See "The Burial within Towns' Limits Act" of 1875 (*Revised Laws of Jamaica*, 1953, Cap. 49, paras. 3, 10). I am grateful to Jeanne Robinson-Foster, Attorney-at-Law, Montego Bay, Jamaica, for providing me with a copy of this legislation. The Burial within Towns' Limits Act not only defines town limits in relation to burial, but also provides a basis for the discontinuation of burial grounds in Jamaican towns and villages.

45. Kettering villagers have varying views about the town limits regulation: some see this change in interment patterns as undermining the identity of family lines, whereas others regard it as making room for the houses of descendants.

46. A square chain is one-tenth of an acre.

47. Thus family land persists, is sold, and continues to be created in the contexts of a persisting land market and overall land scarcity, a point explored more fully, in relation to Martha Brae, in chapters 4–5.

48. Such unrestricted descent also provides scope for the dynamics of amity and of conflict or "crab antics" (cf. Wilson 1995), discussed in chapters 4 and 8 in the context of Martha Brae.

49. The livestock pen on which Granville was founded was said by some villagers to have been Weston Favel Pen. Western Favel was a Trelawny slave estate combining sugar and cattle operations (Craton 1978:42). Today Weston Favel sugar plantation, in the Queen of Spain's Valley, is a tributary of Hampden Estates. The hilly land on which Granville was established may have been the pen for that estate (though see n. 55 below).

50. Cf. *Falmouth Post*, 17 July 1839, on Knibb's class leaders.

51. Mintz (1989:164–65) noted that in the founding of Sturge Town in St. Ann, plots of land varied significantly in size. He suggested a number of reasons: ability of individual purchasers to pay, size of settlers' families, variations in soil quality and topography, favoritism, preexisting differences of economic status, and missionary control and conformity. Oral tradition combined with field data in The Alps and Granville indicates the validity of Mintz's reasoning on the links between church membership, economic differentiation, and landholding among ex-slave settlers. Such internal differentiation of the peasantry has been a continuing theme in the free village of Martha Brae (chapters 4–6).

52. For the Jonkonnu or "John Canoe" masquerade among Jamaican slaves, see Patterson (1973:243–47) and Bilby (1999). The evidence points to a process of Caribbean culture-building incorporating African beliefs and rituals.

53. Here the concept of "war" refers to the potential disputes or "crab antics" that sometimes occur in relation to family land (see chapters 4, 8).

54. The Trelawny Parish Council had recently imposed a similar restriction on yard burial, and the related introduction of a community cemetery, on the village of Daniel Town near Refuge.

55. As stated in n. 49 above, some Granville villagers say that the free village was founded on Weston Favel Pen. However, the reference, in this oral history, to York Pen as the site of the village also has some credence, as York was a Trelawny slave and sugar estate (Craton 1978:43) that in 1778 was owned by the Tharps (Mullin 1994:26). Moreover, York is near Weston Favel and like that plantation is now a tributary of Hampden Estates. Both versions of oral tradition therefore indicate that Granville was founded on a livestock pen that was linked to a sugar estate a few miles inland in the Queen of Spain's Valley.

Chapter Four

1. See also Ogilvie (1954), Fremmer (1968), and Sherlock (1984:119).

2. The title of the Anderson Old Family in Martha Brae (chapter 5) may have been an appropriation of the surname of Mr. Anderson of the Trelawny Parish Vestry who served on this committee, which inquired into squatting on vestry land in the town of Martha Brae.

3. John Kelly may have been the same person, or of the same family, as Daniel Kelly, special justice/stipendiary magistrate for Trelawny in February, March, and July 1839. See *Falmouth Post*, 13 February, 10 July 1839, and R. A. Barrett (2000:104).

4. These core-periphery relations within the Baptist Church were paralleled on an attentuated scale by those between stations and filials or outposts among the Moravians, as in the parish of St. Elizabeth (Besson, forthcoming).

5. These figures are based on the 100 percent census that I collected in 1979. The village population has further expanded since that time.

6. A further 24.3 percent was in forest (such as the wet limestone forest of the Cockpit Country), and 19.7 percent was in scrub and woodland ("Total Area and Land Use in Jamaica," 1993, by courtesy of the Rural Physical Planning Division). I thank Professor Barry Chevannes of the University of the West Indies, Mona, Jamaica, for obtaining these statistics on my behalf.

7. My fieldwork (up to 2001) included interviews in 1995 with officials at Long Pond and with the managing director of Hampden Estates. See also Allen-Vassell and Browne (1992:56).

8. This trade is part of the European Union's Lomé Convention.

9. The other main river-rafting projects in Jamaica are on the Rio Grande in the parish of Portland and the Great River on the boundary of Hanover and St. James.

10. The Friends of the Georgian Society of Jamaica, based in London, are also involved in the restoration of Georgian Falmouth.

11. Part of Maxfield Estate was sold to a small farmer from the Trelawny free village of Schawfield who is the brother of a Martha Brae villager and who has rights with his several siblings to an acre of family land in his natal village.

12. The location of Martha Brae, which is surrounded by estates and near the tourist North Coast and the town of Falmouth, provides some opportunities for wage labor.

13. "Free land" is land that a plantation owner permits another to use free of rental, but generally the land must be returned within a specified time cleared of bush.

14. Nowadays, landless farms vary from ones allowed by estate owners to those persisting in the face of signs declaring that goat trespassers will be shot.

15. The analysis of family land in this chapter draws on my earlier articles — e.g., Besson (1979, 1984a, 1984b, 1987b, 1988, 1992a, 1995b, 1995d, 1997). See also chapters 1, 3, 5, and 8. As will be seen from this chapter (cf. chapter 3), my use of "institution" in the family-land context does not support Michael Smith's static plural society theory as Carnegie (1987) and Crichlow (1994) asserted, but is derived from Mintz and Price's (1992:19) dynamic thesis of Caribbean institution-building. For my response to Carnegie and Crichlow, see Besson (1987a, 1995a).

16. A revised edition of Clarke's study appeared in 1999.

17. See also Greenfield (1960), Comitas (1962:151), and Lowenthal (1972:100–105).

18. Besson (1974, 2:1–113, 1984a:76 [nn. 7, 9], 1987b:38 [n. 3], 1987a, 1988, 1992a). See also Besson (1995a, 1999a, 2000) and Crichlow (1995).

19. Analyses by others for Jamaica (Carnegie 1987 and McKay 1987), St. Vincent (Rubenstein 1987b), and St. Lucia (Crichlow 1994) have reinforced my intersystem approach, rather than refuting the existence of the family-land institution as Carnegie and Crichlow intended.

20. Such loans are available, e.g., for the government's Farm House Scheme.

21. This proverb is quoted on the back cover of Wilson's 1973 book.

22. The 1976 Status of Children Act abolished the Eurocentrically defined status of "illegitimacy."

23. The recognition of such variations clarifies the discrepancy, referred to by William Davenport (1961a:448–49), between Davenport and Edith Clarke (1966) on the issue of shares in undivided land, that Carnegie (1987:86) highlighted and mistakenly assumed was still unclear (but see Besson 1974, 2:68–72, 1987a:111, 126 [n. 6]). This discrepancy parallels to a great extent the legal distinction between joint tenancy and tenancy in common. In the first variation, reported by Clarke, coheirs hold joint rights in undivided land and devolution is initially lateral. This consolidation of rights by surviving members of the same generation resembles the feature of survivorship in the legal estate of joint tenancy. In the next generation, however, the principle of joint rights is reasserted in accordance with tradition, so

that the parallel with the legal system is incomplete. In this variation, coheirs in successive generations retain equal shares to the land. In the second variation, reported by Davenport, coheirs hold specific shares that devolve vertically to their children in an exact parallel with the legal estate of tenancy in common. If individuals have unequal numbers of children, coheirs in successive generations will hold unequal shares to the family property. Davenport failed to recognize this parallel with the legal system, a parallel that challenges his conflict model of customary and legal tenurial systems. I am grateful to "Lawyer" (my late father, Ken McFarlane) for illuminating the distinction between joint tenancy and tenancy in common. Responsibility for the interpretation of family land in relation to these tenures is, however, mine.

24. Through the Family Law Act of 1981. See Carnegie (1987:97 [n. 3]).

25. A similar point regarding the transformation of legal tenure by customary tenure forms the central theme of Michael Smith's (1956b, 1965a) classic analysis of family land in Carriacou, a process so dynamic that it belies his static plural society interpretation of Caribbean land-tenure systems. Moreover, though Smith focused on patrilineages in Carriacou, his evidence on family land clearly indicates a customary cognatic land-transmission system (see chapter 8).

26. For an analysis of Afro-creole conjugality, see chapter 8.

27. Internal differentiation is thus emerging among the squatter peasantry of Zion, as exists in the Martha Brae peasant community.

28. Cf. Turner (1982:90).

29. The title of this Afro-creole descent group is likely to have been an appropriation of the surname of the British West Indian Dawkins planter family, whose members "were survivors of those who claimed to be the first conquerors' of Jamaica" (Craton 1997:99; cf. R. A. Barrett 2000:15). For example, Samuel Goodin Barrett, magistrate for Trelawny, bought sheep from Henry Dawkins's Salt Pond pen in St. Catherine about 1839, one year after emancipation (Craton 1997:120).

30. With no organized amenities, effluence was seeping into the swamp and was in danger of destroying the nutrients that fed the fish life in the sea by Falmouth. Cutting of the mangrove for building and for charcoal burning was having a similar effect.

Chapter Five

1. See also Price (1983) and Price and Price (1991).

2. See also Higman (1998:71, 1999); cf. Thompson (2000).

3. For example, the Mintos were a celebrated Trelawny plantation family (Fremmer 1984c); Robert Minto and James Kelly were Trelawny vestrymen (freeholding/slave-owning planters) in 1782/1791 and 1802 in Martha Brae and Falmouth respectively (Ogilvie 1954:11, 65, 119). See also chapter 4 on the Trelawny magistrates John Kelly (1835) and Daniel Kelly (1839), and on Mr. Anderson of the parish vestry who retrieved captured land in Martha Brae around 1839. Other members of

the Kelly family included "Smith Kelly, Provost Marshal of Jamaica from 1680, his wife Susan, [and] his son John Kelly (c. 1684–1751), . . . who were linked to Colonel Peter Beckford" (Keymer 2001:2).

4. Faircloughs of the master class included Wm. Fairclough, a Trelawny vestryman in 1802 (Ogilvie 1954:119), who was probably the same William Fairclough who was attorney at Good Hope Plantation near Martha Brae in 1817 (Hart 1994:129; and chapter 2).

5. In 2001, however, some individuals in this descent group were "paid up" members of the Anglican church in Falmouth.

6. Some of the Christian names of these Minto ex-slaves suggest appropriations of important individuals in British or colonial Jamaican society.

7. I am grateful to Jackie Ranston for drawing to my attention that the parish records / tax rolls for the neighboring parish of St. Elizabeth did not start until 1875 (personal communications 1995). This suggests that the 1876 Trelawny Land Tax Roll was perhaps the earliest for this parish.

8. Peppercorn sales of land are virtually gifts, but a nominal price is paid to ensure freehold ownership to the recipient.

9. This section of the plantation was named after an earlier tenant of that part of Holland Estate.

10. Such walls were built as protection against hurricanes.

11. As discussed later in this chapter, oral tradition locates the shift from yard burial to a village cemetery in the early decades of the twentieth century. My own exploration of dates of tombstones in the cemetery bears this out. The rationale for this transformation of burial patterns was provided by Jamaican colonial legislation, namely, the Burial within Towns' Limit Act of 1875 (*Revised Laws of Jamaica*, 1953, Cap. 49, paras. 3, 10). See also Besson (1984b) and chapters 3–4. Rhoda, in contrast to her grandmother who was buried in an earthen grave on the family land, was entombed in the Martha Brae cemetery.

12. This land settlement was established around the 1970s through the subdivision and sale of Hague Estate.

13. See E. Clarke (1953, 1966), Fox (1967:156), and Besson (1987b, 1988).

14. To "administer" on the land involved writing to the administrator general, obtaining written and notarized renunciation of land rights from absent coheirs, and advertising in the *Jamaican Gazette* to ensure that there were no further claims to the property.

15. Before my fieldwork I had some knowledge of Lawyer's land sales, which occurred in my childhood and school days, but I was unaware of their significance to the Trelawny peasantry. After becoming familiar with villagers' oral traditions, I asked Lawyer why he had "let down the [planters'] side." He simply said, "it gave me satisfaction to see the people settled on land of their own."

16. When I returned to Martha Brae in 2000, my aging landlady, "Miss Victoria," dispensed with my usual title "Miss Jeanie" and greeted me as "My Daughter!"

thereby indicating a performative dimension of Afro-creole "relatedness" (cf. Carsten 2000).

17. I was initially puzzled by this reference to a picture of Nana Green in a group of other slaves. However, Barry Higman (1998:248) provides evidence of Jamaican and other British West Indian slave and maroon artists in the early nineteenth century who drew or carved pictures, including "the figure of negroes," on paper, calabash, and wood.

18. His maternal grandmother was "Mother Lawrence," who was a slave child on Merrywood Plantation (chapter 3).

19. This hypothesis is reinforced by the oral history account, by Ruth Marshall of the Minto Old Family, that Teacher Roper — who taught her grandmother (born in the 1870s) at the Baptist Prayer House — was the second person to be buried in the Martha Brae cemetery.

20. Cf. Patterson (1973:216–21), Mintz (1989:184–94), Olwig (1981a, 1985:43–81), Brierley (1987:197), Higman (1988:261–66), Tomich (1991), and McDonald (1993:24–26).

Chapter Six

1. See Besson and Momsen (1987), Hills (1988), Mintz (1985:134, 1989:146–47, 223), and Emmer (1995). Except for Emmer, these sources do not agree with such condemnations.

2. Cf. Sahlins (1972) on the domestic mode of production.

3. See Berleant-Schiller and Pulsipher (1986), Armstrong (1990:233–50, 273), Mintz (1996b), and Higman (1998:197).

4. I learned from William Tapper, through trial and error, that "a good planting day" was related not to the sun, but to the phases of the moon as set out in *MacDonald's Almanac*.

5. Salted cod was imported to Jamaica to feed the slaves (Patterson 1973:217), and in 1830 Knibb observed ships from North America bringing pickled fish to Falmouth (Wright 1973:56). The front page of the *Falmouth Post* of 9 January 1839 includes an advertisement from "Falmouth, 11th December, 1838" for "Prime New Codfish" brought on the brig *Greyhound* from Halifax, Nova Scotia. See also Armstrong (1990:273–74).

6. On house size, structure, and roofing in Jamaican slave plantation villages, see Patterson (1973:54), Armstrong (1990:87–132, 268), and Higman (1998:151–72).

7. Cf. Wilson (1973, 1995), but see also Besson (1993) and chapter 1.

8. Cf. Handler (1966).

9. Some of these historical exhibits had been recently excavated by the late Ray Fremmer of Green Park Estate.

10. Rat-bat manure is reputed to be extremely fertile.

11. See also Armstrong (1990:181–84) and Higman (1998:243–44).

12. Mintz (1957) and Katzin (1959a, 1960) reported such "customer" relations in Jamaica, and in the 1990s I was invited (as a stranger) by a higgler in the Mandeville marketplace, in the parish of Manchester, to participate in *brawta*. Mintz (1961) analyzed parallel *pratik* relations in Haiti, and in 1993 I encountered a similar practice called *'rangement* ("arrangement") in the Roseau marketplace in the Windward Island of Dominica.

13. Mintz (1955, 1960, 1989:216); Katzin (1959a, 1960); Laguerre (1982:17); Horowitz (1992:35); Besson (1995g:278–79).

14. On combs in Jamaica, see Chevannes (1995g:106–7).

15. Laguerre (1990:152–53); Besson (1995g); Freeman (1997). In Fort-de-France, French Martinique, for example, higglers (especially market women from Haiti) commute and sell their wares in the marketplace and on the streets (Laguerre 1990:152–53).

16. See Mintz (1960:114, 1989:195–96, 210–12, 216, 223–24) and Mintz and Price (1992:77–80).

17. Simmonds (1987:31–32) noted that on the plantations, whereas male slaves dominated the higher-status roles of drivers and artisans with females filling domestic occupations, the majority of field slaves were given the same work regardless of gender — the gang system being differentiated only by health and age. In contrast, in the towns — where there was a preponderance of women, slave-holding females, and African female slaves (rather than of males and Creoles) — slave women were engaged mainly in domestic work and marketing, while male slaves were generally assigned skilled occupations (cf. Higman 1984:50).

18. Cf. Bush (1990:50).

19. See also M. G. Smith (1956a), Handler (1965, 1966), Frucht (1967), and Fraser (1981).

20. A raft needs to be replaced every six months. Raftsmen employ other men to cut bamboo from farther upriver, buying about a dozen bamboos (36 feet long) for a raft that holds two adults (in addition to the captain) and a child.

21. In the peak tourist season from December to April, an average of 90 rafting trips are made daily on the Martha Brae; this may decrease to about 45 trips per day in the low season from May to November.

22. E.g., tours linking river rafting to a trip to Dunns' River Falls in St. Ann.

23. Good Hope Hotel is now part of Island Outpost, "a group of unique, style-setting properties" (*Simply Caribbean* 1996:69), and "an excursion to Martha Brae for river rafting is just 20 minutes away" (*Caribbean Escapes* 1996:84).

24. See also Chamberlain (1998).

25. The McCarran-Walter Act imposed more rigid restrictions on entry quotas to the United States.

26. Cf. Purcell (1987).

27. During slavery the conch shell was one of the modes used by head drivers to summon plantation slaves for work at dawn (Patterson 1973:67).

28. Herskovits and Herskovits (1947:290–91); Handler (1966:277–78); Horowitz (1992:32–33); Métraux (1971).

29. M. G. Smith and Kruijer (1957); Katzin (1959b); Austin (1984:50); Harrison
(1988:113); Purcell (1998:266, 268 [n. 6]).

30. Such ROSCAs are known as *susu* in Trinidad (Herskovits and Herskovits
1947:76–77, 292), Martinique (spelled *sousou* and *sou sou*) (Laguerre 1990:113–
40), and St. Vincent (Senior 1991:146); *throwing a box* in Guyana (R. T. Smith
1964:315–16) and *boxes* in Montserrat (Philpott 1973:172); *san* in the Dominican
Republic and *esu* in the Bahamas (Norvell and Wehrly 1969); *sangue, solde,* and
comble in Haiti (Laguerre 1982:55–56); and *meeting* in Barbados (Barrow 1986:164).
ROSCAs have also been found among migrants from the West Indies and the Dominican Republic in New York (Light 1972:32–36; Sassen-Koob 1987:283) and among
Jamaicans, Montserratians, and Barbadians in England (Foner 1977:132; Philpott
1973:172, 1977:110–11).

31. The rate of exchange, with rising inflation in the Jamaican economy, was
approximately 55 Jamaican dollars to one pound sterling and 38 Jamaican dollars to
the U.S. dollar.

32. Daisy explained that even small children may participate in partners, and that
"first time" [in the past] she had a children's partners but has discontinued this.

33. In my early fieldwork house-building was itself often achieved through mutual
aid, but the architectural transformation from wooden cottages to concrete houses is
resulting in an increasing reliance on skilled wage labor.

34. This argument could be extended to the Martinican *sousou* (Laguerre 1990)
and to the Bahamian *esu* reported by Daniel Crowley, who interpreted both the *esu*
and Trinidadian *susu* as arriving "more or less simultaneously with Chinese, East
Indian and African immigrants" (personal communication from Daniel J. Crowley
1967, quoted in Norvell and Wehrly 1969:45). But Crowley's assertion that such
ROSCAs were derived simultaneously from Africa and Asia overstretches the cultural
survival thesis. Katzin also argued for the African origins of ROSCAs in Trinidad and
Jamaica, but her "belief" regarding the African origin of Jamaican partners and
Trinidadian *susu* is likewise weakened by her observation that a similar institution exists "among American Indians in Peru" (1959b:440, 440 [n. a]). For a
more recent view of the West African derivation of Caribbean ROSCAs, see Purcell
(1998:266).

35. The new phenomenon of *susu* land in Trinidad (and Tobago), where Herskovits and Herskovits (1947) first identified the *susu*, is being used, e.g., for squatter
regularization in a situation where land is being engrossed by corporate plantations, tourism, and increasing urbanization. Thus not only have ROSCAs in Trinidad
been recognized by law (292), but also their ethos is now guiding sustainable
development.

36. See also Ardener (1964), Besson (1998b), and Purcell (1998).

37. Cf. Turner (1982:89).

38. Although a person may reap the benefits of his or her investment in old age,

individuals are prevented from joining the CTS to secure short-term gain; i.e., when they are elderly and more likely to be sickly or dying. In this way, a viable society is maintained. This viability contrasts favorably with the situation noted by Frazier (1965:376–77) among African Americans in the United States, where "the local societies were found to be unstable [and] were constantly dissolving and reforming and often failed to meet their obligations to their members."

39. Howard Johnson (1991b:192) records an "increased participation of women" in friendly societies in the Bahamas in the late nineteenth and early twentieth centuries—a development similar to the key role of women in wage labor and in the internal marketing system (193). This gender equality parallels the incorporation of both women and men in the Bahamian customary land tenures of "generation property" and commonage, rooted in the protopeasant adaptation (Otterbein 1964; Craton 1987; Besson 1992a; and chapter 8).

40. Olwig (1981a, 1985) identified comparable networks of mutual aid, including death rituals, among protopeasants on different plantations in Danish St. John.

Chapter Seven

1. More recently Chevannes (1995c:7) argues that "there is no religion in Jamaica today to which the name Myal applies," yet Myal exists in the Accompong Maroon society (Besson 1995b, 1995c, 1997).

2. Villagers sometimes call Revival tabernacles "mission houses," a term that derives from the Baptist mission houses during and after slavery. In the Trelawny free village of Refuge, the area where the Baptist mission house was situated is still called "Mission."

3. I use the concept of "ideology" *not* in the sense of "false consciousness," but rather in the anthropological sense of a set of ideas relating to the material/socio-economic conditions of their generation and circulation (see, e.g., Seymour-Smith 1986:145–46)—in this case, the creation of Revivalism by Afro-creole slaves and their descendants in the contexts of colonial plantation slavery, postslavery peasantization, and neocolonial land monopoly.

4. This secondary meaning of Obeah as sorcery is not entirely absent among the Accompong Maroons, where Presbyterian mission Christianity coexists with Myal.

5. Cf. Patterson (1973:182–207) and Schuler (1979a:133).

6. Warsop is said to be the "Mocca" of Edith Clarke's (1953, 1966) classic study.

7. Throughout my early fieldwork Martha Brae's reputed Obeahman was known as "Prof," because he was said to "proform [perform] Science." He was of East Indian descent, an anomaly in Afro-Caribbean Martha Brae. He died shortly after the incident reported by Pastor Roberts, and his scientific work is said, by both the villagers and Prof's family, to be continued by one of his sons.

8. In his introduction to *Rastafari and Other African-Caribbean Worldviews*, Barry Chevannes (1995d:xvi) defines his concept of "worldview." My own use of worldview

is consistent with that of Chevannes (cosmology, ethics, meaning, and symbols) but also, like Thoden van Velzen's (1995:196), includes "ideology" (see n. 3 above).

9. In his early fieldwork Chevannes (1978:7) found that "meaning is attached to each colour: yellow brings on the Spirit, green is for healing, white for purity, blue for prosperity and red for the blood of Jesus and for cutting and clearing evil spirits." In Trelawny, the predominant Revival colors are red and white (with blue as a subsidiary theme), but in 1995 yellow was emphasized in the decorations for the Jacksons' tabernacle during the Revival convention in Martha Brae.

10. Chevannes (1995b:272) defines "croton" as a "shrub, symbolic of the prophet Jeremiah, believed to keep duppies [shadows] in their graves."

11. The "sankeys" derive "from the collection of *Sacred Songs and Solos* by Ira Sankey" (Chevannes 1978:9).

12. The "Rastaman" is said to have shaved off his dreadlocks, attended May's Revival service in Martha Brae and sought baptism, and to have reported that "he feel like a magnet moving his body" when he witnessed the reputed events in Falmouth.

13. Simpson (1957:330), in his classic account of the Jamaican Nine Night Ceremony, observed that "no spirit touches anything that is salted"; this would account for Revivalist practice. Interestingly, despite the Rastafarian rejection of the Revival spirit pantheon, Rastafarian I-tal food is salt-free. Chevannes (1995e:42 [n. 7]) suggests that the Rastafarian taboo against salt may derive from a prejudice against artificial things, and Trelawny Rastafari discussed their taboo on salt with me along similar lines. Here, however, there may be a link with or a reversal of Revivalist ideas.

14. Compare the changes in childbirth practices in relation to the house yard, discussed in chapter 6.

15. Cf. D. Hall (1989:185) on mortuary ritual during slavery. The use of rum, a prime plantation product, in Afro-creole mortuary ritual reflects the significance of the Caribbean context.

16. Return and circulatory migration in relation to such funerary ritual is an increasing practice in Jamaica, as Chevannes found for urban Kingston (see Besson and Chevannes 1996:219, 222).

17. Cf. Beckwith (1929:76). In 1994 in London, a Jamaican migrant told me that similar practices had recently been observed for a deceased parent in the parish of Clarendon, including the cutting of the corpse's Achilles tendons.

18. This elderly widower was not the man of the previous case.

19. Cf. Wardle (2000). Wardle's research in Papine, Kingston, highlights the geographic mobility that typifies modern mortuary ritual in Jamaica as friends and relatives move between Kingston and the countryside for such occasions.

20. There are two Granvilles in western Jamaica involved in the Martha Brae villagers' Revival networking: the neighboring free village in Trelawny and Granville in St. James, a few miles inland from Montego Bay.

21. One male villager commented to me that the event prophesied by Mother

Chisolm had already come to pass. The reputed incident involved elements of both Pukumina and Rastafari.

22. Cf. Beckwith (1929), Abrahams (1983), and Wilson (1995).

23. In 1914 Garvey founded the international Universal Negro Improvement Association (UNIA) in Kingston after traveling in Central America, the Caribbean, and Europe from 1910 to 1914. In 1916 he migrated to the United States, from which he was deported in 1927. He returned to Jamaica from 1927 to 1935, then migrated to London, where he died in 1940.

24. See, e.g., L. E. Barrett (1988), Chevannes (1994, 1995i), Savishinsky (1994), and Besson (1998c).

25. On the symbolic significance of salt in Revival and the possible reversal in Rastafari, see n. 13 above.

26. See also Besson (1995f) and Chevannes (1995e).

27. Cf. L. E. Barrett (1988:210–12, 249–54).

28. See also Seaga (1982:4). Seaga's statistics on membership of Revival cults in "Kingston and Suburbs" and the "Rest of Jamaica" showed a predominance of both Pukumina and Zion membership on the rest of the island (a larger area and mainly rural) compared to urban and suburban Kingston.

Chapter Eight

1. As discussed later in this chapter, the concepts of extraresidential relations and consensual cohabitation, in contrast to legal marriage, derive from Michael Smith (1962b).

2. Laslett (1980:xi), in the preface to his collection (with Karla Oosterveen and Richard Smith) on the comparative history of bastardy, wrote of Hartley's (1980) essay: "Jamaica is included here for an entirely persuasive reason. This is that the proportion of births outside marriage in that country is now, and as Susan Hartley shows in her chapter, has been as far back as the issue can be studied, the highest in the world."

3. Cf. Herskovits and Herskovits (1947:293).

4. See Mintz and Price (1992:62–64). For an early review of this debate and other explanations of the Caribbean family system, see Besson (1974:chap. 2, "West Indian Family Structure: The History of a Controversy," 1:36–107). The debate has continued for a quarter of a century.

5. Edith Clarke (1953, 1966) distinguished these concepts. Raymond Smith (1956) used the term "common-law marriage" for concubinage. Fernando Henriques (1968:109–17) observed that households based on cohabiting unions included "Faithful Concubinage" and the temporary "Keeper Family." Cf. T. S. Simey (1946).

6. The low incidence of consensual cohabitation in Carriacou was attributed to its ambiguous and inconsistent status in relation to "the mating, familial, and [patrilin-

eal] descent systems of Carriacou, . . . with its ritual order" (M. G. Smith 1962a:221). For a fuller discussion of this point, see ibid:216–21.

7. See also Mintz (1989:xviii).

8. Compare my critique of Burton (1999) in chapter 1.

9. See also Barrow (1996).

10. Besson (1979, 1987b, 1989b, 1990, 1995d).

11. See also Besson (1995b, 1999b).

12. See Fox (1967:175–239).

13. Cf. Gutman (1987:360).

14. Morris Freilich (1961), in his analysis of the conjugal patterns of an Afro-Trinidadian peasantry, used the term "serial polygyny" to refer to the widespread characteristic of individuals having *concurrent* unions: Mr. X visiting Mrs. Y while Mr. Y is out visiting Mrs. Z, leaving Mrs. X free to be visited by Mr. Z, etc. My use of "serial polygamy" differs in two respects: it recognizes the high commitment to monogamous relations in any specific marriage (and therefore the truly serial nature of marriages) among the Afro-Jamaican peasantry, and it reflects gender equality in initiating and terminating conjugal unions.

15. Cf. Gutman (1987).

16. It is perhaps this complexity at the empirical level that led to the classic disagreement between Blake (1961) and Roberts (1955) as to the nature of the typical overall "lower class" Jamaican conjugal career.

17. Such bilateral kinship networks tend to dissolve on the death of the individual.

18. See Fox (1967:164–73).

19. Negative rules for sex (an incest prohibition) and marriage (an exogamous or outmarrying rule), though closely linked, may not entirely coincide; that is, it may not be regarded as incestuous to have sexual relations with some persons whom one should not marry.

20. This was the case throughout my fieldwork from 1968 to 1999. However, when I was updating the genealogy of an elderly villager in August 2000, I stumbled on one exception that underlined the rule. Puzzled by the apparent cousinship of her eldest maternal half sister's parents, I assumed I was mistaken and sought clarification. She assured me that I was correct and explained that her late mother, although from a Martha Brae Old Family, did not grow up in the village, but moved there at age twenty-one. It was only after the mother conceived her first child in Martha Brae that she discovered that the baby's father was her first cousin once removed (mother's father's brother's son), or, as the elderly villager put it, "my mother was to call" the baby-father's father "granduncle," so the baby's parents were "two first cousins" and "my mother stopped having children with him."

21. Cf. Gutman (1987).

22. Maine (1861); McLennan (1865); H. L. Morgan (1871).

23. E.g., Malinowski (1913, 1929), Evans-Pritchard (1940), Fortes (1945), and Radcliffe-Brown and Forde (1950).

24. Cognatic descent is traced from an ancestor or ancestress through both males and females and incorporates both women and men. In contrast to ego-focused bilateral kinship, such relations of descent tend to endure in perpetuity. A cognatic descent construct may generate not only cognatic family lines, but also cognatic descent groups or corporations when these family lines hold corporate property, such as family land, reflecting the spatial dimension of the descent line.

25. Such groups can serve as the basis for allocating rights and duties, and for territorial, residential, political, and religious activities.

26. Cf. Webster (1975, 1998) on the contemporary Maori.

27. Cf. Du Boulay (1974:139, 250); Du Boulay and Williams (1987).

28. Cf. Bohannan (1967:59–60).

29. Cf. E. Clarke (1953, 1966).

30. See Fox (1967:147–56), and cf. Webster (1975, 1998).

31. Steven Webster (1975:139) noted a similar dictum among the contemporary Maori who say that their ancestral land, which is based on unrestricted cognatic descent, provides "standing place for the feet."

32. See Mathurin (1967:1–2), Emmer (1995:286), Lowenthal (1972:104), and Craton (1987:107).

33. See Besson (1979:105, 115 [n. 24], 1984a:73, 82 [n. 95], 1987b, 1988, 2001a). My defense of family land, in relation to sustainable development and hidden history, predates Christine Barrow's (1992) and Michaeline Crichlow's (1994) subsequent critiques of Eurocentric perspectives (see Rubenstein 1994 and Besson 1995a). On the substantivist viewpoint, see Sahlins (1972).

34. Besson (1979, 1984a, 1987b, 1988, 1995d).

35. As Lesley McKay (1987) found in Negril, on the border of the parishes of Westmoreland and Hanover, with the transformation of family land from an agricultural to a commercial resource in the context of tourism.

36. Cf. Fox (1967:259, 256).

37. See Davenport (1961a, 1961b), Mintz (1971a:39), Marks (1976:12–13), MacDonald and MacDonald (1978:7), Olwig (1985), Rubenstein (1987a:221), and R. T. Smith (1988, 1996:27–28). Cf. Barrow (1996) and E. Clarke (1966, republished 1999).

38. Cf. R. T. Smith (1996:28). As Goodenough (1955) observed, the concept of the kindred had been used for all kin groups that utilized both genders.

39. Davenport (1961a:449–50) hypothesized that patrilineal innovations, consolidation of shares, and division and conversion into fee simple holdings could serve as restricting mechanisms. He concluded, however, that "so far" the "limiting mechanism in the case of Jamaican family land has not been discovered" (449).

40. Cf. R. T. Smith (1996:27–28).

41. Otterbein's (1964) comparative discussion was based on his own Bahamian data, Greenfield's (1960) work on Barbados, and E. Clarke's (1953) Jamaican study.

42. This intense land scarcity resulted from the highest population density in the Caribbean region (Otterbein 1964:36, 38, quoting Greenfield 1960:166).

43. Besson (1974, 1975, 1979, 1984b, 1987a, 1988).

44. In the case of Trinidad, pronounced urbanization contributes to land scarcity.

45. Robert Dirks (1972:571) identified cognatic descent groups holding family land in the Afro-Caribbean community of Rum Bay in Tortola, arguing that rights to such land were validated by maintaining residence. This initially suggested restricted groups. However, Dirks went on to state that absentee migrants protected their land rights through cash remittances (572), thereby indicating the dispersed and unrestricted nature of the landholding descent group. For a reassessment of Bill Maurer's (1997b) analysis on landholding kin groups in the British Virgin Islands, see Besson (1999c) and chapter 1.

46. For more detailed analyses of unrestricted cognatic landholding kin groups throughout the Caribbean, see Besson (1987b, 1992a, 1995b, 1995d, 1997, 2000, 2001a, 2002). See also chapter 3.

47. Besson (1987b, 1992a, 1995b, 1995d, 2000, 2001a).

48. Price (1975, 1976, 1996); Kobben (1996); Thoden van Velzen and van Wettering (1988:9); Bilby (1989); Hoogbergen (1989); Vernon (1989:209); Mintz and Price (1992:69). Mintz and Price (1992) suggest that "the reasons why uterine [matrilineal] rather than agnatic [patrilineal] descent was chosen" to consolidate corporate communities based on restricted unilineal descent among the Saramaka Maroons were "the great preponderance of men over women among the runaways, as well as the likely prevalence of the uterine principle in those African societies from which these people came" (100 [n. 17], see also p. 69).

49. See, e.g., Radcliffe-Brown (1950:43) for the contention that unilineal systems are necessary for social order in kin-based societies; Solien (1959) and Leach (1960:117) for arguments that nonunilineal/cognatic systems must be restricted; and Besson (1979, 1987b) for fuller discussions of these issues.

Chapter Nine

1. Firth (1963a); Fox (1967); Caplan (1969); Hanson (1971); Hoben (1973); Holy (1996); Parkin (1997); Webster (1975, 1998); Stone (2000).

2. See Forde (1946), Goodenough (1955, 1956), Frake (1956), Worsley (1956), Davenport (1959), Barnes (1962), Meggitt (1965), Allen (1971), and Holy (1996).

3. Otterbein's use of "ambilineal" to refer to descent (through either parent) in restricted nonunilineal descent groups or "ramages" and "bilateral descent" for membership (through both parents) in unrestricted ancestor-focused kin groups was part of the profusion of terms that characterized the initial study of nonunilineal descent systems (see, e.g., Firth 1957, 1963a, Scheffler 1965, and Otterbein's article itself). The use of "bilateral" (which inconsistently referred to both the descent line and the mode of affiliation to descent groups) is more appropriately confined to ego-focused kindreds or kinship networks, rather than to ancestor-oriented kin groups.

4. Otterbein (1964:36) concluded that Jamaica was now typified by "ramages with

ambilineal descent of the exclusive type." For a more detailed critique of Otterbein (1964), see Besson (1979, 1987b).

5. On Otterbein's (1964, 1966) Bahamian study, see Besson (1992a:212 [n. 6]).

6. Cf. Maine (1861), Bohannan (1967:57), Fox (1967:162), Keesing (1975:140–41), and I. M. Lewis (1976:266–67).

7. These arguments beg the question of where to situate the Para case and suggest that the unrestricted cognatic landholding kin groups may have primacy to common land in the Para region of Suriname, at the heart of Dutch West Indian plantation society, in contrast to Guyana, which was the expanding frontier of the British Caribbean.

8. Cf. Hennessy (1993:4), Besson (1995d:93), and Rival (1999).

9. On such burial practices, see, e.g., Larose (1975) on Haiti; Olwig (1985:41) on St. John; Bilby (1989:147) on French Guiana; Tomich (1991:80) on Martinique; Mintz and Price (1992:68–70) on Suriname; and chapters 1, 3–5, including the detailed data, on Jamaica.

10. Hertz's point, however, appears to be borne out in the case of The Alps, Trelawny's first free village, where the postslavery family-land burial grounds contrast with the "cholera ground" where 150 slaves were reputedly buried in unmarked graves — thus remaining "invisible" in death as in life on The Alps slave plantation (chapter 3; Besson 1984b:18).

11. The information, given on the British television news in September 1997, that the queen does not usually attend funerals as she should not come into contact with death suggests an interesting parallel with the Rastafarian mortuary taboo and seems to symbolize the immortality of the "corporation sole" of the British monarchy — summed up in the saying "The King/Queen is dead, long live the King/Queen."

12. See Tonkin, McDonald, and Chapman (1989), Amit-Talai and Knowles (1996), Banks (1996), Holy (1996:6), and Lovejoy (2000) on the cultural construction of identities; Mintz (1989:xvi), Carrithers (1996), and Morris (1991, 1999) on the person and the self; S. Hall (1992), Gilroy (1993), Rapport and Dawson (1998), and Besson (2002) on transnational ethnicities; and Hill (1996) on ethnogenesis.

13. Cf. Besson and Momsen (1987), Escobar (1995), R. Chambers (1997), Purcell (1998), and ASA (2000). The theme of the conference of the Association of Social Anthropologists of the Commonwealth (ASA), held in London in April 2000, was "Participating in Development: Approaches to Indigenous Knowledge."

14. See, e.g., Besson (1999d) and Abramson and Theodossopoulos (2000).

15. Cf. Austin (1984), Gutman (1987), and Wolf (1997).

16. See Foucault (1978), Certeau (1980), Abu-Lughod (1990), and Burton (1997).

17. See also Olwig (1997, 1999) and Besson and Olwig (forthcoming).

REFERENCES

Abrahams, Roger D. 1983. *The Man-of-Words in the West Indies*. Baltimore: Johns Hopkins University Press.

Abramson, Allen, and Dimitris Theodossopoulos, eds. 2000. *Land, Law, and Environment: Mythical Land, Legal Boundaries*. London: Pluto Press.

Abu-Lughod, Lila. 1990. "The Romance of Resistance: Tracing Transformations of Power through Bedouin Women." *American Ethnologist* 17, no. 1:41–55.

Agbasiere, Joseph Thérèse. 2000. *Women in Ibo Life and Thought*. London: Routledge.

Allen, M. 1971. "Descent Groups and Ecology amongst the Nduindui, New Hebrides." In *Anthropology in Oceania: Essays Presented to Ian Hogbin*, edited by L. R. Hiatt and C. Jayawardena, 1–25. Sydney: Angus and Robertson.

Allen-Vassell, Marjorie, and Wintlett Browne. 1992. *Jamaica: A Junior Geography*. Kingston: Carib Publishing Ltd.

Alleyne, Mervyn. 1996. *Africa: Roots of Jamaican Culture*. 1988. Reprint, Chicago: Research Associates School Times Publications.

Amit, Vered, ed. 2000. *Constructing the Field: Ethnographic Fieldwork in the Contemporary World*. London: Routledge.

Amit-Talai, Vered, and Caroline Knowles, eds. 1996. *Resituating Identities: The Politics of Race, Ethnicity, and Culture*. Peterborough, Ontario: Broadview Press.

Ardener, Shirley, 1964. "The Comparative Study of Rotating Credit Associations." *Journal of the Royal Anthropological Institute* 94:201–29.

———. 1995. "Women Making Money Go Round: ROSCAs Revisited." In *Money-Go-Rounds: The Importance of Rotating Savings and Credit Associations for Women*, edited by Shirley Ardener and Sandra Burman, 1–19. Oxford: Berg.

Ardener, Shirley, and Sandra Burman, eds. 1995. *Money-Go-Rounds: The Importance of Rotating Savings and Credit Associations for Women*. Oxford: Berg.

Armstrong, Douglas V. 1990. *The Old Village and the Great House: An Archaeological and Historical Examination of Drax Hall Plantation, St. Ann's Bay, Jamaica*. Urbana: University of Illinois Press.

Asad, Talal, ed. 1973. *Anthropology and the Colonial Encounter*. Ithaca, N.Y.: Ithaca Press.

Association of Social Anthropologists of the Commonwealth (ASA). 2000. Proceedings, Conference on "Participating in Development Approaches to Indigenous Knowledge." London. April.

347

Austin, Diane J. 1984. *Urban Life in Kingston, Jamaica: The Culture and Class Ideology of Two Neighbourhoods*. New York: Gordon and Breach.

———. 1998. "Culture and Ideology in the English-Speaking Caribbean: A View from Jamaica." In *Blackness in Latin America and the Caribbean*, edited by Arlene Torres and Norman E. Whitten Jr., 2:436–59. Bloomington: Indiana University Press.

Banks, Marcus. 1996. *Ethnicity: Anthropological Constructions*. London: Routledge.

Barker, David, and Clinton Beckford. 1998. "Export Yam Production and the Yam Stick Trade in Jamaica: Integrated Problems for Planning and Resource Management." Paper presented at the Third British-Caribbean Seminar of the Royal Geographical Society and the Institute of British Geographers, "Resources, Planning, and Environmental Management in a Changing Caribbean," University of the West Indies, Mona, Jamaica, 8–15 July.

Barker, David, and David J. Miller. 1995. "Farming on the Fringe: Small-Scale Agriculture on the Edge of the Cockpit Country." In *Environment and Development in the Caribbean: Geographical Perspectives*, edited by David Barker and Duncan F. M. McGregor, 271–92. Kingston, Jamaica: University of the West Indies Press.

Barnes, J. A. 1962. "African Models in the New Guinea Highlands." *Man* 62:5–9.

Barrett, Leonard E. 1988. *The Rastafarians: Sounds of Cultural Dissonance*. Boston: Beacon Press.

Barrett, Robert Assheton. 2000. *The Barretts of Jamaica*. Winfield, Kans.: Wedgestone Press.

Barrow, Christine. 1986. "Finding the Support: A Study of Strategies for Survival." *Social and Economic Studies* 35, no. 2:131–76.

———. 1992. *Family Land and Development in St. Lucia*. Cave Hill, Barbados: Institute of Social and Economic Research (Eastern Caribbean), University of the West Indies.

———. 1996. *Family in the Caribbean: Themes and Perspectives*. Oxford: James Currey.

Bastide, Roger. 1972. *African Civilizations in the New World*. New York: Harper and Row.

Bastien, Rémy. 1961. "Haitian Rural Family Organization." *Social and Economic Studies* 10:478–510.

Baxter, Ivy. 1970. *The Arts of an Island*. Metuchen, N.J.: Scarecrow Press.

Beattie, John. 1964. *Other Cultures: Aims, Methods, and Achievements in Social Anthropology*. London: Routledge and Kegan Paul.

Beckford, George L. 1975. "Caribbean Rural Economy." In *Caribbean Economy*, edited by George L. Beckford. Kingston, Jamaica: Institute of Social and Economic Research, University of the West Indies.

———. 1999. *Persistent Poverty: Underdevelopment in Plantation Economies of the Third World*. 1972. 2d ed. Kingston, Jamaica: University of the West Indies Press.

Beckles, Hilary McD. 1988. *Afro-Caribbean Women and Resistance to Slavery in Barbados*. London: Karnak House.

———. 1989. *Natural Rebels: A Social History of Enslaved Black Women in Barbados*. London: Zed Books.

Beckwith, Martha. 1929. *Black Roadways: A Study of Jamaican Folk Life*. Chapel Hill: University of North Carolina Press.

Berleant-Schiller, Riva. 1977. "Production and Division of Labor in a West Indian Peasant Community." *American Ethnologist* 4:253–72.

———. 1978. "The Failure of Agricultural Development in Post-Emancipation Barbuda." *Boletín de Estudios Latinoamericanos y del Caribe* 25:21–36.

———. 1987. "Ecology and Politics in Barbudan Land Tenures." In *Land and Development in the Caribbean*, edited by Jean Besson and Janet Momsen, 116–31. London: Macmillan.

Berleant-Schiller, Riva, and Lydia M. Pulsipher. 1986. "Subsistence Cultivation in the Caribbean." *New West Indian Guide* 60:1–40.

Berlin, Ira. 1987. "Introduction: Herbert G. Gutman and the American Working Class." In *Power and Culture: Essays on the American Working Class, Herbert G. Gutman*, edited by Ira Berlin, 3–69. New York: New Press.

Besson, Jean. 1974. "Land Tenure and Kinship in a Jamaican Village." 2 vols. Ph.D. dissertation, University of Edinburgh.

———. 1975. "Land Tenure and Kinship in 'River Village,' Jamaica." Unpublished paper, University of Edinburgh.

———. 1979. "Symbolic Aspects of Land in the Caribbean: The Tenure and Transmission of Land Rights among Caribbean Peasantries." In *Peasants, Plantations, and Rural Communities in the Caribbean*, edited by Malcom Cross and Arnaud Marks, 86–116. Guildford: University of Surrey, England, and Leiden, Netherlands: Royal Institute of Linguistics and Anthropology.

———. 1984a. "Family Land and Caribbean Society: Toward an Ethnography of Afro-Caribbean Peasantries." In *Perspectives on Caribbean Regional Identity*, edited by Elizabeth M. Thomas-Hope, 57–83. Liverpool: Liverpool University Press.

———. 1984b. "Land Tenure in the Free Villages of Trelawny, Jamaica." *Slavery and Abolition* 5, no. 1:3–23.

———. 1987a. "Family Land as a Model for Martha Brae's New History." In *Afro-Caribbean Villages in Historical Perspective*, edited by Charles V. Carnegie, 100–132. Kingston, Jamaica: African-Caribbean Institute of Jamaica.

———. 1987b. "A Paradox in Caribbean Attitudes to Land." In *Land and Development in the Caribbean*, edited by Jean Besson and Janet Momsen, 13–45. London: Macmillan.

———. 1988. "Agrarian Relations and Perceptions of Land in a Jamaican Peasant Village." In *Small Farming and Peasant Resources in the Caribbean*, edited by John S. Brierley and Hymie Rubenstein, 39–61. Winnipeg, Canada: University of Manitoba.

———. 1989a. Introduction to *Caribbean Reflections: The Life and Times of a Trinidad Scholar, 1901–1986: An Oral History Narrated by William W. Besson*, edited by Jean Besson, 13–30. London: Karia Press.

———. 1989b. Review of *Cultural Adaptation and Resistance on St. John*, by Karen Fog Olwig. *Plantation Society in the Americas* 2, no. 3:345–48.

———. 1990. Review of *Kinship and Class in the West Indies*, by Raymond T. Smith. *Man* 25, no. 2:371.

———. 1992a. "Freedom and Community: The British West Indies." In *The Meaning of Freedom: Economics, Politics, and Culture after Slavery*, edited by Frank McGlynn and Seymour Drescher, 183–219. Pittsburgh, Pa.: University of Pittsburgh Press.

———. 1992b. "Oral Tradition in Caribbean Research: Case Studies from Jamaica, Trinidad, and Guyana." *OPReP Newsletter* No. 18 (June): 3–6. University of the West Indies, St. Augustine, Trinidad and Tobago.

———. 1993. "Reputation and Respectability Reconsidered: A New Perspective on Afro-Caribbean Peasant Women." In *Women and Change in the Caribbean: A Pan-Caribbean Perspective*, edited by Janet H. Momsen, 15–37. London: James Currey.

———. 1995a. "Consensus in the Family Land Controversy: Rejoinder to Michaeline A. Crichlow." *New West Indian Guide* 69, no. 3–4:299–304.

———. 1995b. "The Creolization of African-American Slave Kinship in Jamaican Free Village and Maroon Communities." In *Slave Cultures and the Cultures of Slavery*, edited by Stephan Palmié, 187–209. Knoxville: University of Tennessee Press.

———. 1995c. "Free Villagers, Rastafarians, and Modern Maroons: From Resistance to Identity." In *Born Out of Resistance: On Caribbean Cultural Creativity*, by Wim Hoogbergen, 301–14. Utrecht: ISOR Press.

———. 1995d. "Land, Kinship, and Community in the Post-Emancipation Caribbean: A Regional View of the Leewards." In *Small Islands, Large Questions: Society, Culture, and Resistance in the Post-Emancipation Caribbean*, edited by Karen Fog Olwig, 73–99. London: Frank Cass.

———. 1995e. "The Legacy of George L. Beckford's Plantation Economy Thesis in Jamaica." Review of *Plantation Economy, Land Reform, and the Peasantry in a Historical Perspective, Jamaica, 1838–1980*, edited by Claus Stolberg and Swithin Wilmot. *New West Indian Guide* 69, no. 1–2:111–19.

———. 1995f. "Religion as Resistance in Jamaican Peasant Life: The Baptist Church, Revival Worldview, and Rastafarian Movement." In *Rastafari and Other African-Caribbean Worldviews*, edited by Barry Chevannes, 43–76. London: Macmillan.

———. 1995g. "Women's Use of ROSCAs in the Caribbean: Reassessing the Literature." In *Money-Go-Rounds: The Importance of Rotating Savings and Credit Associations for Women*, edited by Shirley Ardener and Sandra Burman, 263–88. Oxford: Berg.

———. 1997. "Caribbean Common Tenures and Capitalism: The Accompong Maroons of Jamaica." In *Common Land in the Caribbean and Mesoamerica*, edited by Bill Maurer, Special Issue, *Plantation Society in the Americas* 4, no. 2–3: 201–32.

———. 1998a. "Changing Perceptions of Gender in the Caribbean Region: The Case of the Jamaican Peasantry." In *Caribbean Portraits: Essays in Gender Ideologies and Identities*, edited by Christine Barrow, 133–55. Kingston, Jamaica: Ian Randle.

———. 1998b. "Gender and Development in the Jamaican Small-Scale Marketing System: From the 1660s to the Millennium and Beyond." Paper presented at the Third British-Caribbean Seminar of the Royal Geographical Society and the Institute of British Geographers, "Resources, Planning, and Environmental Management in a Changing Caribbean," University of the West Indies, Mona, Jamaica, 8–15 July.

———. 1998c. Review of *Rastafari: Roots and Ideology*, by Barry Chevannes. *Journal of the Royal Anthropological Institute* 4, no. 1:169.

———. 1999a. "Folk Law and Legal Pluralism in Jamaica: A View from the Plantation-Peasant Interface." *Journal of Legal Pluralism and Unofficial Law* 43:31–56.

———. 1999b. "Hidden Histories of the African Diaspora: Kinship and Temporality in Transnational Jamaica." Paper presented at the *Kinship and Temporality Workshop*, Goldsmiths College, University of London, 16–18 December.

———. 1999c. Review of *Recharting the Caribbean: Land, Law, and Citizenship in the British Virgin Islands*, by Bill Maurer. *Journal of the Royal Anthropological Institute* 5, no. 3:506–7.

———. 2000. "The Appropriation of Lands of Law by Lands of Myth in the Caribbean Region." In *Land, Law, and Environment: Mythical Land, Legal Boundaries*, edited by Allen Abramson and Dimitris Theodossopoulos. London: Pluto Press.

———. 2001a. "Empowering and Engendering Hidden Histories in Caribbean Peasant Communities." In *History and Histories in the Caribbean*, edited by Thomas Bremer and Ulrich Fleischmann, 69–113. Madrid: Iberoamericana; Frankfurt am Main: Vervuert.

———. 2001b. "Euro-Creole, Afro-Creole, Meso-Creole: Creolization and Ethnic Identities in West-Central Jamaica." In *Creolization and Creole Identities*, edited by Gordon Collier and Ulrich Fleischmann. Amsterdam: Rodopi Publications.

———. 2001c. "Sacred Sites, Shifting Histories: Narratives, Land, and Globalization in the Cockpit Country, Jamaica." Paper presented at the workshop, "Caribbean Narratives of Belonging: Fields of Relations, Sites of Identity," Goldsmiths College, University of London, 9–10 April.

———. 2002. "Land, Territory, and Identity in the Deterritorialized, Transnational Caribbean." In *Land and Territoriality*, edited by Michael Saltman, 175–208. Oxford: Berg.

———. Forthcoming. *Maroon Town at the Millennium: Transformations of Freedom.*

Besson, Jean, and Barry Chevannes. 1996. "The Continuity-Creativity Debate: The Case of Revival." *New West Indian Guide* 70, no. 3–4:209–28.

Besson, Jean, and Ian McFarlane. 1995. "The Jamaican McFarlanes and Related Families." Unpublished paper, London.

Besson, Jean, and Janet Momsen. 1987. Introduction to *Land and Development in the Caribbean*, edited by Jean Besson and Janet Momsen, 1–9. London: Macmillan.

Besson, Jean, and Karen Fog Olwig, eds. Forthcoming. *Caribbean Narratives of Belonging: Fields of Relations, Sites of Identity.*

Bilby, Kenneth M. 1984. "The Treacherous Feast: A Jamaican Maroon Historical Myth." *Bijdragen tot de Taal, Land- en Volkenkunde* 140:1–31.

———. 1989. "Divided Loyalties: Local Politics and the Play of States among the Aluku." *New West Indian Guide* 63, no. 3–4:143–73.

———. 1993. "The Strange Career of 'Obeah': Defining Magical Power in the West

Indies." Paper presented at the General Seminar, Institute for Global Studies in Culture, Power, and History, Johns Hopkins University, Fall.

——. 1996. "Ethnogenesis in the Guianas and Jamaica: Two Maroon Cases." In *History, Power, and Identity: Ethnogenesis in the Americas, 1492–1992*, edited by Jonathan D. Hill, 119–41. Iowa City: University of Iowa Press.

——. 1999. "Gumbay, Myal, and the Great House: New Evidence on the Religious Background of Jonkonnu in Jamaica." In *African Caribbean Research Review* No. 4, 47–70. Kingston, Jamaica: African Caribbean Institute of Jamaica.

Black, Clinton V. 1979. "Falmouth: Cradle of the Abolition of Slavery." *Daily Gleaner Supplement*, vi–vii. Kingston, Jamaica, 29 August.

——. 1984. *The History of Montego Bay*. Jamaica: Montego Bay Chamber of Commerce.

Blackburn, Robin. 1997. *The Making of New World Slavery: From the Baroque to the Modern, 1492–1800*. London: Verso.

Blain, Douglas. 1989. "Falmouth in Peril: 'An Almost Unspoilt Town.'" In *Georgian Group Annual Report, 1989*. London: Georgian Group.

Blake, Judith. 1961. *Family Structure in Jamaica*. New York: Glencoe.

Bloch, Maurice. 1971. *Placing the Dead: Tombs, Ancestral Villages, and Kinship Organization in Madagascar*. London: Seminar Press.

Bloch, Maurice, and Jonathan Parry. 1982. Introduction to *Death and the Regeneration of Life*, edited by Maurice Bloch and Jonathan Parry, 1–44. Cambridge: Cambridge University Press.

Bohannan, Paul. 1967. "Africa's Land." In *Tribal and Peasant Economies*, edited by George Dalton, 51–60. Garden City, N.Y.: Natural History Press.

Bohannan, Paul, and George Dalton. 1962. Introduction to *Markets in Africa*. Evanston: Northwestern University Press.

Bolland, O. Nigel. 1981. "Systems of Domination after Slavery: The Control of Land and Labor in the British West Indies after 1838." *Comparative Studies in Society and History* 23:591–619.

——. 1992. "Creolization and Creole Societies: A Cultural Nationalist View of Caribbean Social History." In *Intellectuals in the Twentieth Century*, vol. 1, edited by Alistair Hennessy, 50–79. London: Macmillan.

Braithwaite, Lloyd. 1975. *Social Stratification in Trinidad*. 1953. Reprint, Kingston, Jamaica: Institute of Social and Economic Studies, University of the West Indies.

Brana-Shute, Rosemary. 1993. "Neighbourhood Networks and National Politics among Working-Class Afro-Surinamese Women." In *Women and Change in the Caribbean: A Pan-Caribbean Perspective*, edited by Janet H. Momsen, 132–49. London: James Currey.

Brathwaite, Edward. 1971. *The Development of Creole Society in Jamaica, 1770–1820*. Oxford: Clarendon Press.

Brereton, Bridget. 1981. *A History of Modern Trinidad, 1783–1962*. London: Heinemann.

——. 1999. "Family Strategies, Gender, and the Shift to Wage Labour in the British

Caribbean." In *The Colonial Caribbean in Transition: Essays on Postemancipation Social and Cultural History*, edited by Bridget Brereton and Kevin A. Yelvington, 77–107. Gainesville: University Press of Florida.

Brierley, John S. 1987. "Land Fragmentation and Land-Use Patterns in Grenada." In *Land and Development in the Caribbean*, edited by Jean Besson and Janet Momsen, 194–209. London: Macmillan.

———. 1991. "Kitchen Gardens in the Caribbean, Past and Present: Their Role in Small Farm Development." *Caribbean Geography* 3, no. 1:15–28.

British House of Commons. 1842. Select Committee on the West India Colonies, 1842. [London].

Brodber, Erna. 1983. "Oral Sources and the Creation of a Social History of the Caribbean." *Jamaica Journal* 16, no. 4:2–11.

Burnard, Trevor. 1996. "Who Bought Slaves in Early America? Purchasers of Slaves from the Royal African Company in Jamaica, 1674–1708." *Slavery and Abolition* 17, no. 2:68–92.

Burton, Richard D. E. 1997. *Afro-Creole: Power, Opposition, and Play in the Caribbean*. Ithaca, N.Y.: Cornell University Press.

———. 1999. "Names and Naming in Afro-Caribbean Cultures." *New West Indian Guide* 73, no. 1–2:35–58.

Bush, Barbara. 1985. "Towards Emancipation: Slave Women and Resistance to Coercive Labour Regimes in the British West Indian Colonies, 1790–1838." In *Abolition and Its Aftermath: The Historical Context, 1790–1916*, edited by David Richardson, 27–54. London: Frank Cass.

———. 1990. *Slave Women in Caribbean Society, 1650–1838*. London: James Currey.

Campbell, Horace. 1980. "Rastafari: Culture of Resistance." *Race and Class* 22, no. 1:1–22.

———. 1985. *Rasta and Resistance: From Marcus Garvey to Walter Rodney*. London: Hansib.

Caplan, Patricia. 1969. "Cognatic Descent Groups on Mafia Island, Tanzania." *Man* 4, no. 3:419–31.

———. 1995. *Understanding Disputes: The Politics of Argument*. Oxford: Berg.

Caputo, Virginia. 2000. "At 'Home' and 'Away': Reconfiguring the Field for Late-Twentieth-Century Anthropology." In *Constructing the Field: Ethnographic Fieldwork in the Contemporary World*, edited by Vered Amit, 19–31. London: Routledge.

Caribbean Escapes. 1996. Travel brochure. London: Caribtours.

Caribbean Eye Exhibition. 1997. London: Commonwealth Institute.

Carnegie, Charles V. 1987. "Is Family Land an Institution?" In *Afro-Caribbean Villages in Historical Perspective*, edited by Charles V. Carnegie, 83–99. Kingston: African-Caribbean Institute of Jamaica, Research Review No. 2.

Carrithers, Michael. 1996. "Person." In *Encyclopedia of Social and Cultural Anthropology*, edited by Alan Barnard and Jonathan Spencer, 419–23. London: Routledge.

Carsten, Janet. 2000. *Cultures of Relatedness: New Approaches to the Study of Kinship*. Cambridge: Cambridge University Press.

Certeau, Michael de. 1980. "On the Oppositional Practices of Everyday Life." *Social Text* 3:3–43.

Chace, Russel E., Jr. 1984. "The Emergence and Development of an Estate-Based Peasantry in Dominica." Paper presented at the Eighth Annual Conference of the Society for Caribbean Studies, Hoddesdon, Hertfordshire, May.

Chamberlain, Mary, ed. 1998. *Caribbean Migration: Globalised Identities*. London: Routledge.

Chambers, Douglas B. 1997. " 'My Own Nation': Igbo Exiles in the Diaspora." In *Routes to Slavery: Direction, Ethnicity, and Mortality in the Atlantic Slave Trade*, edited by David Eltis and David Richardson, 72–97. London: Frank Cass.

Chambers, Robert. 1997. *Whose Reality Counts? Putting the First Last*. London: Intermediate Technology Publications.

Chambers 20th Century Dictionary. 1983. Edited by M. Kirkpatrick. New ed. Edinburgh: W. and R. Chambers.

Chevannes, Barry. 1978. "Revivalism: A Disappearing Religion." *Caribbean Quarterly* 24, no. 3–4:1–17.

———. 1990. "Rastafari: Towards a New Approach." *New West Indian Guide* 64:127–48.

———. 1994. *Rastafari: Roots and Ideology*. Syracuse, N.Y.: Syracuse University Press.

———. 1995a. Afterword to *Rastafari and Other African-Caribbean Worldviews*, edited by Barry Chevannes, 253–56. London: Macmillan.

———. 1995b. Glossary in *Rastafari and Other African-Caribbean Worldviews*, edited by Barry Chevannes, 272–76. London: Macmillan.

———. 1995c. "Introducing the Native Religions of Jamaica." In *Rastafari and Other African-Caribbean Worldviews*, edited by Barry Chevannes, 1–19. London: Macmillan.

———. 1995d. Introduction to *Rastafari and Other African-Caribbean Worldviews*, edited by Barry Chevannes, xv–xxv. London: Macmillan.

———. 1995e. "New Approach to Rastafari." In *Rastafari and Other African-Caribbean Worldviews*, edited by Barry Chevannes, 20–42. London: Macmillan.

———. 1995f. "The Origin of the Dreadlocks." In *Rastafari and Other African-Caribbean Worldviews*, edited by Barry Chevannes, 77–96. London: Macmillan.

———. 1995g. "The Phallus and the Outcast: The Symbolism of the Dreadlocks in Jamaica." In *Rastafari and Other African-Caribbean Worldviews*, edited by Barry Chevannes, 97–126. London: Macmillan.

———. 1995h. "Revivalism and Identity." In *Born Out of Resistance: On Caribbean Cultural Creativity*, edited by Wim Hoogbergen, 245–52. Utrecht: ISOR Press.

———, ed. 1995i. *Rastafari and Other African-Caribbean Worldviews*. London: Macmillan.

Clarke, Colin G. 1973. "The Slums of Kingston." In *Work and Family Life: West Indian Perspectives*, edited by Lambros Comitas and David Lowenthal, 175–87. Garden City, N.Y.: Anchor Press/Doubleday.

Clarke, Edith. 1953. "Land Tenure and the Family in Four Selected Communities in Jamaica." *Social and Economic Studies* 1, no. 4:81–118.

———. 1966. *My Mother Who Fathered Me: A Study of the Family in Three Selected Communities in Jamaica*. 1957. 2d ed. London: George Allen and Unwin.

Colonial Standard, 27 August 1870.

Comitas, Lambros. 1962. "Fishermen and Co-operation in Rural Jamaica." Ph.D. dissertation, Columbia University.

———. 1973. "Occupational Multiplicity in Rural Jamaica." In *Work and Family Life: West Indian Perspectives*, edited by Lambros Comitas and David Lowenthal, 157–73. Garden City, N.Y.: Anchor Press/Doubleday.

Concannon, T. A. L. 1970. "Introduction: Jamaica's Architectural Heritage." In *Falmouth, 1791–1970*, 4–5. Georgian Society of Jamaica.

Craton, Michael J. 1971. "Jamaican Slave Mortality: Fresh Light from Worthy Park, Longville, and the Tharp Estates." *Journal of Caribbean History* 3:1–27.

———. 1978. *Searching for the Invisible Man: Slaves and Plantation Life in Jamaica*. Cambridge: Harvard University Press.

———. 1982. *Testing the Chains: Resistance to Slavery in the British West Indies*. Ithaca, N.Y.: Cornell University Press.

———. 1987. "White Law and Black Custom: The Evolution of Bahamian Land Tenures." In *Land and Development in the Caribbean*, edited by Jean Besson and Janet Momsen, 88–114. London: Macmillan.

———. 1994. "Reshuffling the Pack: The Transition from Slavery to Other Forms of Labor in the British Caribbean, ca. 1790–1890." *New West Indian Guide* 68, no. 1–2:23–75.

———. 1997. "Property and Propriety: Land Tenure and Slave Property in the Creation of a British West Indian Plantocracy, 1612–1740." In *Empire, Enslavement, and Freedom in the Caribbean*, Michael Craton, 68–103. Kingston, Jamaica: Ian Randle.

Craton, Michael, and D. Gail Saunders. 1991. "Seeking a Life of Their Own: Aspects of Slave Resistance in the Bahamas." *Journal of Caribbean History* 24, no. 1:1–27.

Crichlow, Michaeline A. 1994. "An Alternative Approach to Family Land Tenure in the Anglophone Caribbean: The Case of St. Lucia." *New West Indian Guide* 68, no. 1–2:77–99.

———. 1995. "Reply to Jean Besson." *New West Indian Guide* 69, no. 3–4:305–8.

Cross, Malcolm. 1979. *Urbanization and Urban Growth in the Caribbean*. Cambridge: Cambridge University Press.

Cundall, Frank. 1937. *The Governors of Jamaica in the First Half of the Eighteenth Century*. London: West India Committee.

Curtin, Marguerite, ed. 1991. *Jamaica's Heritage: An Untapped Resource*. Kingston: Mill Press.

Curtin, Philip. 1970. *Two Jamaicas: The Role of Ideas in a Tropical Colony, 1830–1865*. 1955. Reprint, New York: Atheneum.

Dadzie, Stella. 1990. "Searching for the Invisible Woman: Slavery and Resistance in Jamaica." *Race and Class* 32, no. 2:21–38.

Dalton, George. 1967. "Primitive Money." In *Tribal and Peasant Economies*, edited by George Dalton, 254–81. Garden City, N.Y.: Natural History Press.

——. 1971. "Peasantries in Anthropology and History." In *Economic Anthropology and Development*, edited by George Dalton, 217–66. New York: Basic Books

Davenport, William. 1959. "Nonunilinear Descent and Descent Groups." *American Anthropologist* 61, no. 4:557–72.

——. 1961a. "The Family System of Jamaica." *Social and Economic Studies* 10, no. 4:420–54.

——. 1961b. Introduction to *Social and Economic Studies* 10, no. 4:380–85.

de Albuquerque, Klaus. 1980. "Rastafarianism and Cultural Identity in the Caribbean." *Revista/Review Interamericana* 10, no. 2:230–47.

Debien, Gabriel. 1996. "Marronage in the French Caribbean." In *Maroon Societies: Rebel Slave Communities in the Americas*, edited by Richard Price, 107–34. 1973, 1979. 3d ed. Baltimore: Johns Hopkins University Press.

Deeds. 1842. Island Record Office, 851 folio 97, Spanish Town, Jamaica. 12 July.

Dilley, Roy, ed. 1992. *Contesting Markets: Analyses of Ideology, Discourse, and Practice*. Edinburgh: University Press.

Dirks, Robert. 1972. "Networks, Groups, and Adaptation in an Afro-Caribbean Community." *Man*, n.s., 7, no. 4:565–85.

Du Boulay, Juliet. 1974. *Portrait of a Greek Mountain Village*. Oxford: Oxford University Press.

Du Boulay, Juliet, and Rory Williams. 1987. "Amoral Familism and the Image of Limited Good." *Anthropological Quarterly* 60, no. 1:12–24.

Dunn, Richard S. 2000. *Sugar and Slaves: The Rise of the Planter Class in the English West Indies, 1624–1713*. 1973. Reprint, Kingston, Jamaica: University of the West Indies Press.

Edwards, Bryan. 1793. *The History, Civil and Commercial, of the British Colonies in the West Indies*, 2 vols. London: John Stockdale.

Eltis, David. 2000. *The Rise of African Slavery in the Americas*. Cambridge: Cambridge University Press.

Eltis, David, Stephen D. Behrendt, David Richardson, and Herbert S. Klein. 1999. *The Trans-Atlantic Slave Trade: A Database on CD-Rom*. Cambridge: Cambridge University Press.

Eltis, David, and David Richardson. 1997a. "The 'Numbers Game' and Routes to Slavery." In *Routes to Slavery: Direction, Ethnicity, and Mortality in the Atlantic Slave Trade*, edited by David Eltis and David Richardson, 1–15. London: Frank Cass.

——. 1997b. "West Africa and the Transatlantic Slave Trade: New Evidence of Long-Run Trends." In *Routes to Slavery: Direction, Ethnicity, and Mortality in the Atlantic Slave Trade*, edited by David Eltis and David Richardson, 16–35. London: Frank Cass.

Emmer, Pieter C. 1995. "Scholarship or Solidarity? The Post-Emancipation Era in the Caribbean Reconsidered." *New West Indian Guide* 69, no. 3–4:277–90.

"The End of an Era." 1986. *Daily Gleaner*, Kingston, Jamaica, October.

Escobar, Arturo. 1995. *Encountering Development: The Making and Unmaking of the Third World*. Princeton, N.J.: Princeton University Press.

Espeut, Peter. 1992. "Land Reform and the Family Land Debate." In *Plantation Economy, Land Reform, and the Peasantry in a Historical Perspective: Jamaica, 1838–1980*, edited by Claus Stolberg and Swithin Wilmot, 69–84. Kingston: Friedrich Ebert Stiftung.

Evans-Pritchard, E. E. 1940. *The Nuer*. Oxford: Oxford University Press.

Eyre, L. Alan. 1995. "The Cockpit Country: A World Heritage Site?" In *Environment and Development in the Caribbean*, edited by David Barker and Duncan F. M. McGregor, 259–70. Kingston, Jamaica: University of the West Indies Press.

Falmouth Post. 1835–40. Falmouth, Jamaica, selected articles.

Farley, Rawle. 1964. "The Rise of Village Settlements in British Guiana." *Caribbean Quarterly* 10, no. 1:52–61.

Farmers' Register, 1988. 1991. Kingston: Ministry of Agriculture, Data Bank and Evaluation Division.

Feher-Elston, Catherine. 1988. *Children of Sacred Ground: America's Last Indian War*. Flagstaff, Ariz.: Northland.

Finkel, Herman J. 1971. "Patterns of Land Tenure in the Leeward and Windward Islands." In *Peoples and Cultures of the Caribbean*, edited by Michael M. Horowitz, 291–304. Garden City, N.Y.: Natural History Press.

Firth, Raymond. 1957. "A Note on Descent Groups in Polynesia." *Man* 57, no. 2:4–8.

———. 1963a. "Bilateral Descent Groups: An Operational Viewpoint." In *Studies in Kinship and Marriage*, edited by Isaac Schapera, R.A.I. Occasional Paper No. 16, 22–37. London: Royal Anthropological Institute.

———. 1963b. *We, the Tikopia: Kinship in Primitive Polynesia*. 1936. Reprint, Boston: Beacon Press.

———. 1971. *Elements of Social Organization*. 1951. Reprint, London: Tavistock.

Floyd, Barry. 1979. *Jamaica: An Island Microcosm*. London: Macmillan.

Foner, Nancy. 1977. "The Jamaicans: Cultural and Social Change among Migrants in Britain." In *Between Two Cultures: Migrants and Minorities in Britain*, edited by James L. Watson, 120–50. Oxford: Basil Blackwell.

Ford, Joseph C., and Frank Cundall. 1910. *The Handbook of Jamaica*. London.

Forde, C. Daryll. 1946. "The Anthropological Approach to Social Science." *Advancement of Science*, 213–24.

Fortes, Meyer. 1945. *The Dynamics of Clanship among the Tallensi*. Oxford: University Press.

———. 1949. "Time and Social Structure: An Ashanti Case Study." In *Social Structure: Essays Presented to A. R. Radcliffe-Brown*, by Meyer Fortes, 1–32. Oxford: Oxford University Press.

———. 1969. *Kinship and the Social Order: The Legacy of Lewis Henry Morgan*. London: Routledge and Kegan Paul.

Foucault, Michel. 1978. *The History of Sexuality*. Vol. 1, trans. Robert Hurley. London: Allen Lane.

Fox, Robin. 1966. "Kinship and Land Tenure on Tory Island." *Ulster Folk Life* 12:1–17.

——. 1967. *Kinship and Marriage*. Harmondsworth, Middlesex: Penguin Books.

——. 1978. *The Tory Islanders*. Cambridge: Cambridge University Press.

Frake, Charles O. 1956. "Malayo-Polynesian Land Tenure." *American Anthropologist* 58:170–73.

Frank, André Gunder. 1969. *Latin America: Underdevelopment or Revolution*. New York: Monthly Review Press.

——. 1973. *Lumpenbourgeoisie, Lumpendevelopment: Dependence, Class, and Politics in Latin America*. New York: Monthly Review Press.

Fraser, Peter. 1981. "The Fictive Peasantry: Caribbean Rural Groups in the Nineteenth Century." In *Contemporary Caribbean: A Sociological Reader*, edited by Susan Craig, 1:319–47. Trinidad: Susan Craig.

Frazier, Franklin E. 1965. *The Negro in the United States*. 1957. Reprint, New York: Macmillan.

——. 1966. *The Negro Family in the United States*. 1939. Reprint, Chicago: University of Chicago Press.

Freeman, Carla. 1997. "Reinventing Higglering across Transnational Zones: Barbadian Women Juggle the Triple Shift." In *Daughters of Caliban: Caribbean Women in the Twentieth Century*, edited by Consuelo López Springfield, 68–95. Bloomington: Indiana University Press.

Freilich, Morris. 1961. "Serial Polygyny, Negro Peasants, and Model Analysis." *American Anthropologist* 63, no. 5:955–75.

Fremmer, Ray. 1967. "Martha Brae: The P.M.'s Home Town." *Daily Gleaner*, Kingston, Jamaica, 8 August.

——. 1968. "The Origin of Martha Brae." *Daily Gleaner*, Kingston, Jamaica, 21 December.

——. 1980. "Henry Sewell: Heir to an Empire." *Sunday Gleaner Magazine*, Kingston, Jamaica, 17 August.

——. 1984a. "Impressive Hampden." *Daily Gleaner*, Kingston, Jamaica, 1 April.

——. 1984b. "Jamaican Great Houses (2)." *Daily Gleaner*, Kingston, Jamaica, 9 December.

——. 1984c. "Minto's Water Valley Great House." *Daily Gleaner*, Kingston, Jamaica, 15 April.

Frey, Sylvia R., and Betty Wood. 1998. *Come Shouting to Zion: African American Protestantism in the American South and British Caribbean to 1830*. Chapel Hill: University of North Carolina Press.

Frucht, Richard. 1967. "Caribbean Social Types: Neither 'Peasant' nor 'Proletarian.' " *Social and Economic Studies* 16:295–300.

Furnivall, J. S. 1945. "Some Problems of Tropical Economy." In *Fabian Colonial Essays*, edited by R. Hinden, 161–71. London: Allen and Unwin.

——. 1948. *Colonial Policy and Practice: A Comparative Study of Burma and Netherlands India*. London: Cambridge University Press.

Gaspar, David Barry. 1992. "Working the System: Antigua Slaves and Their Struggle to Live." *Slavery and Abolition* 13:131–55.

Gaspar, David Barry, and Darlene Clark Hine, eds. 1996. *More Than Chattel: Black Women and Slavery in the Americas*. Bloomington: Indiana University Press.

Geertz, Clifford. 1962. "The Rotating Credit Association: A 'Middle-Rung' in Development." *Economic Development and Cultural Change* 10, no. 3:241–63.

Genovese, Eugene D. 1971. *In Red and Black: Marxian Explorations in Southern and Afro-American History*. 1968. Reprint, New York: Pantheon Books.

———. 1974. *Roll, Jordan, Roll: The World the Slaves Made*. 1972. Reprint, New York: Pantheon Books.

———. 1981. *From Rebellion to Revolution: Afro-American Slave Revolts in the Making of the Modern World*. 1979. Reprint, Baton Rouge: Louisiana State University Press.

Georgian Society of Jamaica. 1970. *Falmouth, 1791–1970*. [Kingston], Jamaica: Georgian Society of Jamaica.

Giddens, Anthony. 1976. *New Rules of Sociological Method*. London: Hutchinson.

Gilroy, Paul. 1993. *The Black Atlantic: Modernity and Double Consciousness*. London: Verso.

Goode, William J. 1960. "Illegitimacy in the Caribbean Social Structure." *American Sociological Review* 25:21–30.

———. 1961. "Illegitimacy, Anomie, and Cultural Penetration." *American Sociological Review* 26:910–25.

———. 1966. "Notes of Problems in Theory and Method." *American Anthropologist* 68:486–92.

Goodenough, Ward H. 1955. "A Problem in Malayo-Polynesian Social Organization." *American Anthropologist* 57, no. 1:71–83.

———. 1956. "Reply to C. O. Frake, Malayo-Polynesian Land Tenure." *American Anthropologist* 58:173–76.

———. 1970. *Description and Comparison in Cultural Anthropology*. Cambridge: Cambridge University Press.

Goodwin, William B. 1946. *Spanish and English Ruins in Jamaica*. Boston: Meador Publishing Co.

Goody, Jack. 1969. "The Classification of Double Descent Systems." In *Comparative Studies in Kinship*, edited by Jack Goody. London: Routledge and Kegan Paul.

Gough, Kathleen E. 1959. "The Nayars and the Definition of Marriage." *Journal of the Royal Anthropological Institute* 89:23–34.

Green, Pat. 1984. " 'Small Settler' Houses in Chapleton: Microcosm of the Jamaican Vernacular." *Jamaica Journal* 17, no. 3:39–45.

Greene, Jack P. 2000. "Liberty, Slavery, and the Transformation of British Identity in the Eighteenth-Century West Indies." *Slavery and Abolition* 21, no. 1:1–31.

Greenfield, Sidney M. 1960. "Land Tenure and Transmission in Rural Barbados." *Anthropological Quarterly* 33:165–76.

———. 1979. "Plantations, Sugar Cane, and Slavery." In *Roots and Branches: Current Directions in Slave Studies*, edited by Michael Craton, 85–119. Toronto: Pergamon Press.

———. 2000. "Madeira and the Beginnings of New World Sugar Cane Cultivation and Plantation Slavery: A Study in Institution Building." In *Caribbean Slavery in the Atlantic World: A Student Reader*, edited by Verene Shepherd and Hilary McD. Beckles, 42–54, Kingston, Jamaica: Ian Randle.

Greenwood, R., and S. Hamber. 1980. *Emancipation to Emigration*. London: Macmillan Caribbean.

Gullick, C. J. M. R. 1976. "Carib Ethnicity in a Semi-Plural Society." *New Community* 5, no. 3:250–58.

———. 1985. *Myths of a Minority: The Changing Traditions of the Vincentian Caribs*. Assen, Netherlands: Van Gorcum.

Gutman, Herbert G. 1976a. *The Black Family in Slavery and Freedom, 1750–1925*. Oxford: Basil Blackwell.

———. 1976b. *Work, Culture, and Society in Industrializing America: Essays in American Working-Class and Social History*. New York: Knopf.

———. 1987. "The Black Family in Slavery and Freedom: A Revised Perspective." In *Power and Culture: Essays on the American Working Class, Herbert G. Gutman*, edited by Ira Berlin, 357–79. New York: New Press.

Hagelberg, G. B. 1985. "Sugar in the Caribbean: Turning Sunshine into Money." In *Caribbean Contours*, edited by Sidney W. Mintz and Sally Price, 85–126. Baltimore: Johns Hopkins University Press.

Hall, Catherine. 1992–93. "White Visions, Black Lives: The Free Villages of Jamaica." *History Workshop* 34–36, no. 905:100–32.

Hall, Douglas. 1959. *Free Jamaica 1838–1865: An Economic History*. New Haven: Yale University Press.

———. 1971. *Five of the Leewards, 1834–1870*. Barbados: Caribbean Universities Press.

———. 1978. "The Flight from the Estates Reconsidered: The British West Indies, 1838–1842." *Journal of Caribbean History* 10–11:7–24.

———. 1989. *In Miserable Slavery: Thomas Thistlewood in Jamaica, 1750–86*. London: Macmillan.

———. N.d. "The Apprenticeship System in Jamaica, 1834–1838." In *Apprenticeship and Emancipation*. Kingston: Department of Extra-Mural Studies, University of the West Indies, Mona, Jamaica.

Hall, Stuart. 1992. "New Ethnicities." In *Race, Culture, and Difference*, edited by J. Donald and A. Rattansi. London: Sage.

"Hampden Estates." 1995. Hampden, Trelawny, Jamaica.

Handler, Jerome S. 1965. "Some Aspects of Work Organization on Sugar Plantations in Barbados." *Ethnology* 4:16–38.

———. 1966. "Small-Scale Sugar Cane Farming in Barbados." *Ethnology* 5:64–83.

———. 2000. "Slave Medicine and Obeah in Barbados, circa 1650 to 1834." *New West Indian Guide* 74, no. 1–2:57–90.

Handler, Jerome S., and Kenneth M. Bilby. 2001. "On the Early Use and Origin of the Term 'Obeah' in Barbados and the Anglophone Caribbean." *Slavery and Abolition* 22, no. 2:87–100.

Handler, Jerome S., and JoAnn Jacoby. 1996. "Slave Names and Naming in Barbados, 1650–1830." *William and Mary Quarterly*, 3d ser., 53, no. 4: 685–726.

Handler, Jerome S., and Frederick Lange. 1978. *Plantation Slavery in Barbados: An Archaeological and Historical Investigation*. Cambridge: Harvard University Press.

Hanson, F. Allan. 1971. "Nonexclusive Cognatic Descent Systems." In *Polynesia: Readings on a Culture Area*, edited by A. Howard, 109–32. Scranton, Pa.: Chandler.

Harrison, Faye V. 1988. "Women in Jamaica's Urban Informal Economy: Insights from a Kingston Slum." *New West Indian Guide* 62, no. 3–4:103–28.

Hart, Richard. 1994. "Good Hope, Jamaica, 1744–1994." Unpublished MS.

Hartley, Shirley Foster. 1980. "Illegitimacy in Jamaica." In *Bastardy and Its Comparative History*, edited by Peter Laslett, Karla Oosterveen, and Richard M. Smith, 379–96. London: Edward Arnold.

Henderson, George E. 1967. *Goodness and Mercy: A Tale of a Hundred Years*. 1931. 2d ed., Owen Sound, Ontario: Richardson, Bond, and Wright.

Hennessy, Alistair. 1993. Introduction to *The Autobiography of a Runaway Slave Esteban Montejo*, by Miguel Barnet, 1–12. London: Macmillan.

Henriques, Fernando. 1968. *Family and Colour in Jamaica*. 1953. 2d ed., London: MacGibbon and Kee.

Henshall (Momsen), Janet D. 1976. "Post-Emancipation Rural Settlement in the Lesser Antilles." *Proceedings of the Association of American Geographers* 8:37–40.

Herskovits, Melville J. 1937. *Life in a Haitian Valley*. New York: Knopf.

———. 1990. *The Myth of the Negro Past*. 1941. Reprint, Boston: Beacon Press.

Herskovits, Melville J., and Frances S. Herskovits. 1947. *Trinidad Village*. New York: Knopf.

Hertz, R. 1960. "A Contribution to the Study of the Collective Representation of Death." In *Death and the Right Hand*, trans. R. Needham and C. Needham. London: Cohen and West.

Heuman, Gad. 1994. *The Killing Time: The Morant Bay Rebellion in Jamaica*. London: Macmillan.

Higman, Barry W. 1973. "Household Structure and Fertility on Jamaican Slave Plantations: A Nineteenth-Century Example." *Population Studies* 27, no. 3:527–50.

———. 1975. "The Slave Family and Household in the British West Indies, 1800–1834." *Journal of Interdisciplinary History* 6, no. 2:261–87.

———. 1976. *Slave Population and Economy in Jamaica, 1807–1834*. Cambridge: Cambridge University Press.

———. 1984. "Urban Slavery in the British Caribbean." In *Perspectives on Caribbean Regional Identity*, edited by Elizabeth M. Thomas-Hope, 39–56. Liverpool: Centre for Latin-American Studies, University of Liverpool.

———. 1988. *Jamaica Surveyed: Plantation Maps and Plans of the Eighteenth and Nineteenth Centuries*. Kingston: Institute of Jamaica.

———. 1998. *Montpelier, Jamaica: A Plantation Community in Slavery and Freedom, 1739–1912*. Kingston: University of the West Indies Press.

———. 1999. *Writing West Indian Histories*. London: Macmillan.

Hill, Jonathan D., ed. 1996. *History, Power, and Identity: Ethnogenesis in the Americas, 1492–1992.* Iowa City: University of Iowa Press.

Hills, Theo L. 1988. "The Caribbean Peasant Food Forest: Ecological Artistry or Random Chaos?" In *Small Farming and Peasant Resources in the Caribbean*, edited by John S. Brierley and Hymie Rubenstein, 1–28. Winnipeg, Canada: University of Manitoba.

Hinton, John Howard. 1847. *Memoir of William Knibb: Missionary in Jamaica.* London: Houlston and Stoneman.

Hoben, Alan. 1973. *Land Tenure among the Amhara of Ethiopia: The Dynamics of Cognatic Descent.* Chicago: University of Chicago Press.

Hoetink, H. 1985. " 'Race' and Color in the Caribbean." In *Caribbean Contours*, edited by Sidney W. Mintz and Sally Price, 55–84. Baltimore: Johns Hopkins University Press.

Hogg, Peter. 1979. *Slavery: The Afro-American Experience.* London: British Library.

Holt, Thomas C. 1992. *The Problem of Freedom: Race, Labor, and Politics in Jamaica and Britain, 1832–1938.* Baltimore: Johns Hopkins University Press.

Holy, Ladislav. 1996. *Anthropological Perspectives on Kinship.* London: Pluto Press.

Homiak, John P. 1995. "Dub History: Soundings on Rastafari Livity and Language." In *Rastafari and Other African-Caribbean Worldviews*, edited by Barry Chevannes, 127–81. London: Macmillan.

Hoogbergen, Wim. 1989. "Aluku." *New West Indian Guide* 63, no. 3–4:175–97.

Hope, Kempe R. 1989. "Internal Migration and Urbanization in the Caribbean." *Canadian Journal of Latin American and Caribbean Studies* 14, no. 27:5–21.

Horowitz, Michael M. 1971. "A Decision Model of Conjugal Patterns in Martinique." In *Peoples and Cultures of the Caribbean*, edited by Michael M. Horowitz, 476–88. Garden City, N.Y.: Natural History Press.

———. 1992. *Morne-Paysan: Peasant Village in Martinique.* 1967. Rev. ed. Prospect Heights, Ill.: Waveland Press.

Inikori, Joseph E. 1993. *Cahiers d'Etudes Africaines* 32:686.

Innes, Frank C. 1987. "Dimensions of Opportunity for Reducing the Dependency Factor in Caribbean Food Production." In *Land and Development in the Caribbean*, edited by Jean Besson and Janet Momsen, 210–20. London: Macmillan.

Irving of Bonshaw, John Beaufin. 1907. *The Irvings, Irwins, Irvines, or Erinveines; or, Any Other Spelling of the Name: An Old Scots Border Clan.* Aberdeen, Scotland: Rosemount Press.

Isaacs, Valentine. 1996. "History of the Church." In *Trelawny Parish Church of St. Peter the Apostle, 1796–1996*, 11–49. Falmouth, Trelawny, Jamaica.

Island Record Office, Jamaica. Grantors Old Series 4, Lib. 165, fol. 11.

Jacobs, H. P. 1970. "Falmouth." In *Falmouth, 1791–1970*, by H. P. Jacobs and T. A. L. Concannon, 14–16. Kingston, Jamaica: Georgian Society of Jamaica.

Jacoby, Karl. 1994. "Slaves by Nature? Domestic Animals and Human Slaves." *Slavery and Abolition* 15, no. 1:89–99.

Johnson, Howard. 1991a. *The Bahamas in Slavery and Freedom*. Kingston, Jamaica: Ian Randle.

———. 1991b. "Friendly Societies in the Bahamas, 1834–1910." *Slavery and Abolition* 12, no. 3:183–99.

Karasch, Mary. 1979. "Commentary One" on M. Schuler, "Afro-American Slave Culture." In *Roots and Branches: Current Directions in Slave Studies*, edited by Michael Craton, 138–41. Toronto: Pergamon Press.

Karras, Alan L. 1992. *Sojourners in the Sun: Scottish Migrants in Jamaica and the Chesapeake, 1740–1800*. Ithaca, N.Y.: Cornell University Press.

Katzin, Margaret F. 1959a. "The Jamaican Country Higgler." *Social and Economic Studies* 8, no. 4:421–40.

———. 1959b. " 'Partners': An Informal Savings Institution in Jamaica." *Social and Economic Studies* 8:436–40.

———. 1960. "The Business of Higglering in Jamaica." *Social and Economic Studies* 9, no. 3:297–331.

Keesing, Roger M. 1975. *Kin Groups and Social Structure*. New York: Holt, Rinehart and Winston.

Keesing, Roger M., and Andrew J. Strathern. 1998. *Cultural Anthropology: A Contemporary Perspective*. 3d ed. Fort Worth, Tex.: Harcourt Brace College Publishers.

Keymer, Thomas. 2001. "Kelly Family of Jamaica." *Georgian Jamaica* 9, no. 3:2.

Knox, A. J. G. 1977. "Opportunities and Opposition: The Rise of Jamaica's Black Peasantry and the Nature of Planter Resistance." *Canadian Review of Sociology and Anthropology* 14, no. 4:381–95.

Kobben, A. J. F. 1996. "Unity and Disunity: Cottica Djuka Society as a Kinship System." In *Maroon Societies: Rebel Slave Communities in the Americas*, edited by Richard Price, 320–69. 1973, 1979. 3d ed. Baltimore: Johns Hopkins University Press.

Kossek, Brigitte. 1995. Review of *Women and Change in the Caribbean*, edited by Janet H. Momsen. *Journal of the Royal Anthropological Institute*, n.s., 1, no. 1:197–98.

Kroeber, Alfred K. 1946. "The Ancient *Oikoumenê* as a Historic Culture Aggregate." *Journal of the Royal Anthropological Institute* 75:9–20.

Kuper, Adam. 1976. *Changing Jamaica*. London: Routledge and Kegan Paul.

Laguerre, Michel S. 1982. *Urban Life in the Caribbean: A Study of a Haitian Urban Community*. Cambridge, Mass.: Schenkman.

———. 1990. *Urban Poverty in the Caribbean: French Martinique as a Social Laboratory*. London: Macmillan.

Larose, Serge. 1975. "The Haitian Lakou: Land, Family, and Ritual." In *Family and Kinship in Middle America and the Caribbean*, edited by A. F. Marks and R. A. Römer, 482–512. Curaçao: Institute of Higher Studies in Curaçao, West Indies, and Leiden, Netherlands: Royal Institute of Linguistics and Anthropology.

Larson, Brooke, and Olivia Harris, eds., with Enrique Tandeter. 1995. *Ethnicity, Markets, and Migration in the Andes: At the Crossroads of History and Anthropology*. Durham, N.C.: Duke University Press.

Laslett, Peter. 1980. Preface to *Bastardy and Its Comparative History*, edited by Peter Laslett, Karla Oosterveen, and Richard M. Smith, ix–xv. London: Edward Arnold.

Leach, Edmund R. 1960. "The Sinhalese of the Dry Zone of Northern Ceylon." In *Social Structure in Southeast Asia*, edited by George Peter Murdock, 116–26. Chicago: Quadrangle Books.

———. 1961. "Polyandry, Inheritance, and the Definition of Marriage." In *Rethinking Anthropology*, by E. R. Leach, 105–13. London: Athlone Press.

Lévi-Strauss, Claude. 1969. *The Elementary Structures of Kinship*. 1949. Boston: Beacon Press.

Lewis, I. M. 1976. *Social Anthropology in Perspective: The Relevance of Social Anthropology*. Harmondsworth, Middlesex, England: Penguin Books.

Lewis, M. G. 1929. *Journal of a West India Proprietor, 1815–1817*. Boston: Houghton Mifflin.

Light, Ivan. 1972. *Ethnic Enterprise in America*. Berkeley: University of California Press.

Little, Thomas J. 1995. "George Liele and the Rise of Independent Black Baptist Churches in the Lower South and Jamaica." *Slavery and Abolition* 16, no. 2:188–204.

Littlewood, Roland. 1993. *Pathology and Identity: The Work of Mother Earth in Trinidad*. Cambridge: Cambridge University Press.

Long, Edward. 1774. *The History of Jamaica*. 3 vols. London: T. Lowndes.

Lovejoy, Paul E., ed. 2000. *Identity in the Shadow of Slavery*. London: Continuum.

Lowenthal, David. 1961. "Caribbean Views of Caribbean Land." *Canadian Geographer* 5, no. 2:1–9.

———. 1972. *West Indian Societies*. London: Oxford University Press.

———. 1987. Foreword to *Land Development in the Caribbean*, edited by Jean Besson and Janet Momsen, x–xi. London: Macmillan.

MacCormack, Carol P., and Alizon Draper. 1987. "Social and Cognitive Aspects of Female Sexuality in Jamaica." In *The Cultural Construction of Sexuality*, edited by Pat Caplan, 143–65. London: Tavistock.

MacDonald, John Stuart, and Leatrice MacDonald. 1978. "The Black Family in the Americas: A Review of the Literature." *Sage Race Relations Abstracts* 3, no. 1:1–42.

Maine, Henry S. 1861. *Ancient Law*. N.p.: John Murray.

Malinowski, Bronisław. 1913. *The Family among the Australian Aborigines*. London: Hodder.

———. 1922. *Argonauts of the Western Pacific*. London: Routledge and Kegan Paul.

———. 1929. *The Sexual Life of Savages in North-Western Melanesia*. London: Routledge and Kegan Paul.

Marcus, George E., and Michael M. J. Fischer. 1986. "Taking Account of World Historical Political Economy: Knowable Communities in Larger Systems." In *Anthropology as Cultural Critique: An Experimental Moment in the Human Sciences*, 77–110. Chicago: University of Chicago Press.

Marks, A. F. 1976. *Male and Female and the Afro-Curaçaoan Household*. The Hague: Martinus Nijhoff.

Marshall, Woodville K. 1972. "Aspects of the Development of the Peasantry: Peasant Movements and Agrarian Problems in the West Indies." *Caribbean Quarterly* 18:31–58.

———. 1979. Commentary on Sidney W. Mintz, "Slavery and the Rise of Peasantries." In *Roots and Branches: Current Directions in Slave Studies*, edited by Michael Craton, 243–48. Toronto: Pergamon Press.

———. 1985. "Peasant Development in the West Indies since 1838." 1968. Reprint in *Rural Development in the Caribbean*, edited by P. I. Gomes 1–14. Kingston, Jamaica: Heinemann.

———. 1991a. "The Post-Slavery Labour Problem Revisited." The 1990 Elsa Goveia Memorial Lecture. Department of History, University of the West Indies, Mona, Jamaica.

———. 1991b. "Provision Ground and Plantation Labour in Four Windward Islands." In *The Slaves' Economy: Independent Production by Slaves in the Americas*, edited by Ira Berlin and Philip D. Morgan. Special Issue, *Slavery and Abolition* 12, no. 1:48–67.

Mathurin, D. C. Emerson. 1967. "An Unfavourable System of Land Tenure." Paper presented at the Second West Indian Agricultural Economics Conference, St. Augustine, Trinidad. April.

Maurer, Bill. 1996. "The Land, the Law, and Legitimate Children: Thinking Through Gender, Kinship, and Nation in the British Virgin Islands." In *Gender, Kinship, Power: A Comparative and Interdisciplinary History*, edited by Mary Jo Maynes, Ann Waltner, Birgitte Soland, and Ulrike Strasser, 351–63. New York: Routledge.

———. 1997a. "Creolization Redux: The Plural Society Thesis and Offshore Financial Services in the British Caribbean." *New West Indian Guide* 71, no. 3–4:249–64.

———. 1997b. *Recharting the Caribbean: Land, Law, and Citizenship in the British Virgin Islands*. Ann Arbor: University of Michigan Press.

Mauss, Marcel. 1954. *The Gift: Forms and Functions of Exchange in Archaic Societies*. 1925. London: Cohen and West.

McDonald, Roderick A. 1993. *The Economy and Material Culture of Slaves: Goods and Chattels on the Sugar Plantations of Jamaica and Louisiana*. Baton Rouge: Louisiana State University Press.

McGlynn, Frank, and Seymour Drescher, eds. 1992. *The Meaning of Freedom: Economics, Politics, and Culture after Slavery*. Pittsburgh, Pa.: University of Pittsburgh Press.

McKay, Lesley. 1987. "Tourism and Changing Attitudes to Land in Negril, Jamaica." In *Land and Development in the Caribbean*, edited by Jean Besson and Janet Momsen, 132–52. London: Macmillan.

———. 1993. "Women's Contribution to Tourism in Negril, Jamaica." In *Women and Change in the Caribbean: A Pan-Caribbean Perspective*, edited by Janet H. Momsen, 278–86. London: James Currey.

McLennan, John F. 1865. *Primitive Marriage*. Edinburgh: Adam and Charles Black.

Meggitt, M. J. 1965. *The Lineage System of the Mae-Enga of New Guinea*. London: Oliver and Boyd.

Métraux, Alfred. 1971. "Cooperative Labor Groups in Haiti." In *Peoples and Cultures of the Caribbean*, edited by Michael M. Horowitz, 318–39. Garden City, N.Y.: Natural History Press.

Miles, William. 1992. Foreword 1992 to *Morne-Paysan: Peasant Village in Martinique*, by Michael M. Horowitz, ix–xi. Prospect Heights, Ill.: Waveland Press.

Miller, Daniel. 1994. *Modernity: An Ethnographic Approach: Dualism and Mass Consumption in Trinidad*. Oxford: Berg.

Miller, Randall M. 1999. Review Essay, "The Making of African-American Protestantism." *Slavery and Abolition* 20, 3:127–35.

Mintz, Sidney W. 1955. "The Jamaican Internal Marketing Pattern: Some Notes and Hypotheses." *Social and Economic Studies* 4, no. 1:95–103.

———. 1957. "The Role of the Middleman in the Internal Distribution System of a Caribbean Peasant Economy." *Human Organization* 15, no. 2:18–23.

———. 1958. "The Historical Sociology of the Jamaican Church-Founded Free Village System." *New West Indian Guide* 38, 46–70.

———. 1959. "Labor and Sugar in Puerto Rico and Jamaica, 1800–1850." *Comparative Studies in Society and History* 1:273–81.

———. 1960. "Peasant Markets." *Scientific American* 203, no. 2:112–22.

———. 1961. "Pratik: Haitian Personal Economic Relationships." In *Symposium: Patterns of Land Utilization and Other Papers*, Proceedings of the 1961 Annual Spring Meeting of the American Ethnological Society, edited by Viola Garfield, 54–63. Seattle: University of Washington Press.

———. 1971a. "The Caribbean as a Socio-Cultural Area." In *Peoples and Cultures of the Caribbean*, edited by Michael M. Horowitz, 17–46. Garden City, N.Y.: Natural History Press.

———. 1971b. "Toward an Afro-American History." *Cahiers D'Histoire Mondiale* 13:317–31.

———. 1973. "A Note on the Definition of Peasantries." *Journal of Peasant Studies* 1:91–106.

———. 1974a. "The Rural Proletariat and the Problem of Rural Proletarian Consciousness." *Journal of Peasant Studies* 1:291–325.

———. 1974b. *Worker in the Cane: A Puerto Rican Life History*. New York: Norton.

———. 1978. "Was the Plantation Slave a Proletarian?" *Review* 11:81–98.

———. 1979. "Slavery and the Rise of Peasantries." In *Roots and Branches: Current Directions in Slave Studies*, edited by Michael Craton, 213–42. Toronto: Pergamon Press.

———. 1980. "Cultural Resistance and the Labor Force in the Caribbean Region." Paper presented at the Cornell University Conference, "Latin America Today: Heritage of Conquest." 3–5 April.

———. 1985. "From Plantations to Peasantries in the Caribbean." In *Caribbean Con-*

tours, edited by Sidney W. Mintz and Sally Price, 127–53. Baltimore: Johns Hopkins University Press.

——. 1989. *Caribbean Transformations*. 1974. Morningside ed., New York: Columbia University Press.

——. 1995. "Can Haiti Change?" *Foreign Affairs* 74, no. 1:73–86.

——. 1996a. "Enduring Substances, Trying Theories: The Caribbean Region as *Oikoumenê*." *Journal of the Royal Anthropological Institute* 2, no. 2:289–311.

——. 1996b. "Tasting Food, Tasting Freedom." In *Tasting Food, Tasting Freedom: Excursions in Eating, Culture, and the Past*, by Sidney W. Mintz, 33–49. Boston: Beacon Press.

Mintz, Sidney W., and Richard Price. 1992. *The Birth of African-American Culture: An Anthropological Perspective*. 1976. Reprint, Boston: Beacon Press.

Momsen, Janet D. Henshall. 1972. "Land Tenure as a Barrier to Agricultural Innovation: The Case of St. Lucia." *Proceedings of the Seventh West Indian Agricultural Economics Conference*, 103–9, Grand Anse, Grenada. 9–15 April.

——. 1987. "Land Settlement as an Imposed Solution." In *Land and Development in the Caribbean*, edited by Jean Besson and Janet Momsen, 46–69. London: Macmillan.

——. 1988. "Changing Gender Roles in Caribbean Peasant Agriculture." In *Small Farming and Peasant Resources in the Caribbean*, edited by John S. Brierley and Hymie Rubenstein, 83–99. Winnipeg, Canada: University of Manitoba.

Moore, Henrietta L. 1988. *Feminism and Anthropology*. Cambridge: Polity Press.

Morgan, Henry Lewis. 1871. *Systems of Consanguinity and Affinity of the Human Family*. Washington, D.C.: Smithsonian Institution Press.

Morgan, Philip D. 1997. "The Cultural Implications of the Atlantic Slave Trade: African Regional Origins, American Destinations, and New World Developments." In *Routes to Slavery: Direction, Ethnicity, and Mortality in the Atlantic Slave Trade*, edited by David Eltis and David Richardson, 122–45. London: Frank Cass.

Morris, Brian. 1991. *Western Conceptions of the Individual*. Oxford: Berg.

——. 1999. "Being Human Does Not Make You a Person." Inaugural Lecture, Goldsmiths College, University of London, March.

Moynihan, D. 1965. *The Negro Family in the United States: The Case for National Action*. Washington, D.C.: U.S. Government Printing Office.

Mullin, Michael. 1994. *Africa in America: Slave Acculturation and Resistance in the American South and the British Caribbean, 1736–1831*. Urbana: University of Illinois Press.

Murdock, George Peter. 1960. "Cognatic Forms of Social Organization." In *Social Structure in Southeast Asia*, edited by George Peter Murdock, 1–14. Chicago: Quadrangle Books.

Naipaul, V. S. 1973. *The Overcrowded Baracoon*. New York: Knopf.

Ngubane, Harriet. 1977. *Body and Mind in Zulu Medicine: An Ethnography of Health and Disease in Nyuswa-Zulu Thought and Practice*. London: Academic Press.

Norvell, Douglass G., and James S. Wehrly. 1969. "A Rotating Credit Association in the Dominican Republic." *Caribbean Studies* 9, no. 1:45–52.

Ogilvie, Dan L. 1954. *History of the Parish of Trelawny*. Kingston, Jamaica: United Printers.

O'Loughlin, Carleen. 1968. *Economic and Political Change in the Leeward and Windward Islands*. New Haven: Yale University Press.

Olwig, Karen Fog. 1981a. "Finding a Place for the Slave Family: Historical Anthropological Perspectives." *Folk* 23:345–58.

———. 1981b. "Women, 'Matrifocality,' and Systems of Exchange: An Ethnohistorical Study of the Afro-American Family on St. John, Danish West Indies." *Ethnohistory* 28:59–78.

———. 1985. *Cultural Adaptation and Resistance on St John: Three Centuries of Afro-Caribbean Life*. Gainesville: University of Florida Press.

———. 1990. "The Struggle for Respectability: Methodism and Afro-Caribbean Culture on 19th Century Nevis." *New West Indian Guide* 64, no. 3–4:93–114.

———. 1993. *Global Culture, Island Identity: Continuity and Change in the Afro-Caribbean Community of Nevis*. Philadelphia: Harwood.

———. 1997. "Cultural Sites: Sustaining a Home in a Deterritorialized World." In *Siting Culture: The Shifting Anthropological Object*, edited by Karen Fog Olwig and Kirsten Hastrup, 17–37. London: Routledge.

———. 1999. "Caribbean Place Identity: From Family Land to Region and Beyond." *Identities* 5, no. 4:435–67.

Olwig, Karen Fog, and Kirsten Hastrup, eds. 1997. *Siting Culture: The Shifting Anthropological Object*. London: Routledge.

Ortiz, Alfonso. 1972. *New Perspectives on the Pueblos*. Albuquerque: University of New Mexico Press.

Otterbein, Keith F. 1964. "A Comparison of the Land Tenure Systems of the Bahamas, Jamaica, and Barbados: The Implications It Has for the Study of Social Systems Shifting from Bilateral to Ambilineal Descent." *International Archives of Ethnography* 50:31–42.

———. 1965. "Caribbean Family Organization: A Comparative Analysis." *American Anthropologist* 67, no. 1:66–79.

———. 1966. *The Andros Islanders: A Study of Family Organization in the Bahamas*. Lawrence: University of Kansas Press.

Paget, Hugh. 1964. "The Free Village System of Jamaica." *Caribbean Quarterly* 10:38–51.

Parkin, Robert. 1997. *Kinship: An Introduction to Basic Concepts*. Oxford: Blackwell.

Parsons, Talcott. 1952. *The Social System*. Glencoe, Ill.: Free Press.

Patterson, Orlando. 1973. *The Sociology of Slavery: An Analysis of the Origins, Development, and Structure of Negro Slave Society in Jamaica*. 1967. Reprint, London: Granada.

Philpott, Stuart B. 1973. *West Indian Migration: The Montserrat Case*. London: Athlone Press.

———. 1977. "The Montserratians: Migration Dependency and the Maintenance of

Island Ties in England." In *Between Two Cultures: Migrants and Minorities in Britain*, edited by James L. Watson, 90–119. Oxford: Basil Blackwell.

Polanyi, Karl. 1957. "The Economy as Instituted Process." In *Trade and Market in the Early Empires*, edited by K. Polanyi, C. M. Arensberg, and H. W. Pearson, 243–70. Glencoe, Ill.: Free Press.

Pollitt, Brian H. 1985. "Towards the Socialist Transformation of Cuban Agriculture, 1959–82." In *Rural Development in the Caribbean*, edited by P. I. Gomes, 154–72. Kingston, Jamaica: Heinemann.

Price, Richard. 1967. "Studies of Caribbean Family Organization: Problems and Prospects." Manuscript, Department of Anthropology, Johns Hopkins University, Baltimore.

———. 1975. *Saramaka Social Structure: Analysis of a Maroon Society in Surinam*. Rio Piedra: Institute of Caribbean Studies.

———. 1976. *The Guiana Maroons: A Historical and Bibliographical Introduction*. Baltimore: Johns Hopkins University Press.

———. 1983. *First-Time: The Historical Vision of an Afro-American People*. Baltimore: Johns Hopkins University Press.

———. 1990. *Alabi's World*. Baltimore: Johns Hopkins University Press.

———. 2001. "The Miracle of Creolization: A Retrospective." *New West Indian Guide* 75, no. 1–2:35–64.

———, ed. 1996. *Maroon Societies: Rebel Slave Communities in the Americas*. 1973, 1979. 3d ed. Baltimore: Johns Hopkins University Press.

Price, Richard, and Sally Price. 1991. *Two Evenings in Saramaka*. Chicago: Chicago University Press.

Purcell, Trevor W. 1987. "Modern Maroons: Economy and Cultural Survival in a 'Jamaican' Peasant Village in Costa Rica." In *Afro-Caribbean Villages in Historical Perspective*, edited by Charles V. Carnegie, 45–62. Kingston: African-Caribbean Institute of Jamaica.

———. 1998. "Indigenous Knowledge and Applied Anthropology: Questions of Definition and Direction." *Human Organization* 57, no. 3:258–72.

Radcliffe-Brown, A. R. 1950. Introduction to *African Systems of Kinship and Marriage*, edited by A. R. Radcliffe-Brown and Daryll Forde, 1–85. London: Oxford University Press.

Radcliffe-Brown, A. R., and Daryll Forde, eds. 1950. *African Systems of Kinship and Marriage*. London: Oxford University Press.

Rapport, Nigel, and Andrew Dawson, eds. 1998. *Migrants of Identity: Perceptions of Home in a World of Movement*. Oxford: Berg.

Reid, Audley G. 2000. *Community Formation: A Study of the "Village" in Postemancipation Jamaica*. Kingston, Jamaica: University of the West Indies Press.

Richardson, Bonham C. 1992. *The Caribbean in the Wider World, 1492–1992*. Cambridge: Cambridge University Press.

Richardson, David, ed. 1996. *Bristol, Africa, and the Eighteenth-Century Slave Trade to America*. Vol. 4, *The Final Years, 1770–1807*. Bristol: Bristol Record Society, Vol. 47.

Rival, Laura. 1999. "The Social Life of Trees." *Journal of the Royal Anthropological Institute* 5, no. 4:629–30.

Roberts, George W. 1955. "Some Aspects of Mating and Fertility in the West Indies." *Population Studies* 8, no. 3:199–227.

Robinson, Carey. 1969. *The Fighting Maroons of Jamaica*. Kingston, Jamaica: William Collins and Sangster.

Robotham, Don. 1977. "Agrarian Relations in Jamaica." In *Essays on Power and Change in Jamaica*, edited by Carl Stone and Aggrey Brown, 45–57. Kingston: Jamaica Publishing House.

———. 1988. "The Development of a Black Ethnicity in Jamaica." In *Garvey: His Work and Impact*, edited by Rupert Lewis and Patrick Bryan, 23–38. Mona, Jamaica: ISER and Extra-Mural Department, University of the West Indies.

Rodman, Hyman. 1971. *Lower-Class Families: The Culture of Poverty in Negro Trinidad*. London: Oxford University Press.

Rosaldo, Renato. 1993. *Culture and Truth: The Remaking of Social Analysis*. London: Routledge.

Rubenstein, Hymie. 1987a. *Coping with Poverty: Adaptive Strategies in a Caribbean Village*. Boulder, Colo.: Westview Press.

———. 1987b. "Folk and Mainstream Systems of Land Tenure and Use in St. Vincent." In *Land and Development in the Caribbean*, edited by Jean Besson and Janet Momsen, 70–87. London: Macmillan.

———. 1994. Review of Christine Barrow, *Family Land and Development in St. Lucia*. *New West Indian Guide* 68, no. 3–4:369–71.

Sahlins, Marshall. 1972. *Stone Age Economics*. London: Tavistock.

Sassen-Koob, Saskia. 1987. "Formal and Informal Associations: Dominicans and Colombians in New York." In *Caribbean Life in New York City: Sociocultural Dimensions*, edited by Constance R. Sutton and Elsa M. Chaney, 278–96. New York: Centre for Migration Studies of New York.

Satchell, Veront M. 1990. *From Plots to Plantations: Land Transactions in Jamaica, 1866–1900*. Mona, Jamaica: University of the West Indies.

———. 1992. "Government Land Policies in Jamaica during [the] Late Nineteenth Century." In *Plantation Economy, Land Reform, and the Peasantry in a Historical Perspective: Jamaica, 1838–1980*, edited by Claus Stolberg and Swithin Wilmot, 25–38. Kingston, Jamaica: Friedrich Ebert Siftung.

———. 1999. "Government Land-Lease Programs and the Expansion of the Jamaican Peasantry, 1866–1900." *Plantation Society in the Americas* 6, no. 1:47–64.

Savishinsky, Neil J. 1994. "Transnational Popular Culture and the Global Spread of the Jamaican Rastafari Movement." *New West Indian Guide* 68, no. 3–4: 259–81.

Scheffler, H. W. 1965. *Choiseul Island Social Structure*. Berkeley: University of California Press.

Schuler, Monica. 1979a. "Afro-American Slave Culture." In *Roots and Branches: Current Directions in Slave Studies*, edited by Michael Craton, 121–55. Toronto: Pergamon Press.

——. 1979b. "Myalism and the African Religious Tradition in Jamaica." In *Africa and the Caribbean: The Legacies of a Link*, edited by Margaret E. Crahan and Franklin Knight, 65–79. Baltimore: Johns Hopkins University Press.

——. 1980. *"Alas, Alas, Kongo": A Social History of Indentured African Immigration into Jamaica, 1841–1865*. Baltimore: Johns Hopkins University Press.

Schweitzer, Peter P., ed. 2000. *Dividends of Kinship: Meanings and Uses of Social Relatedness*. London: Routledge.

Scott, Rebecca J. 1985. *Slave Emancipation in Cuba: The Transition to Free Labor, 1860–1899*. Princeton, N.J.: Princeton University Press.

Seaga, Edward. 1982. "Revival Cults in Jamaica: Notes towards a Sociology of Religion." 1969. Reprint, *Jamaica Journal* 3, no. 2:3–20.

Senior, Olive. 1991. *Working Miracles: Women's Lives in the English-Speaking Caribbean*. London: James Currey.

Seymour-Smith, Charlotte. 1986. *Macmillan Dictionary of Anthropology*. London: Macmillan.

Sheller, Mimi. 1998. "Quasheba, Mother, Queen: Black Women's Public Leadership and Political Protest in Post-emancipation Jamaica, 1834–65." *Slavery and Abolition* 19, no. 3:90–117.

Shepherd, Verene A. 1998. "Diversity in Caribbean Economy and Society from the Seventeenth to the Nineteenth Centuries." *Plantation Society in the Americas* 5, no. 2–3:175–87.

Shepherd, Verene A., and Kathleen E. A. Monteith. 1998. "Non-Sugar Proprietors in a Sugar-Plantation Society." *Plantation Society in the Americas* 5, no. 2–3:205–25.

Sheridan, Richard B. 1974. *Sugar and Slavery: An Economic History of the British West Indies, 1623–1775*. Barbados: Caribbean Universities Press.

——. 1977. "The Role of the Scots in the Economy and Society of the West Indies." In *Comparative Perspectives on Slavery in New World Plantation Societies*, edited by Vera Rubin and Arthur Tuden, 94–106. New York: New York Academy of Sciences.

——. 1985. *Doctors and Slaves: A Medical and Demographic History of Slavery in the British West Indies, 1680–1834*. Cambridge: Cambridge University Press.

Sherlock, Philip. 1984. *Keeping Company with Jamaica*. London: Macmillan.

Shore, Joseph, and John Stewart. 1952. *In Old St. James (Jamaica): A Book of Parish Chronicles*. 1911. Reprint, Kingston, Jamaica: Sangster.

Sibley, Inez Knibb. 1965. *The Baptists of Jamaica, 1793–1965*. Kingston: Jamaica Baptist Union.

——. 1978. *Dictionary of Place-Names in Jamaica*. Kingston: The Institute of Jamaica.

Sibley, Inez K., and Jasper K. Ogilvie. 1975a. "Early Lodge and Schools." *Daily Gleaner*, Kingston, Jamaica, 19 August.

——. 1975b. "How Falmouth Got Its Name." *Daily Gleaner*, Kingston, Jamaica, 5 August.

——. 1975c. "Trelawny Then and Now." *Daily Gleaner*, Kingston, Jamaica, 28 July.

——. 1980. "A History of Long Pond Sugar Estate." *Sunday Gleaner Magazine*, Kingston, Jamaica, 27 April.

Simey, T. S. 1946. *Welfare and Planning in the West Indies*. Oxford: Clarendon Press.

Simmonds, Lorna. 1987. "Slave Higglering in Jamaica, 1780–1834." *Jamaica Journal* 20:31–38.

Simply Caribbean. 1996. Travel brochure. Harrogate, England.

Simpson, George Eaton. 1956. "Jamaican Revivalist Cults." *Social and Economic Studies* 5:321–442.

———. 1957. "The Nine Night Ceremony in Jamaica." *Journal of American Folklore* 70, no. 278:329–35.

Smith, Kevin D. 1995. "A Fragmented Freedom: The Historiography of Emancipation and Its Aftermath in the British West Indies." *Slavery and Abolition* 16, n. 1:101–30.

Smith, Michael G. 1956a. *A Report on Labour Supply in Rural Jamaica*. Kingston, Jamaica: Government Printer.

———. 1956b. "The Transformation of Land Rights by Transmission in Carriacou." *Social and Economic Studies* 5, no. 2:103–38.

———. 1960. "The African Heritage in the Caribbean." In *Caribbean Studies: A Symposium*, edited by Vera Rubin, 34–46. Seattle: University of Washington Press.

———. 1962a. *Kinship and Community in Carriacou*. New Haven: Yale University Press.

———. 1962b. *West Indian Family Structure*. Seattle: University of Washington Press.

———. 1965a. *The Plural Society in the British West Indies*. Berkeley: University of California Press.

——— 1965b. *Stratification in Grenada*. Berkeley: University of California Press.

———. 1966. Introduction to *My Mother Who Fathered Me: A Study of the Family in Three Selected Communities in Jamaica*, by Edith Clarke, i–xliv. 1957. 2d ed. London: George Allen and Unwin.

———. 1984. *Culture, Race, and Class in the Commonwealth Caribbean*. Mona, Jamaica: Department of Extra-Mural Studies, University of the West Indies.

Smith, M. G., Roy Augier, and Rex Nettleford. 1961. *Report on the Rastafari Movement in Kingston, Jamaica*. Kingston: Institute of Social and Economic Research, University of the West Indies, Mona.

Smith, M. G., and G. J. Kruijer. 1957. *A Sociological Manual for Extension Workers in the Caribbean*. Kingston, Jamaica: University College of the West Indies.

Smith, Raymond T. 1956. *The Negro Family in British Guiana: Family Structure and Social Status in the Villages*. London: Routledge and Kegan Paul.

———. 1964. "Ethnic Difference and Peasant Economy in British Guiana." In *Capital, Saving, and Credit in Peasant Societies*, edited by Raymond Firth and B. S. Yamey, 305–29. London: Allen and Unwin.

———. 1971. "Land Tenure in Three Negro Villages in British Guiana." In *Peoples and Cultures of the Caribbean*, edited by Michael M. Horowitz, 243–66. Garden City, N.Y.: Natural History Press.

———. 1978. "The Family and the Modern World System: Some Observations from the Caribbean." *Journal of Family History* 3, no. 4: 337–60.

———. 1988. *Kinship and Class in the West Indies: A Genealogical Study of Jamaica and Guyana.* Cambridge: Cambridge University Press.

———. 1990. Review of *Afro-Caribbean Villages in Historical Perspective,* edited by Charles V. Carnegie. *Slavery and Abolition* 11, no. 1:121–25.

———. 1996. *The Matrifocal Family: Power, Pluralism, and Politics.* London: Routledge.

Solien, Nancie L. 1959. "The Nonunilineal Descent Group in the Caribbean and Central America." *American Anthropologist* 61:578–83.

Speech of the Rev. William Knibb before the Baptist Missionary Society in Exeter Hall. 1842. London: G. and J. Dyer. 28 April.

Stack, Carol B. 1970. "The Kindred of Viola Jackson: Residence and Family Organization of an Urban Black American Family." In *Afro-American Anthropology: Contemporary Perspectives,* edited by Norman E. Whitten Jr. and John F. Szwed, 303–12. New York: Free Press.

———. 1974. *All Our Kin: Strategies for Survival in a Black Community.* New York: Harper and Row.

Steel, M. J. 1993. "A Philosophy of Fear: The World View of the Jamaican Plantocracy in a Comparative Perspective." *Journal of Caribbean History* 27, no. 1:1–20.

Stewart, John. 1823. *A View of the Past and Present State of the Island of Jamaica.* Edinburgh: Oliver and Boyd.

Stewart, Robert J. 1992. *Religion and Society in Post-Emancipation Jamaica.* Knoxville: University of Tennessee Press.

Stolberg, Claus, and Swithin Wilmot, eds. 1992. *Plantation Economy, Land Reform, and the Peasantry in a Historical Perspective: Jamaica, 1838–1980.* Kingston, Jamaica: Friedrich Ebert Siftung.

Stone, Linda. 2000. *Kinship and Gender: An Introduction.* 2d ed. Boulder, Colo.: Westview Press.

Strang, Veronica. 1997. *Uncommon Ground: Cultural Landscapes and Environmental Values.* Oxford: Berg.

———. 2000. "Not So Black and White: The Effects of Aboriginal Law on Australian Legislation." In *Land, Law, and Environment: Mythical Land, Legal Boundaries,* edited by Allen Abramson and Dimitris Theodossopoulos, 93–115. London: Pluto Press.

Sturge, Joseph, and Thomas Harvey. 1838. *The West Indies in 1837.* London: Hamilton Adams and Co.

Sutton, Constance R. 1974. "Cultural Duality in the Caribbean." Review article on *Crab Antics,* by Peter J. Wilson. *Caribbean Studies* 14, no. 2:96–101.

Tax, Sol. 1953. *Penny Capitalism: A Guatemalan Indian Economy.* Washington, D.C.: Smithsonian Institution Press.

Tenison, Patrick J. 1971. *Good Hope, Jamaica.* Edinburgh and London: Waddie and Co.

———. 1979. *Daily Gleaner Supplement,* vi–vii, Kingston, Jamaica, 29 August.

Thoden van Velzen, H. U. E. 1995. "African-American Worldviews in the Caribbean." In *Rastafari and Other African-Caribbean Worldviews*, edited by Barry Chevannes, 196–210. London: Macmillan.

Thoden van Velzen, H. U. E., and W. van Wetering. 1988. *The Great Father and the Danger: Religious Cults, Material Forces, and Collective Fantasies in the World of the Surinamese Maroons*. Dordrecht, Netherlands: Foris.

Thomas-Hope, Elizabeth M. 1978. "The Establishment of a Migration Tradition: British West Indian Movements to the Hispanic Caribbean in the Century after Emancipation." In *Caribbean Social Relations*, edited by Colin G. Clarke, 66–81. Liverpool: Centre for Latin American Studies, University of Liverpool, Monograph Series, No. 8.

——. 1980. "Hopes and Realities in the West Indian Migration to Britain." *Oral History: Journal of the Oral History Society* 8, no. 1:35–42.

——. 1992. *Explanation in Caribbean Migration. Perception and the Image: Jamaica, Barbados, St. Vincent*. London: Macmillan.

——. 1995. "Island Systems and the Paradox of Freedom: Migration in the Post-Emancipation Leeward Islands." In *Small Islands, Large Questions: Society, Culture, and Resistance in the Post-Emancipation Caribbean*, edited by Karen Fog Olwig, 161–75. London: Frank Cass.

Thompson, Paul. 2000. *The Voice of the Past: Oral History*. 1978, 1988. 3d ed. Oxford: Oxford University Press.

Tomich, Dale. 1991. "*Une Petite Guinée*: Provision Ground and Plantation in Martinique, 1830–1848." In *The Slaves' Economy: Independent Production by Slaves in the Americas*, edited by Ira Berlin and Philip D. Morgan. Special Issue, *Slavery and Abolition* 12, no. 1:68–91.

Tonkin, Elizabeth, Maryon McDonald, and Malcolm Chapman, eds. 1989. *History and Ethnicity*. London: Routledge.

Total Area and Land Use in Jamaica. 1993. Kingston: Rural Physical Planning Division, September.

Trouillot, Michel-Rolph. 1984. "Labour and Emancipation in Dominica: Contribution to a Debate." *Caribbean Quarterly* 30:73–84.

——. 1988. *Peasants and Capital: Dominica in the World Economy*. Baltimore: Johns Hopkins University Press.

——. 1989. Review of *Afro-Caribbean Villages in Historical Perspective*, edited by Charles V. Carnegie. *Social and Economic Studies* 38:321–25.

——. 1992a. "The Caribbean Region: An Open Frontier in Anthropological Theory." *Annual Review of Anthropology* 21:19–42.

——. 1992b. "The Inconvenience of Freedom: Free People of Color and the Political Aftermath of Slavery in Dominica and Saint-Domingue/Haiti." In *The Meaning of Freedom: Economics, Politics, and Culture after Slavery*, edited by Frank McGlynn and Seymour Drescher, 147–82. Pittsburgh, Pa.: University of Pittsburgh Press.

——. 1998. "Culture on the Edges: Creolization in the Plantation Context." *Plantation Society in the Americas* 5:8–28.

Turner, Mary. 1982. *Slaves and Missionaries: The Disintegration of Jamaican Slave Society, 1787–1834*. Urbana: University of Illinois Press.

———. 1988. "Chattel Slaves into Wage Slaves: A Jamaican Case Study." In *Labour in the Caribbean*, edited by Malcolm Cross and Gad Heuman, 14–31. London: Macmillan.

———. 1995. Introduction to *From Chattel Slaves to Wage Slaves: The Dynamics of Labour Bargaining in the Americas*, edited by Mary Turner, 1–30. Kingston, Jamaica: Ian Randle.

Underhill, Edward B. 1862. *The West Indies: Their Social and Religious Condition*. London: Jackson, Walford and Hodder.

van den Bor, Wout. 1979. "Peasantry in Isolation: The Agrarian Development of St. Eustatius and Saba." In *Peasants, Plantations, and Rural Communities in the Caribbean*, edited by Malcom Cross and Arnaud Marks, 117–41. Guildford, England: University of Surrey, and Leiden, Netherlands: Royal Institute of Linguistics and Anthropology.

———. 1981. *Island Adrift: The Social Organization of a Small Caribbean Community: The Case of St. Eustatius*. Department of Caribbean Studies, Royal Institute of Linguistics and Anthropology, Leiden, Netherlands. The Hague: Smits Drukkers-Uitgevers B.V.

Vernon, Diane. 1989. "Some Prominent Features of Ndjuka Maroon Medicine." *New West Indian Guide* 63, no. 3–4:209–21.

Wagley, Charles, 1960. "Plantation-America: A Culture Sphere." In *Caribbean Studies: A Symposium*, edited by Vera Rubin, 3–13. 1957. 2d ed. Seattle: University of Washington Press.

Wallerstein, Immanuel. 1974. *The Modern World-System I: Capitalist Agriculture and the Origins of the European World-Economy in the Sixteenth Century*. San Diego: Academic Press.

———. 1980. *The Modern World-System II: Mercantilism and the Consolidation of the European World-Economy, 1600–1750*. Boston: Academic Press.

Wardle, Huon. 2000. *An Ethnography of Cosmopolitanism in Kingston, Jamaica*. Lewiston, N.Y.: Edwin Mellen Press.

Webster, Steven. 1975. "Cognatic Descent Groups and the Contemporary Maori: A Preliminary Reassessment." *Journal of the Polynesian Society* 84, no. 2:121–52.

———. 1998. *Patrons of Maori Culture: Power, Theory, and Ideology in the Maori Renaissance*. Dunedin: University of Otago Press.

Whitaker, Mark P. 1998. "Reflexivity." In *Encyclopedia of Social and Cultural Anthropology*, edited by Alan Barnard and Jonathan Spencer, 470–73. 1996. Reprint, London: Routledge.

Williams, Eric. 1964. *Capitalism and Slavery*. 1944. Reprint, London: Andre Deutsch.

Wilmot, Swithin. 1982. "The Peacemakers: Baptist Missionaries and Ex-Slaves in Western Jamaica, 1838–40." *Jamaican Historical Review* 13:42–48.

———. 1992. "Black Space/Room to Manoeuvre: Land and Politics in Trelawny in the Immediate Post-Emancipation Period." In *Plantation Economy, Land Reform, and the Peasantry in a Historical Perspective: Jamaica, 1838–1980*, edited by Claus Stolberg and Swithin Wilmot, 15–24. Kingston, Jamaica: Friedrich Ebert Siftung.

Wilson, Peter J. 1969. "Reputation and Respectability: A Suggestion for Caribbean Ethnology." *Man* 4, no. 1:70–84.

———. 1973. *Crab Antics: The Social Anthropology of English-Speaking Negro Societies of the Caribbean*. New Haven: Yale University Press.

———. 1995. *Crab Antics: A Caribbean Case Study of the Conflict of Reputation and Respectability*. 1973. Rev. ed., Prospect Heights, Ill.: Waveland Press.

Wolf, Eric R. 1982. *Europe and the People without History*. Berkeley: University of California Press.

Worsley, Peter M. 1956. "The Kinship System of the Tallensi: A Revaluation." *Journal of the Royal Anthropological Institute* 86:37–75.

Wright, Philip. 1973. *Knibb "The Notorious": Slaves' Missionary, 1803–1845*. London: Sidgwick and Jackson.

Wright, Philip, and Paul F. White. 1969. *Exploring Jamaica*. London: Andre Deutsch.

Wulff, Helena. 1995. "Introducing Youth Culture in Its Own Right: The State of the Art and New Possibilities." In *Youth Cultures: A Cross-Cultural Perspective*, edited by Vered Amit-Talai and Helena Wulff, 1–18. London: Routledge.

Yelvington, Kevin A. 1993. "Gender and Ethnicity at Work in a Trinidadian Factory." In *Women and Change in the Caribbean: A Pan-Caribbean Perspective*, edited by Janet H. Momsen, 263–77. London: James Currey.

———. 1995. *Producing Power: Ethnicity, Gender, and Class in a Caribbean Workplace*. Philadelphia: Temple University Press.

———. 1996. "Flirting in the Factory." *Journal of the Royal Anthropological Institute*, n.s., 2, no. 2:313–33.

———. 1998. "Caribbean." In *Encyclopedia of Social and Cultural Anthropology*, edited by Alan Barnard and Jonathan Spencer, 86–90. 1996. Reprint, London: Routledge.

Young, Virginia Heyer. 1993. *Becoming West Indian: Culture, Self, and Nation in St. Vincent*. Washington, D.C.: Smithsonian Institution Press.

INDEX

313; and oral traditions, 19, 121–22; and surnames, 24, 143; and burial grounds, 28, 30, 31, 32, 86, 88, 110, 115, 123–24, 300; and protopeasantry, 32, 84, 88, 291; cross-cultural study of, 34–35; and maroons, 86; and lakou, 91; in British Honduras, 96; and migration, 107, 110, 117, 121, 122, 123, 193, 217–18, 304–5; and Refuge, 114; and Old Families, 161; and funeral rituals, 236; and Revival-Zion, 259–60; and family structure, 281, 289–305, 344 (n. 24); and paradoxical attitudes toward land, 291–92, 315–16; and family land as specific resource, 292–93; and immortal land, 293–94; and inalienable freehold rights, 295–98; and joint estate, 298–300; and adaptive land use, 300–303; and crab antics, 303–4; and land access, 313–15, 345 (n. 3)

Come To-Gather Society (CTS), 231–38, 257

Comitas, Lambros, 11, 214, 215

Commonwealth Immigrants Act (1962), 219

Cosmologies, 8, 28, 31, 238. *See also* Religion

Crab antics, 14, 16, 23, 144, 146–47, 150, 302–4, 305, 317, 318

Craton, Michael, 26, 52, 53, 141, 325 (n. 6)

Creole culture, 8, 14, 21, 22

Creole language, 20, 160

Creole planters, 66, 67

Creolization: and Caribbean region, xvi; and Besson's positioned subjectivity, xxv; and land tenure, 8, 9; and functionalist-pluralist debate, 11, 18; and culture-building, 22; and naming, 23, 24, 26, 143; and cultural anthropology, 34; and religion, 36; and

plantation society, 53; and capitalist class relations, 160; and cooking, 198; and architecture, 199

Cross, Malcolm, 20, 275

Cuba, xvii, 38, 39, 83, 86, 136, 219, 220, 221, 326–27 (n. 3)

Cultural anthropology, xiii, xiv, xv, 34, 313

Culture-building: and gender, 16–18, 24, 25, 41, 274, 318; and cognatic descent groups, 19; and capitalist class relations, 20, 22, 150–51; and class, 20–22; and economic system, 22, 36, 195; and primogeniture, 26; and marriage, 27, 283; and law, 33, 34; and slave trade, 46; and family-land institution, 144; and oral traditions, 160; and Emancipation Vigil, 208; and rotating savings and credit associations, 231; and friendly societies, 238; and Revival-Zion, 256, 263, 274; and Rastafarian movement, 264

Cuniffe, Henry, 55–56, 57, 68, 79

Curtin, Philip, 30, 31, 321 (n. 1)

Dalton, George, 205, 215

Davenport, William, 280, 281, 288, 308, 309, 314

Dawkins Old Family, 155, 161, 183, 295, 335 (n. 29)

Denmark, xviii, 38, 85, 97

Dexter, Benjamin, 105, 108, 109–10

Dominica, xxiv, 7, 83, 95, 142, 310, 312

Dutch Guiana, 87, 88, 98

Dutch West Indies, 39, 85, 97–98

Ecology, 35, 313

Economic system: economic production, xvi, xviii, xxi, 133, 135, 198; and peasants, 7, 195; and social stratification, 10; and functionalist-pluralist debate, 11; and family-land institution, 19, 317; cross-cultural study of,

and functionalist-pluralist debate, 12–14; and respectability-reputation dichotomy, 13–16, 18, 23; and titles, 14, 17, 18; and culture-building, 16–18, 24, 25, 274, 318; and cognatic descent groups, 17, 27, 28, 29, 34, 41, 88, 143, 322 (n. 3); and marketing, 17, 29, 200, 206, 208, 211–12; and migration, 17, 218–19, 222; and peasants, 22; and provision grounds, 29, 200; and marriage, 35, 283, 284; and slave trade, 41, 43, 71; and slavery, 41, 51; and urban slaves, 53; and postemancipation labor force, 91, 327–28 (n. 9); and institution-building, 111; and division of labor, 200–201, 212–13, 284, 338 (n. 17); and occupational multiplicity, 214, 215–16; and rotating savings and credit associations, 229, 230; and friendly societies, 232; and Revival-Zion, 254, 255, 274–75; and Rastafarian movement, 266, 267, 273; and family structure, 281; and race, 318

Genovese, Eugene, 5, 280, 319

Georgia Estate, 64, 65, 67

Georgian Society of Jamaica, 63, 80

Gilmore, Pam, 156, 170, 210–11, 222, 230, 269

Gold Coast, 42, 43, 46

Goodenough, Ward, 290–91, 308, 309, 313, 314–15

Good Hope Estate, 58–61, 67, 136

Goodin family, 63, 67

Grant, Francis, 64, 65–66, 67

Granville/Grumble Pen: study of, xxiii, 107; and oral traditions, 17, 120–21, 124–25, 160, 333 (n. 55); and dual naming, 25, 124–25; and Cunningham surname, 66; founding of, 106, 119, 120, 128, 130, 131; and Old Families, 115, 120–24, 161, 162, 163, 183; and Kettering, 117; and Martha

Brae, 131; and land tenure, 137; and burial grounds, 141, 145, 201; and Baptist Church, 171, 240; and Samuels Old Family, 178; and Revival-Zion, 241, 245, 252, 255, 261, 262; and funeral rituals, 258; and Rastafarian movement, 267–68

Greater Antilles, 7, 37, 38

Green, Nana, 182–83, 185

Greenfield, Sidney, 33, 141, 314

Green Park Plantation, 61, 119, 172

Grenada, 95, 278, 310

Grimes, Stephen, 163, 165

Gutman, Herbert, 5, 280

Haiti, xvii, 22, 29, 38–39, 90–91, 201, 213, 227, 307–8, 310

Hall, Catherine, 329 (n. 19)

Hall, Douglas, 24–25, 81–83, 85, 87

Hampden Estates, 64–65, 67, 133, 135, 198

Handler, Jerome S., 25–26, 31

Harmony Hall Estate, 118, 119

Hart, Richard, 50, 71–72

Henriques, Fernando, xxii, 10, 50, 286

Herskovits, Frances, xvii, 227, 230

Herskovits, Melville J., xiv–xv, xvi, xvii, 20, 227, 230, 278

Higman, Barry, 29, 47, 48, 52, 53, 159, 196, 199, 212, 231, 280

Hispaniola, 38, 86

Hogmeat gangs, 51, 109, 119

Holland Estate: and Zion, 7, 9, 156, 157; and Martha Brae, 55, 129, 130, 131, 137, 192, 196; and Tharp, 59; and Granville, 119; and oral tradition, 164–65, 172

Holy, Ladislav, 289, 314

Horowitz, Michael, 142, 279, 286, 287

House yards: and peasant economy, 16, 196–202; as symbol of autonomy, 16, 201; and kinship, 19–20; and plantation society, 49; and cognatic descent groups, 86, 142; and marketing system, 87, 203; and protopeasantry, 88, 197; and apprenticeship, 95; and land tenure, 96, 137; and legislation, 103; and burial grounds, 117, 124, 145; and squatters, 152; and family-land institution, 166; provision grounds distinguished from, 196–98; and internal differentiation, 198–200; and division of labor, 200–201, 213; symbolism of, 201–2

Howell, Leonard, 266, 273

Identity: and land as symbol, 13, 14; and nicknames, 24; and naming, 26, 143; and law, 33, 34; and family-land institution, 33, 115, 117, 118, 122, 140, 143, 163, 293, 315, 317; and English plantocracy, 52; and opposition, 85; and kinship and land, 87; and family-land graveyards, 110, 111; and Kettering, 116; and migration, 218; and friendly societies, 237; and family structure, 282; and ego-focused bilateral kinship networks, 288, 289

Indenture, 6, 38, 39, 41, 92, 253

Informal commercial importers (ICIs), 195, 203, 205, 207, 208, 230

Institution-building: and family-land institution, 8; and African American culture, 9, 20; and slaves, 20–23, 31, 323 (n. 13); and shared/separate value systems, 21–22, 31–32, 319; and resistance to slavery, 22–23; and law, 34; and protopeasantry, 34, 84, 111, 142, 150–51, 161, 191, 231, 237; and friendly societies, 237–38

Irving Tower Plantation, 55, 59, 129, 130, 131, 161–65, 172, 176, 196

Jackson, Joe, 148, 246, 248–54, 260–63

Jackson, May, 209, 245, 248–54, 260–63, 274

Jamaica: and Beckwith, xv; and sugar, xviii, 47–48; and class, xxv, xxviii, 10, 18–20; and protopeasants, 7, 86–88, 90; and family-land institution, 8, 12; and functionalist-pluralist debate, 10, 12; and creole culture, 21; and power, 22; and marketing, 29; and religion, 30–31; legal system of, 33; and plantation system, 37, 38, 39, 46–47; and slave trade, 42, 43, 46, 47; plantation society in, 47–54; and estate flight, 81, 82; and maroon treaties, 86; and postslavery peasantization, 90–94, 106; agrarian structure of, 132–33, 134; and family structure, 278

Johnson, Howard, 237–38

Kane, Shirley, 178–79

Karasch, Mary, 21–22, 238

Katzin, Margaret, 228, 230

Kelly Old Family, 129, 130, 145, 161, 165, 169, 183, 187–93, 304

Kettering: and Knibb, 106, 115–19; as free village, 107, 128; founding of, 115, 131; and burial grounds, 117, 118, 141, 145, 170, 201, 301; and occupational multiplicity, 214; and Rastafarian movement, 267

Kingston, Jamaica, 43, 53, 135, 241

Kinship: and land tenure, xix, 8–9, 26–34, 88, 89, 103, 315, 317; and family structure, xxii, 280, 281; and functionalist-pluralist debate, 10, 18–20; and equality, 13; and ego-focused bilateral kinship networks, 19, 21, 27, 28, 34, 35, 280, 281, 288–89, 305–6; and cognatic descent groups, 19, 27, 28, 29–30, 90, 313; and marriage, 19, 27–28, 323 (n. 18); and shipmate bond, 20, 27, 28, 282, 283, 289, 323 (n. 14); and peasants, 22; and slaves, 23, 26–27, 30, 32, 85, 279, 280, 289; Hawaiianized Eskimo kinship terminology, 35, 282, 305–7, 313; and planter class, 67; and identity, 87; and lakou, 90–91; and migration, 115, 219; and house yards, 201; and Revival-Zion, 251; bilateral kinship networks, 288–89; and ecology, 313

Knibb, Mary, 116, 119, 122, 130

Knibb, William: and Refuge, 25, 111–12, 114, 119; and Baptist Church, 100, 102, 172; and Baptist War, 101; and abolition, 102, 104, 173, 187–88, 239, 266; and wages, 102–3, 106; and free villages, 103, 104–7, 128, 131; and Kettering, 106, 115–19; and The Alps, 107–9; and Granville, 119–25; and Martha Brae, 129, 130, 131, 132, 189; and Falmouth marketplace, 203

Land access: and Afro-Caribbean women, 15; and free villages, 89, 110, 125; and planter class, 91, 104–5; and Morant Bay Rebellion, 106; and tourist industry, 136; and Martha Brae, 139, 156, 170, 189, 196, 197; and peasant economy, 214; and migration, 218; and Rastafarian movement, 272; and cognatic descent groups, 313–15, 345 (n. 3)

Land acquisition, xxvi, 16, 84

Land as symbol, 13, 186, 315–16

Land monopoly: peasants as oppositional to, xxvi; resistance to, 6; and family-land institution, 8, 19, 143, 291; and British West Indies, 96; and tourist industry, 107, 137, 195, 310, 315; and diversified cultivation, 198

Land patents, 54

Land tenure: and kinship, xix, 8–9, 26–34, 88, 89, 103, 315, 317; and family structure, xxii; and Kenneth Murdoch McFarlane, xxv; and agrarian legal code, xxvi, 11, 12, 36; and peas-

ants, 6, 22; and family-land institution, 8, 9, 11; and crab antics, 14; and gender, 18, 29, 41; and cognatic descent systems, 19, 27; and creole culture, 22; cross-cultural study of, 35; and slavery, 40; and plantation-peasant interface, 83, 86, 125, 137, 181–82, 318; and protopeasantry, 86, 88, 147; and identity, 87; and slaves, 89, 327 (n. 5); and free villages, 104; and Martha Brae, 137–39; and land use, 197

Land use patterns, 48–49, 197

Larose, Serge, 91, 310

Law: and agrarian legal code, xxvi, 11, 12, 36; state law, 9, 22, 144, 147, 150–51, 317–18; and identity, 33, 34; and slavery, 51–52; and planter class, 67; and family-land institution, 140, 144–51, 317. *See also* Legislation

Leeward Maroons, 47, 54, 160, 315

Leeward Maroon treaty, 55, 86, 91, 128

Legal freeholds, 103, 140, 144, 151, 156, 191, 195

Legislation: and land tenure, 91, 94; and provision grounds, 92, 103; and estate-based peasants, 93; and estate flight, 94, 103; and land access, 96; and burial grounds, 117, 124, 140, 145. *See also* Law

Legitimacy: and family-land institution, 9, 33–34, 140, 146, 147, 149, 150, 311; and respectability, 16, 323 (n. 9); and plantation system, 17; and domestic groups, 277, 278; importance of, 279; and complex marriage system, 284, 287–88; and Baptist Church, 285

Lesser Antilles, 7, 37–38, 43

Lévi-Strauss, Claude, 28, 35, 282, 283, 313, 323 (n. 18)

Lewis, M. G. "Monk," 25, 50

Liele, George, 99, 264

Lindo Old Family, 161, 168–69, 183, 223, 240

Littlewood, Roland, 15, 23

Long, Edward, 51, 56–57, 204

Long Pond Estates, 62, 64, 113, 133, 331 (n. 39)

Lowenthal, David, 11–12

Lyon Old Family, 112, 113, 115, 117, 331 (n. 37)

Mahogany Hall Estate, 62, 110

Malinowski, Bronisław, xiv

Manley, Norman, 187–88

Mann, James, 99–100

Manumission, 53, 66

Marketing system: and gender, 17, 29, 200, 206, 208, 211–13; and slaves, 53, 86–87, 90; and protopeasantry, 86–87, 91, 203, 204; and postslavery peasantization, 106; and land monopoly, 137; internal marketing system, 195, 202; and Falmouth marketplace, 203–8, 317; and higglers, 205–10, 212, 213, 230, 338 (n. 15); and Martha Brae marketers, 208–12; and rotating savings and credit associations, 230, 231

Maroon communities, xxiii, 25, 85–86, 88, 95, 98, 266, 315

Maroons: as peasants, 7; and resistance to slavery, 47, 52, 84, 85; and protopeasantry, 88; and estate flight, 89; and Jamaica, 90, 91; in British West Indies, 95; in Danish West Indies, 97

Maroon Town, St. James, xxiii, 201

Maroon wars, 6, 52, 67

Marriage: and respectability, 13, 14, 16; and kinship, 19, 27–28, 34, 35, 323 (n. 18); and age, 27, 28, 35, 279, 284–85; and planter class, 67; and family-land institution, 140; and house yards, 201; and domestic groups, 277, 278–79; and complex marriage system,

281, 282–88, 313; and bilateral kinship networks, 288–89

Marshall, Ruth, 169–70, 188, 192–93, 222, 295

Marshall, Woodville, 7, 82–83, 237

Martha Brae: Afro-Caribbean cultural history of, xxi, 8, 9, 22, 24, 80, 81–125, 319; oral traditions of, xxi, 8, 125, 132, 157, 159–93; and slave trade, xxi, 43, 53, 55, 67, 69–71, 78; Euro-Caribbean plantation history of, xxi, 54–58, 73–80, 159, 172; establishment of, xxi, 55–56; and peasants, 8, 80, 81; as free village, 8, 81, 127–32; derivation of name, 56–57; and planter class, 67–68; dissatisfaction with, 73–80; architecture of, 80, 167–69, 199–200; and marketing system, 87, 208–12; and Kettering, 117; and Old Families, 124, 129, 132, 137, 138, 157, 295; transformation of, 125, 127–32, 151, 157, 173, 188; and Baptist Church, 127, 129, 130–31, 171–72, 185, 187–88, 239–40, 275; contemporary context of, 132–37; and internal differentiation, 137–39, 161, 332 (n. 51); and family-land institution, 138, 139, 140–44; and Minto Old Family, 161–71; and Thompson Old Family, 171–82; and Anderson Old Family, 182–87; and Kelly Old Family, 187–93; and migration, 219; and Revival-Zion, 245, 252, 255, 260–63, 275; and Rastafarian movement, 267, 268, 272, 274, 275

Martinique, xvii, xxiv, 87, 97, 142, 227, 279, 310

Maxfield Estate, 66, 119, 137, 172

McCarran-Walter Act (1952), 219

McFarlane, Edith Adair Baxter, xxvii

McFarlane, George Lindsay, xxv

McFarlane, Kenneth Murdoch, xxv–xxvi

McFarlane, Meg Myers, xxvii–xxviii
McIntosh, Morgan, 163–68, 170, 176, 292, 295
Meggitt, M. J., 313, 314
Merrywood Estate, 59, 119
Methodist mission, 76, 98
Migration: and gender, 17, 218–19; and plantation system, 39; and Scottish ethnicity, 49–50, 63–64; and British West Indies, 95–96; and estate flight, 98, 217; and cognatic descent groups, 107, 110, 117, 121, 122, 123, 193, 217–18, 292, 304–5; and kinship, 115, 219; and peasant economy, 195, 217–26, 295; and house types, 199; and marketing system, 207, 208; early twentieth-century migrations, 220–21; North American migrations, 221–22; and United States, 222, 223, 224; to Britain, 222–26; and rotating savings and credit associations, 231; and funeral rituals, 258, 260; and family structure, 280
Minto, Christine, 163, 224–25
Minto, Edna, 163
Minto, Evadne, 163
Minto, George Finlayson, 162, 169, 170, 188
Minto, Isobel, 163
Minto, John Jarvis, 162
Minto, Rebecca, 169, 170
Minto, Rhoda, 162–63, 165–67, 169
Minto, William Shakespeare, 162, 163, 165–68, 190, 224, 225, 226
Minto Old Family, 67, 124, 145, 149, 156, 160–71, 176, 188, 189–90, 192, 199, 224, 226, 295
Mintz, Sidney W., xxii, xxv, 6–9, 20, 21, 22–23, 27, 29, 82, 83, 87, 90–91, 143, 144, 196, 199, 201, 211, 212, 213, 214, 215, 227, 279, 290, 307–8, 309, 310, 312, 319
Missionaries: and "primitive" societies,

xiii; and Moravian mission church, xxiii, 98; and Hampden Estate, 65; Methodist mission, 76, 98; Nonconformist missionaries, 93, 98, 101, 102, 103, 266, 275; Baptist missionaries, 98–100, 103, 107, 108, 112, 116, 239; and abolition movement, 102, 328–29 (n. 18)
Montego Bay, Jamaica, 43, 53, 55, 69, 72, 136
Montpelier Plantation, 48, 49, 51, 52–53, 55, 198, 199, 201
Montserrat, 95, 96, 310
Morant Bay Rebellion (1865), 16, 93, 106
Moravian Church, xxiii, 98, 243
Morrison, Irene, 262, 263
Moynihan, Daniel, 279, 280
Murdock, George, 305
Mutual aid: and peasant economy, 195, 226–31; and agricultural labor exchange, 226–27; rotating savings and credit associations, 227–31, 317; and friendly societies, 231–38; and family structure, 282; and ego-focused bilateral kinship networks, 288, 289
Myalism, 17, 21, 27, 30–31, 242–43, 261, 263, 273, 274, 316
Myers, Albert Angelo, xxvi–xxvii
Myers, Elizabeth Murton Philpott, xxvii
Myers, Michael S., xxvii

Native Americans, xiv, 5, 316
Native Baptist Christianity, 28, 32, 100, 101, 242, 260, 264, 266, 273, 274
Nelson, Lloyd, 162, 163, 167, 168–69, 170, 224–26, 295
Netherlands, xviii, 38, 40, 41, 86, 142
Nevis, 95, 96, 310, 328 (n. 12)
Nicknames, 14, 17, 18, 23, 26, 269, 271
Nonconformist Baptist Church, 16, 32, 93, 98

resistant response to plantation system, xxvi, 6, 7, 22, 82, 84, 90, 97; and land acquisition, xxvi, 84; estate-based peasants, xxvi, 88, 93–94, 96; and Besson's positioned subjectivity, xxvi–xxviii; and land tenure, 6, 22, 94; definition of, 6–7; and estate flight, 8, 9–10, 215; and family-land institution, 9–10, 94, 95; and creole culture, 22; and marketing, 87; of Haiti, 90–91; and postslavery peasantization, 90–98, 132, 191–92; and free villages, 105; and occupational multiplicity, 214, 215

Persian Wheel, 76, 80, 167

Phillippo, James, 103, 104, 105, 329 (n. 19)

Philpott, Sir John, xxvii

Plantation-peasant interface: Mintz on, xxii; and Besson's positioned subjectivity, xxv, xxvi; and peasants' resistant response, xxvi, 6, 7, 16, 22, 82, 84; and Afro-Caribbean culture, 8; conflict in, 20, 30; and cognatic descent groups, 32, 291; and poverty, 39; and land tenure, 83, 86, 125, 137, 181–82, 318; and Martha Brae, 127; and wage labor, 179; and Revival-Zion, 243; and land monopoly, 310

Plantation society, xxv, 11, 47–54, 274

Plantation system: and European colonies, 6; and squatters, 7; and functionalist-pluralist debate, 11; and family structure, 21, 279; variants of, 37–39, 83; and slave trade, 39–47; and economic system, 61, 92, 107, 132, 195; and corporate plantations, 107, 132, 133; and migration, 218. *See also* Estate flight

Planter class: and Kenneth Murdoch McFarlane, xxv, xxvi; and English plantocracy, 52, 54, 59, 61–63, 67, 69; and Scottish planters, 63–66, 67, 68, 76; and planters of slave descent, 66; and creole planters, 66, 67; consolidation of, 67–72; and Falmouth, 76, 77; and labor recruitment policy, 82, 83, 84; and postemancipation labor force, 82, 89, 91–93, 95, 107; and land access, 91, 94, 104–5; and missionaries, 98–99

Political action, 15–16, 106, 274

Postemancipation labor force: and planter class, 82, 89, 91–93, 95, 107; and wage labor, 102–3, 106, 195, 200, 214, 215–16, 227, 257; supply of, 131; and free villages, 196; and gender, 200

Power: and Afro-Caribbean culture, 22; and resistance to slavery, 23; and surnames, 24, 25; and institution-building, 31; and free villages, 106, 329 (n. 24); and agency, 319

Price, Richard, xxii, 8–9, 20, 21, 22–23, 27, 29, 85, 91, 159, 213, 290, 307–8, 309, 310, 312, 319

Primogeniture: and plantation society, xxv, 51; and family-land institution, 9, 24, 26, 33, 140, 143, 144, 150; and culture-building, 26, 32; and gender, 41; and friendly societies, 237; abolition of, 285

Procreation, 18, 27, 28, 283, 285

Protopeasantry: as peasants, 7; and family structure, 16; and religion, 30; and cognatic descent groups, 32, 84, 88, 291; and institution-building, 34, 84, 111, 142, 150–51, 161, 191, 231, 237; postslavery peasants linked with, 82, 83; and resistance to slavery, 84; adaptations of, 85, 86–87, 95, 96, 97–98; and land tenure, 86, 88, 96, 147, 197; and marketing, 86–87, 91, 203, 204, 212, 213; and provision grounds, 88, 191; and economic system, 195; and occupational multiplicity, 214; and agricultural labor exchange, 227; and friendly societies, 237, 238; and Rastafarian movement, 264; and marriage, 289

Providencia, 12–14, 17, 142, 146

Provision grounds: and family-land institution, 9; as male domain, 16; and cognatic descent groups, 28, 86, 88, 142; and gender, 29, 200, 213; and plantation system, 48; and labor recruitment policy, 82, 83; and marketing system, 87, 90, 203; and proto-peasantry, 88, 191; and postemancipation labor force, 91–93; and legislation, 92, 103; and apprenticeship, 95; and Martha Brae, 139; house yards distinguished from, 196–98; and agricultural labor exchange, 226–27

Puerto Rico, xvii, 38, 39, 83, 196

Pukumina, 243–48, 250, 258–59, 261

Race: and functionalist-pluralist debate, 10–11, 12; in Caribbean region, 10–34; and respectability-reputation dichotomy, 13; and slave trade, 39–40; and miscegenation, 50; and colonial legal system, 51; and colored transformed into whites, 52; and planter class, 66; and gender, 318

Radcliffe-Brown, Alfred, 290

Rasheed, Lily, 249–50, 252, 254, 255, 256, 262, 263

Rastafarian movement: and gender, 16, 18; and nicknaming, 17, 24; and Babylon/Zion dichotomy, 153, 267; and marketing, 211; and Revival-Zion, 264, 267–68, 270, 272–75; and Baptist Church, 264, 267–68, 271, 272–75; origins of, 264–66; in twentieth century, 266–67; in Trelawny Parish, 267–72

Refuge/Wilberforce: study of, xxiii,

107; and Knibb, 25, 111–12, 114, 119; founding of, 106, 128, 131; and oral traditions, 112, 113–15; Kettering compared to, 116; and burial grounds, 141, 201; and Revival-Zion, 241

Religion: interpretation of, 10; and institution-building, 20, 21, 323 (n. 13); and slaves, 21, 32, 264, 274; and peasants, 22; and land tenure, 30; and creolization, 36; and gender, 200; and Great Revival, 243, 260. *See also* Baptist Church; Missionaries; Myalism; Obeah-Myal magico-religious complex; Rastafarian movement; Revival-Zion

Reputation, 12–18, 23, 24, 318

Resistance to slavery: and plantation system, xviii–xix; and peasants' response to plantation system, xxvi, 6, 22, 84, 90, 97; of Afro-Caribbean women, 15; and family structure, 21; and religion, 21; and institution-building, 22–23; and Myalism, 31; and mortality, 40; and Igbo, 43; in Jamaica, 47; and maroons, 47, 52, 84, 85; planters' fear of, 52; and identity, 85; and estate flight, 88–90, 91; and land tenure, 94; and free villages, 103, 111, 127; and family-land institution, 143

Respectability, 12–16, 18, 23, 24, 318

Revival-Zion: and Besson's positioned subjectivity, xxvi; and gender, 16, 18; and titles, 17, 18; adherence to, 32; participation in, 152; and Obeah-Myal magico-religious complex, 153, 242, 243, 253, 255, 263; and Zion, 154–55; and house yards, 200; and burial grounds, 202; and friendly societies, 233, 234, 235, 236, 237; and funeral rituals, 235–36, 237, 256–60, 316; and Baptist Church, 240–44, 256, 263; and balm-yards, 241, 250;

and Great Revival, 243; spirit pantheon of, 244–48; leaders, healers, and evangelists of, 248–51; meetings and ritual symbols of, 251–56, 341 (n. 9); dynamics of, 260–63; and Rastafarian movement, 264, 267–68, 270, 272–75; and family-land institution, 304

Richardson, David, xxi, 42, 43, 46, 69, 71

Rosaldo, Renato, xxiv

Rotating savings and credit associations (ROSCAs), 17, 202, 227–31, 317

Rowe, John, 76, 99

Rum, xviii, 135

Rural proletariat, 39, 97, 214

St. Croix, 38, 97, 98

Saint Domingue, 7, 38, 47, 85, 86, 87, 90

St. Elizabeth Parish, xxiii

St. Eustatius, 87, 97–98, 310

St. James Parish: peasant communities of, xxiii; and functionalist-pluralist debate, 11; and Myal cult, 21; and religion, 30; and slave trade, 43; and provision grounds, 48; and Scottish migrants, 50; and creolization, 53; as old St. James, 54–55, 57–58; and Baptist missionaries, 98

St. John, 21, 27, 38, 87, 88, 97, 310

St. Kitts, xxiv, 39, 95, 96

St. Lucia, xxiv, 95, 310

St. Vincent, 95, 96, 310, 312

Samuels Old Family, 177, 178–79

Saramaka, 98, 159, 308, 315

Schuler, Monica, 21, 31, 242, 319

Scottish ethnicity, 48, 49–50, 51, 56, 63–66, 67, 68, 76, 142

Scott Old Family, 117, 118

Second Maroon War of 1795–96, xxiii, 60

Select Committee of the House of Commons on the West India Colonies (1842), 81–82

Senegambia, 42, 46, 69

Shared/separate value systems, 12–14, 21–22, 31–32, 319

Sharpe, Granville, 106, 119

Sharpe, Sam, 101

Shearer, Hugh, 168–69, 239–40

Sheller, Mimi, 15, 23, 89

Shipmate bond, 20, 27, 28, 282, 283, 289, 323 (n. 14)

Simmonds, Madeline, 145, 182–87, 292, 293, 296, 301, 302, 303

Slave rebellions: as resistance, 6; and surnames, 24; and Obeah, 31; and Obeah-Myal complex, 32; in Jamaica, 52, 90, 91; and planter class, 67; in British West Indies, 85, 94, 95; in Saint Domingue, 90; and religion, 100

Slave revolutions, 38, 90

Slavery: and European expansion, xiv; effects of, xvi; and European colonies, 6; and peasants, 7; and institution-building, 20; and religion, 32; and race, 39–40; and Scottish migrants, 50; and law, 51–52; and protopeasantry, 87; and oral traditions, 114–15; and Obeah-Myal complex, 242; and Revival-Zion, 253; and family structure, 278. *See also* Opposition to slavery; Resistance to slavery

Slaves: population of, xviii; as protopeasants, 7; and family-land institution, 9; and autonomy, 16, 91; and institution-building, 20–23, 31, 323 (n. 13); and religion, 21, 32, 264, 274; and naming, 23, 24–26; and nicknames, 23, 26; and kinship, 23, 26–27, 30, 32, 85, 279, 280, 289; and surnames, 24–25, 26; agency of, 25, 83; employment in urban centers, 48, 53; ethnic differences of, 50, 52; oc-